Lake District
Grid Squares Explored

Lake District Grid Squares Explored

Peter Bryant Danby

The Pentland Press
Edinburgh – Cambridge – Durham

Dedicated to the Memory of my Daughter
Sue
who died in tragic circumstances
15th February 1988

First published in 1994
by The Pentland Press Ltd
1 Hutton Close
South Church
Bishop Auckland
Durham

ISBN 1-85821-173-5

Cover photograph : Grange Bridge, Borrowdale

Typeset by Carnegie Publishing Ltd, 18 Maynard St, Preston
Printed in Great Britain by BPC Wheatons Ltd, Exeter

Contents

Acknowledgements

The grid on the map at page 14 is the National Grid taken from the Ordnance Survey map with the permission of the Controller of Her Majesty's Stationery Office.

I am indeed fortunate that during the countless hours of research both on the ground and in print I have been given every help and encouragement by my wife Marjorie and my children Heather and Ross.

My thanks too to Peter Adamson for reading the manuscript and for prompting improvements.

I am very much indebted to Rosemary Liddle for her kind permission to use her photographs.

Preface

Many books have been written about the Lake District—so why one more? During the last thirty years, and more, I have made many pilgrimages to various locations within the Lake District National Park and, whilst my fund of knowledge has increased—so has my library, which invariably travels with me.

For a long time I have felt that what I needed was a more detailed reference book of the National Park and peripheral area—and I've searched in vain. So the only solution was to create one! Whilst I have to accept that it cannot be complete in every detail I have endeavoured to locate, grid square by grid square, as much as possible.

Purposely, I have not ventured very much (in print that is) on to the high fells, as all that is recorded in faithful detail by the late Alfred Wainwright who, unknowingly, was part inspiration for this book. Nor have I mentioned, over-much, that which is to be seen in the larger areas of population, for that is covered in detail in localized publications.

I trust that you, fellow traveller, will find this reference book helpful in increasing your knowledge of this delightful corner of England.

Willoughby on the Wolds. September 1993.

How to use this book

The purpose of this book is to record as accurately as possible the relative Grid Reference (consisting mainly of 6 figures) of any given objective so that the reader may locate it on the ground more easily—with a maximum error of 264ft/80m.

The National Grid is a reference system of squares overprinted on all Ordnance Survey maps and gives each feature or place a unique reference which is always the same no matter which scale of map is used.

The reference lines across a map from north to south are known as "eastings" and increase in number from west to east. They form the first component of a grid reference. The reference lines across a map from east to west are known as "northings" and increase in number from south to north. They form the second component of a grid reference.

In the preparation of this book reference has been made to the 4 Ordnance Survey Leisure maps covering the English Lakes. These are on a scale of 2½ inches to 1 mile—4cm to 1 km. The map in this book is not produced to scale but gives an indication of the relevant areas covered.

The text refers to each Grid square where there is something of interest under various headings which, in the main, are self-explanatory but perhaps a little more detail on some of these may be helpful.

">" means greater than and "<" means less than.

ARCHAEOLOGY. Study of human antiquities, especially of the pre-historic period and usually by excavation.

ARCHITECTURE. Structure or style of building.

CHURCH. Embraces buildings of all religious faiths. Some are therefore Chapels, Quaker Meeting Houses etc.

CRAFTS. Source details in the main.

FISH. References have been made to the fishing readily available to the visitor. Not unnaturally, much of the better fishing is under the control of Angling Associations, who may be prepared to give limited membership, details of which is best available from specialized publications or from Information Centres. In all circumstances, it is the duty of every angler to be in possession of all necessary licences and permits BEFORE commencing to fish and to use only the methods so prescribed for a particular fish species, and to honour bag limits if applicable.

GEOLOGY. Science of the earth's crust, its strata and their relationship and changes. Geological features of the District. First detailed survey of the Lake District 1859/65 produced first accurate figures for the height of the mountains. Under this heading is recorded Minerals.

HISTORIC. Famous in history—normally used for past events.

HISTORICAL. Historical evidence, belonging to history not legend.

I

LEGEND. Traditional story popularly regarded as historical: popular, but unfounded belief. Fable, myth, fiction, doubtful narrative. Fictional story.

LITERARY. Generally refers to the writers and poets of the area and covers their residences.

MINE. Excavation in rock and earth to extract minerals. Initial works where a vein exposed at surface, known as outcrop or in depth by cross-cutting (horizontal tunnel driven to intersect vein). The horizontal entrance or passage known as an adit. Many of these exist on the Lake District fell-sides and caution is urged that unless the reader is qualified and accompanied, exploration of them should be resisted, for disturbance of old roof supports may bring about collapse with disastrous results. However, surface exploration of sites and spoil heaps may produce interesting mineral specimens. At all times it is incumbent on the reader to ensure that access is not prohibited. The main entrance to a particular mine has been allotted its relevant grid reference but there can be other smaller adits etc., on the adjacent fell-side, which relate to the mine.

REFRESHMENT. Mention has been made to Inns and Public Houses where an agreeable meal may be obtained: in many instances limited accommodation may also be available dependent on time of year and numbers in the party. Some entries relate to accommodation as opposed to just bar meals. As the reader will readily appreciate there are very many places prepared to cater for the visitors' needs and it is not the purpose of this book to provide a guide to such places but only to indicate to the weary traveller where he or she might be revictualled.

TOPOGRAPHIC. Description of map representation.

Literary Plaudits

Ille terrarum mihi praeter omnes angulus ridet.
(That corner of the earth to me smiles sweetest of all).

Horace Ode.11. V1. 13–14.

I do not indeed know any tract of country in which, within so narrow a compass, may be found an equal variety in the influences of light and shadow upon the sublime or beautiful features of landscape... Yet, though clustered together, every valley has its distinct and separate character; in some circumstances, as if they had been formed in studied contrast to each other, and in others with the united pleasing differences and resemblances of a sisterly rivalship.

William Wordsworth.
Guide to the Lakes. 1810.

Such as spend their lives in cities, and their time in crowds, will here meet with contrasts that engage the mind, by contemplation of sublime objects and raise it from nature to nature's first source.

Father Thomas West.
(In the first Lake District guide book 1778).

There are so many things to see and to do in Lakeland and so much to learn that a lifetime can be too short for fitting them all in, but this is no reason why we should not look around us and do our best to find out what it is all about. For, by making the conscious effort we can add immeasurably to our enjoyment and build up a permanent interest.

A. H. Griffin.
Still The Real Lakeland. 1970.

Even the guide-books compiled by the "masters" although they are veritable mines of information, never quite succeed in capturing all the essence of Lakeland, for country such as this, meaning so many different things to so many people; disclosing secrets to one but withholding them from another, defies description by the written or spoken word. For Lakeland is, after all, in the eye of the individual beholder, and therein lies much of its charm.

Arthur Knowles.
Lakeland Today. 1973.

Yet it is not just the landscape which changes in just a few miles, lush pastures to open heather to wild crags and frightening mountains. It is also the buildings. You see twee cottages in a wide variety of styles, farmhouses in all materials, village houses in a variety of design.

Hunter Davies.
The National Trust Magazine Autumn 1986.

... Size is not Lakeland's claim to be placed high among the beautiful regions of Britain; exquisite proportion, infinite variety of form and colour, and an atmosphere of enchantment—these are her chief attributes.

Jessica Lofthouse.
The Curious Traveller through Lakeland. 1954.

In the small area of the Lake District are tranquil lakes, quiet valleys, gently rolling vales and awesome mountains, each individual and with its own special character. Today it is still a working community of farmers and sheep where the Trust's protection of so much of this glorious landscape is aimed at maintaining the delicate balance between man and nature.

The National Trust Handbook.

Anyone who visits Grasmere and Rydal without having read Dorothy's Journals and William's poems has lost more than he can dream, for they re-create not only the life of their day, but point the way to a far closer observation and keener appreciation of the natural beauties of the district which they knew so intimately.

Maxwell Fraser.
Companion into Lakeland. 1937.

A region where the capricious pattern of sun and shower, the magnificent sculpture of the mountains, the narrow, placid lakes compose an immutable yet ever-changing vista. Man, with all his creative genius, cannot compete with the timeless natural forces which have given us the English Lakes.

Vera Burden.
History, People and Places in The Lake District. 1976.

Much of the magic of the district also lies in a wonderful kaleidoscopic quality that can make the landscape change in appearance not only from day to day but virtually from hour to hour.

Molly Lefebure.
The English Lake District. 1964.

Bibliography

Acknowledgements are due to, and further reading suggested of, the works of the following authors:

ADAMS John: *Mines of the Lake District Fells.*

BOWKER Tom: *Mountain Lakeland.*

BRACEBRIDGE Brian: *The Archaeology of the Industrial Revolution.*

BRAGG Melvyn: *Land of the Lakes.*

BROOKS J. A: *Ghosts and Legends of the Lake District.*

BRUNSKILL R. W. Professor: *Vernacular Architecture of the Lake Counties.*

BURDEN Vera: *History, People and Places in the Lake District.*

BURTON Anthony: *The National Trust Guide to our Industrial Past.*

CARRUTHERS F. J: *Around the Lakeland Hills.*
  Lore of the Lake Country.

CLARE T: *Archaeological sites of the Lake District.*

COLLINGWOOD W. G: *The Lake Counties.*

DAVIES Hunter: *The Good Guide to The Lakes.*
  Beatrix Potter's Lakeland.
  William Wordsworth.

DENYER Susan: *Traditional Buildings and Life in the Lake District.*

DUERDEN Frank: *Best Walks in the Lake District.*

DUNKLING Leslie & WRIGHT Gordon: *A Dictionary of Pub Names.*

FRASER Maxwell: *Companion into Lakeland.*

GELLING Margaret: *Place-names in the Landscape.*

GITTINGS Robert & MANTON Jo: *Dorothy Wordsworth.*

GRIFFIN A. H: *Still The Real Lakeland.*

HARDY Eric: *The Naturalist in Lakeland.*

HARRINGTON Edward: *The Meaning of English Place Names.*

HOLGATE James & PARKINSON Geoff: *Anglers' Guide to the Lake District.*

HOPKINS Tony: *Walks to remember.*

KNOWLES Arthur: *Lakeland Today.*

LARWOOD Jacob & HOTTEN John Camden: *English Inn Signs.*

LEFEBURE Molly: *The English Lake District.*
  Cumberland Heritage.

LOFTHOUSE Jessica: *Lancashire Villages.*
  The Curious Traveller through Lakeland.

McCRACKEN David: *Wordsworth and the Lake District.*

McINTIRE Walter. T: *Lakeland and the Borders of Long Ago.*

MEE Arthur: *The Lake Counties.*

NICHOLSON Norman: *Greater Lakeland.*
  Portrait of the Lakes.

ORRELL Robert: *Saddle Tramp in the Lake District.*
Over the Fells.

PAGE Jim Taylor. MBE., BSc: *A Field Guide to the Lake District.*

PALMER J. H: *Historic Farmhouses in and around Westmorland.*

PARKER John: *Lake District Walks for Motorists. Walk the Lakes.*

PARSON William & WHITE William: *History, Directory and Gazetteer of Cumberland & Westmorland. 1829.*

PEVSNER Sir Nikolaus: *The Buildings of England-North Lancashire. The Buildings of England-Cumberland and Westmorland.*

RICE H. A. L: *Lake Country Portraits. Lake Country Towns.*

ROBERTSON Dawn & KORONKA Peter: *Secrets and Legends of Old Westmorland.*

ROLLINSON William. Dr: *Life and Tradition in the Lake District.*
A History of Cumberland and Westmorland.

ROOM Adrian: *Dictionary of Place Names in the British Isles.*

ROWLING Marjorie: *The Folklore of the Lake District.*

SANDS Ronald: *Portrait of the Wordsworth Country.*

SCOTT David. M. A.: *The Laker's A. B. C.*

SHAW W. T: *Mining in the Lake Counties.*

SHELBOURN Colin: *Lake District Walks with a Point.*
Lakeland Towns & Villages.

SLACK Margaret: *Lakeland Discovered. From No Man's Land to National Park.*

SMITH Kenneth: *Cumbrian Villages.*

SMITHERS Tom: *Living in Lakeland.*

SPENCER Brian: *The Visitor's Guide to The Lake District.*

UNSWORTH W: *An Illustrated Companion into Lakeland.*

WAINWRIGHT A: *Westmorland Heritage.*
Wainwright in the Valleys of Lakeland.

WATSON Jim: *Lakeland Villages.*

WELSH Frank: *The Companion Guide to The Lake District.*

WELSH Mary: *Naturalist's Guide to Lakeland Waterfalls throughout the year. Volumes I to IV.*

WHITE Tom Pagen: *Lays and Legends of the English Lake Country.*

WORDSWORTH Dorothy: *Illustrated Lakeland Journals.*

WORDSWORTH William: *Guide to the Lakes.*

Various authors: *Chambers's Encyclopaedia.*

Meticulous research has gone into the preparation of the information ascribed to each Grid Square, but neither the author nor publishers can be held responsible for alterations, errors or omissions; although they would welcome notification of such for future editions.

Where dates and times have been included every effort has been made to ensure correctness of entries at the time of writing. However, they can be subject to modification without notice and intending visitors should check with local information centres. Actual admission charges have been omitted for they are subject to revision.

Practical Information

ACCIDENT

To summon help: 6 long blasts on whistle or 6 long torch flashes. Can use mirror if sunny. Repeat after 1 minute.
Send for help: after making patient comfortable and protected from the elements. Know your exact grid reference location.
Telephone the Police 999: they will do what is then necessary. Listen carefully to their instructions AND OBEY.

MOUNTAIN ACCIDENTS ASSOCIATION RECOMMENDA-TIONS

ARE YOU WEARING
Brightly coloured wind and rain-proof clothing?
Suitable boots?

DO YOU KNOW
How to use your equipment?
What time it gets dark?
The International Mountain Distress Signal? [See *ACCIDENT*].

HAVE YOU GOT

Map?	Compass?	Whistle?	Torch?
Spare food?	Spare warm clothing?	First Aid?	Watch?

Ice axe if snow or ice on the fells?

HAVE YOU left information about where you are going with someone who will miss you if you don't return?

MEASUREMENT

On Ordnance Survey Maps the Grid Lines are usually at one kilometre intervals. It follows, then, that the diagonal of a square is about 1½ kilometres.

Miles	0.621	1.243	1.864	2.485	3.107	6.214	9.320
km/mi.	1	2	3	4	5	10	15
Km	1.609	3.219	4.828	6.437	8.047	16.093	24.139

The average person walks about 50 metres in 75 strides.

Naismith's formula measures time over distance travelled and height gained. Roughly, 5 kms are walked every hour and half an hour is added every 300 metres climbed.

Height - Rough guide.

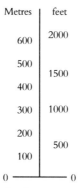

Metres	feet
600	2000
500	
	1500
400	
300	1000
200	
	500
100	
0	0

Temperature falls as height is gained:

In clear and dry weather by as much as 6F° for every 1000ft (3.3C° for every 300 metres). These values may be halved if very cloudy. Beware of wind-chill which reduces the perceptible temperature to the surface of the skin according to the strength of the wind. There are low-cost gadgets available which indicate such temperatures.

Wind Chill

				Factors		
	60	−7	−13	−19	−26	−32
Wind	50	−6	−12	−18	−25	−31
Speed						
Km/H	40	−5	−11	−17	−23	−29
	30	−3	− 8	−14	−20	−25
	20	0	−5	−10	−15	−21
	10	5	0	−4	−8	−13
Air temp°C		8	4	0	−4	−8

Rough conversion of Centigrade to Fahrenheit: Double the Centigrade reading and add 30.

Freezing point of water = 32°F or 0°C.

Depth of snow

Roughly 2.54cms/1 inch of rainfall is equivalent to 25.40cms/10 inches of snow. Wet snow obviously packs tighter than dry snow but in the long run the formula is about right.

The Beaufort Wind Scale

		Force	mph	km/h
Calm:	Smoke rises vertically	0	0	0
Light:	Smoke moves in wind	1	1–3	1.5–5
	Weather vane not affected			
Light breeze:	Can be felt on face	2	4–7	2.5–11
	Leaves rustle			
	Weather vane moves			
Gentle breeeze:	Small twigs move constantly	3	8–12	13–19
Moderate breeze:	Small branches move	4	13–18	21–29
	Dust/paper blows about			
Fresh breeze:	Small trees sway	5	19–24	30–39
Strong breeze:	Large branches move	6	25–31	40–50
Moderate gale:	Hard to walk against	7	32–38	51–61
	Whole trees move			
Fresh gale:	Walking difficult	8	39–46	62–74
	Twigs break off trees			
Strong gale:	Loose tiles etc removed	9	47–54	75–87
Fierce gale:	Trees uprooted	10	55–63	88–101
	Serious structural damage			
Storm:	Widespread damage	11	64–75	102–121
Hurricane:	Devastation	12	76+	122+

CAR PROBLEMS

Automobile Association:
24 hour breakdown service — Freephone 0800 887766
— Mobile phone users 0345 887766

Information service — Phone 0345 500600
— Mon/Fri 0700/1900hrs. Sat/Sun 0800/1700hrs

Royal Automobile Club:
24 hour breakdown service — Freephone 0800 828282

COUNTRY CODE—UK

Enjoy the countryside and respect its life and work
Guard against all risk of fire
Fasten all gates
Keep your dogs under close control
Keep to public paths across farmland
Use gates and stiles to cross fences, hedges and walls
Leave livestock, crops and machinery alone
Take your litter home
Help to keep all water clean
Protect wildlife, plants and trees
Take especial care on country roads
Make no unnecessary noise.

COUNTRY CODE—USA

Take nothing but pictures
Leave nothing but footprints
Kill nothing but time.

TOURIST INFORMATION

Windermere.   Phone 05394 46499
Ambleside.   Phone 05394 32582
Brockhole.   Phone 05394 46601

Radio Cumbria: 266 and 397m (Medium Wave). 95.6 (VHF).
Radio Furness: 358 (Medium Wave). 96.1 (VHF).

Weather Forecast. Phone 05394 45151
The day's weather from 0800hrs and the morrow's outlook from 1600hrs. (Very often the weather improves as the day progresses).

What's on in Cumbria. Phone 05394 46363

Useful Addresses

Association of County Councils. Eaton House, 66a Eaton Square, London SW1W 9BH.

Association of District Councils. 9 Buckingham Gate, London SW1W 6LE.

British Mountaineering Council. Crawford House, Precinct Centre Booth St East. Manchester M13 9RZ.

British Railways Board. Rail House, Euston Square, PO Box 100 London NW1 2DZ.

British Tourist Authority. Information Centre. 64 St James's St. London SW1.

British Travel Centre. 4–12 Regent Street, Piccadilly, London SW1Y 4PQ.

British Trust for Conservation Volunteers. 36 St Mary's Street, Wallingford, Oxon OX10 0EU.

Byways and Bridleways Trust. 9 Queen Anne's Gate, London SW1H 9BY.

Calvert Trust (Challenge for the disabled). Little Crosthwaite, Underskiddaw, Keswick. CA12 4QD.

Camping and Caravanning Club of Great Britain. 11 Lower Grosvenor Place. London SW1 OEY.

Caravan Club. East Grinstead House, London Road, East Grinstead. Sussex. RH19 1UA.

Council for British Archaeology. 112 Kennington Road, London N1 9AG

Council for Environmental Conservation. 80 York Way, London N1 9AG.

Council for National Parks. 4 Hobart Place, London. SW1W 0HY.

Council for the Preservation of Rural England. 4 Hobart Place, London SW1W OHY.

Country Landowners' Association. 16 Belgrave Square, London SW1X 8PQ.

Countryside Commission. John Dower House, Crescent Place, Cheltenham. Glos. Concerned with development/improvement of facilities for enjoyment of the countryside.

County Naturalists' Trusts. For Cumbria–Rydal Road, Ambleside. Concerned with nature conservation; manages nature reserves.

Cumbria Tourist Board. Ashleigh Holly Road, Windermere. LA23 2AQ

Cumbria Wildlife Trust. The Badger's Paw, Church St Ambleside. LA22 OBU. Phone 05394 32476. Publications on the Lake District, nature trails and reserves.

Cyclists' Touring Club. 69 Meadrow, Godalming. Surrey GU7 3HS.

The Dalesman Publishing Co. Ltd. Clapham, Lancaster. LA2 8EB. Publications on the life of Cumbria.

Department of the Environment. 2 Marsham Street, London SW1P 3EB.

English Heritage. N Off. Carlisle Castle, Carlisle. CA3 8UR. Head Office: 23 Saville Row, London. W1X 2HE.

English Tourist Board. Thames Tower, Black's Road, London W6 9EL.

Fell Bus. 25 Manor Park, Keswick. CA12 4AB.

Forestry Commission. 231, Corstophine Road, Edinburgh EH12 7AT. Publishes guides to forest walks, nature trails and recreational facilities on their land.

Friends of the Lake District. No.3. Yard 77 Highgate. Kendal. LA9 4ED. Phone 0539 20788.

Geologists' Association. Burlington House, Piccadilly, London W1V 9AG.

Health and Safety Executive. Baynards House, Chepstow Place, London W2 4TF.

Holiday Fellowship. 142 Great North Way, London NW4 1EG.

Keswick on Derwent Water Launch Co., 29 Manor Park, Keswick. (Launches sail Easter to early November).

Lake District Leisure Pursuits Ltd. Fall Barrow Hall, Windermere LA23 3DL.

Lake District National Park Information Service. Bank House, High St. Windermere. Cumbria.

Lake District Special Planning Board. Busher Walk. Kendal.

Local Ombudsman (England). 21 Queen Anne's Gate, London SW1 9BU

Long Distance Walkers' Association. Wayfarers, 13 The Moorings Close, Park Gate. South Wirral. L64 6TL.

National Association of Local Councils. 108 Great Russell St. London WC1 3LD.

National Council for Metal Detecting. 105 Bradwall Road, Sandbach, Cheshire CW11 9AN.

National Farmers' Union. Agriculture House, Knightsbridge, London SW1X 7NJ

National Trust. 36 Queen Anne's Gate, London. SW1H 9AS.

Nature Conservancy Council. Northminster House, Peterborough PE1 1UA. Government body responsible for nature conservation in UK. Publishes guides on national nature reserves and pamphlets on conservation topics. Regional Office—Blackwell, Bowness on Windermere. Cumbria.

North West Water Ltd. New Town House, Buttermarket Street, Warrington, Cheshire. Phone 0925 234000.

Open Spaces Society. 25a Bell Street, Henley on Thames. Oxon RG9 2BA.

Ordnance Survey. Romsey Road, Maybush, Southampton SO9 4DH.

Outward Bound Trust. 14 Oxford Street, London W1.

Ramblers' Association. 1/5 Wandsworth Road, London. SW8 2XX.

Royal Society for Nature Conservation. The Green, Nettleham, Lincoln LN2 2NR.

Royal Society for the Protection of Birds. The Lodge, Sandy. Beds SG19 2DL. Manages nature reserves and organizes educational facilities.

Sports Council. 16 Upper Woburn Place, London WC1H 0QP.

Woodland Trust. Autumn Park, Dysart Road, Grantham. Lincs. NG31 6LL.

YMCA National Centre. Lakeside, Ulverston LA1Z 8BD

Youth Hostels Association. Trevelyan House. 8 St Stephen's Hill. St Albans. Herts. AL1 2DY.

Youth Hostels Association Lake District Area Office. Elleray, Windermere LA23 1AW.

Youth Hostels Association Bookshop. 14 Southampton Street London WC2E 7HY.

When writing requesting information or literature it would be appropriate to enclose a stamped addressed envelope.

NOTES

LAKE DISTRICT GRID SQUARES REPRESENTED

KEY

[1] Cockermouth	[2] Bassenthwaite	[3] Mungrisdale
[4] Skelton	[5] Penrith	[6] Lorton
[7] Keswick	[8] Threlkeld	[9] Pooley Bridge
[10] Askham	[11] Buttermere	[12] Borrowdale
[13] Thirlmere	[14] Haweswater	[15] Bampton
[16] Wast Water	[17] Langdales	[18] Ambleside
[19] Kentmere	[20] Shap Fells	[21] Ulpha
[22] Torver	[23] Hawkshead	[24] Windermere
[25] Kendal	[26] Bootle	[27] Broughton/Furness
[28] Newby Bridge	[29] Levens	[30] Stainton

14

AREA 1 – Cockermouth

08 30

CHURCH. St Bridget. Brigham (the homestead by the bridge). Late Norman, early C14 additions. Anglo-Danish cross socket with carvings. Crossheads.

NY 089304

10 30

ARCHAEOLOGY. Fort with oval rampart and ditch. Fitz Wood. Cockermouth.

NY 102305

10 31

ARCHAEOLOGY. Site of Roman Fort—Dervento. Papcastle. Originally of considerable size and importance but stones plundered to build Cockermouth Castle. Many artefacts have been unearthed although site not fully excavated save for barracks and bath-house in 1961. Castle Gardens (old people's housing) now stands on main site.

NY 108316

HISTORICAL. In C12 Alice de Romilli, sister of William, destined to be King (being nephew of King David I of Scotland), inherited lands comprising Barony of Allerdale when William drowned in The Strid near Bolton Abbey. Alice married Gilbert Pipard (a Judge to Henry II) and it was he who built Pipard's Castle on the ruined Roman Fort site which very probably accounts for the present village's name Papcastle. Wordsworth, in his poem, "The White Doe of Rylstone" referred to the brother as "... The noble Boy of Egremound..." (line 230). Alice founded Bolton Abbey in her brother's memory.

NY 1031

10 35

ARCHITECTURE. Tallentire Hall. c1770 and later. Centre front recessed. Ionic columns.

NY 104352

REFRESHMENT. The Bush Inn. Tallentire.

NY 109354

11 30

CHURCH. Christ Church. South St. Cockermouth ("Kukra": confluence of rivers). 1865. Plain tower, large pinnacles. The interior is very interesting.

NY 118306

St Joseph. (R. C.) 1856. Bellcote. Apse. Low interior, hammer beam roof. Crown St. Cockermouth.

NY 118306

Congregational. 1856. Gothic. Steep pinnacles. Main St. Cockermouth.

NY 119307

CRAFTS. Metalwork. Balnakeil Forge. Lamplugh Corner. Cockermouth. Phone 0900 823169. Mon/Sat. 0800–1730 hrs.

NY 1130

11 31

ARCHITECTURE. Hames Hall. Cockermouth. Tudor. 3 bays. Turrets. Battlements.   NY 116314

11 33

CHURCH. St Bride. Bridekirk. 1868–70. Neo-Norman, part early Norman Church incorporated. Magnificent C12 font decorated with beasts and birds, the baptism of Christ and the expulsion from Eden and the artist's portrait. Sculptured by Master Richard of Durham the best north country craftsman of the C12. The Runic inscription reads "Rikarth he me wrokte, and to dis merthe gernr me brokte." (Richard has wrought me and to this glory brought me). Reredos has fleur-de-lys patterned tiles with background of terracotta interlaced arches. Trinity stone. Grave slabs.   NY 116337

HISTORICAL. The Vicarage. Bridekirk. Birthplace of Sir Joseph Williamson (1633–1701) President of the Royal Society. Buried Westminster Abbey. The Vicarage also the birthplace of Thomas Tickell (1686–1740) poet and statesman.
                                                                        NY 117336

LITERARY. Thomas Tickell, poet, born 1686 in Bridekirk Vicarage. Educated Queen's College, Oxford. In 1710 obtained a post in Dublin under Joseph Addison (1672 to 1719—poet, essayist and statesman, his grave and monument are in Westminster Abbey, London). In 1711 Tickell was elected Professor of Poetry at Queen's College, Oxford. Died 1740—buried in Dublin. Best works: *On the Prospect of Peace* 1712, *On the death of Mr Addison* 1721.   NY 117336

11 37

REFRESHMENT. The Masons Arms. Gilcrux. Phone 06973 20765. NY 115379

11 38

CHURCH. St Mary. Gilcrux [pronounced Gilcruce]. (C "Gilcruc": a retreat by a hill). C12 to C19. Bellcote, nave, chancel. Anglo-Danish Cross. Reredos—a copy in glass of The Last Supper by Leonardo da Vinci. Chancel arch has hagioscope. Royal Arms of George II. 1836 sundial above porch.   NY 114380

Wesleyan Chapel 1875 said to be on the site from which John Wesley preached to an assembled throng. Gilcrux.   NY 117381

HISTORICAL. Birthplace of Joseph Jackson (died 1789). Scientist and philosopher, vociferous in refuting Newton's theories. Gilcrux.   NY 1138

12 30

ARCHITECTURE. Town Hall, previously Methodist Church 1841. Three bays. Greek Doric Columns. Main St. Cockermouth.   NY 124306

CASTLE. Located above confluence of River Derwent and Cocker. Built 1134 by Waltheof, son of Earl of Dunbar. Mostly ruins but part still inhabited by Dowager Lady Egremont. It is thought that much of the stone was plundered from the Roman fort at Papcastle. Rarely open to the public, though viewing permitted during Cockermouth's Festival in third week of August. Outer gate-house 1440 by Percy whose heraldic devices are above arch. Mostly Percy work on inner gatehouse, kitchen tower & flag tower. Round tower is c1250. "Oubli-ette" dungeons housed forgotten prisoners. Besieged by Royalists in Civil War. Cockermouth. NY 124309

CHURCH. All Saints. Cockermouth. 1852–4. Large, sandstone and with recessed 180ft/54m spire in crossing tower, 8 bell peal. Colourful west window by Kempe c1897. Memorial window to Wordsworth. Church Room contains wall tablet "On this site stood the Grammar School which William Wordsworth attended as a boy. To this school also came Fletcher Christian, Leader of the Mutiny of the *Bounty*, April 28th 1788." Churchyard—grave of John Wordsworth (William's father) died 30 December 1783 aged 42, five years after his wife. Also grave of Fearon Fellows who in 1820 became the first Astronomer Royal at the Cape of Good Hope, where he died aged 43 years. NY 124306

EVENT. Cockermouth and District Agricultural Show. Saturday prior to 1st Monday of August at Greenlands. Livestock, Sheep, Show Jumping, Dogs, Hound Trail, Handicrafts, Produce, Vintage Machinery and Trade Stands. NY 1230

Cockermouth Festival. Literary and musical events. All July. NY 1230

HISTORICAL. Market bell—"butter bell" rung to indicate the start of the market still hangs in the Market Place 15ft/4.5m up on right hand side corner of a shop. Market Charter granted 1221 and markets still held on Mondays and Wednesdays. Cockermouth. NY 124307

LITERARY. Wordsworth's birthplace, Wordsworth House. Main Street Cock-ermouth. Built 1746 for Joshua Lucock, Sheriff of Cumberland, and shortly after sold to the Lowther family and rented to John Wordsworth when appointed land agent and attorney to Sir James Lowther in 1766. Five children were born here, Richard 1768; William 7th April 1770; Dorothy 25th December 1771; John 1772 and Christopher 1774. The latter became Master of Trinity College, Cambridge. His three sons also achieved renown—John, the eldest, became Classical Lecturer at Trinity College, Cambridge; Christopher became Bishop of Lincoln [his eldest daughter, Elizabeth, appointed first principal of Lady Margaret Hall, Oxford], and Charles became Bishop of St Andrews following his achievements as a Master of Winchester College. House cared for by National Trust and open Easter–mid Oct daily (not Thursdays) 1100–1700hrs. Sundays 1400–1700hrs. Fee. Phone 0900 824805. NY 124307

MEMORIAL. Statue of Richard Southall Bourke—6th Earl of Mayo. In 1872 when Viceroy and Governor General of India, assassinated by a convict whilst in the Andaman Islands. Main Street. Cockermouth. NY 122307

Statue of Wordsworth's sister Dorothy as a child. Harris Park, Cockermouth. NY 121301

"On 17th May 1568 There came to this house As a guest of Henry Fletcher Esq

Mary Queen of Scots On her journey from Workington to Carlisle." Car park. Cockermouth. NY 122301

MUSEUM. Castlegate House Gallery. Cockermouth. The only art gallery in Cumbria which is also a home. Castlegate House may once have been the dower house for the widows from Cockermouth Castle, opposite. Georgian building— above the back door is written the date 1739 followed by a poem "I love this dear old house because/It offers after dark/A pause for rest/A rest for paws/A place to moor my barque." Cumbrian paintings a speciality: purchases may be made. Open March–mid October Mon–Sat 1030–1630hrs except Wed when open 1030–1900hrs. Closed Thursdays. Free. Phone 0900 822149. NY 123308

The Toy & Doll Museum. In a narrow alleyway off Market Place, Cockermouth. 300 Dolls in regional costume. Display of British toys spanning the whole of C20. Other toys, tinplate model railway and Scalextric track. Open lst Feb–30th Nov daily 1000–1700hrs. Winter by appointment. Fee. Curator and owner Rod Moore. Phone 0900 827606. NY 123307

REFRESHMENT. The Globe Hotel 1750. On site of earlier wooden hostelry. Main St. Cockermouth. Phone 0900 822126. NY 122307

Trout Hotel. Crown St. Cockermouth. Phone 0900 823591. NY 120307

Ship Inn. Market Place. Cockermouth. Phone 0900 823091. NY 125307

TOURIST INFORMATION CENTRE. Riverside Car Park. Market Street. Cockermouth. Phone 0900 822634. NY 122306

14 34

CHURCH. Methodist Chapel 1894. Blindcrake (meaning top rock). NY 147346

CUSTOMS. Unusual custom at Blindcrake of burying its horses within the village boundary. Gravestone inscribed "Marmaduke 1900" the then Vicar (Revd W. A. Sharpe) of Isel's horse. NY 149347

HISTORICAL. Inscribed tablet to long vanished village water pump "As birds drink, and straight lift up their head,/So must man, sip and think, of better drink,/He may attain to, after he is dead." Easter Cottage. Blindcrake. NY 148345

14 38

REFRESHMENT. The Horse & Jockey Inn. Parsonby. Phone 06973 20482. NY 143388

14 39

CHURCH. St Cuthbert. Plumbland. 1870 on site of Norman church 1130 and possibly on Saxon site of C8. Some Norman architecture. Plate, cup and cover c1600. Hogsback tombstones AD 980. NY 142393

15 32

ARCHITECTURE. C16 Hewthwaite Hall, now a farmhouse. Inscribed on doorway lintel "John Swynburn Esquire and Elizabeth his wyfe Did make cost of this work in the dais of ther lyfe Ano Domini 1581 Ano Rae 23." The whole topped by figures of bishops in niches and two shields, one reversed. Figures also flank the inscription. Such early stone dating uncommon. NY 152328

15 33

ARCHITECTURE. Isel Hall. Isel. Spectacular C16 building. Pele tower. Family home of the Lawson's since Elizabeth I. NY 158337

15 39

REFRESHMENT. Last Man Inn. Plumbland. Former landlord and family cricketing enthusiasts. NY 152392

16 30

MINE. Embleton Mine. High in mineral content although little lead. Mined since 1749 at least, until abandoned in 1856. NY 169306

16 33

CHURCH. St Michael. Isel. 1130. Unusual for its size has 15 windows. Present belfry replaced a tower. Anglo-Danish cross shaft with rounded swastika. Royal Arms 1721, white horse of Hanover, given it is opined, by Sir Wilfred Lawson of Isel Hall, Groom to the Bedchamber to George I. Triskele Stone—sadly represented by a photograph due to the theft of the actual stone in 1986. (Triskeles—three lines radiating from a central point, three linked knot, Thor's thunderbolt and a Swastika—which predates Christianity). Some of the altar frontal fabric originally hangings used in Westminster Abbey for coronation of Edward VII in 1902. Black marble tablet in chancel:

> Hic jacet ille cinis qui Modo Lawson erat
> Even such is Time which takes in trust
> Our Youth, and Joyes, and all we have;
> And payes us but with Age and Dust
> Within the Dark and Silent Grave
> When we have wander'd all our Wayes
> Shuts up the Story of our dayes;
> And from which Earth, and Grave and Dust
> The Lord will raise me up, I Trust.
> Wilfridus Lawson Miles obijt 16 die
> Aprilis Anno aetatis suae 87. Annoque
> Salutis 1632.   NY 162333

17 30

CHURCH. St Margaret. Wythop. 1865. Nave, bellcote and chancel. Good stained glass. NY 176306

REFRESHMENT. The Wheatsheaf Inn. Embleton. Phone 07687 76408.
NY 171304

17 31

ARCHAEOLOGY. Early type large stone circle. 100ft/30m diameter. Elva Plain. Bassenthwaite. NY 178317

18 30

MINE. Behind Close House—a run in level in all probability made by lessees of Embleton mine (q.v. NY 169306). NY 182309

18 31

ARCHITECTURE. Higham School, a Cumbria Adult Educational Residential College, near Embleton. c1800. Gothic. 11 symmetrical bays. Towers. NY 185316

18 32

CHURCH. St Barnabas. Setmurthy (Murdoch's shieling). 1794 restored 1870. Nave and chancel in one. Polygonal NW turret and polygonal SW baptistery. Font 1661. From 1852 to 1880 Charles C. Southey, son of the poet, was Vicar. NY 184322

18 38

CHURCH. St Michael. 1120. Bothel. NY 182389

18 39

REFRESHMENT. The Greyhound Inn. Bothel. Phone 06973 20601. NY 183393

19 30

REFRESHMENT. Pheasant Inn. C16. Bassenthwaite Lake. Phone 07687 76234 NY 199307

WALKS. Sale Fell. Bassenthwaite. Circuit 6 miles/9.6km. Ascent 900ft/274m. Strenuous. Superb views from summit cairn—Scotland, Skiddaw, Helvellyn, Grisedale Pike. Start: Pheasant Inn. NY 199307

19 32

HISTORICAL. 200 years ago a popular water sport "horse-racing" was in vogue at Ouse Bridge, Bassenthwaite Lake. Several horses in barges were towed towards middle of the lake. The barges then sunk, and the first horse to swim ashore was declared the winner. Much betting took place at such events. NY 199321

19 37

PLANTS. Acid moorland habitat. Bothel. NY 1937

AREA 2 – Bassenthwaite

20 30

ARCHAEOLOGY. Fortified settlement site, with triple ramparts. Castle How. Bassenthwaite. NY 202308

BIRDS. Around Bassenthwaite and Derwent Water in winter and spring: bittern, buzzard, chiffchaff, cormorant. Ducks: goosander, mallard, merganser, pochard, scaup, teal, tufted & wigeon; pied flycatcher. Geese: barnacle, canada, greylag & pinkfoot; goldcrest; great crested & little grebe; herring & lesser black-backed gulls, sparrow hawk, water pipit, raven, whooper swan. Tits: blue, coal, great, long-tailed, marsh & willow; willow warbler and wren. NY 2030

20 31

FISH. Bassenthwaite (OE/ON: Bastun's Lake). 4 miles/6.4km long and ¾ miles/ 1.2km wide. Maximum depth 70ft/21.3m. Average depth 18ft/5.48m. Height above sea-level 223ft/68m. Eel, perch, pike, salmon, 3-spined stickleback, brown trout and vendace. Ouse Bridge and eastern shore best. Permits/licence from Temple Sports or Field & Stream, Keswick or Gunshop and D. W. Lothian. Cockermouth. The whole lake is a Site of Special Scientific Interest and is owned by the National Park Authority. Southern part of the lake is a nature reserve, the middle section is used for various non-boating activities and the northern part is used for sailing connected with the Bass Lake Sailing Club. Boat hire at Piel Wyke ("bay of the castle") harbour. Public access to Bassenthwaite Lake only at Ouse Bridge, Wythop and Woodend. Footpath along NE shore. NY 2031

20 32

ARCHITECTURE. Armathwaite Hall, near Bassenthwaite. 1881. Castellated Victorian/Tudor mansion, but now a hotel. During the last war used as a school. Formerly seat of the Vanes, then the Bowsteads and later still the Hartleys. Phone 07687 76551. NY 208325

20 36

ARCHAEOLOGY. Site of Roman turf-built fort. Circa AD 70. Caermot, Binsey Fell. Bassenthwaite. NY 202368

21 32

REFRESHMENT. Castle Inn. Bassenthwaite. Phone 07687 76401. NY 215327

22 31

CHURCH. St John. Bassenthwaite. 1878. Small spire, polygonal apse and lancet windows. NY 228316

22 32

CHURCH. Methodist Chapel. 1865. Near village green. Bassenthwaite.

NY 229321

22 33

HISTORICAL. Sheep stealers were hanged at Cobblers Hollow named so because its trees provided wood for clog soles. Bassenthwaite.   NY 229335

MINE. Robin Hood Mine. Antimony—about 20 tons during 1840s.

NY 227330

22 35

ARCHAEOLOGY. Tumulus. Binsey.   NY 225355

23 31

MINE. High Mill Trial; level. Antimony samples 1840s.   NY 239319

23 32

ARCHITECTURE. Orchard Cottage has plaque over door "This house done by John Grave 1736." Bassenthwaite.   NY 231323

REFRESHMENT. Sun Inn. Bassenthwaite. Phone 07687 76439.   NY 231323

23 35

WALL. Believed to be the last wall built (late C19) to enclose land. 3 miles/ 4.82km long it took a farmer and his three sons 5 years to complete. Binsey near Ruthwaite. Dating enclosure walls without documentary evidence is difficult but, in general, a wall with rounded corners was easier to build in the absence of accurate surveying—only possible from c1760. In this region most of the fell walls were built mainly by itinerant labour following the General Enclosure Act of 1801 when common rights were abolished. The first meaningful survey executed in Scotland after 1745 rebellion when lack of maps caused grave problems to Royalist commanders, and the Lake District re-surveyed accurately on the scale of 1 inch to 1 mile.   NY 2335

23 36

HISTORICAL. Mary White, a successful Ruthwaite farmer's daughter, in 1797 married (the later famous) John Peel after eloping to Gretna Green because of parental objections to her suitor.   NY 238368

MINE. Ruthwaite Barytes Mine. 1870s to 1920.   NY 238369

23 37

CHURCH. St James. Uldale Mill. 1730—some C16. Nave, chancel and twin bellcote. White. Chalice 1571 with rare leather cover. Permission to view from Vicar of Ireby. 1915 Lych-gate.   NY 239379

23 38

ARCHITECTURE. Market Cross and Moot Hall. Market Charter granted 1237. Important centre for corn trade in C18. Ireby. NY 238387

CHURCH. St James. Ireby (settlement of the Irish). 1847. Nave, bellcote & chancel. Lancet windows. Font with four carved roundels. Interesting porch stones, one to John de Ireby who died 700 years ago, carved with cross and sword.
NY 238389

REFRESHMENT. Black Lion Inn. Ireby. NY 239387

24 34

ARCHAEOLOGY. Roman camp site, remains of. Orthwaite. NY 248345

ARCHITECTURE. Whitefield House. Bassenthwaite. 1840. Castellated. Roman Doric columns. Interesting fenestration. NY 244346

25 34

ARCHITECTURE. Orthwaite Hall. Bassenthwaite. 1675. Interesting features. One time home of William George Browne, intrepid middle-eastern voyager murdered in Persia 1812. NY 253342

25 35

EVENT. Marathon fell run includes the area's 27 lakes, meres & waters. In July 1983 Jos Naylor MBE set a new record for the 106 miles/170km run plus 18,000ft/5486m of ascent at 19 hours 14 mins 25 secs. Overwater near Uldale. (Refer NY 259139). NY 2535

FISH. Overwater. Depth 60 ft/18.2m. Rainbow trout. Permit from Mr. S. G. Payne. Rydal Mount Racing Stables. Gilcrux. Phone 06973 20010. NY 2535

25 36

REFRESHMENT. Snooty Fox. Uldale. Phone 09657 479. NY 250369

26 30

BIRDS. Peregrine falcon nest site. Dead Crags. Skiddaw Forest. NY 268308

26 31

MINE. Dead Beck Trial—for lead—not proven. NY 262312

26 38

ARCHAEOLOGY. Bronze Age/Roman. 3 huts circles and enclosures—suggest a farm settlement; evidence of a droveway. 12 urns excavated. Aughertree Fell.
NY 263380

27 31

WATERFALLS. Whitewater Dash, 100ft/30m. Near gated road from Bassenthwaite which leads to Skiddaw House thence to Threlkeld and Keswick.
NY 272314

27 35

MINE. Longlands Copper Mine. Trial levels. 1841–1857. Now used as a small reservoir. NY 271352, NY 272356 and NY 273351

28 37

CRAFTS. Weaving. Greenrigg cottage. NY 288374

29 32

MINE. Little Wiley Gill Mine, Caldbeck Fells. Confluence of Red Gill and Little Wiley Gill. Little found other than clusters of quartz crystals. NY 297322

29 33

MINE. Roughtongill Mine at Balliway Rigg, Caldbeck Fells. C16 & abandoned 1894. Lead, copper and zinc plus barytes and umber. 30/60oz of silver per ton of lead metal. NY 298339

29 34

MINE. Red Gill Mine. Caldbeck Fells. Small quantities of lead and copper plus the rare mineral linarite. Closed 1871. Recent application to reopen refused on safety grounds. NY 295348

29 35

MINE. Braefell Mine. Worked several times in C19 but unsuccessfully. Spoil heaps contain some galena and other minerals. NY 298357

Area 3 – Mungrisdale

30 34

MINE. Roughtongill Mine. A level east of Clints Gill. C12—abandoned 1894. Lead, copper and zinc plus small quantities of barytes, umber and mixed mineral clays. 30/60 oz of silver per ton of lead metal. Here German miners erected one of the first crushing and dressing plants in the Lake District. NY 309345

WATERFALLS. Roughtongill. Series of small falls near to old mine workings. Sign-posted path from Fell Side Farm (NY 305375). 2¼ miles/3.62km. Circuit. Moderate. NY 302346

30 36

INDUSTRIAL ARCHAEOLOGY. Roughtongill Mine smelting works (remains of) could process 100 tons of lead ore a month. NY 301362

MINE. Hay Gill Mine. There are many related trial levels hereabouts. 1785–1874. Lead and copper. NY 308360

30 38

REFRESHMENT. C17 farmhouse Parkend. Home made food. NY 301389

30 39

CHURCH. Friends Meeting House. Whelpo. Near to east side of the bridge; single storied cottage, three bay. 1698. NY 3039

31 30

GEOLOGY. Schist. NY 318306

31 34

MEMORIAL. A slate bench atop High Pike 2159ft/658m bears two plaques: one to Mick Lewis of Nether Row. Died 1944 aged 16 "who loved all these hills." The other to his mother who outlived him by several years. Caldbeck Fells. NY 319349

MINE. China Clay Mine. Originally known as Hare Stones Umber Mine. First worked 1883 for umber but little found though much white clay. Closed 1894. NY 311347

1818 Level. Its spoil heaps in steep-sided gill east of China Clay Mine. Stone-arched in initial footage near to end of which is chiselled an inscription "SR/1818: Aged/58." NY 315347

31 37

MINE. Old Potts Gill Copper Mine. 1867–1871. Very small amounts of lead and copper ores. Spoil heaps contain good specimens of chalcopyrites. NY 318371

31 39

INDUSTRIAL ARCHAEOLOGY. Remains of Howk Bobbin Mill in limestone gorge, Caldbeck. NY 319398

32 32

GEOLOGY. Quartz and Apatite. Caldew Valley. NY 323329

Wolfram. To be found in mine tip at Brandy Gill. Caldew Valley. NY 326329

MINE. Carrock Tungsten Mine. Tungsten, some arsenopyrite-arsenic and wolframite plus bismuth, gold and scheelite. Some 23 different mineral species have been found here. 1850s–1981. The importance of this mine and its tungsten necessitates a "care and maintenance" regime until such time as other sources of tungsten are unavailable resulting in increased world prices. NY 324329

32 33

MINE. Upper Brandy Gill Mine. c1724–1877. Mainly copper, some lead, plus 23 varieties of minerals. NY 322338

WATERFALLS. Brandy Gill. Carrock Fell. Follow mine road at Mosedale's telephone box—sign-posted Swineside. Park at Grainsgill Beck and climb track beside old mine workings. 3 miles/4.82km. Circuit. Moderate. NY 324335

32 34

MINE. Dry Gill Mine. Last worked 1894. Lead plus rare mineral campylite. Spoil heaps contain good specimens of barytes and malachite. Hereabouts is an area of Cardocian Shale containing fossils. NY 325346

32 35

MINE. Driggith Mine. 30 fathom level. 1791–1940s. Mainly lead—some copper. Also No. 12 level at NY 324353 (Refer NY 331362). Up to 60 oz of silver per ton of lead metal. NY 327353

32 36

MINE. Old Potts Gill. 1871–1947. Barytes. The only mine in the Caldbeck Fells to have produced the greatest variety of minerals. NY 320361 and NY 320365

East Potts Gill Mine. Barytes. 1942–1966. NY 321361

32 39

ARCHITECTURE. Rectory 1785. Caldbeck. Two tripartite windows face the churchyard. Built on site of C12 hospice dissolved under King John. NY 326399

CHURCH. St Kentigern. Caldbeck (ON "Cold brook"). Medieval tower, Norman doorway. Inside—six bays with octagonal piers on S side and round piers on N side. Other interesting architectural differences. Royal Arms of George IV. Saxon well site below steps to river named after St Mungo. Churchyard—grave of John Peel of Ruthwaite. Headstone portrays hunting horns. Died November 13th 1854, aged 78 years, after hunting accident at Ruthwaite—3,000 attended his funeral. His friend John Woodcock Graves, Manager of a Caldbeck woollen mill (1671 and now a ruin)

26

produced the grey cloth mentioned in his song "D'ye Ken John Peel ..." he wrote in 1828 in the Caldbeck cottage bearing "TBB 1718" over the door lintel. The air to the song was "Bonnie Annie" an old Border tune, but rearranged in 1868 by William Metcalfe, a choral member and then organist of Carlisle Cathedral, where he was buried 1909. Graves emigrated to Australia, died aged 91 and is buried beside the Derwent River which flows beneath Mount Wellington, Hobart, Tasmania. Also, grave of Mary Harrison (*née* Robinson) "The Beauty of Buttermere". (Refer Area 11. 1717 Historical) Eventually she had married Richard Harrison, a Caldbeck farmer, by whom she had quite a large family. Died 1837 aged 58.   NY 326399

Methodist Chapel—previously Wesleyan Chapel. 1832. Plaque—"Remember now Thy Creator." Caldbeck.   NY 3239

CRAFT CENTRE. In Priests Mill built 1702 as a cornmill, later used as a sawmill and joiners workshop. Mining Museum and Cafe. Gift shop and local crafts. Photography studio. Operating watermill. Caldbeck. N from church then left down lane. Open Tues/Sun. 1100/1700hrs. Phone 06998 369.   NY 327399

REFRESHMENT. The Oddfellow's Arms, originally the John Peel Inn. Caldbeck. Has portrait of John Peel. Phone 06998 227.   NY 322397

33 32

TREES. Junipers, growing on Borrowdale Volcanic Series screes. Caldew Valley.
NY 3332

St Bega Church, Bassenthwaite. (Author)

33 35
MINE. Driggith Mine. 60 fathom level. Mainly lead, some copper. (Refer NY 327353).   NY 330359

33 36
MINE. Driggith Mine. 90 fathom level. Mainly lead, some copper. Virtually non-productive. (Refer NY 327353).   NY 331362

Sandbeds East Mine. Barytes. 1946–1966.   NY 333362

Sandbeds West Mine. Barytes. 1952–1966.   NY 331362

33 38
ARCHITECTURE. C18 market cross—four round pillars surmounted by a pyramidal roof. Hesket Newmarket "Ash tree headland".   NY 339385

Hesket Newmarket Hall. Built by Sir Wilfred Lawson c1635 so that the sun on the twelve angled walls and the circular roof indicate the time, in the manner of a sun dial.   NY 339386

34 32
GEOLOGY. Magnetite. Carrock Fell.   NY 3432

34 33
ARCHAEOLOGY. Carrock Fell. Largest Cumbrian Romano-Iron Age fort covering 5 acres/2ha. There is a small cairn in form of an Early Bronze Age Burial cairn. No visible traces of hut circles; fort possibly only used in summer—transhumance.   NY 343337

GEOLOGY. Borrowdale volcanic series. Carrock Fell.   NY 3433

Diorite.   NY 3433

Gabbro.   NY 3433

34 34
MINE. Dry Gill Mine. Level driven 1868. (Refer NY 325346).   NY 345346

34 38
EVENT. Hesket Newmarket Agricultural Show. Last Saturday in August. Livestock, Sheep, Fell Ponies and Horses, Dogs, Wrestling, Handicrafts, Produce, Vintage Machinery, Trade Stands.   NY 3438

REFRESHMENT. Old Crown Inn. Hesket Newmarket. 400 years old. Excellent beer brewed on the premises. Unusually a lending library in the bar. Phone 06998 288.   NY 340386

35 32
CHURCH. Quaker Meeting House, Mosedale. 1702—enlarged 1884, restored 1973. Regular Meetings for Worship are held. Light refreshments are served daily except Mondays and Sunday afternoons from May to September.   NY 357323

GEOLOGY. Feldspar in Gabbro found on Carrock Fell   NY 355323

35 33

ARCHAEOLOGY. Carrock Fell. Cremation burial sites. Approx 200 cairn circles.   NY 350330

35 34

MINE. Carrock End Mine. First worked c1700—abandoned 1869. 4 cross-cut levels hereabouts. Copper.   NY 351343

REFRESHMENT. Carrock Fell Hotel.   NY 352344

WALKS. Carrock Fell. Circuit 8¾ miles/14km. Ascent 1400ft/426m. Strenuous. Extensive views of "back o' Skidda". Start: Carrock Fell Hotel.   NY 352344

35 35

INDUSTRIAL ARCHAEOLOGY. Remains of a small smelting works for Driggith Mine beside Carrock Beck. (Refer NY 327353).   NY 352350

YOUTH HOSTEL. Carrock Fell. High Row Cottages. Haltcliff. Hesket New-market. Wigton. Phone 06998 325.   NY 358355

36 30

CHURCH. St Kentigern. Mungrisdale. (C "Mung": dearer one, and refers to St Kentigern; ON "Grisdale": young-pig valley). 1756. Nave, chancel and bellcote with C15 bell. Three decker pulpit earliest panel of which is 1679. Box pews. Cover Paten and Cup inscribed "Mounge Grieesdell 1600". Black Letter Bible of 1617. Cobbled porch. On site of earlier church AD 552. Memorial tablet to Raisley Calvert, whose son, also Raisley, nursed by Wordsworth when dying of consumption, died 1795. The Poet was beneficiary under his Will in the sum of £900. Wordsworth was moved to write a 14 line Sonnet entitled "To the Memory of Raisley Calvert"; "Calvert! it must not be unheard by them/Who may respect my name; that I to thee/Owed many years of early liberty..."   NY 364305

GEOLOGY. Skiddaw slates. Mungrisdale.   NY 3630

REFRESHMENT. Mill Inn. C16. Mungrisdale. Phone 07687 79632 Originally a Mill. Popular venue of Charles Dickens and Wilkie Collins. (Charles Dickens 1812–70 novelist, born Portsmouth educated Chatham. Died in Gad's Hill. Buried Westminster Abbey. London. William Wilkie Collins 1824–89 originator of the modern mystery novel. Buried Kensall Green. London).   NY 363302

WALKS. Souther Fell. (Pronounced "Sowter" Fell). Circuit 5 miles/8km. Moderate. Some wet areas. Start: Mill Inn Mungrisdale.   NY 362303

Good views of River Glenderamackin, Blencathra (Saddleback) and its Sharp Edge. Good weather essential.   NY 363302

36 31

GEOLOGY. Site of earlier glacial lake. Mosedale (ON "mosi": the dale of peat moss).   NY 3631

36 36

GEOLOGY. Limestone, cut through by River Caldew. Haltcliff Bridge.

NY 367367

37 33

GEOLOGY. Limestone. Greystoke.   NY 3733

37 35

ARCHITECTURE. Thwaite Hall, Mungrisdale. Rebuilt 1555 and modernised 1870. Large stone chimney.   NY 375350

37 36

CHURCH. St Kentigern. Castle Sowerby. C12/13. Low. Porch entrance C14/15. Double bellcote.   NY 379362

39 33

MAMMALS. Red deer—best at dusk. Greystoke Forest.   NY 3933

39 34

MAMMALS. Roe deer. Greystoke Forest. Observation hide. Permit from Head Forester, Millfield Lodge. Hutton Roof.   NY 3934

Helm Crag, Grasmere. (Author)

Area 4 – Skelton

41 31

ARCHAEOLOGY. Remains of a camp. Berrier Hill.   NY 416313

42 35

NATURE RESERVE/TRAIL. Scrub and woodland. Roe deer. Butterflies. Managed by Cumbria Wildlife Trust and open to Public all year. Ellonby.

NY 423359

42 36

ARCHITECTURE. Hardrigg Hall near Skelton now a farm. Near ruined Pele tower.   NY 425362

43 30

ARCHITECTURE. Greenthwaite Hall. Greystoke. From 1380s seat of the Haltons. Mullioned windows. Diagonally set chimneys. Three storied porch with heraldic and inscribed door.   NY 432302

CASTLE. Greystoke. Part medieval, part C19. Original Pele tower C14—for which William Lord Greystoke was given permission to crenellate in 1353. During reign of Queen Elizabeth I, Philip Howard, Earl of Arundel acquired the castle through marriage to the heiress of Lord Dacre. It is still the Howard family home. Not open to the public.   NY 436308

LEGEND. Greystoke Castle is said to be haunted by The Devil who visits once a year one night in February. Charles Howard, the then Duke of Norfolk, followed hounds, even on the Sabbath, which could only result in tragedy, according to the locals. During one such hunt a strange gentleman on a black horse enquired whether he might join the Duke's party—he proved such an entertaining person that the Duke invited him to stay overnight—in the Pele Tower. Next morning there was no sign of the stranger although his neatly folded clothes were there and the bed had been slept in. Likewise, his black horse had disappeared from the locked stable where it had been bedded overnight. The Duke and his entourage were perplexed but the locals were convinced that it was The Devil. Unknowing visitors who have since stayed overnight in that Peel Tower room on a certain February night have claimed to be disturbed by a spectre with cloven hooves and horned goat's head. The room now stands empty.   NY 436308

REFRESHMENT. The Boot & Shoe Inn. C16. Greystoke. Run by the third generation of the Tweedle family. Phone 07684 83343.   NY 439309

43 32

ARCHITECTURE. Johnby Hall Greystoke. Built by William Musgrave c1584 around a Pele Tower. Later additions. Doorway inscription.   NY 434327

43 35

CHURCH. St Michael. Skelton ("place on a hill/bank"). 1794. C14 tower. C18 pulpit. Font octagonal baluster. Ornate east window. South wall sundial c1750. Peace Memorial lych-gate.   NY 439356

Primitive Methodist chapel. 1865. Skelton.   NY 437357

REFRESHMENT. The Dog & Gun Inn. Skelton. Phone 07687 73463.
                                                                              NY 437354

44 30

CHURCH. St Andrew. Greystoke (C "crei": fresh/clear and OE "stoc": a place/settlement). C13/17. Founded as a Collegiate Church. W tower appears medieval but rebuilt in 1848. E window nearly all C15 glass—rare appearance in a church window of the devil trampled on by a Saint. Oak stalls have carved misericords. Ancient bells. Early artifacts and brasses—one, a memorial to Henry Askew killed in France and buried by the Germans who inscribed the cross "Here lies a brave British Officer." Other brasses, to Margaret Moresby (c1540), Richard Newport (1551) and Winifred Newport (1547). Also a brass of Dr John Whelpdale 1526, a Master of the College of Greystoke founded by Sir William de Greystoke in 1358. Alabaster effigies of William 14th Baron of Greystoke (died 1359) and John, 4th Baron Greystoke. Finely carved rood screen. Medieval sanctuary stone, of blue whinstone, marked the boundary beyond which fugitives from justice could claim sanctuary of the church. The stone is now protected by a wrought iron grill in nearby wall. Plague stone (known locally as "Spillers") where, during The Plague which nearly decimated the villagers, coins were "purified" in vinegar before changing hands. The hollowed out stone lies beside path N of the church.   NY 442307

44 32

ARCHITECTURE. Blencow Hall. Between two low towers. Centre of house doorway lintel bears date 1590. Mullioned windows. Pele Tower.   NY 449326

45 30

ARCHITECTURE. Fort Putnam farm. Greystoke. Named after General Israel "Puffing" Putnam. Turret, castellations, tall Gothic window. Arches. Interesting wall screening C18 farm buildings. Planning Application for change of use.   NY 452309

45 32

CHURCH. Methodist chapel—originally Wesleyan chapel. 1877. Little Blencow.
                                                                              NY 454327

CRAFTS. Old Smithy. Blencow. Brass & copper artefacts manufactured. NY 454328

HISTORICAL. Farm building with square cupola once a renowned Grammar School, founded by Thomas Burbank. Over the door may still be seen "Ye Youthe rejoice at this foundation/Being made for your education. AD 1577." In 1913 it merged with Penrith Grammar School. Two famous scholars: Edward Law (1750–1818) created Lord Ellenborough later Lord Chief Justice of England and George Whitehead (c1636–1723), celebrated Quaker. Great Blencow.   NY 456322

REFRESHMENT. The Crown Inn. Little Blencow. NY 453327

45 36

CHURCH. St James. Hutton in the Forest (OE "hoh": the farm on the spur of land—in the forest). Originally 1714 (on site of earlier chapel) but much rebuilt. Chancel imitation C15, nave windows imitation C16. C10 cross fragment embedded in masonry. C17 Memorial to Sir George Fletcher who was "Knight of the Shire near 40 years." C17 Communion rails. NY 459364

46 30

ARCHITECTURE. Bunkers Hill Farm. Name derived from Battle of Bunkers Hill in USA, in which the Howards fought. Centre part, castellated to three sides. Pointed windows. NY 465303

REFRESHMENT. Clickham Inn. Blencow. Phone 07684 406. NY 467309

46 31

ARCHITECTURE. Spire House Farm. Greystoke. Castellations to part of the facade with arches below, 2 round blind, 2 double pointed. Polygonal storey supports lead spire—resembling that of a church. It is said that the resident tenant told his landlord, the Duke of Norfolk, that his religious beliefs did not necessitate church attendance for worship, as his own house would suffice, whereupon the Duke had erected for him a "church-like" building. NY 463313

46 32

INDUSTRIAL ARCHAEOLOGY. The original grain mill converted to the present day timber mill. Laithes. NY 463328

46 35

EVENT. Skelton Agricultural Show. Old Park, Hutton-in-the-Forest. Livestock, Show Jumping, Crafts, Produce and Trade Stands, Carriage Driving. 3rd Saturday in August. NY 4635

HISTORIC HOUSE. Hutton-in-the-Forest. Part medieval with C17 additions. C14 Pele tower, long gallery. Previously the residence of the Fletchers and the Vanes; now the private home of Lord and Lady Inglewood, whose family seat it has been since C17. Fine collection of furniture, paintings and tapestries. Cupid room, magnificent recently restored plaster ceiling. Open end of May/end of Sept. Thurs, Fri & Sun and Bank Holiday Mondays, 1300–1600hrs. Fee. In winter by appointment. Phone 08534 84449. Woodland walk, C17 Dovecot and gardens open all year. 1100–1700hrs except Saturdays. NY 4635

WALKS. Inglewood Forest, relict of. Hutton-in-the-Forest. NY 460358

47 31

ARCHITECTURE. Farmhouse—typical longhouse (living quarters, byre & barn under one roof). Opposite St John's Church. Newton Reigny. NY 479317

CHURCH. St John. Newton Reigny (from the De Reigny family who possessed the area 1185–1275). C12. Nave, twin bellcote (one of these bells is from Shap Abbey when the Monastery was dissolved), aisles and chancel. Cover Paten and Cup 1568. A beam next to chancel bears a carving "The Naymes of the Carpynteis that have builded the Roofe An Domi 1583. Videlict John Atkenson and Henere Bymert." Vault of Vaux family of Catterlen and Richmond tombs.   NY 479316

REFRESHMENT. The Sun Inn. Newton Reigny. Phone 0768 67055.

NY 479315

47 32

ARCHITECTURE. Catterlen Hall Newton Reigny, now a farmhouse. C15/16. Pele tower range with Henry VIII window. Manorial residence of the De Vaux family from c1160.   NY 478321

47 38

ARCHITECTURE. Brackenburgh Tower. 1903. Built in Tudor tradition. Pele tower. Oriel above entrance.   NY 476384

48 30

ARCHAEOLOGY. Newton Reigny. Long cairn. Burial urns have been found.

NY 483304

GEOLOGY. Sandstone—dark red. In Penrith used with limestone. "Throughs" in walls. Newton Reigny.   NY 4830

Borrowdale from Latrigg. (Author)

48 31

ARCHAEOLOGY. Newton Reigny. Enclosure. NY 482316

REFRESHMENT. George III Inn. Newton Reigny. NY 480314

49 30

FARM. Cumbria College of Agriculture and Forestry. Newton Rigg. Open days.
Phone 0768 63791. NY 492309

49 37

CHURCH. St John Evangelist. Plumpton Wall. 1907. Wagon roof richly carved
with roses. Much linenfold carvings. Beautiful and of high architectural merit.
  NY 497372

HISTORICAL. Percy Topliss the "Monocled Mutineer", well known fraudster
and murderer, died 1920 in gunfire exchange with Inspector Riche and Sergeant
Bertram, on roadside by Romanway Farm, Plumpton. NY 497374

49 38

ARCHAEOLOGY. Castlesteads. Roman fort—Voreda. Not fully excavated. Inscriptions found indicate that fort was garrisoned in C3 by 2nd Cohort of Gauls guarding the
important highway between Chester and Hadrians Wall. NY 494384

Buttermere and Haystacks. (Rosemary Liddle)

AREA 5 – Penrith

50 36

ARCHAEOLOGY. Site of Roman camp. Plumpton Wall.   NY 500363

51 30

CHURCH. St Andrew. Penrith (C "penrhudd": red hill & OE "chief ford"). 1720–2. Red sandstone. Only the C12 west tower remains from the previous building. Probably a chapel on this site in C6. Wall paintings by local artist Jack Thompson 1845. C15 fragments of stained glass in N aisle window. S aisle window 2 heads, parents of Cicely Neville mother of Richard III and Edward IV. Two chandeliers 1745 given by the Duke of Portland in gratitude for the rout on Clifton Moor of Bonnie Prince Charles. C11 crosses & Hogsback coffins perhaps combined produced what is popularly known as the Giants Grave. The giant: Tarquin (ON "Thorfinn") supposedly killed by Sir Lancelot du Lac. Late in C16 the grave was opened and very large bones found. The grave thought to be of Owain Caesarius, King of Cumbria 920/937. Gothic mausoleum. Grave of Wordsworth's mother who died when he was 8. She was Anne, daughter of William Cookson, textile dealer of Penrith who was only 31 when she died in 1778. Memorial to Robert Virtue (John Stephenson's superintendent of works during construction of Lancaster & Carlisle Railway), who died 1846. The pinnacled Gothic screen is a feature of the churchyard.   NY 516302

Quaker Meeting House C18. Meeting House Lane. Penrith. Two galleries formed from original stables—handsome woodwork.   NY 516305

CRAFTS. Eden's Craft Gallery in old Grammar School. St Andrew's Churchyard. Penrith. Phone 0768 67955.   NY 516303

EVENT. Penrith Agricultural Society Show on 4th Saturday July. Livestock, Sheep Dog Trials, Show Jumping, Carriage Driving, Produce, Handicrafts, Horticulture, Trade Stands, Vintage Machinery.   NY 5130

LITERARY. Home of Wordsworth's maternal grandparents, William and Dorothy Cookson and Mary Hutchinson. Arnison's shop. Middlegate, Penrith.

NY 516302

Dame Anne Birkett's School in 1777, overlooking St Andrew's, where William and Dorothy Wordsworth and Mary Hutchinson were school chums. Tudor House Cafe. Penrith.   NY 516302

Wordsworth nursed Raisley Calvert (son of Duke of Norfolk's agent) during terminal illness 1795 at the Robin Hood Inn. Penrith. He left Wordsworth £900 which freed the poet from penury. Wordsworth later wrote "I should have been forced by necessity into one of the professions, had not a friend left me £900. This bequest was from a young man with whom, though I call him friend, I had but little connection; and the act was done entirely from a confidence on his part that I had power and attainments which might be of some use to mankind."

NY 516302

MEMORIAL. Victorian clock tower commemorating Philip Musgrave of Eden Hall, on site of original market cross, demolished early C19. Penrith.   NY 516301

REFRESHMENT. The Gloucester Arms. 1477. Once Dockray Hall. Great Dockray, Penrith. One of the oldest inns in England. Over the entrance, Arms of Richard III (two boars rampant). He lived here when visiting Penrith as Warden of the North. He was crowned King of England in 1483 and defeated in 1485 at The Battle of Bosworth Field. The main bar is the original hall which still retains interesting panelling. Phone 0768 62150.   NY 516300

Penrith is famous for its FUDGE—exports world wide. The Toffee Shop. Brunswick Road. Penrith.   NY 514304

TOURIST INFORMATION CENTRE. In Robinson's School 1670–1970. Also has a small Museum. Middlegate, Penrith. Phone 0768 64671.   NY 514304

52 31

ARCHITECTURE. Penrith Beacon of Sandstone. 1715. On same site as earlier warning tower against Scottish raiders. Square, pyramidal roof, round arched windows. In 1805 beacon lighted to warn of Napoleonic invasion—proved false. Scott, then touring the Lakes, immediately returned to Dalkeith to join his regiment.   NY 522314

53 35

QUARRY. Last working quarry in Penrith Sandstone.   NY 533353

54 35

INDUSTRIAL ARCHAEOLOGY. Horse Engine House (local name "Gin Case"). Beckbank.   NY 546358

HISTORICAL. A brass dish of 1417, resembling a platter or a shield, 16in/40cm in diameter, given to the daughter of the house on her marriage to a "King of Mardale" (Refer NY 456115). With effaced boss inscription which read "Mary, Mother of Jesus. Saviour of Men. If e'er this dish be sold or gi'en, Farewell the Luck of Burrell Green." Burrellgreen farm near Great Salkeld.   NY 546353

54 39

CHURCH. St Michael. Lazonby. C14/15 perhaps. The original medieval church was swept away by River Eden flood waters. Interesting artefacts and churchyard curios. Much of the woodwork was carved by Canon Wilson buried here in 1921 after an incumbency of 40 years.   NY 547395

55 30

BIRDS. Goosander nesting site. Whins Pond.   NY 5530

FISH. Whins Pond. Rainbow trout—on fly. Bag limit. Permit from adjacent house. Mrs E. Siddle. Ewanway, Edenhall, Penrith. Phone 0768 62671.   NY 5530

HISTORICAL. Traditional cell of St Ninian. Early Christian community site across river. Isis Parlis (Giants Graves) caves. They can only be approached by passing along narrow ledges of the cliff. The first cave is only a narrow recess but the other is capacious and appears to have had a door and a window. Near Penrith.
NY 559303

55 35

ARCHITECTURE. Nunwick Hall. 1892. Tudor style. Red sandstone. Gables. Mullioned windows, arched lights.   NY 554359

55 36

CHURCH. St Cuthbert. Great Salkeld ("a large sallow wood"). C14 tower, immense for the size of the church, with embattled parapet—stronghold or refuge during border raids. Some C17 armour preserved therein. Dungeon. Nave & chancel. Fine Norman doorway. Roman altar in porch. Fireplace on 1st floor. Artefacts from Civil War. Windows—St Cuthbert & William Nicholson (1655–1727) Bishop of Carlisle. Effigies of Thomas de Caldbec, Archdeacon of Carlisle, died 1319; Anthony Hutton died 1637 and his wife. The building of the church said to have been financed by Sir Richard Whittington, three times Lord Mayor of London.   NY 552368

Barn Dovecot. Low Snab Farm, Newlands. (Author)

HISTORICAL. Rectory. Great Salkeld. Birthplace of Edward Law (1750–1818), later Lord Ellenborough and, following successful defence of Warren Hastings 1st Governor General of Bengal India, Lord Chief Justice of England. Hastings was impeached for collusion at Westminster Hall in 1788—resulted in 6 year trial. (See G. R. Gleig *Life of Warren Hastings* 3 Volumes 1841; Sir G. W. Forrest *Selections from the State Papers of Warren Hastings* 2 Volumes 1910; G. W. Hastings *A Vindication of Warren Hastings* 1909; A. Mervyn Davies *Warren Hastings* 1935).

NY 552368

REFRESHMENT. The Highland Drove Inn. Great Salkeld. Phone 0768 83349.

NY 551369

AREA 6 – Lorton

08 20

CHURCH. St Michael. Lamplugh ("bare valley"). 1870. Large double bellcote. Stained glass by Kempe. Notable artefacts. 3 gargoyles. NY 089208

HISTORICAL. The superstition and beliefs of local populace in C17 well illustrated by this extract from the Register of Deaths in Lamplugh parish from "janry ye 1, 1658 to Janye ye 1, 1663—Frightened to death by fairies 6/Bewitched 4/Old women drowned upon a trial for witchcraft 3/Led into a horse pond by a will o' the wisp 1." NY 089208

REFRESHMENT. The Lamplugh Arms. Lamplugh. NY 089209

The Pack of Hounds Inn. Lamplugh. Phone 0946 861232 NY 089209

09 28

CHURCH. Christchurch. Eaglesfield (OE "Ecgel's Feld": Eagles Field.) 1872. Round apse, steeple. George III plate. NY 095282

HISTORICAL. Birthplace of Robert de Egglesfield, chaplain to Queen Philippa of Hainault, founder of Queen's College, Oxford—buried there 1349. Eaglesfield. NY 0928

Birthplace of John Dalton (1766–1844). Scientist. Developed Atomic Theory. A child prodigy he taught at Pardshaw Hall School when only 13. Memorial tablet above doorway of his home—"John Dalton DCL LLD The Discoverer of The Atomic Theory Was born here 5th September 1766 Died at Manchester 27th July 1844." The Carlisle Public Library has a sheet of coloured ribbons as seen by Dalton, who was colour-blind. Eaglesfield. NY 0928

REFRESHMENT. The Black Cock Inn. Eaglesfield. Phone 0900 822989. NY 096281

10 23

MINE. Sosgill Trial—level. Lead. NY 103237

10 25

HISTORICAL. At Pardshaw Crag SE of Eaglesfield, George Fox the Quaker founder, using the natural acoustic properties of the rocks preached to a multitude c1653. Here also, in 1857 Neale Dow the American temperance reformer, addressed over 5000 people. NY 104256

10 28

CHURCH. John Dalton Memorial Church erected by the Royal Society in commemoration. Nave with bellcote & chancel. Eaglesfield. NY 107280

HISTORICAL. Birthplace of Fletcher Christian 1764, who led the Mutiny on the *Bounty* against Captain Bligh in 1789 and afterwards founded the Pitcairn Island colony. Moorland Close. NY 108286

PLANTS. Lowland moss habitat. Dubb's Moss. (Cumbria Wildlife Trust.) Permit required from Church St Ambleside. NY 102288

WALL. Incorporates bee-boles. Eaglesfield. NY 108286

11 21

WATERFALLS. Holme Force. Loweswater. Sign-posted path adjacent to lay-by between Grange Hotel and Loweswater Hall, leads to Hudson Place beyond which a lane gives way to a path to the Force in Holme Wood. 2½ miles/4.02km. Circuit. Easy. NY 118217

11 22

REFRESHMENT. The Grange Hotel. Waterend. Loweswater.
Phone 0946 861211. NY 116226

11 23

WELL. St Ninian's Well; the Celtic saint was also known as St Ringan. Tradition has it that the Cumbrian born saint preached to and converted the local people circa AD 390. Fangs Brow. Loweswater. NY 110236

11 24

CHURCH. St Michael. Mosser ("the sheiling in the peat moss"). 1773. Small. Nave bellcote & chancel. NY 114242

11 29

YOUTH HOSTEL. Double Mills. Cockermouth. Phone 0900 822561.
NY 118298

12 21

ARCHITECTURE. Barn with Dovecot. Watergate Farm. Loweswater.
NY 127210

FISH. Loweswater. (ON "Laghi's Water": Laghi a personal name. Also ON "Laufs-saer-vatn": leafy lake). Owned by National Trust. 1½ miles/2.4km long, ½ mile/0.8km wide. 429ft/130m above sea-level. Maximum depth 60ft/18.2m. Eel, perch, pike and brown trout. Rowing boats available from Watergate Farm.
NY 1221

MEMORIAL. Wooden seat inscribed "Roy Barret." Carved boots and oak leaves. Corpse Road from Fangs Brow above Loweswater. NY 121217

PLANTS. Oakwood habitat—Holme. (National Trust). NY 1221

TREES. Oakwood. Holme and Watering Woods Loweswater. NY 1221

12 22

WALKS. Loweswater. Circuit 4 miles/6.4km. Easy. Start: lay-by NE of Lake. Holme Wood on SW shore has wide variety of Hardwood Trees. Lake flows into

Crummock Water, i.e. inwards towards the District's centre; all other lake flows are outwards.   NY 121223

13 20

ARCHAEOLOGY. Earthworks, south of Loweswater. It is thought that they may relate to a Dark Age church connected with St Ninian but their very size (approximately 150ft/45m by 80ft/24m) may suggest otherwise, although very possibly a sacred enclosure.   NY 139203

MINE. Kirkgill Wood Mine. Lead. (Refer NY 146216).   NY 139209

14 20

CHURCH. St Bartholomew. Loweswater. 1827, built by the villagers. Polygonal apse. Some geometric tracery. C14 bell. Cover Paten and Cup, 1570, the only relics in this form by John Freeman (noted silver smith) make them extremely valuable.   NY 141209

EVENT. Loweswater & Brackenthwaite Agricultural Show held annually on third Thursday of September in school field. Livestock, Show Jumping, Sheepdog Trial, Hound Trail, Carriage Driving, Fell Race, Handicrafts, Produce, Trade Stands.   NY 1420

MINE. Kirkgill Wood Mine. 1839–1860s. (Refer NY 139209).   NY 140208

REFRESHMENT. Kirkstile Inn (originally "The Hare and Hounds"). Loweswater. Phone 0900 85219.   NY 141209

14 21

MINE. Kirkgill Wood Mine. Buried level. Lead. Reputed that "Batey's Cave", as it is locally known, runs under nearby Scale Hill. Above car park at Scalehill Bridge.   NY 149215

Loweswater Lead Mine. 1819–1841. Shafts infilled. Lead. Adjacent to Moss Cottage (partly constructed from old mine buildings).   NY 146216

14 22

MINE. Kirkgill Wood Mine. Exploratory level on quartz vein below Cold Keld.   NY 148221

15 20

FISH. Crummock Water. (OE "Cromboc Water": Crooked Water). Owned by National Trust. 2½ miles/4km long, ½ mile/0.8km wide. 321ft/97m above sea-level. Maximum depth 144ft/43m. Average depth 88ft/26m. Charr, eel, perch, pike, brown trout and sea trout. Permit from Rannerdale Farm overlooking the water. Rowing boats for hire. North West Water Ltd licence required for sea trout.   NY 1520

HISTORICAL. Traces of C12 house (the Lindsays') at Peel, which name suggests some form of defensive tower.   NY 150203

PLANTS. Lake habitat—Crummock Water.   NY 1520

Aira Force. Ullswater. (Author)

Oakwood habitat—Lanthwaite (ME "longthwaite" [corrupted]: long clearing).
NY 1520

TREES. Oakwood. Lanthwaite. Crummock Water. NY 1520

WALKS. Crummock Water and Lanthwaite Wood. 4 miles/6.5km. Easy. Park in a lay-by and walk N several 100 yards/91m then past Lanthwaite Farm. Splendid views of Haystacks and Great Gable from lake shore. NY 158207

15 21

VIEWPOINT. Brackenthwaite Hows. 674ft/205m. Fine prospect of the serried ranks of mountains to S & E especially. NY 1521

15 22

ARCHAEOLOGY. Hut circle enclosure, 200ft/61m diameter. Brackenthwaite. Lorton Vale. NY 158220

ARCHITECTURE. Low Hollins. Brackenthwaite. 1687. Mullioned windows.
NY 158226

MINE. Liza Beck Trial. Some galena. NY 157222

15 25

ARCHITECTURE. Lorton Hall. Pele Tower. 7 bays. Mullion windowed living range. 1663 with later additions. Priest hole. Oak panelling. Carolingian & Jacobean furniture. It is said that on this site King Malcolm III (1057–93) and Queen Margaret stayed while touring Strathclyde which formed part of their kingdom. Open to the public by appointment only. Phone 0900 85252.
NY 153258

Pack-horse cottage 1734. Low Lorton. NY 153259

CHURCH. St Cuthbert. Lorton (OE "hlora": roaring stream). C19. Rendered. Embraced west tower. Short chancel, lancet windows. Unusual 1851 long-handled collecting shovel. Much heraldry on corbels, pews and pulpit. NY 155259

EVENT. Sheep Dog Trials. 3rd Saturday of July. Lorton. NY 1525

REFRESHMENT. Wheatsheaf Inn. Low Lorton. Phone 0900 85268.
NY 152259

15 26

EVENT. Melbreak Hunt Show. Dogs, Sheep Dog Trials, Hound Trail and Trade Stands. 4th Saturday of July. Lorton. NY 153268

16 20

ARCHAEOLOGY. Clustered settlement with banked enclosures. Lanthwaite Green. Grasmoor. NY 161209

16 21

GEOLOGY. Truncated spurs. Whiteside. Crummock Water. NY 1621

MINE. Gasgale Gill Trial. 10ft/3m inroad unsuccessful. NY 164210

16 25

CHURCH. Wesleyan Chapel 1840. High Lorton.   NY 160258

CRAFTS. White Ash Barn. High Lorton. Work by local artists, hand made crafts and pressed flower work. Open daily 1200–1700hrs week before Easter to end of October. Small restaurant. Phone 0900 85236.   NY 161257

HISTORICAL. The village hall was the site of the first Jennings Brewery. High Lorton.   NY 161255

TOURIST INFORMATION CENTRE. Post Office. High Lorton. Phone 0900 85220.   NY 162255

TREES. In field next to the Telephone Kiosk at High Lorton is the yew tree, mentioned by Wordsworth in the "Yew Trees" 1804 "There is a Yew tree, pride of Lorton Vale/Which to this day stands single, in the midst/Of its own darkness, as it stood of yore..." (lines 1–13). Its girth now exceeds 13ft/4m. Under this tree George Fox (1624–1691) who lived at Swarthmoor Hall, Ulverston, founder of the Society of Friends (Quakers), addressed a large crowd in 1653. In 1759 John Wesley preached from the same spot.   NY 162255

16 29

CHURCH. St Cuthbert. Embleton (OE "Eanbalds Tun": enclosed land). 1806. Slim tower. Interesting C18 artefacts.   NY 162294

17 20

GEOLOGY. Stone stripes. Grasmoor.   NY 1720

18 21

WATERFALLS. Gasgale Gill. Crummock Water. Start opposite car park at Lanthwaite Green Farm. 3½ miles/5.63km.   NY 184214

18 22

PLANTS. Only known English location of red alpine catchfly (*Viscaria alpina*). Hopegill Head.   NY 189223

18 26

WATERFALLS. 25ft/7m in woodland. Forestry Commission. Spout Force. High Lorton.   NY 183260

18 29

ARCHAEOLOGY. Circa C1 iron sword with jewelled hilt and bronze engraved scabbard found near Wythop Mill. It is now in the British Museum.   NY 1829

INDUSTRIAL ARCHAEOLOGY. Overshot water wheel powered corn mill, but used as a sawmill from 1860. Display of old hand tools and wood-working machinery. Wythop Mill. Embleton.   NY 180294

REFRESHMENT. Small cafe. Wine licence. Wythop Mill. Embleton. Phone

07687 76394. Very small car park. Open Easter-October. Sunday–Thursday. 1300–1700hrs. NY 180294

19 21

GEOLOGY. Zinc Blende, at Force Crag mine—in mining days known as "Black Jack". NY 193215

MINE. Force Crag Mine. High Force Workings. Barytes (principally barium sulphate) used in glass, rubber and paint manufacture, also as a lubricant for oil well drilling. At one time yielded 35oz of silver per ton of lead metal. New Coledale Mining Ltd is the present occupant but there have been many since 1578 when first ore analysis prepared. Connected to Low Force workings (NY 200216) by a tunnel known as Laporte Incline constructed by Laporte Chemicals in early 1950s. No 1 level has a spring at its end which, since discovery in 1855, has welled up 100 gallons a minute, the water slightly warm accompanied by carbon dioxide gas. NY 193214

WATERFALLS. Low Force & High Force. Coledale. Path to falls beyond Braithwaite and at start of Whinlatter Pass. Follow the track to New Coledale Mine beyond which is Low Force (NY 196215). Take path to left of mine building which necessitates crossing the Coledale by stepping stones, keeping Force Crag on the right. 6 miles/9.6km. Circuit. Strenuous. NY 192215

19 23

PLANTS. Mountain habitat. Rare alpine campion. Hobcarton Crag. NY 1923

19 24

VIEWPOINT. Brow of Whinlatter Pass. Views to North. NY 198245

AREA 7 – Keswick

20 20

MINE. Cobalt Mine. Opened c1848 by Keswick Mining Company to abstract cobalt but inconclusive though much arsenic found. Mining soon abandoned. Near Scar Crag. NY 206207

20 21

MINE. Force Crag Mine. Low Force workings. Zinc. New Coledale Mining Ltd is present occupant. (Refer NY 193215). NY 200216

20 24

NATURE RESERVE/TRAIL. Whinlatter forest trail. Circuit 1½ miles/2.5km. Fox, badger & pine marten. Thornthwaite Forest guide/map from Information Centre. NY 207245

PLANTS. Pinewood habitat. Whinlatter. (Forestry Commission. Permit required). NY 2024

TOURIST INFORMATION CENTRE. Whinlatter Pass. Thornthwaite. Interpretative displays. Free. Shop. (Forestry Commission). Open Easter–October daily 1000–1700hrs. Phone 07687 78469. NY 209245

WALKS. Whinlatter Top. Circuit 2½ miles/4km. Ascent 670ft/204m. Strenuous. Good views. Hobcarton, Grisedale Pike & Scotland. Start: Information Centre, Whinlatter. NY 207245

Wheelchair walks provided from Information Centre. NY 207245

20 25

BIRDS. The now rare corncrake has been heard calling over several years. Thornthwaite Forest. NY 2025

20 28

INDUSTRIAL ARCHAEOLOGY. Scant remains of 1930s Silica Brick Works which were non-viable. Wythop Hall. Bassenthwaite Lake. NY 206281

21 20

PLANTS. Oak wood habitat. Birkrigg. NY 2120

TREES. Relict sessile oak wood. Near to limit of their climatic range in UK at 1640ft/500m. Very possibly descendants of original wood 7000 years ago. Birkrigg. NY 2120

21 24

GEOLOGY. Skiddaw slate. Whinlatter Pass. NY 2124

21 26

BIRDS. Peregrine falcon nest site. Slape Crag. Bassenthwaite Lake. NY 216266

GEOLOGY. Skiddaw slate. Barf. NY 2126

Lakelands oldest fossils found in shale below Bishop of Barf rock. Thornthwaite Forest. NY 2126

LEGEND. Below the summit of Barf, 1536ft/468m, in Thornthwaite Forest, is a pinnacle of rock 7ft/2m high known as The Bishop, regularly whitewashed by the landlord of the Swan Hotel and the Corps of Royal Engineers. Legend has it that the newly appointed Bishop of Derry rode his horse up the steep crag to demonstrate his faith in God; both horse and rider were killed. Lower down the slope is a much smaller pinnacle known as The Clerk (listening patiently to the interminable sermon from on high). It is said that the Bishop and his horse are buried beneath this stone. Bassenthwaite Lake. NY 216264

MINE. Beckstones Mine. Old, superficial exploration—abandoned 1870s. Lead and zinc ore. NY 219263

Beckstones Level. First recorded mining 1532 and abandoned 1891. Blende, cerussite and galena. 8 oz of silver per ton of lead metal. NY 218263

Windyhill Mine. First record of mining 1532 and abandoned 1891. Blende, cerussite and galena. 8 oz of silver per ton of lead metal. NY 219267

WATERFALLS. Beckstones Gill. Bassenthwaite Lake. Take track opposite car park in Powterhow Wood, then over second stile on right. (Among the trees is The Clerk—see Legend above). On reaching the Gill follow indistinct path upwards. At top of the waterfall, over stile into forest and take first track down. 3½ miles/5.63km. Circuit. Strenuous. NY 213265

21 27

MINE. Woodend Mine. First record of mining 1532. Blende, cerussite and galena. 8oz of silver per ton of lead metal. Abandoned 1891. NY 219271

22 23

CHURCH. St Herbert. Braithwaite. NY 229236

REFRESHMENT. Coledale Inn. Braithwaite. Georgian bar of 1824 and Victorian lounge. Long ago served ale to the thirsty workers of the Cumberland Pencil Company established in the village from 1868 until factory burned down in 1898. The business then moved to present site in Keswick. Phone 07687 78272. NY 229235

WALKS. Coledale Horseshoe. Circuit 10½ miles/17km. Ascent 4400ft/1340m. Strenuous. Finest ridge walk on the North West fells with excellent views. Start: Braithwaite. NY 227238

22 25

CHURCH. St Mary. Thornthwaite. c1760. Remodelled. Cruciform, bellcote, lancet windows. NY 226254

Slope Stone. Little Town, Newlands. (Author)

CRAFTS. Thornthwaite Galleries in converted C18 barn—ceramics, paintings (oil and water-colour), sculpture, hand embroidery and lace & weaving. Open daily except Tuesdays 10.30–1700 hrs. All year. Thornthwaite. Phone 059682 78248.   NY 224256

HISTORICAL. Anthony Wilson, mining consultant and entrepreneur, used the water power from the abandoned Thornthwaite Mine to generate electricity for his home, Thornthwaite Grange and other neighbouring properties. Thornthwaite.
NY 224255

MEMORIAL. "In Memory of Anthony Wilson 1871–1953. Jessie Wilson 1873–1952 of Thornthwaite Grange." Bus shelter. Thornthwaite.   NY 224254

MINE. Ladstock Mine. Old—abandoned 1870s. Lead and zinc ores.NY 220251

Rachel Wood Mine. Just below Seldom Seen Road—Thornthwaite Forest Trail. Old. Outcrop workings abandoned 1870s and deep workings abandoned 1920. Lead and zinc ores.   NY 223256

Thornthwaite Mine. Abandoned 1920. Lead and zinc ores. 10 oz of silver per ton of lead metal.   NY 223258

Thornthwaite Mine worked from an engine shaft over which is now Thornthwaite Garage, the foundations and lower course being part of the pit head structure.
NY 224256

22 26

REFRESHMENT. Swan Hotel. Thornthwaite. Part C17.
Phone 07687 78256.   NY 222265

22 28

ARCHITECTURE. Tennyson Theatre. Mire House, Bassenthwaite. A small open-air theatre constructed by the Tennyson Society in 1974 to mark the place where the poet supposedly composed "Morte d'Arthur".   NY 227284

CHURCH. St Bega. (OE "Beag"; Ring. In medieval times, oaths were sworn on it as they were on arm-rings in pagan Scandinavian temples). Bassenthwaite. Norman, restored. C12 chancel arch. Lead Crucifix, probably C14. Royal Arms George II. Circular churchyard and position by stream may suggest pagan origins. St Bega, daughter of an Irish king fled to England rather than marry the Norwegian prince her father had chosen and founded the Benedictine nunnery on west coast of Cumbria circa AD 850, giving name to nearby village, St Bees.   NY 227287

LITERARY. Tennyson was inspired by the view near St Bega's church to write the closing scene of his *Idylls of the King* (1859). Alfred Tennyson, 1st Baron Tennyson, was born at Somersby in Lincolnshire in 1809. Educated at Somersby, Louth Grammar School and Trinity College, Cambridge. Died 1892 and buried in Westminster Abbey, London. Memorials in Haslemere, where in 1868 he built Aldworth and lived there until his death. Memorial also near Farringford. His works include: "The Devil and the Lady", *Poems by Two Brothers* (with his brother Charles) 1827, "Timbucktoo" 1829, "The Lotos-Eaters" 1833, "The Lord of

Burleigh" 1833, "Love and Duty" 1840, "In Memoriam" 1850, "Ode on the Death of the Duke of Wellington" 1852, "The Charge of the Light Brigade" 1854, *Maud* 1855, *Enoch Arden* 1864 and "Locksley Hall Sixty Years After" 1886.

NY 227287

23 20

GEOLOGY. Malachite. Newlands Valley. NY 2320

TREES. Ash—hollow, because tops cut off in winter to feed sheep. NY 236204

23 21

GEOLOGY. Chalcopyrites—copper pyrites. Occurs around Newlands mine.

NY 2321

HISTORICAL. Farm Uzzicar. Situated close by the tarn known as Husaker or Uzzicar until drained for cultivation and then known as Neuland (newly cleared land) in 1323. NY 234218

Farmhouse at Stair bears the inscription "TF 1647" said to be the initials of Thomas Fairfax who commanded the Parliamentary forces in the Civil War and who stayed there. In 1651, Parliamentary forces destroyed the Brigham (Keswick) forge where all the Newlands mines ore was smelted. This was the death knell of the Newlands Valley industry. NY 237212

INDUSTRIAL ARCHAEOLOGY. Long ago, woollen mills at Stair. Newlands Valley. NY 237212

MINE. Barrow Mine—disused but was prosperous in 1880s. Galena, cerussite & blende. Self-employed miners. Spoil heaps remain. NY 234217

Stoneycroft Mine. Lead. Mine not worked since 1854 due to financial losses. 22 oz/623g of silver per ton of lead metal. Also a collapsed level at NY 230211.

NY 231212

23 22

MINE. Barrow Mine. Derwent Water. Closed 1889. Lead, argentiferous galena, blende, cerussite, pyromorphite and iron pyrites. NY 232222

23 23

REFRESHMENT. Royal Oak Inn. Braithwaite (ON "breith-tveit": the broad clearing). Phone 07687 78533. NY 232237

WALKS. Coledale and Causey Pike. Circuit 9 miles/14.5km. Ascent 2500ft/762m. Strenuous. A demanding ridge walk dangerous in bad weather. Start: Braithwaite. NY 232236

23 27

BIRDS. Possible nest site of bittern. Bassenthwaite Lake. NY 232272

23 28

ARCHITECTURE. Mire House, Bassenthwaite. Late Georgian, 7 bays, porch, 4 Tuscan columns. Family home of the Speddings. Open to the Public from April–October Wednesdays, Sundays and Bank Holiday Mondays. 1400–1700 hrs. Phone 07687 72287. NY 228284

LITERARY. Mire House. Bassenthwaite Lake. Originally a hunting lodge built 1666 by 8th Earl of Derby. In 1802 left to John Spedding of Armathwaite Hall. John Spedding and William Wordsworth were in the same class at Hawkshead Grammar School. House remains in the Spedding family. James Spedding author of 14 Volume biography of Francis Bacon. Thomas Carlyle, Edward Fitzgerald, Tennyson and other literary men of the time equally valued James Spedding's wise counsel. House open Easter–October Wednesdays, Sundays & Bank Holiday Mondays. 1400–1700hrs. Grounds open daily 1030–1730hrs—best for rhododendrons in May and June. Phone 07687 72287. NY 232284

MAMMALS. Roe deer. Dodd Wood. (Instances where roe bucks have scraped the bark off young trees with their antlers to mark their territories). NY 235282

NATURE RESERVE/TRAIL. Dodd Wood Forest Trail. Circuit 1½ miles/ 2.5km. Guide obtainable at start—Old Sawmill adjacent to car park. Good photography. NY 235282

REFRESHMENT. The Old Sawmill. Dodd Wood car park. Phone 07687 74317. NY 235282

WALKS. Bassenthwaite Lake. Start: forest near Mire House. 3 miles/5km. Easy. To Ravenstone and return via St Bega's. NY 236281

23 29

REFRESHMENT. Ravenstone Hotel near Bassenthwaite.
Phone 07687 76240. NY 236297

24 20

GEOLOGY. Galena. Around Catbells. NY 2420

HISTORICAL. The ancient sheep farm, Skelgill, has been in the Grave family since 1347. Newlands Valley. NY 243208

MEMORIAL. Catbells. In memory of "Thomas Arthur Leonard. Founder of Co-operative and Communal Holidays and 'Father' of the open-air movement in this country. Born London March 12th 1864. Died Conway July 19th 1948. Believing that The best things any mortal man hath are those which every mortal shares, he endeavoured to promote Joy in widest commonality spread." (In 1891 T. A. Leonard, a Congregational Church Minister, organized holidays for local mill people leading to formation of Co-operative Holidays Association in 1892. Later, this became the Countrywide Holidays Association—C. H. A.). NY 246209

MINE. Brandley Mine. Long since abandoned. Lead up to 83% and small percentage of silver plus fluorite (very rare in the Lake District)—often found as cubic crystals, colourless and translucent. Impurities produce yellow, green, blue and violet hues. East flank of Skelgill Bank. NY 247204

Minersputt Mine. Mining commenced c1560s, date abandoned unknown. Lead. NY 244202

24 21

REFRESHMENT. Swinside Inn. Swinside, Newlands Valley. Original carved cupboard c1600, built into passage wall. Exposed beams & ships timbers. Phone 07687 78253. NY 243218

WALKS. Catbells (OE "catt" and ME "belde": den of the wild cat). Summit 1481ft/451m. Ascent 1400ft/420m. Circuit 4 miles/ 6.5km. Moderate but some steep sections. Panoramic views. Start: near Hawse End. Derwent Water.
NY 247213

Newlands Horseshoe. Circuit 10 miles/16km. Ascent 3000ft/910m. Strenuous. Panoramic views to three sides. Start: near Portinscale. NY 247213

24 22

MAMMALS. Red squirrels. Swinside woods. Derwent Water. NY 2422

TREES. Birch Wood. Ullock. NY 2422

24 23

REFRESHMENT. The Farmers Arms. Portinscale (ON "portcwene": harlot's hut). Phone 07687 73442. NY 249237

24 26

HISTORICAL. A hermit known as the Dod Man, a native of Banffshire whose real name was George Smith, (born c1825 and died in his home county 1875) lived in a "home" built of sticks, stones and withered tree branches on a rocky ledge above Scalebeck Gill. His bed was of leaves. He had neither boots, coat nor hat. Skilled in portraiture, in pencil, oil and water-colour paint. To provide for his very modest needs he sold portraits to visitors who went out of their way to find him. Dancing Gate. Dodd. Skiddaw. NY 2426

PLANTS. Deciduous mixed habitat. Ivy Crag. Dodd Wood. (Cumbria Trust for Nature Conservation. Permit required). NY 2426

WALKS. Forest trail from car park at Dodd Wood. NY 2426

24 27

GEOLOGY. Skiddaw (C "ska-da": sun god; ON "skyti": crag, "haugr": height). Slate. Dodd Wood. Skiddaw. NY 2427

PLANTS. Pinewood habitat. Dodd Wood. Skiddaw. (Forestry Commission. Permit required). NY 2427

WATERFALLS. Skill Beck. Dodd Wood. Thornthwaite Forest. Series of small falls. Path from Mirehouse (Historic House) car park on A 591. Follow trail to No. 4 marker post then bear left. 2½ miles/4.0km. Circuit. Moderate. NY 242278

25 20

HISTORICAL. Brandlehow Park was the first purchase of the National Trust in 1902 to guarantee public access to Derwent Water shore. Cost £6,500 (Approximately £250,000 in today's values). A Plaque marks the occasion "Brandlehow/The First Property of the National Trust in this District/was opened on 16th October 1902 by/H. R. H. The Princess Louise/Four Oaks were planted here by/Princess Louise/Miss Octavia Hill/Sir Robert Hunter/Canon H. D. Rawnsley". NY 2520

MAMMALS. Red squirrels. Brandlehow Park. NY 2520

25 21

ARCHITECTURE. St Herbert's Island on Derwent Water; remains of Gothic oratory. Keswick. NY 259213

HISTORICAL. Otterbield Island. Derwent Water. Once the home of the otter; bield meaning place or shelter. NY 253211

St Herbert's Island, Derwent Water. St Cuthbert's disciple, St Herbert, thought to have lived here as a hermit. Both died at the same hour on 19th March 687. C14 pilgrims were ferried across the lake from Nichol End to the small oratory on the island. Here they bought small crucifixes to be blessed; a mould for making these found at Nichol End in recent times (now in Keswick museum). NY 259213

25 22

GARDEN. Lingholme, Portinscale. Keswick. Victorian mansion formerly used for summer lets (Beatrix Potter and family stayed several times; she wrote *Squirrel Nutkin* on one holiday). Now the home of Lord and Lady Rochdale. Phone 07687 72003. Formal & informal gardens. Rhododendrons, shrubs & trees overlooking Derwent Water. 1½ mile/2.4km garden walk. Open daily except Sundays April–October 1000–1700hrs. Fee. NY 254222

25 23

ARCHAEOLOGY. In 1901 a hoard of Neolithic stone axes were found at Portinscale. NY 2523

FISH. Derwent Water (C "dwr": water and "gwyn": clear). Half the lake is owned by National Trust, the remainder, privately). 3 miles/4.8km long & 1¼ miles/2km wide. 244ft/74m above sea-level. Maximum depth 72ft/22m. Average depth 18ft/5.4m—so it can freeze over in winter—at one time for 15 weeks. Eel, perch, pike, 3–spined stickleback, vendace, brown trout & sea trout. Vendace may perhaps be extinct as none reported caught in recent years. (The River Derwent is 35 miles/56km in length draining about 30 small tarns and 100 streams from its source on Scafell to the sea. It holds salmon, trout and sea trout). Permit from Temple's Sports shop, Station Street, Keswick. Game licence from North West Water Ltd. New Town House, Buttermarket Street, Warrington. Cheshire. Phone 0925 234000. NY 2523

WELL. Portinscale. One, Dorothy Well, the other unnamed but inscribed

"Whosoever drinketh of this water shall thirst again But whosoever drinketh of the water that I shall give shall never thirst." NY 252236

25 24

CHURCH. St Kentigern. Crosthwaite (ON "kross": a wayside cross in a clearing). Late Perpendicular save for 1557 chapel. Stands on site of St Kentigern's Church of 553. Half a C15 figure (of St Anthony?) in stained glass N aisle. E window by Kempe 1897. Finely carved C14 Font. Chalice c1660. C15 figures of Sir John Derwentwater and his wife. C14 bell from Loweswater Church. One handed clock. Floor bears 4 symbols of St Kentigern—bell, bird, fish and tree—this design (Glasgow's Arms, for St Kentigern is patron saint of that city) incorporated into church gates. Preserved in tower—quaint bellringing instructions in verse by Thomas Martin when aged 86, informing the bell-ringers that "they would be fined for overturning a bell, swearing or coming to ring in spurs and a hat". An unusual feature—incised Consecration crosses, where the Bishop anointed the fabric on Dedication—9 inside & 12 outside. Brass to Sir John Radcliffe (leader of local militia at Battle of Flodden Field) died 1527, and his wife Dame Alice, who is buried in Salisbury Cathedral. Monument to Robert Southey, the poet, died 1843 (with an inscription by Wordsworth). Memorial paid for by Brazillian Government because Southey had written its first official history although he had never visited that country. Southey is buried in the churchyard as is Elizabeth Lynn Linton (1822–98), novelist and writer on the Lake District. She was the first woman writer to be on a newspaper payroll. Also buried nearby is Jonathan Otley the "father" of Lakeland geology although a basket maker and clock maker by trade and Canon Hardwicke Drummond Rawnsley (1851–1920), a founder member of the National Trust, who was Vicar here in 1883–1917. His self-written epitaph "Here rests at last a man whose best/Was done because he could not rest./His wish to work, his will to serve/Were things from which he could not swerve;/Till death came with gentle hand And said 'Sleep now—and under-stand'". He was also Chaplain to George V, a County Councillor, founder of Keswick School of Industrial Art and established many other entities and published 38 books. Also buried here although tomb destroyed, is Peter Crosthwaite, "guide, geographer and hydrographer to the nobility and gentry". NY 258243

LITERARY. Robert Southey born in Bristol 1774, where his father was an unsuccessful linen draper. Educated Corston, Westminster School, London & Balliol College, Oxford, financed by an Uncle living in Lisbon. In 1795 married Edith, (sister of Sarah Coleridge, Samuel Taylor's wife). In 1839 married his second wife, Caroline Bowles in Boldre, Hants. Died 21 March 1843 and buried Crosthwaite church (see above). Commemorated in Westminster Abbey, London. His best works—"The Retrospect" 1793, "Joan of Arc" 1796, "To a Dear Friend" 1797, *Letters from Spain and Portugal* 1797, *Thalaba the Destroyer* 1801, *Madoc* 1805, *The Curse of Kehama* 1810, *Roderick the last of the Goths* 1814, *History of Brazil* 1810–19. In 1813 Southey became Poet Laureate after Sir Walter Scott rejected the honour in deference to him. NY 258243

25 26

MINE. Carl Side Trial—level. Mainly barytes.   NY 256269

26 20

ARCHITECTURE. Barrow House. Derwent Water. Built 1787 at a cost of £1655.3.6d by Joseph Pocklington, previously of Derwent Island. Charming Adam room.   NY 268200

BIRDS. Treecreeper roost in Californian redwood. Barrow Wood. NY 268200

GEOLOGY. Agglomerate. Derwent Water   NY 269202

TREES. Californian redwood with treecreeper roost. Barrow Wood.
              NY 268200

WATERFALLS. Barrow House. Derwent Water. Within the grounds of the Youth Hostel are waterfalls with 100ft/30m fall mostly made by blasting.
              NY 268200

YOUTH HOSTEL. Barrow House. Borrowdale. Keswick. Phone 07687 77246.
              NY 268200

26 21

ARCHAEOLOGY. Lord's Island on Derwent Water—remains of medieval Settlement. Sir Francis Radcliffe fled here from Parliamentary forces from his Northumberland home—but to no avail as his home on Lord's Island was destroyed in 1640. His descendant James Radcliffe, third and last Earl of Derwent Water was only 27 when beheaded in 1716 for not acknowledging George I and Protestantism.   NY 266218

BIRDS. Cormorants, especially, roost here. Scarf Stones. Derwent Water.
              NY 263210

GEOLOGY. Borrowdale volcanic series. Catgill. Derwent Water.   NY 269211

HISTORICAL. Lord's Island. Derwent Water. Remains of Manor house, once the home of Earl of Derwent Water. Much of the stone from the sacked residence said to have been used in building Keswick's Town Hall.   NY 265219

Rampsholme Island. Derwent Water. (Ramps is garlic). Given to the National Trust by Mr H. W. Walker with the request that the public be allowed to land upon it.   NY 264214

LEGEND. The Derwent Water family supported the Stuarts but the 2nd Earl, James Radcliffe, beheaded on Tower Hill London 24 February 1716 following the rebellion of 1715. The night following his execution it is said that there was a great display of the Aurora Borealis (Northern Lights) which henceforth were known as Derwent Water's lights. After the 1745 rebellion, Charles Radcliffe brother of James, executed and his lands confiscated by the Crown and bestowed on Greenwich Hospital.   NY 265219

26 22

GEOLOGY. Friar's Crag. Derwent Water. Made up of dolerite, an igneous rock and with tiny crystals of augite. NY 262223

Castle Head. Derwent Water. A volcanic lava "plug". NY 269227

HISTORICAL. Derwent Island. National Trust—no public access. In C16 German miners from Augsberg settled here, to work surrounding mines. In 1781 Joseph Pocklington (friend of Peter Crosthwaite, an early exploiter of the area's tourism) bought the island (until then known as Vicar's Island and previously, Hest Holme) and proclaimed himself to be Governor of Pocklington Island. To maintain his position he built a fort and battery along with chapel, druids circle and a boat house resembling a chapel. Barely visible ruins today. NY 261224

Friar's Crag. During C7 friars would gather here to be blessed by St Herbert who lived in his hermitage on St Herbert's Island. NY 262223

MEMORIAL. Friar's Crag. Derwent Water. On Borrowdale slate pillar low-re-lief portrait bronze by A. C. Lucchesi, designed by W. G. Collingwood. Inscribed "John Ruskin MDCCCXIX–MDCCCC (1819–1900). The first thing which I remember As an event in my life was being taken by my nurse to the brow of Friar's Crag on Derwent Water." Later in his poem, "The intense joy mingled with awe,/that I had in looking through the hollow in the mossy roots,/over the crag into the dark lake,/has ever associated itself more or less/with all twining roots of trees ever since." Also inscribed is early Christian symbol "Chi-Rho". NY 264223

Memorial near Friar's Crag. Derwent Water. To Hardwicke Drummond Rawn-sley (1851–1920) "who, greatly loving the fair things of Nature and Art Set all his love to the service of God and man." Many achievements but most important as founder of the National Trust in 1895 together with Miss Octavia Hill and Sir Robert Hunter. NY 264224

NATURE RESERVE/TRAIL. Friar's Crag. Derwent Water. Circuit 2 miles/ 3km. The Friar's Crag Nature Walk guide obtainable from Trust Lakeside Information centre near the start at the car park in Keswick. NY 265229

TRANSPORT. Derwent Water Launch Co. Lakeside. Phone 07687 72263 or 73013 at Registered Office, 29 Manor Park, Keswick. Provides regular service to various landing stages on the lake—Ashness Bridge, Lodore Falls, High Brandle-how, Low Brandlehow, Hawse End & Nichol End. Round trip about 50 minutes. Service—week prior to Easter until end of November. NY 265228

VIEWPOINT. Friar's Crag. Derwent Water. Purchased 1922 in memory of Canon Hardwicke Drummond Rawnsley, a founder member of the National Trust. NY 263222

WALKS. Friar's Crag—east of boat landing stage. (National Trust). Keswick. Route for wheelchairs. NY 264222

Keswick-Cockshot Wood-Great Wood-Friar's Crag. Circuit 3.4 mls/ 5.5km. Easy. Start: Cockshot Wood. NY 266229

26 23

ARCHITECTURE. Moot Hall Keswick. 1813 replaced C16 courthouse which acted as the Receiving House where copper was given the Queen's mark. Island site in Main St. Incorporates materials from ruined mansion on Lord's Island, Derwent Water. Ground floor had open archways wherein a small market used to be held although once it was a prison. Clock tower with one handed clock. Bell in clock tower dated 1601 possibly from the Radcliffe mansion on Lord's Island. Now National Park Information Centre. NY 266234

CHURCH. St John Evangelist. Keswick. (OE "cese-wic": the cheese dairy farm [of Fountains Abbey]). 1838 with additions. Tower with recessed spire. Beautiful stained glass 1888/9 East especially, by Holiday. Churchyard grave of Sir Hugh Walpole. NY 264234

CRAFTS. Lakeland Stonecraft. Open Mon–Fri. Keswick. NY 2623

Skiddaw Pottery. Open daily. Sat & Sun p.m. Keswick. NY 2623

EVENT. Keswick Agricultural Show. Cattle, Horses, Sheep, Cumberland and Westmorland Wrestling, Hound Trailing, Handicrafts Carriage Driving, Produce and Trade Stands. August Bank Holiday Monday. NY 2623

Keswick Carnival. Floats, Trade Stands, Bands, Morris Dancing. Mid-June Sunday. NY 2623

Keswick Victorian Fair. Christmas stalls etc., 1st Sunday December. NY 2623

Keswick Religious Convention. 2nd to 3rd Sats. July. NY 2623

LITERARY. Greta Hall, Keswick, now part of Keswick School, was the home of Coleridge, Shelley and Southey (Refer NY 258243). **Samuel Taylor Coleridge** was born Ottery St Mary 1772. Died 1834 and buried at St Michael's, Highgate, London. Educated at Christ's Hospital London and Jesus College Cambridge. Married Sara Fricker 1795. Lived at Keswick 1800–03 but after falling in love with Sarah Hutchinson (Wordsworth's wife's sister) his marriage virtually ended. In 1809 he left his family at Greta Hall to be cared for by the Southeys. His best works, "The Watchman" 1796, "Frost at Midnight", "To the River Otter", "The Rime of the Ancient Mariner", "The Foster-Mother's Tale", all in *Lyrical Ballads* 1798. "Remorse" 1813, "Kubla Khan" 1816, *Biographia Literaria* 1817. **Percy Bysshe Shelley** born Warnham 1792. Drowned in the Gulf of Spezia, Italy, when his boat overturned in a squall 1822—his heart is buried in Bournemouth. Educated at Eton and University College, Oxford. Married Harriet Westbrook, the daughter of a London coffee-house keeper, in Edinburgh 1811. She drowned in Serpentine (Kensington Gardens) 1816. He forfeited his income of £6,000 per annum [much later reinstated] from his father for marrying without parental consent and for being "sent down" for writing a pamphlet on atheism. Lived in various locations, but Keswick 1811–13. His works included— *Original Poetry* (with his sister) 1810, "Zastrozzi" 1810, "St Irvyne" 1810, "The Necessity of Atheism" 1811, "The Retrospect" 1812, *Queen Mab* 1813, "Alastor or the Spirit of Solitude" 1816 and *The Revolt of Islam* 1818. NY 264237

MEMORIAL. Sir Hugh Walpole (1884–1941) buried SW corner of St John's churchyard. Keswick. NY 264234

Plaque let into pavement outside Pitlochry Wool Shop, Main St. Keswick. "Peter Crosthwaite's original Museum situated here 1780–1870. Peter Crosthwaite 1735–1808, his grandson John Fisher Crosthwaite J. P., F. S. A., 1819–1897." NY 265236

MUSEUM. Fitzpark, Station Road. Keswick. Phone 07687 72645. Established 1779 by Peter Crosthwaite, ill-tempered and irascible but he paid meticulous attention to detail in recording the natural world around him. He called himself "Admiral of the Keswick Regatta, Keeper of the Museum, Guide, Pilot, Geographer and Hydrographer to the Nobility and Gentry." He produced the first accurate survey of some of Lakeland—3 inches to 1 mile in 1780s. Born at Crosthwaite 1735 apprenticed as a weaver and then joined East India Company. Became a Customs official on his return to England. Married a Keswick girl and then opened his museum. Lake District connections—geology, ornithology, Roman & manuscripts etc; of De Quincey, Ruskin, Southey, Sir Hugh Walpole and Wordsworth (mostly facsimiles on display—to preserve originals). Scale model of the Lake District by Joseph Flintoft (1867) who took his own measurements and 17 years in the making of it. Open daily (not Sundays) April–October. 1000–1230hrs & 1400–1730 hrs. Fee. NY 269237

Cumberland Pencil Museum, now part of Rexel Pencil factory. Southey Works, Keswick. History from C16 to present day & manufacture of the pencil. Graphite now imported. Open all year daily (except 25/26 Dec and 1 Jan) 0930–1600hrs. Fee. Phone 07687 73626. NY 263238

Keswick Railway Museum. 1st floor (above National Westminster Bank) 28 Main Street, Keswick. Memorabilia illustrating Cumbrian Railway history. Open during summer 1400–1700hrs. Fee. NY 266232

REFRESHMENT. George Hotel. Keswick. C16. Originally named Bunch of Grapes (when illicit wad/plumbago traded) then George and Dragon and, in 1714 on the accession of George I, The George. During reins of Elizabeth I and James I, used as a Revenue office to receive German miners dues from silver production. NY 266234

Dog & Gun Inn. Lake Rd, Keswick. Phone 07687 73463. NY 265230

TOURIST INFORMATION CENTRE. Moot Hall. Market Place, Keswick. National Park Centre. Leaflets, displays, guided walks. Phone 07687 72645. Open daily Easter–September. NY 266234

WALKS. Circuit of Derwent Water. 10 miles/16km. Ascent 150ft/ 50m. Moderate. A classic Lake District walk. Journey can be broken by using the regular lake launches. Start from Moot Hall, Keswick. NY 266234

YOUTH HOSTEL. Station Rd. Keswick. Phone 07687 72484. NY 267235

26 24

WALKS. Spooney Lane-Latrigg-Brundholme-Windebrowe. Keswick. Circuit 5 miles/8km. Ascent 886ft/270m. Moderate. Start: NY 267242

26 25

ARCHITECTURE. Ormathwaite Hall. Ormathwaite. 2 Georgian houses at right angles overlooking a square lawn. 7 and 5 bays. Farm building has turret dated 1769.   NY 268253

LITERARY. The Ghyll. In 1802 Sir George Beaumont (a founder of the National Gallery) gave the site to William Wordsworth so that he would be near Coleridge who lived in Keswick. However, he chose not to live there but immortalised Applethwaite in his sonnet "At Applethwaite near Keswick". Wordsworth planted yew tree in 1808. Applethwaite.   NY 266258

26 26

WATERFALLS. Slades Beck. Millbeck. Skiddaw. Series of small cascades. Path from Millbeck Farm. 2 miles/3.21km. Circuit. Moderate.   NY 261268

26 27

PLANTS. Rare alpine campion. Little Man. Skiddaw.   NY 2627

26 29

LITERARY. To celebrate victory at Waterloo in 1815, Southey and Wordsworth with their respective families and retinue consumed roast beef and plum pudding on the summit of Skiddaw 2837ft/864m on 21 August 1815. It seemed a popular pastime to dine in style on mountain summits but it required many people to carry up all that was required—they even carried up a cannon to signal "a Toast".   NY 261291

Mrs Ann Radcliffe (nee Ward) 1764–1823, buried Bayswater, London. Novelist *Mysteries of Udolpho* 1794. First woman to ride a horse to summit of Skiddaw— 1794. Peter Crosthwaite's diary records that "the Oak Galloway [a pony] carried a woman of twenty-four stone weight unto the top of Skiddaw."   NY 261291

27 20

WATERFALLS. Cat Gill below Walla Crag. Keswick.   NY 275208

27 21

BIRDS. Peregrine falcon nest site. Walla Crag. Derwent Water.   NY 277214

GEOLOGY. Breccia, with slate content can be found at the junction of volcanic and slate rocks on the path to Falcon Crag on the east side of Derwent Water.
                                                                 NY 270211

LEGEND. Lady's Rake. Walla Crag. Derwent Water. Supposed route of Lady Radcliffe in C18 fleeing with family treasure from Parliamentary forces (then attacking Lord's Island). Some gold coins subsequently found.   NY 274212

WALKS. Great Wood (originally an oak wood), Ashness Bridge, Walla Crag and

Rakefoot. Circuit 4 miles/6.5km. Ascent 984ft/300m. Fine views over Derwent Water. Passes Falcon Crag once the home of peregrine falcons. Start: Great Wood.

NY 272213

27 22

GEOLOGY. Borrowdale volcanic series. Dolerite. Castle Head. Keswick.

NY 270228

VIEWPOINT. Excellent views into Borrowdale from Castle Head. Keswick.

NY 270227

27 24

HISTORICAL. C16 farmhouse—Windebrowe, Keswick. At one time occupied by miners from Augsberg working at nearby Brigham Forge. Then, home of William Calvert, brother of Raisley (Germanic origin "Ritseler") whom Wordsworth nursed during his terminal illness (Refer NY 516302). William and Dorothy stayed here in 1794. Sold to the Speddings in 1833. Now owned by The Calvert Trust. Two rooms furnished—known as the Wordsworths' rooms. Open Wednesdays 1400–1630hrs Easter to 31st October. Also by appointment. Phone 07687 72112.

NY 277240

MAMMALS. Red squirrel. Latrigg. Keswick

NY 2724

VIEWPOINT. Particularly fine views into Borrowdale from Latrigg's summit at 1203ft/366m. Keswick.

NY 278247

27 25

ARCHITECTURE. Italianate villa built for William Oxley of Liverpool 1856/63. Centre—3 bays and central tower. Underscar.

NY 271256

27 26

MINE. Applethwaite Gill Trial. C16 shaft, level and surface works.

NY 270265

28 24

PLANTS. Deciduous mixed habitat. Brundholme. (Cumbria Trust for Nature Conservation. Permit required).

NY 2824

28 25

MEMORIAL. Runic wayside cross on Lonscale Fell. Erected 1891 by Canon Hardwick Drummond Rawnsley in memory of two Skiddaw shepherds—Edward Hawell of Lonscale born 21 October 1815 and died 2 June 1889, and his son Joseph Hawell of Lonscale born 24 December 1854 & died 20 February 1891. Noted breeders of prize Herdwick sheep. Also to Robert Walker Hawell born 16 March and died 29 December 1911. Inscribed verse from Rawnsley's "Great Shepherd" — "Great Shepherd of Thy heavenly flock,/These men have left our hill/Their feet were on the living rock,/Oh guide and bless them, still."

NY 282257

28 29

HISTORICAL. Skiddaw House. One of the loneliest houses in England. Here, for nearly 47 years, lived Pearson Dalton, shepherd for 5 days a week, with only his dogs for company. Every weekend he walked some 8 miles across the fells to stay from Saturday afternoon to Monday morning with his sister at Fellside, near Caldbeck. In 1969, when aged 75 he retired to live with her. His home is now a Youth Hostel. NY 287291

YOUTH HOSTEL. Skiddaw House. NY 287291

29 21

EVENT. Hound trailing competitions. Autumn. Dale Bottom Farm, near Keswick. In 1906 Hound Trailing Association established. Trail hounds being lighter than foxhounds can average 20mph/32kmh over 10 mile/16km of fell-side following an aniseed trail. NY 296217

29 23

ARCHAEOLOGY. Castle Rigg. Keswick. circa 1500 BC stone circle (of a species of granite not found locally) 110ft/33m diameter approx, comprises 38 irregularly shaped stones with 10 stones in an internal triangle, all standing perpendicularly. Not only was it a prehistoric meeting place, possibly to dispense law, it may also have been an early astronomical observatory to measure Solstices/Equinoxes—pairs of stones pointing to the sunrise at midsummer and midwinter. Certain geometric configurations suggest its purpose in that a line drawn on the Ordnance Survey map, from the summit of Helvellyn to Skiddaw's summit, passes through the centre of the circle bounded by its two tallest stones. Another line drawn from the SW outlying stone of the circle meets Long Meg near Penrith and is the exact position of the rising sun on 1st May. The smallest stones set out as a rectangle parallel with other stone circles/henges. The field in which the "circle" stands was purchased by Canon Rawnsley, a co-founder of the National Trust. From the circle there are splendid views south of transition from Skiddaw Slate to Borrowdale Volcanic rocks. NY 292236

WALKS. Castlerigg, St John's in the Vale Church and Twet Tarn. (Known locally as Tewfit Tarn perhaps after the name of Lapwing —Tewatt, Tewet, Teucht, Teuchet, Teafit, Tewhit, Tewfit). Circuit 3.7 miles/ 6km. Ascent 558ft/170m. Moderate. A charming walk. Start: opposite Castlerigg Stone Circle. NY 292237

29 25

GEOLOGY. Truncated spurs—west of Threlkeld. NY 2925

29 26

GEOLOGY. Erratics—among Skiddaw slates—quarry. NY 299262

MINE. Blencathra Mine. 1840s–1880. Lead, copper and barytes. NY 297267

29 27

GEOLOGY. Barytes. Can be found in lead mines spoil heaps. NY 297271

Chalcopyrites. NY 297271 and NY 297275

Chiastolite. Clearly seen on exposures at this location. Blencathra.   NY 299270

Malachite. Confluence of Roughten Gill and Glenderaterra Beck.   NY 297275

Mica.   NY 297278

At Roughten Gill, Blencathra, spotted slates (Hornfels) produce a ringing sound when struck. Such slates as these, carefully selected form the set of musical stones to be seen in Keswick Museum.   NY 298276

Skiddaw slate. Glenderaterra Valley (C "Glyn-derataran": the valley of the angel or demon of execution.)   NY 2927

Skiddaw granite outcrop. Sinen Gill.   NY 297278

MINE. Brundholme Mine, Lonscale Fell. 1872–1920. Shafts and levels. Lead, copper and barytes.   NY 296273 and NY 296277

Ashness Bridge. (Rosemary Liddle)

Area 8 – Threlkeld

30 21

.\TERFALLS. Brown Beck below High Rigg. St John's in the Vale. Path hind diocesan youth centre, near church. 5 miles/ 8.04km. Circuit. Strenuous.

NY 305215

30 22

CHURCH. St John. St John's Vale. 1845. Small and low overall. West tower. Chancel and nave in one. Canopied pulpit. Written evidence of a church here 1554, possibly built by Knights Hospitallers of the Order of St John of Jerusalem in C13.

NY 306225

MEMORIAL. John Richardson. Born 1817 and died 1866 at nearby Bridge House. Mason turned schoolmaster for 27 years, he assisted in the building of the present church St John's in the Vale. Also a talented dialect poet; at 54 his first book published *Cummerland Talk* (1871) being short tales and rhymes in the dialect of that county. Other writings followed. Memorial opposite E window.

NY 306225

WELL. St John. St John's Vale. SW of churchyard.

NY 306225

Well. Portinscale. (Author)

30 27

WATERFALLS. Roughten Gill. Blencathra. Path north from Blencathra Centre—a National Park Residential Centre, (NY 304256). When near sheepfold take path east and follow sheep trod beside Gill. 4 miles/6.43km. Circuit. Moderate.

NY 309279

31 20

VIEWPOINT. From Wren Crag Thirlmere, between Great How and Raven Crag, framed by Scots Pines. St John's in the Vale.　　　　NY 317201

31 21

ARCHITECTURE. Sosgill Bridge. Naddle Fell. Fine stone arch. Photographic view of Blencathra.　　　　NY 315210

31 25

WATERFALLS. Kilnhow Beck and Gate Gill. Blencathra. Path from car park in Threlkeld, to Blease Gill. 3 miles/4.82km. Circuit. Moderate.　　NY 316258

31 26

MINE. Blease Gill Trial—level. Lead.　　　　NY 315267

32 20

MINE. Fornside Mine. Level at NY 323209 in barren quartz vein and behind Fornside Farm a longer level with some copper ores.　　　NY 323205

32 22

MINE. Wanthwaite Crag Mine. Trial levels hereabouts. Copper and lead.

NY 325225

32 23

GEOLOGY. Microgranite extracted for road-making. Threlkeld Quarries.

NY 3223

32 24

ARCHAEOLOGY. Probably Iron Age farm. Threlkeld Common.　NY 329240

Iron Age settlement. Well. Hut circles. Threlkeld Knotts.　　　NY 328243

GEOLOGY. Borrowdale volcanic series. Threlkeld Quarries.　　NY 3224

32 25

CHURCH. St Mary. Threlkeld ("Thralls spring"). [Thrall means a native of Briton]. 1777. Replaced a thatched church. West tower two bells, each at least 500 years old. Oblong nave and chancel in one. Late Georgian organ. Black Letter Bible 1613. Parish records from Elizabeth I. Churchyard cenotaph to 45 huntsmen giving names and ages—many were long lived. "Also of John Crozier of the Riddings/died 5 March 1903, aged 80, for 64 years he was the beloved Master/of the Blencathra Foxhounds/and mainly through his instrumentality/this monument was erected." Atop the memorial is inscribed "Around them stand the old familiar mountains." Also inscribed "The Forest Music is to hear the hounds/Rend the thin air, and with lusty cry/Awake the drowsy echo and confound/Their perfect language is a mingled cry." NY 322254

HISTORICAL. Threlkeld Hall, now a farmhouse, was once in ownership of Sir Lancelot Threlkeld, stepfather of "The Shepherd" Lord Clifford. (Refer NY 538288). "Sir Lancelot was wont to say that he had three noble houses, one for pleasure, Crosby, in Westmorland, where he had a park full of deer; one for profit and warmth, wherein to reside in winter, namely, Yanwath, nigh Penrith; and the third, Threlkeld—well stocked with tenants to go with him to the wars." (William Wordsworth *Guide to the Lakes*). NY 329258

REFRESHMENT. Horse and Farrier Inn. Threlkeld. Mounting block. Over the door an inscription "CIG 1688". The initials are those of Christopher and Grace Irton of Threlkeld Hall. De Quincey and Wordsworth used often to take refreshment here and William sometimes stayed the night if inclement weather occurred during his weekly visit from his home in Grasmere to Penrith Head Post Office. Phone 07687 79688. NY 324255

Salutation Inn. Threlkeld. Phone 07687 79614. NY 323254

32 26

GEOLOGY. Cerussite in lead veins at mines near Blencathra. NY 324260

MINE. Threlkeld Mine. C17–1928. Lead and zinc. The only Lakeland mine to employ mules to draw the bogies—on Long Horse level. Other mines using railed bogies employed ponies to haul them. NY 325261

TOPOGRAPHIC. Blencathra Foxhound kennels. Threlkeld. NY 325261

32 27

GEOLOGY. Stone stripes. Blencathra. NY 323277

32 28

GEOLOGY. Arete. Blencathra. (C "Blen-y-cathern": the peak of witches). NY 3228

MEMORIAL. Quartzite cross 16ft x 10ft (4.8m x 3m) laid out in memory of an unknown climber by Harold Robinson of Threlkeld, who regularly climbed Blencathra. NY 324281

33 28

MINE. Saddleback Old Mine. Scales Tarn. Lead in quantity not found. (Refer NY 344276). NY 332286

33 29

MINE. Bannerhead Mine. Lead and some graphite. NY 335295

34 22

WATERFALLS. Mosedale Beck. Matterdale Common. Park at Red Moss (NY

380219) and follow Old Coach Road west and then south west up Mosedale Beck. 6 miles/9.65km. Circuit. Easy. NY 347224

34 26

REFRESHMENT. Scales Inn. Blencathra. NY 344269

34 27

MINE. Saddleback Old Mine. Mousethwaite Comb. Lead in quantity not found. (Refer NY 332286). NY 344276

34 28

WATERFALLS. Glenderamackin River. Bridle path from Bannerdale Cottage, Mungrisdale then fell path. 5 miles/8.04km. Circuit. Moderate. Can be very wet. NY 346281

35 22

MINE. Wolf Crags. Matterdale Common. One level on quartz vein. NY 357223

PLANTS. Acid moorland habitat. Matterdale Common. NY 3522

35 29

LEGEND. Midsummers's eve apparition of marching soldiers led by mounted officers on Souther fell-side, so steep no horse could have retained its footing. First seen in 1735 and supposedly on several midsummer's eves since: 1745 and 1774. The spectacle lasted for some two hours on each occasion. As many as 26 respectable citizens witnessed the apparition at the same time between 2000–2200 hrs. (In 1735 later reports indicated that Bonnie Prince Charles was manoeuvring his troops very many miles away on the other side of the Solway Firth, prior to marching on London. Perhaps what was seen was a reflected mirage—though later sightings cannot be so explained!). Throughout history similar sightings have been recorded—refer Judges IX.36. NY 355291

36 20

WATERFALLS. Coegill Beck and Rush Gill. Dowthwaitehead. Ullswater. Park at Bank (NY 386219) near Dockray. Downhill is signposted track to Dowthwaite-head. Coegill Beck lies south west and Rush Gill (NY 368208) lies north west. An indistinct path across the fells joins the two falls. 5 miles/8.04km. Circuit. Moderate. NY 365204

36 22

GEOLOGY. Site of earlier glacial lakes. Matterdale. NY 3622

36 27

ARCHITECTURE. 1719 date stone, Hutton Moor End, Threlkeld, inscribed

THIS BUILDING'S AGE
THESE LETTERS SHOW
M D CC XIX

THOUGH MANY GAZE
YET FEW WILL KNOW.

(M=1000; D=500; CC= 200; XIX= 19).   NY 364271

36 29

PLANTS. Barberry (rare), bedstraw, brooklime, broom, butterwort, clover, forget-me-not, foxglove, germander speedwell, golden saxifrage, herb bennet, lady's smock, lesser and greater stitchwort, moss campion, spearmint, tormentil and wild rose. Mungrisdale.   NY 3629

TREES. Aspen grove. Mungrisdale.   NY 3629

38 21

ARCHITECTURE. Castellated and folly-like property of Penrith RDC. Waterworks.   NY 380218

WALKS. Dowthwaitehead, Ullswater. Circuit 2 miles/4.4. M. Easy. Start: Red Moss cross roads.   NY 380219

38 27

ARCHAEOLOGY. Extensive site of three Roman camps. Threlkeld—Old Roman road just off A 66. First identified by Father Thomas West in C18.
                    NY 3827

FARMING. Troutbeck Sheep market; mainly Herdwicks & Swaledales.
                    NY 389272

38 29

GEOLOGY. Borrowdale volcanic series. Eycott Hill.   NY 387295

39 20

MEMORIAL. Enclosing land given to National Trust. In memory of Walter Costclay, barrister and mountaineer, died in Gran Paradiso mountains in Italy.
                    NY 399208

WATERFALLS. Aira Force. Ullswater. 70ft/21m fall. National Trust car park & refreshments.   NY 399205

39 21

REFRESHMENT. The Royal Hotel. Dockray. Mary Queen of Scots reputed to have stayed here. Phone 07684 82356.   NY 393216

TREES. Alder. Its charcoal superior to others in making gun powder.
                    NY 399213

39 22

ARCHITECTURE. Hollows Farm previously an inn with brew-house. Matterdale.   NY 392228

CHURCH. Matterdale (ME "madderdock": madder [a red-rooted plant used in dye production]). 1573, consecrated by Bishop Meye in 1580. Undedicated. Nave and chancel in one. Slate W tower originally of thatch but now stepped gables. C18 pulpit with canopy. Stained glass by Kempe depicting the Holy Nativity. Norman font.   NY 395224

39 25

ARCHAEOLOGY. Great Mell Fell (C "moel": a bare hill) at height of 1760ft/536m a low cairn, 25ft/7m diameter surrounded by 60ft/18m diameter ditch 3ft/1m wide.   NY 396254

AREA 9 – Pooley Bridge

40 20

ARCHITECTURE. Lyulph's Tower (L'ulf's Tower). Ullswater. 1780. Three sides of an octagon. Four castellated hexagonal towers. Round arched windows. Built by an Earl of Surrey, The Rt. Hon Charles Howard, afterwards Duke of Norfolk, as a hunting box. It stands on the site of the medieval tower of Baron de L'Ulf of Greystoke (1st Baron of Ullswater). Wordsworth wrote of the tower in "The Somnambulist"—1st line "List, ye who pass by Lyulph's Tower…"

NY 404202

FISH. Aira Beck. N.T. Brown trout. Free.   NY 4020

LEGEND. Emma, a local beauty, betrothed to Sir Eglamore, took to sleep walking during his long absence. On return he found her beside the Force but, not knowing she was asleep, touched her whereupon she overbalanced and fell to her death. (Wordsworth wrote of this in "The Somnambulist" (line 132) "…The soft touch snapped the thread/Of slumber-shrieking back she fell,/And the Stream whirled her down the dell/Along its foaming bed…"). Heartbroken, the Knight built a cell beside the fall and lived there many years.   NY 4020

De Quincey related the remarkable incident of Elizabeth Smith who, walking alone, found herself unable to climb neither upwards nor downwards on the rocks slippery with the torrent of water. Through the mist a shadowy figure appeared whom she recognised as her sister who guided her to safety and then vanished. On reaching home her enquiries revealed that her sister had not left the premises that day.   NY 4020

LITERARY. Aira Force. Patterdale. Here in 1836 Wordsworth wrote "Airey Force Valley". "Not a breath of air, ruffled the bosom of this leafy glen…"   NY 4020

MEMORIAL. Bridge—Aira Force. Lower fall. In memory of Cecil Spring Rice. Poet, Privy Councillor and H. M. Ambassador to the USA during the Great War. Built by his friends.   NY 400206

Bridge—Aira Force. Upper fall. In memory of Stephen Edward Rice. CB. 1856–1902.   NY 400209

TREES. Whitebeam plantation. Aira Force car park.   NY 401201

WALKS. Aira Beck Force. Dockray. Circuit 3.1 miles/5km. Ascent 442ft/135m. Easy. Start: National Trust car park.   NY 401200

40 21

LITERARY. Gowbarrow Park, a medieval deer park. Here Wordsworth saw and wrote "Host of Golden Daffodils". 1802 Journal.   NY 4021

40 27

REFRESHMENT. Sportsmans Inn. C18. Cumberland Wrestling sign. Troutbeck. Phone 07684 83231. NY 405279

41 21

GEOLOGY. Rhyolite. Gowbarrow Fell. NY 412218

41 28

ARCHAEOLOGY. Stone Carr. Motherby (ON "mothirs": personal name plus farm). Remains of stone circle. Settlement site. NY 419282

42 24

GEOLOGY. Conglomerate. Little Mell Fell. NY 4224

42 27

CHURCH. All Saints. Penruddock (C "a ruddy hill"). 1902. Nave and chancel in one. Bellcote. Earlier windows. Kist. NY 426275

Presbyterian-now United Reform. 1789. On earlier site. Penruddock. NY 429277

HISTORICAL. At High Farm (1695) Penruddock, many years ago in an unused room was found a chest, now known as the Penruddock Kist, for it contained deeds and documents, relating to the village, spanning many generations. The Kist is now in the church and Carlisle Archives hold the documents. NY 424275

REFRESHMENT. The Norfolk Arms. Penruddock. NY 427277

43 20

FISH. Skelly (Schelly) [*Coregonus lavaretus*] a kind of fresh water herring. Used to be netted from Skelly Neb to NY 436204 Kailpot Crag. Ullswater. William Wordsworth in his *Guide to the Lakes* writes of this in his "Excursion on the banks of Ullswater" on 9 November 1805. NY 438208

43 22

CHURCH. All Saints. Watermillock. 1884. Sandstone and slate. Tower, nave & chancel. Lancet windows. Cup 1581. Royal Arms George II. Diamond Jubilee (1897) of Queen Victoria commemorated by a bell. Memorial to Sir Cecil A. S. Rice. (1859–1918), Ambassador to USA 1913–18. He wrote the hymn "I vow to thee my country..." Collection of photographs dated 1936, of all parishioners. Mode of dress worthy of study! Sun dial supported by cross shaft/coffin lid.
NY 432229

VIEWPOINT. Ullswater from Watermillock church. NY 432229

43 27

ARCHITECTURE. Hutton John C14. Pele tower. Mullioned and transomed windows in Jacobean style. Dovecot. From C14 held by the Huttons, then by marriage to the Huddlestons in reign of Queen Elizabeth I. Still in family ownership. View by appointment only. Phone 07684 83326. NY 439270

44 22

ARCHITECTURE. Watermillock House. 1689. 3 light mullioned windows.

NY 446224

44 29

CRAFTS. Beckstones Art Gallery, Greystoke Gill, near Penrith. Over 200 original oil and water-colour paintings by more than 30 professional artists. A selection of C19 work and a range of limited edition prints. Phone 07684 83601. Open daily except Mondays. 1000–1800hrs. April/November. NY 446296

45 20

MINE. Swarthbeck Gill Iron Trial. 200yd/182m level near foot of waterfall.

NY 455206

WATERFALLS. Swarthbeck Gill. Ullswater. 40ft/12.19m. Path from Howtown. 3½ miles/5.63km. Circuit. Moderate. NY 455205

45 21

LEISURE. Ullswater Yacht Club. Thwaithill Bay. NY 456218

45 26

CHURCH. St Andrew. Dacre ("deigr": a tear, hence trickling stream). Norman. West tower, rebuilt 1810. Late C12 chancel. Doorway with thin shafts—one waterleaf and one crocker capital. Interior—piers on north side mostly round and all octagonal on south side. Communion Rail late C17 with twisted balusters. Churchyard has fragments of two crosses. One, C8 Anglian Cross, the other C10 Viking which bears carvings of Adam and Eve and the sacrifice of Isaac. Also, two men said to represent King Athelstan & King Constantine. Church stands on site of Saxon monastery mentioned by the Venerable Bede in his Ecclesiastical History AD 731—some traces of foundations. Stone in south of chancel said to be token in respect of "Peace of Dacre" signed in 926 between Athelstan of England and Constantine of Scotland. Memorial tablet by Sir Francis Chantrey to Edward Hassell of Dalemain, died 1825. Lady Anne Clifford (Anne of Pembroke) gave the large wooden lock (1671) on SW door. 4 bears mark the corners of the original churchyard—NW corner bear asleep with head on pillar, SW corner bear attacked by a cat, SE corner bear endeavours to shake off the cat and NE corner bear eats the cat. These may be relics from the monastery and may have been guardians of the dead or pinnacles of Dacre Castle walls. A Christian cemetery recently excavated, produced C9 coins and an C8 stylus/pen. NY 457263

REFRESHMENT. Horse and Farrier Inn. Dacre. Horse riders' mounting blocks. Notice in porchway reads "Members of the Lake District Special Planning Board, Friends of the Earth and similar organizations are not welcome in this pub." Phone 07684 86541. NY 458266

46 24

ARCHAEOLOGY. Iron-Age Fort on Dunmallard Hill "hill of slaughter"—first settlement at Pooley Bridge. Its outline, double ramparts, still visible. NY 467246

ARCHITECTURE. Waterfoot. 7 bayed house of c1800. Venetian windows, Ionic columns. NY 460245

GEOLOGY. Conglomerate. Excellent specimens alongside road by lake at Pooley Bridge. NY 468242

HISTORICAL. Eusemere (ON "oss": outfall of lake). Pooley Bridge. Was the home of Thomas Clarkson, the anti-slave trade campaigner. His portrait hangs in Dove Cottage—his wife befriended Dorothy Wordsworth. NY 469241

WALKS. Pooley Bridge-Dacre-Dalemain Park. Circuit 5½ miles/ 8.8km. Easy. Start: car park West of Pooley Bridge. NY 469245

46 26

CASTLE. Dacre. Early C14 Pele tower, walls 7ft/2m thick and 66ft/20m high. Arms of the Earl of Sussex over the entrance. Ground floor; horses/stores. 1st & 2nd floors—family/tenants. Fighting organised from the roof. Original Border defence system. Battlements. Unusually well preserved. Flemish tapestry, Chippendale, Sheraton furniture. Lord Dacre added large windows C17. A family member served at the siege of Acre in the Holy Land—hence D'Acre. It was here on 12 June 927 that King Athelstan of England, Constantine King of Alba, Owain King of Strathclyde and Eadwulf Lord of Bamburgh agreed to suppress heathenism— soon afterwards Constantine's son became Christian. 10 years later King Athelstan crushed the invasion mounted by the two Scottish kings and Olaf of Dublin, at Broomborough on the Wirral. Perhaps one of the most important battles in English history. Private—it passed to Edward Hasell of nearby Dalemain in 1723 and still is part of the estate but viewing appointments may be made through Dalemain (Refer NY 478269). NY 461265

LEGEND. Sir Guy Dacre's wife, Eloise, ran off with an Italian but both apprehended by Lyulph who retained them at his tower beside Ullswater until Sir Guy brought her back to Dacre Castle. She was led to a dungeon where the Italian was chained to the wall. She rushed to embrace him but his head fell to her feet. She was left with the decomposing corpse until she died of madness. Both are said to haunt the castle. NY 461265

46 28

ARCHAEOLOGY. in 1785 a Viking "penannular" thistle brooch with a pin some 22 inches/55cms long, in excellent condition, found in Silver Field, Flusco Pike, near New Biggin. This treasure now in British Museum. NY 464287

47 22

GEOLOGY. Drift—deposits left after retreat of glacier. Askham Fell. NY 4722

47 24

ARCHITECTURE. Pooley Bridge, a C16 3 arched bridge marked the border between the old counties of Cumberland & Westmorland. It replaced a weir with fish trap. A fish market used to be held in the Square in front of Crown Inn. NY 470244

Weathervane in shape of a fish. Market Square. Pooley Bridge   NY 472244

CHURCH. St Paul. Pooley Bridge ("pool how": the bridge by the hill by the stream). 1868. Overall small. Bell turret with spire. Lancet windows.   NY 472244

INDUSTRIAL ARCHAEOLOGY. Remains of octagonal horse-engine house but no machinery. Mains House Farm. Pooley Bridge.   NY 476246

REFRESHMENT. Sun Hotel. C16. Pooley Bridge. Phone 07684 86205
      NY 471245

Crown Inn. Pooley Bridge. Phone 07684 86495.   NY 470245

Chalet Hotel. Pooley Bridge.   NY 471244

TOURIST INFORMATION CENTRE. National Park Centre. Leaflets, displays etc. Open daily Easter–September. The Square. Pooley Bridge. Phone 07684 86530.   NY 470243

WALKS. Pooley Bridge to Heughscar—1213ft/370m and to Askham Fell. 4 miles/6.4km. Easy. Good vantage point to view lake and even Yorkshire.
      NY 471244

47 25

ARCHITECTURE. Barton Hall near Pooley Bridge. 1710 and 1868. 5 bays. Curved broken pediment to doorway. Windows—stone crosses. Fine oak panelling and splendid plaster ceiling with carvings of oak leaves, roses, thistles and vines.   NY 479252

47 26

HISTORIC HOUSE. Dalemain. Ullswater. Medieval to Georgian. In C12 John de Morville owned the initial buildings (it was his brother Hugh who, with three other Knights, murdered Beckett), but has been the Seat of the Hasell family since 1679, though the Laytons owned it prior to them. Some fine wooden chimney pieces and a Jacobean plaster ceiling. Front door lock, by George Dent of Appleby, given by Lady Anne Clifford. Priest's hole rediscovered 1851. C16 barn. Picnic sites. Fallow deer. Museum. Shop. Cafe in the medieval Old Hall. Open Easter/mid Oct daily except Friday and Saturday 1115–1700hrs. Fee. Phone 07684 864450.   NY 478269

MAMMALS. Fallow deer herd. Dalemain Park.   NY 4726

47 27

LITERARY. In 1805 William Wordsworth's in-laws, the Hutchinsons made their home here. Park House. Dacre.   NY 471271

47 28

LEGEND. Barons Cross Quarry—disused. So called after one of the Barons of Dacre who fell from his horse here and died of his injuries. A memorial cross was erected but does not now exist. Stainton.   NY 479282

Sharrow Bay, Ullswater. (Rosemary Liddle)

48 22

ARCHAEOLOGY. Settlement site. Cockpit. Moor Divock.   NY 483223

48 26

ARCHITECTURE. Barton Church Farm. Once the Vicarage. Coat of Arms of the Dawes family 1701. Above the porch door is inscribed "L and A. D. Non est haec requies. 1628. T and E. D. 1693." Plaque over a door—1637 "Non mihi sed successoribus" (not for me but my successors). Buildings L shaped configuration. Of the once fine plaster ceiling on 1st floor only part remains.   NY 485264

Kirkbarrow. Medieval farmhouse, much rebuilt in C16 but some evidence of original cruck construction can be seen. Ornamented two storey porch.   NY 489262

CHURCH. St Michael. Barton (OE "baertun": a barley field/outlying grange) near Penrith. C11. Of red sandstone. The siting of the church within an oval enclosure suggests a pre-Christian site. Late C13–early C14 massive arches strengthen original Norman arches of the uncommon central tower. Handsomely carved stone reredos. C13 font. Quartered shield—Lowther, Lancaster, Beauchamp and Hartson—above C17 porch. Royal Arms of George II. Brass inscription to Francisca, wife of Lancelot Dawes who died 1673 aged 23 "At her appearance the noone sun/Blush'd and shrunke because was quite undone,/In her concentr'd did all graces dwell./God pluckt my rose yt He might take a smell." Memorials to John Wordsworth died 1819 and his wife Anne died 1815, both of Penrith. Sundial on south wall. Mounting block to N side. 1920 lych-gate in memory of 1914—18 war. Grave of Wordsworth's grandfather, Richard (born 1690–died 25 June 1760), who was Receiver-General for Westmorland and grave of his wife Mary. Also grave of Richard's daughter, Ann Myers, (William's Aunt) died 1787.   NY 488264

48 28

CHURCH. Methodist chapel. 1877. Stainton (place on stony ground).   NY 486284

REFRESHMENT. The Kings Arms. 1721. Mounting steps. Stainton. Near Penrith. Phone 0768 62778.   NY 486282

48 29

ARCHAEOLOGY. Newton Reigny. Standing stones.   NY 489299

49 20

ARCHAEOLOGY. Tumulus. Moor Divock.   NY 499203

49 21

ARCHAEOLOGY. Cop stone 4¾ft/1.4m high, part of original stone circle/ stone avenue. Tarn Moor.   NY 494216

Burial chamber. White Raise. Crouched skeleton exhumed—middle to late Bronze Age.   NY 494212

Many remains of cairn circles. Moor Divock.   NY 4921

49 22

PLANTS. Acid moorland habitat. Moor Divock. NY 4922

49 23

ARCHAEOLOGY. Hill settlements (Roman/British)—embanked enclosures contain hut circles & internal banks. Skirsgill. Askham. NY 498231

49 27

FISH. Trout rearing farm. Sockbridge Mill. Open to the public for fishing.

NY 497277

Area 10 — Askham

50 21

GEOLOGY. Conglomerate. Helton. NY 5021

50 26

ARCHITECTURE. Sockbridge Hall. C15. Mullioned and transomed windows and one Henry VIII window. Now a farm. NY 504269

CHURCH. Wesleyan chapel. 1879. Tirril. NY 504267

The Old Meeting House 1733. Single storied cottage now a private residence. To the front is an enclosure, formerly a cemetery which contained the grave of Charles Gough, killed on Helvellyn 1805. (Refer NY 344149). NY 503267

LITERARY. Wordsworth House, formerly Sockbridge House, near Penrith. Private. Once was home of Wordsworth's grandfather and birthplace of his father, before being a private boarding school. Built 1699 for Reginald and Elizabeth Dobson. NY 504269

REFRESHMENT. The Queens Head. 1719. Once a pair of cottages and home of William Wordsworth. Tirril. Phone 0768 63219. NY 503266

50 27

PLANTS. Pinewood habitat. Whinfell. (Private). NY 5027

50 28

ARCHITECTURE. Yanwath Hall, Penrith. 1322 Battlemented Pele Tower with turrets, built by John de Sutton. At one time a prison and hangings took place here. Sandstone roof slabs affixed to laths by sheep bones. C15 hall—possibly the finest manorial hall in the country. Royal Tudor coat of Arms in plaster over the fireplace. Elizabethan five light mullioned and transomed windows and an oriel window. Well preserved interior. Original minstrel gallery. Queen's room where Mary Queen of Scots rested on her journey across the border into England. Rare brick oven. In ownership of the Threlkelds C15 and by marriage to the Dudleys in C16 and to the Lowthers 1671 and still part of the Lowther estate. Now a farmhouse but originally guarded the Roman crossing point of the River Eamont which led north from High Street. NY 508282

Skirsgill Hall. Penrith. 1795. Originally with wings but now 2 wide bow windows and three windows with blind central arcade. NY 509287

FARM. Yanwath Hall. Open days. Phone 0768 62692. NY 508282

HISTORICAL. The Luck of Skirsgill Hall—large armorial goblet engraved "The Luck of Skirsgill. September 1st ANNO 1732". Arms of Whelpdale of Skirsgill are engraved between a fruiting vine and a tulip. Commemorates engagement of

John Brougham's daughter Mary with William Whelpdale. The Luck was sold a quarter of a century ago and its whereabouts not known.　　　NY 509287

51 21

ARCHAEOLOGY. Medieval camp—Setterah Park. Roman relics have been found.　　　NY 514212

REFRESHMENT. The Helton Inn. Helton. Phone 09312 232.　NY 511219

51 22

CHURCH. Wesleyan Chapel. 1867. Helton (OE "helde": sloping ground).　　　NY 511221

51 23

ARCHITECTURE. Askham Hall. Three irregular wings around oblong court-yard. Tower at S end of E wing. This and adjoining, C14. Some remodelling around 1685 to S front of tower after conversion to Elizabethan mansion 1574 by Thomas Sandford, whose family's name continued until 1680—from 1375. The Sandford Arms inscribed "Thomas Sandford Esquyr for this payd meat and hyr The year of our Savyore XV hundreth seventy-four" emblazoned on the west wing. Then a Rectory. Mullioned and transomed windows. The Earl of Lonsdale in residence. Not open to the Public. Askham.　　　NY 516239

White washed cottages in Askham. Many date from 1650–1750.　　NY 5123

CHURCH. St Peter. Askham (the place with the ash trees). Rebuilt 1832 by Robert Smirke, the designer of the British Museum. Pseudo Norman although some remains of the original C13 church (then dedicated to St Columba). Interesting earlier artefacts—Elizabethan tomb chest. C17 altar-table. Flagon 1711. Font 1661. Gallery at W end. Several tablets to the Sandfords of Askham Hall. The cost of creating the baptistery in 1950 met by a native of Askham long since emigrated to USA. Lighting in commemoration of Allied Victory 1945. Charles Southey, son of Robert the poet, Vicar here until he died in 1888.　　　NY 518238

FARMING. Good examples of old agricultural strip pattern of fields north & south of Main Street. Askham.　　　NY 5123

MUSEUM. Lakeland Country Base. Askham. March/October. Phone 09312 400.　　　NY 514237

REFRESHMENT. The Queens Head. 1682. Askham. Gabled porch portrait of Elizabeth I. Wagon wheels of old Bampton hearse. Phone 09312 225.　　　NY 513237

The Punch Bowl Hotel. Askham. Phone 09312 443.　　　NY 516238

WALKS. Askham and Lowther Estate. Circuit 3¼ miles/5.2km. Easy. Takes in church and chapel. Start: Askham church.　　　NY 517238

51 24

BIRDS. Chiffchaff, crossbill, curlew, dipper, dunnock, goldcrest, heron, jackdaw, kingfisher, lapwing, magpie, mallard, moorhen, oyster catcher, partridge, pheasant, redshank, common sandpiper, skylark, snipe, starling, blue, great & long tailed tits, treecreeper, grey & yellow wagtails, garden & willow warblers and yellow hammer. Summer. Lowther Valley. NY 5124

CHURCH. St Michael. Lowther (ON "lauthra-a": the foaming river). C12. Exterior much altered. Interesting C17 artefacts. Oddly carved columns with grotesque beasts. Anglo-Norse Hogsback tombstones in porch. Saxon Cross. Behind the organ, statue of the first Lord Lonsdale, died 1700. North transept— Brass to Henry, Lord Lowther in his Life Guards uniform, who died 1887. In churchyard—Mausoleum 1857. Corner turrets. Inside, figure of William Earl of Lonsdale (1757–1844). It was to him that Wordsworth dedicated his poem "The Excursion". Yellow banner of Lonsdales displayed. "The Yellow Earl" Hugh Cecil (1857–1944) patron of boxing, he beat the then world heavyweight champion John L. Sullivan, (Lonsdale Belt first fought for 1909) and first President of Automobile Association, whose vehicles still display "his" livery. Epitaph to Thomas Cook died 1695 aged 24: "Hast thou, Health, Strength, Art, Industry, Yet dye thou must, for these had I." Grave of Jacob Thompson, Lake District landscape painter. NY 519244

51 25

ARCHAEOLOGY. Yanwath Woodhouse. Iron Age settlement site. NY 519259

Also a fortified site. Castlesteads. Yanwath. NY 518252

51 27

REFRESHMENT. The Gate Inn. Yanwath. The inn sign—a hanging gate and wall inscription "This gate hangs well/and hinders none,/ Refresh and Pay/and Travel on." Phone 0768 62386. NY 512277

51 28

ARCHAEOLOGY. Mayburgh Henge "maidens fortification". Eamont Bridge. Its circular stone banks with diameter of 383ft/116m rise to 15ft/4.5m. No ditch. Single standing stone 9ft/3m. Probably late Neolithic—stone and bronze implements found. Possibly the "Fort of Union" meeting place of three Kings by "Eamot-side" AD 926. NY 519284

FISH. Trout rearing farm. Southwaite Green. Eamont Bridge. NY 5128

51 29

CASTLE. Castlegate, Penrith. Built in 1399 by William Strickland Bishop of Carlisle. Was the home of the Nevilles, among them Richard Neville, Earl of Warwick, who, in the C15 at the age of 21, was the richest man in England—later he was known as "Warwick the King Maker". Once occupied by Richard, Duke of Gloucester, who became Richard III; he died on Bosworth Field. NY 513299

MUSEUM. Penrith Steam Museum in Castlegate Foundry operated by the Stalker family from 1858/1959. Varied vintage machinery, static and working. Furnished

Victorian cottage. April/Sept. Monday to Friday 1000–1630hrs. Saturday & Sunday only on Bank Holidays. Fee. Phone 0768 62154.   NY 513299

REFRESHMENT. Two Lions Inn. Princes St Penrith. Once Gerard Lowther's town house, built on site of previous building incorporated into present one. The old dining room now a bar, has original plaster ceiling of 1585 adorned with ensigns armorial of the Dudleys, Lowthers, Radcliffes, Threlkelds and others. Fire-place in the hall has three Heraldic shields. An outhouse was the original kitchen—huge fire-place. Bowling Green at rear. Phone 0768 64446.   NY 516299

52 20

WALL. Very good example of 3 course construction. Whale.   NY 521205

52 23

CASTLE. Spectacular C17 ruin. Lowther. The first commission of Robert Smirke, (who when aged 25, designed the British Museum), for the Lowther family, whose home it was from 1784 until 1936. Their fortunes, arising in the main from coal from C17–20, made them one of the richest families in England, but dwindling royalties on account of nationalization and estate duties led to the castle becoming the ruin it is today. Not open to the public.   NY 522239

52 24

FARM. Lowther Home Farm. Guided tours. The Warden. Forge Cottage. Askham. Phone 09312 400.   NY 526242

52 28

ARCHAEOLOGY. "King Arthur's Round Table". At one time the venue for jousting etc., and one time campsite of Scot's army *en route* to Worcester accompanied by Charles II. Tradition has it that Sir Lancelot du Lac killed the giant Tarquin here—his grave is in Penrith churchyard. Probable early Bronze Age henge—300ft/91m diameter earthworks and ditch on the inside. Central platform with one surviving entrance. Possibly shrine to the war god Camulos. Excavation has revealed cremations and also Bronze Age and Stone Age axes. Eamont Bridge, Penrith.   NY 523284

ARCHITECTURE. First house into what was Westmorland i.e. south of the River Eden, is dated 1671. Bears Latin inscription "Omne solum forti patria est" (Every soil is a fatherland to a brave man). Eamont Bridge.   NY 522287

Eamont Bridge C16. 3 segmental arches, with span of 120ft/36.5m. Triangular cut waters. A bridge at this point mentioned in Calendar of Inquisitions in 1291.   NY 523287

Mansion House. Eamont Bridge. 1686. 2½ storeys and 5 bays. Interesting interior.   NY 522288

Brougham Hall—restored. Ancestral home of the Broughams. Lord Chancellor Henry Peter Brougham c1840 designed a four wheeled horse-drawn carriage, named after him and much in use up to early part of C20. Magnificent hall with gilded roof. Pele tower c1600. (Carbon and ring-dating suggest that the oak used in the tower's construction, was planted in 1425 and felled in 1586). Impressive gateway. Once known as "The Windsor of the North" its former stables and servants' quarters now form a large craft centre. NY 528284

Old toll house where City of Carlisle claimed the revenue "For horses, mares, geldings, cattle, sheep and rams led, driven or carried out of the County of Cumberland, or that pass out of the County to be sold. Twopence for every horse, mare, gelding (one penny). For every score of sheep or lambs—twopence." NY 522288

CHURCH. St Wilfreds. Brougham near Eamont Bridge. (OE "ea[ge]mot": the meeting of the rivers). C14 but rebuilt by Lady Anne Clifford 1658 (very few churches of this period exist). Long & low. Splendid medieval wood carvings brought back from the Continent by Lord Brougham and Vaux c1840. Font C17. Screen c1500. Pulpit—some C17. Lectern & bronze with Brougham Arms. C17 German plate. Some C14 Glass, C15 Flemish altar piece—a rare triptych with sculptured and guilded Crucifixion scenes—has been exhibited at Victoria & Albert Museum. Hoard of debased Roman coins circa C600 found by grave-digger. NY 527284

CRAFTS. Brougham Hall. Open daily. Art gallery; prints, sculpture; Phone 0768 899091. Goldsmith. Chocolate truffle-maker. Wood-turner. Art; metal worker; Phone 0768 890558. Country furnishings; Phone 0768 890144. NY 528284

MEMORIAL. To 4 Volunteers from Eamont Bridge who served in the South African War. NY 524283

REFRESHMENT. The Crown Hotel. 1720. Eamont Bridge. Phone 0768 62566. NY 524283

The Beehive Inn. 1727. Eamont Bridge. Rhyme over door "Within this hive we are all alive,/Good liquor makes us funny;/If you be dry, step in and try,/The flavour of our honey." A reference to the days when ales sweetened with honey before sugar was available. Phone 0768 62081. NY 524283

52 29

ARCHITECTURE. Hornby Hall built by the Birbeck family in C16. Arched lights. West wall doorway lintel 1602. Eamont Bridge. NY 526292

53 22

EVENT. Lowther Horse Trials and Country Fair. 2nd Fri/Sat/Sun of August annually. Carriage Driving, Gun Dogs, Hounds, Fishing, Falconry, Clay Pigeon Shooting, Trade Stands etc., Phone 09312 378. NY 5322

LEISURE. Lowther Park. Fun fair. Miniature railway. Open Easter and then weekends. Late May–mid Sept daily 1000–1800hrs. Phone 09312 523. NY 5322

MAMMALS. Lowther Park. Deer—red, fallow, Japanese and Formosan sika plus indigenous British mammals. Birds. Shop. Cafe. Picnic area. Open daily Easter–October. 1000–1800hrs. Fee. NY 5322

TREES. Oaks, ancient. In very early deer park. Lowther Park.　　NY 5322

53 23

ARCHITECTURE. Model village to C18 architecture. Near Lowther Newtown.　　NY 537236

53 24

ARCHAEOLOGY. Long cairn. Lowther.　　NY 538243

53 26

CUSTOMS. Shaking Bottle or Sugar Water Sunday (the first after Ascension) celebrated at Clifton's Well, the return of Spring. People drank well water mixed with Spanish or sugar and decorated the well with flowers. The practice banned in 1824 by Bishop of Penrith when cock fighting and wrestling ensued.　　NY 536263

REFRESHMENT. George & Dragon. Clifton. Phone 0768 65381.　　NY 537262

The Clifton Hill Hotel (a motel). Phone 0768 62717.　　NY 536265

53 27

ARCHITECTURE. Clifton Manor. Pele tower, C15—restored. Family seat of the Wybergs from C14–C19. The farmhouse nearby has Roman slab, inscription and carved figures, built into its structure. Nearby is site of Battle of Clifton Moor, rebellion 1745. Open to the public, daily.　　NY 531271

CHURCH. St Cuthbert. Clifton (the place on a hill). Tradition has it that the Lindisfarne monks bearing St Cuthbert's body when fleeing from the Danes in C9 rested here. Norman and later additions. Interesting C18 artefacts. Window bears portrait of Eleanor Engayne, mistress of Clifton Manor, married 1365. Also memorial tablet on N wall. Pulpit carving of The Adoration given by Lord Clifford. Churchyard Memorial to 11 Dragoons of Bland's Regiment who died at Clifton Moor 18th December 1745. Medieval Cross near porch.　　NY 532271

HISTORICAL. On 18th December 1745 Bonnie Prince Charles's rear guard troops under the command of Lord George Murray were overtaken by advance party under command of Duke of Cumberland with Lord Cobham's, Lord Mark Kerr's and General Bland's Dragoons and although some Scots were able to retreat across Lowther Bridge this was the last skirmish on English soil. The Scots are buried under an oak tree on Town End Farm.　　NY 532271

53 28

ARCHAEOLOGY. Brougham (Brocavum). Roman fort founded by Agricola used as a provisioning centre for Hadrian's Wall. Abutts the castle.　　NY 538288

CASTLE. Brougham—pronounced "Broom". (OE "burgh-ham": a fortified farm). Rectangular C12 Keep. Inscription on outer gatehouse "Thys Made Roger". (Roger Clifford, killed at Bannockburn 1314). At the end of the C13 passed by marriage to Robert Lord Clifford, Edward I's confidant who created it the strongest fortress in the valley of the Eden. In 1617 James I said to have stayed here for 3 days. After the Civil War restored by its last great owner Lady Anne Clifford, (born 1590) only daughter of George, 3rd Earl of Cumberland and 13th Lord Clifford. Married Earl of Dorset, then Earl of Pembroke and Montgomery. Of her five children only two girls reached adulthood. When nearly 60, after the death of her uncle the 4th Earl of Cumberland and her cousin the 5th Earl of Cumberland she inherited vast wealth and used it mainly on her passion for building. She restored her castles at Appleby, Bardon, Brough, Brougham, Pendragon & Skipton, plus numerous churches and almshouses. Cromwell said of her "Let her build what she will, she shall have no hindrance from me." Lady Anne died here 1675 aged 86. The ceiling in the passage from the stairs to the second floor has a Roman tombstone embedded within it which bears Christian inscription though difficult to decipher. Indoor—period additions, unusual in plan. Open Apr/Sept daily; Oct/Mar closed Mondays. Phone 0768 62488. In care of English Heritage.   NY 538288

LEGEND. The Shepherd Lord. Lady Margaret Clifford's husband (the Black-faced Clifford—on account of his complexion) was killed in a skirmish at Dittingdale just prior to battle at Towton on 29 March 1461, fighting for the Red Rose of Lancaster, leaving a daughter and two sons. But the Yorkist Edward IV ascended the throne and quickly wreaked vengeance upon his enemies, actual and potential, and so the two Clifford boys were ordered to be put to death. The widow (daughter and sole heiress of Henry de Bromflete, Baron de Vesci) declared to the enemy troops that her servant had taken the children overseas though, in reality, only the younger son had been sent to the Netherlands, where he later died. His sister much later became the wife of Sir Robert Aske. Henry, the elder son, at the age of 7 was sent to Lonsborrow where he lived with a shepherd who had married the attendant to his nurse. When aged 14, his mother had married Sir Lancelot Threlkeld and about this time rumours reached the Court of Edward IV that her son was alive. She anticipated the King's actions and had the shepherd and her boy move to a remote part of Cumberland where the lad grew up as a shepherd. 15 years later at the Battle of Bosworth, the Yorkists were defeated and Henry VII came to the throne whereupon Lady Margaret announced that her elder son lived. Summoned to appear at the House of Lords, this simple dalesman who could neither read nor write had his title and his land restored to him. He then availed himself of the teachings of the Bolton Abbey monks so at the age of 31 was exalted from a poor shepherd lad into a rich and powerful lord. In 1513, when aged 60, he was appointed commander of the army which fought victoriously on 9th September 1513 at Flodden during which 10,000 Scotsmen died along with 4,000 English. He died peacefully on 23rd April 1523 when aged 70. Wordsworth was moved to write "Song at the Feast of Brougham Castle upon the Restoration of Lord Clifford, the Shepherd, to the Estates and Honours of His Ancestors."   NY 538288

54 22

ARCHITECTURE. Hackthorpe Hall, Strickland. C17. Jacobean four-light mullioned and transomed windows. 3 storied porch. St John Lowther born here, succeeded to Lowther Hall.   NY 545228

LEGEND. The Boggle of Hackthorpe Hall—in the form of a calf. It led the farmer to treasure buried beneath a trough. Thereafter no further disturbance for the calf was then able to rest in peace. Boggles in human form or otherwise were feared more than "Dobbies" (ghosts), and only one person at a time could see them.   NY 545228

54 23

REFRESHMENT. Lowther Castle Hotel. The Court lounge bar was once used on Mondays fortnightly for sittings by the West Ward Justices transferred to Shap 1963. Hackthorpe. Phone 09312 339.   NY 543230

54 29

MONUMENT. Countess Pillar. Eamont Bridge. 14ft/4.26m high octagonal pillar with pyramidal roof and finial—1656. On cube atop pillar are shields and a sundial, plus an inscription commemorating Lady Anne Clifford's, Dowager of Pembroke, last farewell from her mother on 2 April 1616 "a woman of greate naturall wit and judgement, of a swete disposition, truly religious and virtuous, and endowed with a large share of those four moral virtues, prudence, justice, fortitude and temperance." Her mother, Margaret Countess of Cumberland died 1617. The commemorative bequest of £4 is still paid over to the poor on the adjoining dole stone tablet.   NY 548290

55 20

ARCHITECTURE. Thrimby Hall 1676. Much rebuilt.   NY 555204

GEOLOGY. Coal measures. Thrimby.   NY 5520

55 22

CHURCH. St Barnabas. 1872. Great Strickland (in Domesday Book—Stircaland: "pasture for young bullocks"). Lancet windows. Wooden bell turret.   NY 556228

55 25

GARDEN. Larch Cottage Nurseries. Melkinthorpe Penrith CA10 2DR. Phone 09312 404. Extensive range of unusual and old-fashioned cottage garden plants, shrubs and alpines.   NY 556252

55 26

CRAFTS. Wetheriggs Country Pottery. Clifton Dykes. Penrith. C19 clay works originally developed to manufacture bricks and tiles for Brougham Hall estate. Daily 1000–1800hrs. (Closed Christmas Day). Pottery, weaving, museum, (displaying old machines and tools; potter's wheels available for visitors to practice the art of "throwing" clay), gallery, cafe, shop and picnic area. Video of clay pottery history since 1855. Fee. Phone 0768 62946   NY 555263

INDUSTRIAL ARCHAEOLOGY. Wetheriggs County Pottery built in 1855 by a Mr Binings and now worked as a Studio Pottery. Many C19 relics and a Beehive-kiln which was in regular use from 1855 to 1959. To bring the kiln up to 1100°C over a period of 36 hours, six tons of coal were required. Also preserved is an 1855 steam blunger, where clay and water mixed and then agitated by the blunger to create a suspension. The resultant creamy liquid was then run off into a sunpan to allow the water to evaporate. Tramway and also a steam engine. Early products included Barm pots, salt kits and drain pipes but now more ornamental wares.   NY 555263

55 29

CHURCH. St Ninian. Ninekirk. Completely rebuilt 1660 by Lady Anne Clifford. Tall canopied box pews, screen, benches, font (1662) & pulpit poor box of that period. Nave & chancel in one. Collar beamed roof. East wall wreath bearing initials of A. P. (Anne Pembroke) 1660. Lady Anne's diary records (of the Church) "it would in all likehood have fallen down, it was soe ruinous, if it had not bin repard by me." There is no electric light nor heating and therefore cannot be used during the winter. The Churchyard is still open for funerals. (Lady Anne's mother's bowels are buried here—her body at Appleby). Ninekirk is thought to relate to the Celtic saint, Ninian, who was (by some considered) a native of Strathclyde. He studied in Rome and on his return became a missionary in the north, living in a cave in the C5.   NY 559299

Area 11 – Buttermere

09 18

MINE. Kelton Fell Mine. Haematite. Along with its "sister" mine at Kelton Park (NY 085183) very productive. NY 095180

09 19

FISH. Cogra Moss. Depth 30ft/9.1m. Lamplugh Fell. Brown trout. Day permits: D. W. Lothian. Tackle Shop. 35 Main St, Cockermouth. Phone 0900 822006. NY 0919

MINE. Knock Murton Fell Mine. Haematite. Highly productive. 1853–1914. NY 095190

10 13

MINE. Old Crag Fell Mine. Haematite. NY 105139

10 14

GEOLOGY. Haematite. NY 1014

MAMMALS. Pine marten. Ennerdale. NY 1014

10 15

EVENT. Ennerdale Show. Bowness Knot. Last Wednesday in August. NY 1015

FISH. Ennerdale Water (ON "Eghnar-dalr": the dale of the River Ehen). Lake owned by North West Water Ltd. Water supplied to West Cumbrian industry. 2½ miles/ 4km long, ¾ mile/1.2km wide. 368ft/112m above sea level. Maximum depth 148ft/45m. Average depth 62ft/18m. Charr & brown trout. The freshwater shrimp (*Mysis relicta*) inhabits this lake and no other in England. Day permits—Mrs Phyllis Humphreys. High Bridge Farm, Ennerdale. NY 1015

NATURE RESERVE/TRAIL. Smithy Beck Forest Trails—waymarked. Circuits of 1¼ miles/2km and also 2½ miles/3.5km. Forest ecology—Japanese larch, Scots pine & most common coniferous trees. Extreme northern limit of holly blue butterfly. Good for mosses and lichens. Deer—red & roe, red squirrel & badger. Forestry Commission Guide. Start: Bowness Knot. NY 109153

WALKS. Nine Becks Walk. Circuit 9 miles/15km. Waymarked paths through forest follow River Liza—impressive after rain. Forestry Commission Map— "Walking in Ennerdale Forest." Start: Bowness Knot. NY 109153

Ennerdale Water circuit. 7½ miles/12km. Strenuous. Some rough and wet sections. Good views of Pillar and Steeple. Start: Bowness Knot. NY 109153

11 15

GEOLOGY. Granophyre. Ennerdale. NY 1115

12 12

MINE. Iron Crag Mine. c1864–1881. Haematite.   NY 129124

12 17

MINE. Redgill level.   NY 128170

13 13

WATERFALLS. Woundell Beck and Low Beck. Ennerdale. Park at Bowness Knot. Path alongside lake to bridge across River Liza (ON "lysa": bright water). On S shore cross Woundell Beck to reach falls where Deep Gill and Silverdale Beck unite. Continue on path, very indistinct at times, through Deep Gill to reach highest fall (NY 147115) from which a path leads to plateau between Haycock and Scoat Fell. At wall turn NE for cairn for Steeple 2687ft/819m and descend via Long Crag returning to lake via Ennerdale Forest. 11 miles/17.70km. Circuit. Strenuous.   NY 134132

13 16

MINE. Gale Fell level. Not viable and closed 1873. Further level refer NY 140167.   NY 139167

13 18

MINE. Mosedale Mine. Lead. Last worked c1891—unsuccessful.   NY 136186

13 19

MINE. Whiteoak Mine. Several levels and one shaft. Leased 1864 and last worked 1891. Lead.   NY 130199

14 14

YOUTH HOSTEL. Cat Crag, Gillerthwaite, Ennerdale. Phone 0946 861237.
                                                                 NY 142141

14 16

MINE. Gale Fell Level. 1863–1873. Iron ore, not viable. Further level—refer NY 139167.   NY 140167

14 19

MINE. Melbreak Trials. Iron ore. Only a few feet into mountain.
                                               NY 142192 and NY 148196

15 10

FISH. Trout. Free. Much favoured. Scoat Tarn. Depth 65½ ft/20m.   NY 1510

15 14

GEOLOGY. Arete. Red Pike.   NY 1514

15 17

MINE. Scale Force Level. 1863–1873. Iron ore. Uneconomic. Near foot of waterfall.   NY 151171

WATERFALLS. 125ft/38m. Scale Force, Lakelands highest waterfall. Crummock Water.	NY 151171

15 18

GEOLOGY. Roches moutonnées. Low Ling Crag. Crummock Water.
	NY 157183

TREES. Austrian pines. Crummock Water shore. Larger cones than Scots pine and bark not so red.	NY 1518

VIEWPOINT. Low Ling Crag. Crummock Water.	NY 157183

16 13

MEMORIAL. To Members of the Fell and Rock Climbing Club who died in the 2nd World War. Bridge over River Liza. Ennerdale Forest.	NY 165135

16 15

GEOLOGY. Hanging Valley. Sour Milk Gill. Buttermere.	NY 169158

WATERFALLS. Sourmilk Gill. Buttermere. From village take path to lake across water meadows. As lake is reached follow path through Burtness Wood on a rock path/ladder of syenite rocks from Ennerdale—granophyre [medium grain size of granite family in which quartz and feldspar are intergrown] which appear red when wet. Alpine lady's mantle grows beside the path. 3 miles/4.82km Circuit. Strenuous.	NY 169158

16 16

TREES. Oakwood. Scale, Buttermere.	NY 1616

WATERFALLS. Far Ruddy Beck. Crummock Water. From Buttermere car park take path on left of Fish Hotel and via stile to a lane towards the double-arched Scale Bridge, at which turn NW beside Crummock Water before climbing the fell towards the beck. 3 miles/4.82km. Circuit. Strenuous.
	NY 163168

16 17

ARCHITECTURE. Watergate, of wood, prevents sheep from wandering.
	NY 169172

Scale Bridge. Double-arched, one small. Crummock Water.	NY 163170

BIRDS. Summer—kingfisher, heron & common sandpiper. Winter—greylag goose, pochard & whooper swan. Crummock Water.	NY 1617

16 18

GEOLOGY. Skiddaw slates. Crummock Water.	NY 1618

Alluvial fan. Rannerdale. Crummock Water.	NY 162186

MINE. Rannerdale Trial. 6ft/1.8m inroad unsuccessful.	NY 163183

16 19

HISTORICAL. Cinderdale—Iron ore smelted, hence its name.   NY 1619

WALKS. Crummock Water. Circuit 8½ miles/13.7km. Strenuous. Rough and wet underfoot. Good view of the virtually inaccessible Scale Force, 125ft/38m fall. Start: Cinderdale Common.   NY 162194

17 11

GEOLOGY. Borrowdale volcanic series. Pillar.   NY 1711

17 12

MEMORIAL. Plaque and Cairn erected by Fell and Rock Climbing Club members in memory of John Wilson Robinson (1853–1907) a pioneer cragsman of Lorton, who reputedly made a hundred ascents of Pillar.   NY 177123

PLANTS. Mountain habitat—Pillar.   NY 1712

17 14

GEOLOGY. Borrowdale volcanic series. High Stile.   NY 1714

Hanging valley.   NY 1714

MAMMALS. Pine martens. Burtness Combe. Buttermere.   NY 176146

17 15

TREES. Oakwoods. Burtness and Horseclose. Buttermere.   NY 1715

Pillar from Innominate Tarn. (Author)

17 16

ARCHITECTURE. Bank barn. Wilkinsyke farm. Buttermere.   NY 174169

FISH. Buttermere. (Dairy Pasture Lake—older style, ancient Norse, owner Buthar). Owned by the National Trust. 1½ miles/ 2.4km long, ½ mile/0.8km wide. 329ft/100m above sea-level. Maximum depth 94ft/28.6m. Average depth 55ft/16m. Charr, eel, perch, roach and brown trout. Permit from Gatesgarth Farm, Buttermere.   NY 1716

WALKS. Red Pike Ridge-Buttermere. Circuit (via lake side) 9½ miles/15km. Ascent 3450ft/1050m. Strenuous. Start: Fish Hotel, Buttermere.   NY 174169

WATERFALLS. A series of small cascades. Sourmilk Gill. Buttermere.
NY 172162

YOUTH HOSTEL. King George VI Memorial Hostel. Buttermere. Phone 059685 70245.   NY 178169

17 17

ARCHITECTURE. Slate built house with "corbie stepped" gables. Buttermere.
NY 174172

Norman cottages—named after John Norman, a local, who sailed on HMS *Bounty*. Buttermere.   NY 174172

CHURCH. St James. Buttermere. 1841. Very small—lower chancel. Bellcote— two bells. Entrance pillar and font of earlier date. 16 carved angels in ceiling. Wrought iron porch gate depicts shepherd with his ewe and lamb. Memorial to Alfred Wainwright: "Pause and Remember Alfred Wainwright Fellwalker, Guide Book Author and Illustrator who loved this valley, Lift your eyes to Haystacks His favourite place. 1907–1991." Burials at Lorton 5 miles/8km north north west.
NY 176170

EVENT. Buttermere Show. 3rd Saturday in October. Held opposite Fish Hotel. Sheep, Dogs, Fell Race, Hound Trail, Trade Stands.   NY 176170

HISTORICAL. In 1792, Captain Joseph Budworth (veteran of the Siege of Gibraltar and first pedestrian tourist worthy of note, wrote of his wanderings under the pen-name "A Rambler") published his book *A Fortnights Ramble to the Lakes*. In it he made a great deal of the innkeeper's 15 year old daughter, Mary Robinson, "Her face was a fine oval, with full eyes and lips as red as vermilion. Her cheeks had more of the lily than the rose..."; resulting in much publicity. On 2nd October 1802, James Hatfield aged 44, impersonating Colonel The Honourable Alexander Augustus Hope, MP for Linlithgow, wooed Mary and married her in Lorton church meanwhile running up huge debts. During their honeymoon Hatfield was exposed as a swindler and bigamist and was arrested on their return. (He was already married to Lord Robert Manning's daughter by whom he had three children and had left them to marry a Miss Nation). He escaped to Ravenglass and thence to Wales, but rearrested, and tried, not for bigamy, but for falsely franking his letters as an M. P. He was hanged on 3rd September 1803 from a dung cart on the "Sands", a little island formed by the River Eden, between the two bridges on the N side of Carlisle. He is buried in St Mary's graveyard close to the N gate. Mary was left with child, which was stillborn. In 1808 she married Richard Harrison, a farmer of Todcrofts by whom she had quite a large family. She died aged 58 on 7th February 1837 at Todcrofts, Caldbeck and is buried in Caldbeck churchyard. Wordsworth praised her in *The Prelude* Book VII (1805/6) line 321. NY 176170

REFRESHMENT. Fish Hotel, Buttermere. Phone 07687 70253. NY 176170

Bridge Hotel. Buttermere. Previously The Queen, The Victoria Hotel and before that a corn mill; traces of millpond and races in adjacent wood above the bridge. Phone 07676 70252. NY 175170

WALKS. Red Pike, High Stile, Buttermere. Circuit 6 miles/9.5km. Ascent 2400ft/731m. Very strenuous. Dramatic and rugged but superlative ridge walk of 1½ miles/2.4km. Difficult in bad weather. Panoramic views. Start: car park, Buttermere. NY 176170

17 18

HISTORICAL. Site of C11 battle. English v Normans, the former victorious. The Norman Army Commander, William Rufus, was led to believe that he was leading his men over a pass instead of the cul-de-sac that it is. Rannerdale—Crummock Water. NY 171187

LITERARY. Rannerdale was the setting of "The Secret Valley" by Nicholas Size, former landlord of the Bridge Hotel, Buttermere. NY 1718

18 14

MINE. Low Wax Knott Trial. Level and openworks at Scarth Gap. In C19 two men worked this but one is presumed to have murdered the other—a body was found in a deep pool at Warnscale Bottom and the suspect was never again seen. NY 188141

18 15

ARCHITECTURE. Hassness tunnel on north shore of Buttermere. Built by George Benson then owner of Hassness House, who wished to complete the existing path around the lake and also to maintain his labour force in work during the winter. NY 186158

GEOLOGY. Alluvial fan. Hassness. Buttermere. NY 187157

MINE. Buttermere Mine. C16. Copper. NY 180157

WATERFALLS. Comb Beck. Buttermere. Cascades. NY 183152

18 16

BIRDS. Golden eagles nesting site over a century ago. Crags— Hassness How Beck. Buttermere. NY 189163

GEOLOGY. Skiddaw Slate. Buttermere. NY 1816

19 12

TREES. The first plantation of the Forestry Commission in 1926. Black Sail. Ennerdale.   NY 1912

YOUTH HOSTEL. Black Sail Hut. (ON "sel": mountain hut). Ennerdale. Below summit ridge of Haystacks. Isolated. Previously a shepherd's bothy. Accommodates 18. March–October. No telephone.   NY 195124

19 14

ARCHITECTURE. Salving House. Gatesgarth Farm. Buttermere. Refer NY 544042 for details of salving.   NY 194149

MEMORIAL. Small white cross—inscription reads "Erected by Friends of Fanny Mercer. Accidentally killed 1887." On the 8th September Fanny, aged 18, and fellow servants of Reverend P. Bowden Smith, climbed Honister Crag and descended via Fleetwith Pike. The alpenstock she was carrying jammed in rock crevice and, acting as a vaulting pole, propelled her off the rock face. She fell about 20ft/6m onto her head and rolled a further 130ft/40m. Cross maintained by Cockermouth Mountain Rescue Team. Fleetwith Pike.   NY 197147

19 15

MINE. Beckside Trial. Lead. Opposite small car park Buttermere, made out of flattened spoil heaps. 2 well hidden levels.   NY 192154

WALKS. Buttermere. Circuit 4 miles/6.4km. Easy. Good views of Fleetwith Pike, High Crag, High Stile and Red Pike. Photogenic. Start: Gatesgarth (ME "Gatescartheved"; top of the road gap) or Buttermere village.   NY 195150

Haystacks. Circuit 4½ miles/7.5km. Ascent 1700ft/520m. Strenuous. Superior views from this lesser height though the real "gem" is Innominate Tarn so called by the Fell and Rock Climbing Club early this century unaware that it was already named Loaf Tarn due to the dough-like appearance of the raised clumps of peat in its waters. Alfred Wainwright's Ashes (1907–20.1.91) were scattered hereabouts. Start: Gatesgarth Farm.   NY 195150

Pillar—high level route. Circuit 11 miles/18km. Ascent 4800ft/1460m. Strenuous. Impressive rock face. Pillar rock summit—High Man 750ft/230m—recorded first climb 9th July 1826 by John Atkinson, a local shepherd. A retired clergyman, Reverend James Jackson climbed Pillar up the W side—known today as "The Old West Climb" in May 1875 when aged 78 and again in 1876. In 1878 he was killed at his third attempt. That legend of rock-climbing W. P. Haskett Smith claimed it to be one of the four best climbs in England; the others being Gable, Mickledore and Wast Water screes.   NY 195150

19 17

WATERFALLS. Moss Force. Newlands Hause.   NY 194174

AREA 12 – Borrowdale

20 10

PLANTS. Mountain habitat. Great Gable. NY 2010

20 13

MINE. Blackbeck Trial. Galena. NY 201131

WATERFALLS. Warnscale Bottom. Haystacks. Path from Gatesgarth Farm (NY 194149). At circular sheep pen follow grass track and cross Warnscale Beck to falls. Return can be made via Haystacks and Scarth Gap Pass. 5 miles/8.04km. Circuit. Strenuous. NY 201136

20 14

LEGEND. The Graemes—a border clan of noted repute, stole sheep and cattle in Borrowdale and attempted escape via Honister Pass. Dalesmen enjoined battle and the clan chief's son was killed. His body said to have been buried high on Honister Crag, marked with his bonnet, claymore and shield. Others recount that a cairn on Hindscarth (NY 216166) marks the burial. NY 2014

20 19

FUNGI. Over 30 species recorded on this acid soil. Keskadale. NY 2019

PLANTS. Oak wood habitat. Keskadale. NY 2019

TREES. Relict sessile oak wood. Near to limit of their climatic range in UK at 1640ft/500m. Very possibly descendants of original wood 7,000 years ago. Keskadale. Newlands Valley. NY 2019

21 10

CAIRN. Westmorland Cairn. Great Gable. Built by the father and brother of Colonel "Rusty" Westmorland, eminent climber and mountain rescuer in 1876, who decided that the finest Lakeland mountain view was from this spot. NY 211102

MEMORIAL. Summit of Great Gable, 2949ft/898m bronze relief map showing Kirk Fell, Great Gable, Lingmell, Broad Crag and Great End together with names of 20 members of the Fell and Rock Climbing Club of the Lake District who lost their lives in the First World War. Unveiled Whit Sunday 1924. Commemorative service is still held on the summit every Remembrance Sunday. NY 211103

21 13

GEOLOGY. Roches moutonnées. Dubs Bottom. NY 210131

QUARRY. Dubs Quarry. Green slate. Quarrymen lived in small huts e.g. at Dubs, only going home on Sundays. Linked to the Hause (NY 224135) by self-acting inclined tramway (descending full wagons hauled up lighter empty wagons). Now a stepped fellwalkers' path. NY 210135

21 14

QUARRY. Honister Crag Quarry. Green slate. Closed 1985 having been open for perhaps two centuries. Harriet Martineau (1802–1876) records that "nearly forty years ago (c1854) there was a man named Joseph Clark at Honister, who made seventeen journeys (including seventeen miles of climbing up and scrambling down) in one day, bringing down 10,880lbs (4,935kg) of slate. In ascending he carried the hurdle, weighing 80lbs (36kg); and in descending each time he brought down 640lbs (290kg) of slate. At another time he carried down, in three successive journeys, 1280lbs (580kg) each time. His greatest day's work was bringing down 11,717lbs (5314kg) in how many journeys is not remembered, but in fewer than seventeen." NY 215140

21 17

WATERFALLS. Scope Beck. Little Dale. Newlands. Park at Chapel Bridge, Newlands. Follow path to Newlands church and on to Low High Snab, then track alongside Scope Beck. 4 miles/6.43km. Circuit. Moderate. NY 214177

22 10

WATERFALLS. Taylor Force. 140ft/42m. Viewpoint; Stockley Bridge. Known locally as the White Maid of Borrowdale. NY 229109

22 12

GEOLOGY. Hanging Valley. Sour Milk Gill. Seathwaite. NY 229122

22 13

MINE. Honister Trial Level. Copper. NY 223137

QUARRY. Honister Hause. The slate from Yew Crag, Dubs and Honister Crag quarries was processed here. (This slate was used on roof of House of Commons). In operation from 1643 until recently. NY 224135

WALKS. Great Gable via Windy Gap. Circuit 6 miles/9.5km. Ascent 2450ft/750m. Strenuous. Some of track used by pack-horse trains for quarried slate and illicit whisky smuggling in bygone days. Start: car park Honister Hause.
NY 225135

YOUTH HOSTEL. Honister Hause, Seatoller. Keswick. On site of old quarry men's barracks. Phone 07687 77267. NY 225135

22 14

QUARRY. Yew Crag Quarry. Green slate. In operation since C17 until closure in 1966 when conditions became unsafe. NY 224143

22 15

MINE. Dalehead Mine. Ruins of. Spoil heaps. NY 222157

Dalehead Mine Level. Spoil heap. NY 225155

22 16

MINE. Long Work. Copper. Mining commenced c1565 and continued intermittently until abandoned 1922. The above open works also at NY 225162.

NY 228162

WATERFALLS. Newlands Beck. Newlands. From Chapel Bridge (NY 231194) follow gated mine road. 5½ miles/8.85km. Circuit. Easy. NY 229161

22 17

MINE. Castle Nook Mine. Lead. Closed 1864, re-opened 1917 and finally closed 1918. NY 227170

22 18

ARCHITECTURE. Pigeon Loft above C16 byre door. Low Snab farm. Newlands Valley. NY 229186

HISTORICAL. Goldscope Mines. Newlands Valley. Thomas Percy, Earl of Northumberland, owned land embracing the mine but did not authorize mineral extraction nor did he receive financial benefit. His attempts to prevent operations resulted in a trial in 1568, judgement being found in favour of the Crown. His dissatisfaction resulted in his leading an armed rebellion and subsequent defeat and his execution in 1569. NY 226185

MINE. Goldscope Mine. Originally named "Gottesgab" (God's Gift) by German miners but corrupted over the years via Gowd Scalp/Gold Scalp to Goldscope. Situated on E and W flanks of Scope End. Old land records suggest there was mining here in C13 but the only level on the east side, a copper vein adit, was started in 1564 by German miners employed by the Company of Mines Royal. Over the centuries several lessees were involved and in 1852 Clarke drove the original level forward and discovered a rich lead vein—over 20ft/6.09m wide in places. This produced 7 oz/198g of silver per ton of lead metal with minuscule amounts of gold. In 1854 a huge collapse necessitated working at greater depths with consequential water problems which resulted in the closure of the mine in 1864. NY 226185

REFRESHMENT. Low Snab Farm. Newlands Valley. NY 229186

22 19

CHURCH. Newlands. 1843 restored 1885. Low, white. Small gallery, panelled pulpit and desk—1610. Round headed windows. Surrounded by sycamore trees within walled enclosure. Wordsworth visited May 1826 and wrote "How delicate the leafy veil/Through which yon house of God/Gleams 'mid the peace of this deep dale/By few but shepherds trod!/And lowly huts, near beaten ways,/No sooner stand attired/In thy fresh wreaths, than they for praise/Peep forth, and are admired." ("To May" lines 81–88). Tiny schoolroom added to left side. Tutelage ceased 1967. NY 229193

23 10

ARCHITECTURE. Stockley Bridge—on old pack-horse bridge route from Borrowdale to Wasdale. Destroyed in August 1966 (now restored) when about 5 in/130mm of rain fell within an hour.   NY 235109

GEOLOGY. Moraine. Seathwaite Fell.   NY 235100

Kettle moraine. Stockley Bridge.   NY 235109

23 12

ARCHITECTURE. Seathwaite (the clearing with the "saetr"). This hamlet is the wettest inhabited place in Britain with an annual rainfall of 125 in/3175mm. Nearby Sprinkling Tarn near Sty Head has recorded over 200 in/5080mm per annum. Whilst cottages and farm houses might be limewashed almost annually the outbuildings and barns are not, for this allows air to circulate freely through gaps and maintains the hay at a "safe" temperature. Cattle and sheep, too, are less prone to disease. The lime often had dung added to enable the mixture to adhere better to the stonework.   NY 235122

GEOLOGY. Graphite (plumbago), found only at Seathwaite and one other site. Soft steel-grey substance, significant in Lake District history and industry for casting cannon balls, glazing pottery and later, the manufacture of "lead" pencils.   NY 234127

HISTORICAL. Seathwaite Farm has been occupied by three generations of Edmondsons.   NY 235122

MINE. Disused. Start date not known but workings recorded in 1555—last mined c1891. Graphite known as plumbago, wad, black cawke or black lead. Its early use for marking sheep and black-leading kitchen ranges, but later in crucible and refractory mould construction and in metal casting. In powdered form used as a remedie for colic. Its value per ton prime quality increased from £18 in 1646 to £3,920 per ton in 1804. (The net profit of the mining company in 1803 was £92,690 after striking a rich "pipe" which yielded 31¼ tons). Sent to London in barrels on waggons, some of it being stored in the cellars of the Unitarian Chapel in Essex Street. Sold by auction conducted in the upper room of local public-house on 1st Monday monthly. Illicit working and theft presented major problems which necessitated draconian action. An Act of Parliament, passed after an armed attack on the mine in 1752 declared that theft from or illegal entry to be a felony, resulting in public whipping and one year's hard labour or seven years' transportation. Given to National Trust by the Bankes family in 1981 as were their Kingston Lacey and Corfe Castle Estates (both in Dorset). National Resource for Keswick pencil industry from 1790 onwards. Borrowdale.   NY 234127

TREES. Borrowdale yews. Seathwaite. Wordsworth wrote of these in 'Yew Trees' "But worthier still of note/Are those fraternal Four of Borrowdale,/Joined in one solemn and capacious grove;/Huge trunks! And each particular trunk a growth/Of intertwisted fibres serpentine." In 1883 a severe gale damaged all but three which are now battered remnants although regeneration is now well advanced. NY 238128

WALKS. Great Gable from Climbers Traverse. Circuit 7 miles/11 km. Ascent 2700ft/820m. Strenuous. This route, although difficult, gives unsurpassed views of the Napes, together with other vertical rock faces beloved of climbers, for it was here that true Lake District rock climbing came of age around 1880, some routes being up to Hard Very Severe Standard. In 1936 Hesket Smith, a pioneer of true rock climbing, climbed the Needles when aged 76 to celebrate his first climb of that rock 50 years previously. Start: Seathwaite. NY 235123

23 13
GEOLOGY. Kettle moraine. Honister. NY 230136

23 15
QUARRY. Rigghead Quarry. Slate. 1864, now disused. On High Scawdel. Borrowdale. NY 237153

23 16
MINE. St Thomas's Work. Open works for copper. Castlenook. NY 230166

23 17
MINE. Castlenook Mine. Trial level adit. NY 231170

Castlenook Mine. Trial level adit at waterfall foot. NY 231171

23 18
GEOLOGY. Erratics. Maiden Moor. Borrowdale. NY 2318

MEMORIAL. Low Snab Farm. Newlands Valley. Footbridge over Newlands Beck. Stone inscribed "Peter John Ingrams 1936–1975. Death shall have no dominion." NY 230184

23 19
ARCHITECTURE. Slope Stone. Good example at Little Town. Newlands Valley. NY 231193

MINE. Little Mine Crag. Copper pyrites. NY 233190

WALKS. Newlands valley. Circuit—Chapel Bridge, Low Snab, Skelgill and Little Town. Easy. Start: Chapel Bridge. Views of Causey Pike, Hindscarth and Catbells. NY 231194

Dale Head and Robinson. Circuit 7½ miles/12km. Ascent 2800ft/ 860m. Strenuous. Route takes in the once famous mines of Goldscope, Castlenook and Dale Head, first worked in C16. Start: Chapel Bridge, Little Town. Newlands Valley. NY 231194

24 13
GEOLOGY. Moraine. Borrowdale. NY 2413

PLANTS. Deciduous mixed habitat. Borrowdale. NY 2413

REFRESHMENT. Yew Tree Inn. Seatoller (ON "saetr": high summer pasture, of the alder trees). Phone 07687 77634.   NY 244138

TOURIST INFORMATION CENTRE. National Park Daleshead Base. Seatoller Barn. Open daily Easter–September. Phone 07687 77294. Illustrated talks, demonstration of crafts by local people, guided walks, walksheets & leaflets.
NY 245137

WALKS. Seatoller-Rosthwaite and return. 3 miles/4.8km. Mainly easy. Start from bend in road to Honister then bear right. Good views of Castle Crag, Grange Fell, Rosthwaite Fell & Glaramara.   NY 246137

Seatoller-Johnny Wood-Scaleclose. 2.1 miles/3.5km. Ascent 492ft/150m. Start: Seatoller car park, take path between farm buildings.   NY 247138

Eel Crags and High Spy. Borrowdale. Circuit 9 miles/14.5km. Ascent 1800ft/548m. Strenuous. Superlative views. Start: car park Seatoller.   NY 246137

Scafell from Borrowdale. Circuit 12 miles/19.3km. Ascent 3100ft/950m. Start: Seatoller.   NY 246137

24 14

WATERFALLS. Scaleclose Force. Borrowdale. Start from Seatoller Barn (a National Trust car park) and take path north east into Johnny Wood. At gap in wall follow upward path west to open fell below High Doat. Then north across contours to a stile at which point the beck is clearly heard, although the Force is within a ravine. 3½ miles/5.63km. Circuit. Moderate.   NY 246147

24 15

ARCHAEOLOGY. Fort. Castle Crag, Borrowdale (ON "borgardalr": the valley of the fort). Most of remains destroyed by quarrying. Father Thomas West, author of the first Lake District Guide book in 1778 wrote that the fort measured 70yds/64m east to west and 40yds/36m north to south. Keswick Museum has some of the findings—red glazed Samian ware, broken rims and handles of water jars and a copy of a Roman spoon, which suggests that the site was occupied by Romanized Britons.   NY 249158

MEMORIAL. At base of Castle Crag, Borrowdale. By a seat a plaque "The land surrounding the summit of Castle Crag was given to the nation in memory of Sir William Hamer M.A., M.D., F.R.C.P. by his wife Agnes, whom this seat commemorates. 1939."   NY 249159

24 17

ARCHITECTURE. Hollows Farm Grange. C17 oak staircase.   NY 247171

GEOLOGY. Skiddaw slates. Hollows Farm. Grange.   NY 247171

MINE. High Close. Copper. Open works and two levels—Ellers Beck Grange. First worked 1566 and in 1567 ownership won by Queen Elizabeth against the Earl of Northumberland.   NY 246178

High Close. Very old 50ft/15m level. Near Greenup.   NY 244177

WATERFALLS. Above Ellers Beck. Maiden Moor. Derwent Water. Path from Grange. 2 miles/3.21km. Circuit. Moderate.   NY 245175

24 18

MINE. Yewthwaite High Adit. Trap Knotts. 350ft/106m long but CARE a shaft was sunk 80ft/24m from the entrance.   NY 243189

Black Crag Trial. Superficial open work at the top of a scree gully. NY 246186

24 19

LITERARY. Brackenburn (built 1919) Derwent Water, (now a private home and not open to the public) was the home of Sir Hugh Seymour Walpole from 1923 until his death on lst June 1941. Born in Auckland, New Zealand, in March 1884, where his father was an Anglican Clergyman who returned to UK on his appointment as Principle of Bede College, Durham and later Bishop of Edinburgh. Hugh was educated at King's School, Canterbury & Emmanuel College Cambridge. Soon became full-time author. His works include *The Cathedral* 1922, *The Old Ladies* 1924, *Harmer John* 1926. His saga *The Herries Chronicle* (*Rogue Herries* 1930, *Judith Paris* 1931, *The Fortress* 1932 and *Vanessa* 1933) is set in Borrowdale and surrounding valleys. Lesser known novels—*Bright Pavilions* and *Katharine Christian* portray Tudor life in Keswick.   NY 249192

MEMORIAL. Beside a seat "To the memory of Sir Hugh Walpole. CBE. of Brackenburn. This seat is erected by his friend Harold Cheevers, September 1941." Overlooking Derwent Water.   NY 249195

MINE. Yewthwaite. C18 closed 1893. Low adit at 850ft/259m and the Trustees Level at 700ft/213m. Very profitable and productive—galena, cerussite and pyrites.   NY 240194

PLANTS. Alpine polypody—alongside path above road. Derwent Water.
                     NY 249199

25 11

GEOLOGY. Dovenest Crag, Comb Gill. Borrowdale Fells. Unique in Lake District and possibly in Britain, this massive crag detached from parent rock above, slid down fellside to present site, where it rests uneasily—some recent movement being observed.   NY 253117

25 13

ARCHITECTURE. Narrow hump-backed bridge with lop-sided arch, over tributary of River Derwent, behind Mountain View, Seatoller. A Folly. A John Braithwaite donated £25 for its building in 1781. Peculiar inscription on stone "This bridge was built at the/expence of John Braithwaite/of Seatoller in the Year of/our Lord 1781./By Thomas Hayton and/Richard Bowness./I count this folly You have done/As You have neither Wife or Son/Daughter I have, God give her Grace/And I Heaven for her Resting place."   NY 251139

The eight houses at Mountain View built for quarry workers. Originally named Leconfield Terrace after Lord Leconfield who bought the Manor of Borrowdale.

NY 251137

CHURCH. C19. On site of 1505 church. Bellcote. Jacobean Pulpit removed from now drowned Mardale church. Borrowdale NY 258139

INDUSTRIAL ARCHAEOLOGY. Grain Mill, remains of in Comb Gill. Possibly from 1546. Overshot wheel. Millstones of St Bee's red sandstone. Closed over 100 years ago but then taken over as a saw mill for Honister Quarry.

NY 254135

MEMORIAL. "Bob Graham of Keswick 1889–1966. Holder of the Lake District Climbing Record 1932–1964. 42 peaks 32000ft/9753m. 130 miles/209km in 23 hours 39 minutes. Amongst Fells he loved." Green slate headstone SE of Borrowdale church. Circuit comprised the summits of: Skiddaw, Great Calva, Saddleback, Wanthwaite Pike, Dodds of Helvellyn, Dolleywagon Pike, Fairfield, Seat Sandal, Steel Fell, Calf Crag, High White Stones, High Raise, Sergeant Man, Harrison Stickle, Pike o'Stickle, Rossett Pike, Hanging Knotts, Bowfell, Esk Pike, Great End, Scafell Pike, Mickledore, Broadstand, Scafell, Yewbarrow, Red Pike, Steeple, Pillar mountain, Kirk Fell, Great Gable, Green Gable, Brandreth, Dale Head, Hindscarth, Robinson and High Snab. Total height in excess of Everest—in one day! (Official records would suggest 27000ft/8229m of ascent over 72 miles/115km in the same time. Whichever, his record stood until 1960 when the same circuit was completed in 22 hours 18 minutes by Alan Heaton. (Refer NY 2535). NY 259139

WATERFALLS. Comb Beck Gill. Park at Seatoller Barn and follow path towards Stonethwaite. Through gate beyond house named Mountain View, across bridge and through gate directly ahead. Turn right towards an old mill, after which, strike up fellside to indistinct path which leads to waterfalls. Path climbs upwards to Tarn at Leaves, below Bessyboot. 3½ miles/5.63km. Circuit. Moderate. NY 253131

25 14

EVENT. Borrowdale Show on 3rd Sunday September. Sheep, Fell Ponies, Dogs, Sheepdog Trial, Hound Trail, Fell Race, Wrestling and Handicrafts. Trade Stands.

NY 257148

GEOLOGY. Moraine. Rosthwaite. NY 257147 and NY 258145

Very large Roches moutonnées—The How. Rosthwaite. NY 258147

MEMORIAL. Plaque let into Vicarage garden wall E side of Keswick/Seatoller road near turn off for Stonethwaite. "1914–1918. This tablet records the names of those of this parish who went forth to the Great War."

N. B. Ashworth	S. Edmondson	J. Plaskett
Flor Ashworth	E. Feirn	T. Richardson
E. J. Boow	W. Gaskell	I. Richardson
R. H. Boow	J. Hind	T. Robinson
E. Bird	F. Hindmoor	J. W. Rigg
W. S. Bird	B. Jenkinson	T. R. Rigg

E. Bird	G. Jenkinson	J. R. Rigg
T. Brown	F. Jenkinson	M. A. Slee
W. N. Brown	W. Jenkinson	A. Smith
F. E. Darvell	T. Jenkinson	E. Smith
G. Dover	H. E. Leyland	A. E. Wilson
J. H. Dover	J. W. Mounsey	R. B. Woodend
J. Edmondson	W. Nicholson	R. Zanazzi NY 257142

Memorial seat inscribed "Given by his family in memory of T. W. (Tommy) Thompson A. C. I. S. Treasurer of the Lakeland YHA for thirty years 1972." Longthwaite Youth Hostel. NY 255142

Memorial slate seat inscribed "Presented to the Longthwaite Hostel to treasure the memory of our beloved son Paul K. Brookes aged 17 years who was killed in a fall from Heron Crag on 26th August 1978 whilst on his way to this hostel on a fell-walking holiday with his Parents and Sister Sally Anne." Longthwaite Youth Hostel. Borrowdale. NY 255142

PLANTS. Oak wood habitat. Johnny Wood. Borrowdale. (National Trust). Site of Special Scientific Interest (SSSI) on account of uncommon mosses and liverworts; forked spleenwort, oak and brittle bladder. NY 2514

REFRESHMENT. Scafell Hotel. Rosthwaite. Former coaching inn. Snacks in Riverside bar and draught beer from the wood. Phone 07687 77208. NY 259148

Royal Oak Hotel. Rosthwaite. Phone 07687 77214. NY 259148

TREES. Once pollarded ash & sycamore; other tree species have rooted in resultant hollowness—high up. Ash leaves still form an important fodder crop in Borrowdale and the Langdales. The trees are pollarded at about 10ft/3m approximately every 12 years. A pollarded tree may possibly live 400/500 years longer than one left to grow normally. NY 255143

Oakwood. Johnny Wood. Borrowdale. NY 2514

WALKS. Rosthwaite-Low Hows Wood-Castle Crag. Circuit 3.1 miles/ 5km. Ascent 656ft/200m. Moderate. Panoramic views from this isolated platform in Borrowdale. Start: Rosthwaite. NY 258149

Rosthwaite-Willygrass Gill-Dock Tarn-Watendlath. Circuit 4.6 miles/7.5km. Ascent 1280ft/390m. Strenuous. Clear visibility essential. Start: Rosthwaite, near Hazel Bank Hotel. NY 258149

Rosthwaite-Stonethwaite. Circuit 4 miles/6.4km. Easy, though some rough ground. Limited parking. Good views of Eagle Crag with Bull Crag across the valley. NY 258147

YOUTH HOSTEL. Longthwaite. Borrowdale. Phone 07687 77257.
NY 254142

25 15

ARCHITECTURE. Watergate of slatted wood to prevent sheep straying along Tongue Gill. NY 252151

HISTORICAL. High Hows Quarry—cave. The eccentric Millican Dalton,

(Professor of Adventure) pre-war mountaineer, lived here during the summer months. Born 1867 not far from Alston and died 1947. Above the cave entrance is carved "Don't!! waste worrds, or jump to conclusions." (The mis-spelling a whim of Dalton's friend who chiselled the lettering in the 1930s). In his early years he was in commerce in London but opted very early in youth to commune with Nature. A happy man which radiated to others to whom he passed on his self acquired knowledge of the locality and regions further afield. He had the courage to live the sort of life he believed in. NY 250157

25 16

GEOLOGY. The Bowder Stone (ME "bulder stan": large boulder). 1771 tons/1743 tonnes of metamorphic rock finely balanced on its end. 62ft/18.8m long & 84ft/25.6m circumference. Once presumed to have fallen from neighbouring cliffs but now thought to have been transported to its present position by glacial action from Scotland—"glacial erratic". John Pocklington commissioned a hole to be cut through the boulder base so that a little old woman whom he employed, living in a nearby cottage, could shake visitors' hands, from the other side. On the south corner of the stone it is possible to make out a strange face, which is said to be of Balder, (may be derived from Boethar) son of Odin. May be climbed by 29 wooden steps. NY 254164

INSECTS. Small heath & mountain ringlet butterflies. Orange tailed bumblebee. Long Moss. Borrowdale. NY 259166

MEMORIAL. King's How. Borrowdale. Inscribed on rock below summit "In loving memory of King Edward VII/Grange Fell is dedicated by his sister Louise" (Duchess of Argyll, one of Queen Victoria's children who died in 1939 aged 91) "As a sanctuary of rest and peace/Here may all beings gather strength and/Find in scenes of beautiful nature a cause/For gratitude and love to God giving them/Courage and vigour to carry out His Will." (In 1910 when King Edward VII died the National Trust purchased, through subscription, King's How, Bowder Stone and Borrowdale Birches). NY 258166

QUARRY. Quayfoot Quarry. 1880–1936. Its building stone from the Fairy Cave used in the construction of Keswick Railway station and bridges. NY 253167

WALKS. King's How. Circuit 3½ miles/5.5km. Ascent 110ft/340m. Good views. Start: Bowder Stone car park. Borrowdale. NY 252169

25 17

ARCHITECTURE. 2 segmented arched bridge between which is a small island called the Whins. 1675. Grange. NY 254175

School 1894 erected in memory of Miss M. Heathcote. A plaque reads, "This school was erected to the memory of Miss Margaret Heathcote, mainly by the subscription of personal friends and others who thus recognised a life of good works spent among and for the inhabitants of this neighbourhood." Grange. NY 251175

Slope Stone. Beside track from Grange to Castle Crag.   NY 252173

CHURCH. Holy Trinity. Grange (Furness Abbey monks stored their grain in "Grangia"—hence, Grange). 1860. Nave & chancel in one. Bellcote. Tunnel shaped beamed ceiling has a plethora of imitation Norman dogtooth decoration carried over into arched windows internally and externally. Churchyard perimeter delineated by upright slate slabs. The first stone was laid October 4th 1894 by Miss Langton of Barrow House.   NY 252175

Methodist Chapel 1894 on site of Wesleyan chapel of 1859. Grange.   NY 253175

GEOLOGY. Roches moutonnées. Grange. Borrowdale.   NY 253175

LITERARY. Grange farm—supposed home of Rogue Herries in *The Herries Chronicle* by Sir Hugh Walpole. Grange.   NY 253174

MEMORIAL. "In memoriam W. Hodgson./He prayeth well who loveth well/ Both man and bird and beast/For the dear God who loveth us/He made and loveth all./September 1878." There is a small horse trough to the front of the stone. Beside the Keswick to Seatoller Road.   NY 254171

Memorial seat inscribed along its top "This seat was repaired by the National Trust 1912." Also inscribed on the back rest "Here traveller rest and feel/the potent charm, of fell and valley, bridge and clustered farm,/Make them thine own no absence shall destroy,/the hamlets peace—the ancient rivers joy." Main road near Grange Bridge.   NY 255176

REFRESHMENT. Borrowdale Gates Country House Hotel. Grange in Borrowdale. Phone 07687 77204.   NY 253174

WALKS. Castle Crag. Borrowdale. Circuit 2½ miles/4km. Ascent 951ft/290m. Strenuous. Very steep ascent & descent. Once the stronghold of a Celtic Lord of Borrowdale. In 1920 the then owner Sir William Hamer gave Castle Crag to the National Trust in memory of his son John Hamer, 2nd Lieut 6th KSLI (born 8th July 1897, killed in action 22nd March 1918), and also in memory of 10 other Borrowdale men killed in the first World War. Start: Grange.   NY 252174

25 18

MINE. Saltwell Mine. Derwent Water. Copper and lead.   NY 255189

PLANTS. Lake habitat, east end of Derwent Water.   NY 2518

25 19

GEOLOGY. Fluorspar. Brandlehow.   NY 250194

HISTORICAL. Manesty Park purchased by the National Trust in 1905.
                                                                    NY 2519

MAMMALS. Badgers (local names "pates" or "grays"). Manesty Park, Derwent Water. Virtually extinct by end of C18 following bounty of one shilling (5p) per head. Now on increase.   NY 2519

MINE. Brandlehow Mine. Derwent Water. Lead. 7oz/198g of silver per ton of lead metal. Water problems; maximum flow of 150 gallons per minute resulted in very high costs of pumping and forced abandonment in 1891. Waste tips reveal barytes, cerussite, fluorspar, galena pyrite and zinc blende.   NY 250196

26 13

MEMORIAL. Plaque in barn wall at entrance to Stonethwaite—"H. F. Fisher 1963. The National Trust."   NY 262137

WALKS. Stonethwaite to Smithymire Island. Circuit 4 miles/6.4km. Moderate. Best avoided in wet weather. Views of Bull Crag and Glaramara 2560ft/780m. Start: Stonethwaite.   NY 262138

26 15

HISTORICAL. Hazel Bank Hotel. The Simpsons, who owned Hazel Bank prior to it being a hotel, were the first in Borrowdale to own a car.   NY 260150

LITERARY. Hazel Bank Hotel—subject in Sir Hugh Walpole's *Rogue Herries*.
                    NY 260150

REFRESHMENT. Hazel Bank Hotel. Rosthwaite. Phone 07687 77248.
                    NY 260150

26 16

GEOLOGY. Erratics—several good specimens. Grange Fell. Borrowdale.
                    NY 2616

26 17

HISTORICAL. All that remains of Dr. Parnaby's Troutdale salmon fishery hatchery are long, rectangular slate-lined tanks let into the ground beside Comb Gill. Started c1856 its boom year reached 1869 when, under management of a Mr. J. J. Armistead (who reared other game fish) American brown trout eyed ova sold for £100 per thousand but prices fell away and project wound down by 1883. Troutdale, Borrowdale.   NY 262176

26 18

FISH. Watendlath Beck. Brown trout. Free.   NY 2618

REFRESHMENT. The Lodore Swiss Hotel (ON "Lagr": low & "dore": gap). Borrowdale. In C19 when known as the Lodore Inn, a small cannon was kept for the purpose of demonstrating the echoes promoted by the surrounding fells, for the gratification of its patrons, at 4 shillings/20p a discharge. Phone 07687 77285.
                    NY 264188

High Lodore Farm. Snacks available throughout the day from Easter to end of October and then at weekends. Phone 07687 77221.   NY 262183

Borrowdale Hotel. Phone 07687 77224.   NY 261182

TREES. Oakwood. Ashness.   NY 2618

WALKS. Derwent Water west shore. 3 miles/4.8km. Easy. From Lodore Hotel (limited parking) clockwise to Hawse End, passing through Brandlehow Woods, the first purchase of the National Trust in 1902. Frequent boat service back to Lodore; time table at pier head. As a diversion, Catbells may be climbed from the paths immediately after crossing the shallows. NY 264188

Lodore-Watendlath-Ashness. Circuit 4½ miles/7.2km. Ascent 600ft/182m. Moderate. Limited parking. Start Lodore Hotel. NY 264188

Troutdale-Grange Fell-Watendlath-High Lodore. Circuit 4.6 miles /7.4km. Ascent 1082ft/330m. Strenuous. Start: near Borrowdale Hotel. NY 262183

WATERFALLS. Lodore Falls. Borrowdale. 90ft/27m fall, down wooded hillside. Private; 5p charge to view, box in Lodore Hotel wall. Best after heavy rain. Robert Southey in his "How does the water come down at Lodore" 1820, delighted by this spectacle in full spate, wrote "...Retreating and beating and meeting and sheeting, Delaying and straying and playing and spraying, Advancing and prancing and glancing and dancing, Recoiling, turmoiling and toiling and boiling, And gleaming and streaming and steaming and beaming, And rushing and lushing, brushing and gushing, And flapping and rapping and clapping and slapping, And curling and whirling and pushing and twirling, And thumping and plumping and bumping and jumping, And dashing and flashing and splashing and clashing; And so never ending, but always descending, Sounds and motions for ever and ever are blending, All at once and all o'er with a mighty uproar, And this way the Water comes down at Lodore." NY 265188

26 19

GEOLOGY. Alluvial fan. Derwent Water. NY 2619

PLANTS. Periodically, usually about mid-October, a Floating Island appears in the bay off Lodore. It consists of water plants forced to the surface by decomposition gasses. NY 263194

WALKS. Lodore Falls and Ashness. Circuit 3 miles/4.8km. Best after heavy rain. "Surprise View" offers superb vantage point—Derwent Water, Bassenthwaite, Skiddaw, Catbells, Great Gable and Grisedale Pike. Ashness Bridge—much photographed. NY 267195

WATERFALLS. Barrow Falls. Catgill. Derwent Water. NY 268199

27 12

MEMORIAL. Bridge at confluence of Langstrath Beck and Greenup Gill "This bridge was re-erected in Memory of Gordon Hallworth. Aged 21 years. A devoted member of the Manchester University Mountaineering Club who during the night following 7th January 1939 Died of exhaustion in this Dale Notwithstanding the self-sacrificing assistance of his two companions and the strenuous effort of a Relief Party of their friends. May 1939." NY 274129

27 13

INDUSTRIAL ARCHAEOLOGY. Ancient bloomery used by Furness Abbey monks. Iron ore from their mine at Ure Gap, Bowfell, brought down Langstrath to Smithymire Island. Despite the not inconsiderable distance involved it was very much cheaper and far less heavy to bring ore down from Bowfell to this spot where the supply of wood was (then) plentiful, for 5 tons/5080kg of wood produced 1 ton/1016kg of charcoal of which 11 cwt/558kg produced 3 cwt/ 152kg of iron from ½ ton/508kg of ore.   NY 273131

WATERFALLS. Galleny Force. Langstrath. 6ft/1.8m spout—Stonethwaite Beck. A further waterfall is on Greenup Gill (NY 281122) and may be reached by following Langstrath Beck, at its confluence with Stonethwaite Beck. Cross at footbridge, then north east towards Stonethwaite Beck which cross by bridge and follow east bank of Greenup Gill. Altogether 5 miles/8.04km. from Stonethwaite. Circuit. Moderate.   NY 272131

27 15

FARMING. Ancient field system still recognisable—south end of Watendlath tarn.   NY 2715

27 16

FISH. The Tarn. Watendlath (ON "vatns endi": end of the lake). Perch, pike, brown & rainbow trout. Day & evening permits. Bag limits. Permit from Borrowdale Fisheries. Phone 07687 77293.   NY 2716

GEOLOGY. Hanging valley—above Borrowdale.   NY 2716

LITERARY. Greenhow farm, Watendlath, was the birthplace of Judith Paris, heroine in *Rogue Herries* (1930) by Sir Hugh Walpole.   NY 276163

27 18

ARCHAEOLOGY. Unexcavated hill fort—possibly Iron Age. Borrowdale.
                                        NY 274180

WALL. Incorporating terrain, rock traverse. Stones horizontal regardless of slope. Watendlath.   NY 270180

27 19

ARCHITECTURE. Ashness Bridge. Famous pack-horse bridge—single arch. View very photogenic.   NY 270196

VIEWPOINT. Surprise View. Spectacular, of Derwent Water from Watendlath Road.   NY 270194

29 14

FISH. Blea Tarn. Watendlath Fell. Brown trout. Free.   NY 2914

29 16

GEOLOGY. Garnets. Cockrigg Crags. Thirlmere.   NY 299168

29 18

WATERFALLS. Mere Gill. Thirlmere. Permissive path beside Beck from Shoulthwaite Farm (NY 300206). 3 miles/4.82km. Circuit. Moderate.   NY 298188

Area 13 – Thirlmere

30 11

WATERFALLS. Wythburn Valley. Thirlmere. Path from west side of Thirlmere, cross bridge and through gate onto permissive path across the meadows. Follow path to falls. Very wet after rain. 3½ miles/5.63km. Circuit. Moderate.

NY 307116

30 14

MAMMALS. Red deer. Thirlmere Forest.　　　　　　　　　　　　NY 3014

30 15

NATURE RESERVE/TRAIL. Launchy Gill. Thirlmere. Circuit 1 mile/ 1.6km.　　　　　　　　　　　　　　　　　　　　　　　　　　　NY 308158

PLANTS. Pine wood habitat. Thirlmere. (North West Water Ltd. Permit required).　　　　　　　　　　　　　　　　　　　　　　　NY 3015

WATERFALLS. 100ft/30m cascades, in woodland. Launchy Gill. Thirlmere. The path passes near to a huge precariously balanced boulder—the "Tottling" stone (D: "unsteady").　　　　　　　　　　　　　　　　NY 307156

30 17

HISTORICAL. Monkey puzzle tree (beside car park) "marks" the grounds of Armboth House, once owned by Countess Ossalinsky. Was the setting for *The Shadow of Crime* by Sir Hugh Cain. In 1890/2 two small lakes [Leathe's Water (named after the historic owners, The Leathes family of Dalehead Hall) and Wythburn Water] integrated and water level raised 54ft/16m and nearly all properties comprising the villages of Armboth and Wythburn submerged. Only Wythburn church and 3 properties at Steel End remain. John Ruskin & Thomas Carlyle at forefront of public outcry and protestations—though to no avail it helped form a united public front—hence the National Trust formed 1895.

NY 305172

30 18

ARCHAEOLOGY. Iron Age hill fort. Shoulthwaite Gill. Thirlmere. Probably occupied by Britons hostile to the Romans.　　　　　　　NY 300188

VIEWPOINT. Raven Crag. Thirlmere.　　　　　　　　　　　　NY 301189

31 13

FISH. Harrop Tarn. Thirlmere. Depth 16½ft/5m. Perch & brown trout. Free.

NY 310137

WALKS. Harrop Tarn. Thirlmere. Circuit 2 miles/3.2km. Moderate. Wet areas. Good views of Helvellyn and Thirlmere. Start: car park.　　NY 316139

31 14

FISH. Thirlmere (OE "thyrel": a hole/narrow waist of water). Owned by North West Water Ltd. 3½ miles/5.6km long & ½ mile/0.8km wide. 583ft/177m above sea-level. Maximum depth 158ft/48m. Eel, perch, pike, brown trout and white-fish. Free. Methods of fishing are restricted and bailiffs vigilant. Car park.

NY 316142

31 15

MINE. Launchy Gill Mine. Its difficulty of access, requiring strenuous scrambling, just north of Rough Crag and below White Crags, has resulted in the survival of a superb example of Elizabethan stope and feather working.   NY 312154

31 16

WALKS. Thirlmere shore and Great How. Circuit 5 miles/8km. Ascent 1092ft/ 332m. Strenuous. Start: east side of Thirlmere at Swirls.   NY 316169

31 17

REFRESHMENT. King's Head. Thirlspot. Contains C17 furniture from farm-houses submerged when Thirlmere Reservoir flooded. Also displayed are pictures of the area before flooding. The landlord regularly whitewashes the stones marking the footpath via Browncove Crags to Helvellyn.   NY 316177

Dalehead Hall. Thirlspot. Phone 07687 72478.   NY 312175

31 18

ARCHITECTURE. Thirlmere dam wall, 260yds/237m long, 100ft/30m high and its base 50ft/15m wide. The reservoir took 10 years to build, cost £3 million and opened October 1894.   NY 310189

31 19

WALKS. Naddle Fell. Circuit 4½ miles/7.2km. Ascent 700ft/213m. Strenuous. Good visibility essential to obtain Alpine Views. Start: from car park of North West Water Ltd.   NY 317196

YOUTH HOSTEL. The Old School. Stanah Cross. Thirlmere.

Phone 07687 73224.   NY 318190

32 10

WATERFALLS. Greenburn. North of Grasmere.   NY 324101

32 11

LEGEND. Dunmail Raise. Cairn marks the boundary between old Cumberland & Westmorland (fact) but has also represented the demarcation between England and Scotland. It also commemorates Duvenald's (Dunmail) defeat and (supposed) death in 945 when last King of Cumberland, at the hand of Edmund of Northumbria and Leoline of South Wales. (Other researchers suggest that Dunmail lived on for thirty years after this battle, [some say in Strathclyde] supposedly dying on a pilgrimage to Rome). Edmund then gave Cumberland to Malcolm of

Scotland but the county became independent again in 1032 when it was handed back to Knut (Canute). NY 327117

32 12

MEMORIAL. Stone plaque inset into wall at Thirlmere beside main road. "30th of NMO 1843. Fallen from his fellows side/The steed beneath is lying/Harnessed here he died/His only fault was dying." WB. Directly underneath a further stone inscribed "This stone was re-erected on this site by the Manchester Corporation Water-works Committee 1948." NY 325125

WATERFALLS. Birkside Gill. Thirlmere. Start at Wythburn Chapel on A 591. Follow path through forest; waterfalls at southern extremity. 2 miles/3.21km. NY 328125

32 13

CHURCH. Wythburn Chapel. (ON "vithir brun": the willow valley). 1640 on 1554 site, restored 1872. White. Low. Apse. Stained glass by Holiday 1892. Wordsworth wrote of the church in *The Waggoner* (2nd Canto. Lines 1–10). NY 324136

MEMORIAL. Beside telephone kiosk on main road, Thirlmere. "A record of the two walks from hence over The Armboth Fells July 1833–43 which inspired Matthew Arnold's poem 'Resignation' and in reverent memory of the poet born 24 December 1822, died 15 April 1888." "We left us ten years since you say/That wayside inn left today/And now behold in front outspread/Those upper regions we must tread/Mild hollows and clear healthy swells/The cheerful silence of the fells." MA. NY 324136

32 14

MINE. Wythburn Mine. 1839–1880. Lead. Several levels at increasing altitude. NY 325148

WATERFALLS. Helvellyn Screes. Path from car park at Wythburn Chapel signposted Helvellyn then right to a permissive path which follow north. 2½ miles/4.02km. Circuit. Easy. NY 324148

32 16

WATERFALLS. Helvellyn Gill. Thirlmere. Long series of small falls. Start from car park on A 591 opposite Station Coppice. 1½ miles/2.41km. NY 322167

32 18

MINE. Thirlspot Copper Mine. C16 openworks. NY 322180

WATERFALLS. Fisher Gill. Thirlmere. Start from car park at High Park Wood—follow path up fellside. 3 miles/4.82km. NY 323183

32 19

WATERFALLS. Mill Gill. St John's in the Vale. Path from car park at Legburthwaite. NY 325199

33 10

ARCHITECTURE. Automobile Association sentry-type Telephone Box. Pre-war and now scheduled as a building of special historical and architectural interest by Department of Environment. One of 7 so scheduled, others: Aysgarth (Yorkshire), Porlock Hill (Somerset), Halfway House (Woodbury, Devon), Beadnell (Northumberland), Mere Corner (Cheshire) & Brancaster Staithe (Norfolk). There are 30 others not scheduled. NY 332105

MINE. Providence Mine. Haematite. c1700–1876. NY 339105

Dunmail Rise Level. Copper trial. Barren. NY 333104

33 12

MINE. Birkside Gill copper mine. c1850s. NY 330126

33 13

WATERFALLS. Whelpside Gill. Thirlmere. Path from NE corner of car park at Wythburn chapel in direction of Helvellyn. Cross Comb Gill to slope of Middle Tongue beyond which lies Whelpside Gill. 1½ miles/2.41km. Circuit. Moderate. NY 331139

33 15

PLANTS. Very rare shrubby cinquefoil (*Potentilla fruticosa*). Helvellyn. NY 3315

34 11

MINE. To the left of the pack-horse track up Little Tongue Gill to Grisedale Tarn are the remains of Providence Iron Mine. Grasmere. NY 347112

WATERFALLS. Tongue Gill, south of Grisedale Tarn. Park at Mill Bridge on A 591 ½ mile/0.8km north of Grasmere. 5 miles/8.04km. Circuit. Strenuous. NY 348111

34 12

FISH. Grisedale Tarn. Maximum depth 100ft/30m. Brown trout. Free. NY 3412

34 14

MEMORIAL. To Charles Gough, poet and Quaker, who on 18 April 1805 fell to his death from Striding Edge, Helvellyn ("the hill of Willan", mentioned in a C11 Charter). "Beneath this spot were found in 1805 the remains of Charles Gough, killed by a fall from the rocks. His dog was still guarding the skeleton." (Canon Hardwicke Drummond Rawnsley). Also inscribed are lines from William Wordsworth's "Fidelity". It was on 20 July 1805 when a shepherd discovered the remains. The Irish terrier (Foxey) had given birth to pups which lay dead beside the corpse. She was unable to feed them and she herself only existed on remnants of carrion found far and wide. She had not touched her master's body. Despite every care and attention after rescue she died several days afterwards at Kendal. Sir Walter Scott was moved to write "How long didst thou think that his silence was slumber? When the wind waved his garments how oft didst thou start?" (Refer NY 503267). Memorial erected 1890 NY 344149

The Dixon Memorial "In Memory of Robert Dixon, Rookings, Patterdale who was killed on this place on the 27th day April 1858 when following fox hounds", stands on a rock platform on Striding Edge overlooking Nethermost Cove.

NY 349149

34 15

ARCHITECTURAL. Red Tarn, below Striding Edge and Swirral Edge long ago dammed to supply water to Glenridding lead mine. NY 3415

FISH. Red Tarn. Helvellyn. Maximum Depth 60ft/18m. Charr, schelly and brown trout. NY 345153

LITERARY. William Wordsworth climbed to summit of Helvellyn—3,116ft/950m when aged 74 having walked from Rydal Mount. The material to build the Ordnance Survey column was carried up by one of Tommy Dickinson's Clydesdales. NY 342151

MEMORIAL. Helvellyn. "The first aeroplane to land on a mountain in Great Britain did so on this spot on December 22, 1926. Bert Hinkler and John Leeming in an Avro-Alpha landed here and after a short stay flew back to Woodford."

NY 343151

MINE. Brown Cove Mine. Level with stone-arched entrance. NY 340156

PLANTS. Mountain habitat. Helvellyn—east side. NY 3415

Brothers Water from Boardale Hause (Author)

34 17

ARCHITECTURE. Small ski hut belonging to the Lake District Ski Club. Day use only. Raise. NY 346178

35 11

PLANTS. Mountain habitat. Fairfield. NY 3511

35 12

INSECTS. Caddis creeper (*Phryganea obsoleta*). Grisedale Tarn. NY 351122

LEGEND. Edmund, King of the Saxons is reputed to have thrown into Grisedale Tarn the golden crown of Dunmail, the last King of Cumberland, whom he had slain in battle AD 945. NY 3512

MEMORIAL. Grisedale Tarn. Stone of Parting—1800, commemorates the place where William Wordsworth bade farewell to John, his brother, later drowned on 5th February 1805 when the East Indiaman, *The Earl of Abergavenny* of which John was Captain, struck a rock off Portland Bill, Dorset and sank with the loss of nearly 300 passengers and crew. John Wordsworth is buried in an unmarked grave at Wyke Regis near Weymouth. Original stone removed by vandals or "Treasure Seekers" but it bore William's grief in "Brother and friend, if verse of mine/Have power to make thy virtues known/Here let a monumental stone/Stand—sacred as a Shrine;/And to the few who pass this way,/Traveller or Shepherd, let it stay/Long as these mighty rocks endure,/—Oh do not thou too fondly brood,/Although deserving of all good,/on any earthly hope, however pure!" NY 352122

35 13

MINE. Ruthwaite Lodge Mine. Grisedale. Workings near climbing hut. C16–1870s. NY 355136

WATERFALLS. Ruthwaite Gill. Grisedale. Path from Grisedale Bridge (NY 390161). Follow lane upwards to a path leading to the falls. 6½ miles/10.46km. Circuit. Moderate. NY 355136

35 14

MINE. Eagle Crag Mine. Grisedale. Lead. C16–1870s. NY 358142

WATERFALLS. Nethermostcove Beck. Grisedale. From Glenridding car park take path to Lanty's Tarn and, beyond, follow Grisedale Beck on an indistinct path to the falls. 7 miles/11.26km. Circuit. Moderate. NY 354145

35 15

WATERFALLS. Red Tarn Beck. Helvellyn. From Glenridding car park follow path to Greenside Mine and then follow path SW towards Red Tarn. 7 miles/11.26km. Circuit. Strenuous. NY 357159

36 11

HISTORICAL. Flinty Grave, Fairfield. Two young girls fell to their death on

Easter Monday 1951 and for many weeks their bodies lay undiscovered in the snow. NY 361117

36 12

WATERFALLS. Deepdale. Ullswater. Track over bridge from telephone box at Deepdale Bridge to reach head of Deepdale and cascades. 6 miles/9.65km. Circuit. Moderate. NY 368125

36 13

PLANTS. Rare oblong woodsia (*Woodsia ilvensis*). St Sunday Crag. NY 3613

36 17

GEOLOGY. Barytes. Found on Greenside lead mine spoil heaps. NY 365175

MINE. Glenridding. Greenside lead mine. C17. 3000ft/914m deep, and extensive tunnelling even into Helvellyn. Produced 8 ounces of silver for every ton of lead. In 1875 the mine produced lead and silver ore worth in excess of £1 million. Over 200 years a single vein yielded 2,400,000 tons of ore and 2,000,000 oz of silver. Worked out and abandoned 1962 its main problem being transportation of the ore. In its early days the ore, was carried by pack-horses to Stoneycroft smelter at Keswick via Sticks Pass but after 1820 the dressed ore was hauled to Alston Moor smelter. In 1867 the Penrith/Keswick railway line (now axed) enabled a link with Newcastle on Tyne; the ore being traction engine hauled to Troutbeck station and then railed to Messrs Walkers Parkers Smelting Works. This was one of England's most profitable lead and silver mines, although in the 1870s the Top Dam burst and the resulting flood of water carried away the mine's silver refining house and with it 1,000 oz/28,350g plate of silver which was never recovered. Water power was provided from Red Tarn and Kepple Cove Tarn. This latter's dam burst in 1927 during a severe storm and smashed through the village. No lives lost. It created the promontory upon which the steamer pier now stands. In 1862, above the High Horse Level, massive roof-fall brought down 120,000 tons of rock, resulting in the chasm at NY 359186. No injuries, and £80,000 worth of dressed ore resulted. Electric locomotive 1892, first in any British mine, used in Lucy Level. Also a first in a UK mine was the use of an electric winder on Smith's shaft. In 1959 the mine was used by the Atomic Energy Authority to test conventional explosives during which two men died. NY 365174

YOUTH HOSTEL. Helvellyn. Former home of Greenside lead mine manager. Phone 07684 82269. NY 365174

36 18

GEOLOGY. Hanging valley. Glencoynedale. NY 3618

36 19

HISTORICAL. Birkett Fell renamed after Lord Birkett who argued in the Lords, 1962, against the proposal to create a reservoir out of Ullswater. Memorial cairn NY 365198. NY 364197

WATERFALLS. Hart Side. Ullswater. Path from Aira Force car park (NY 398205) to Spying How, Brown Hills and Scot Crag. Return via Swineside Knott and Round How. 7½ miles/12.06km. Circuit. Moderate.　　　NY 360191

37 10

PLANTS. Alpine meadow rue, alpine lady's mantle and sea campion. Dove Crag. Fairfield.　　　NY 3710

37 12

GEOLOGY. Glaciated valley. Deepdale.　　　NY 3712

38 11

WATERFALLS. Dove Falls. Dovedale. Brothers Water. Path from Cow Bridge. 4 miles/6.43km. Circuit. Easy.　　　NY 387116

38 16

ARCHITECTURE. Patterdale Hall. C17. Owned by the Mounseys (known as the Kings of Patterdale and the Hall, their Palace). Now much extended and used as YMCA outdoor activity centre.　　　NY 389161

CHURCH. Methodist Chapel, originally Wesleyan. 1890. Glenridding.
　　　NY 386169

REFRESHMENT. Travellers Rest. Glenridding. Phone 07684 82298.
　　　NY 385169

Ullswater Hotel. Glenridding. Phone 07684 82444.　　　NY 387169

Glenridding Hotel. Glenridding. Phone 07684 82228.　　　NY 387168

TOURIST INFORMATION CENTRE. National Park Centre. Leaflets, books, displays; has a relief model of Helvellyn range. Open daily Easter–September. Beckside car park. Glenridding. Phone 07684 82414.　　　NY 385169

WALKS. Greenside. Circuit 3½ miles/5.6km. Easy. Start: Glenridding car park (turn left and left again out of the village).　　　NY 387169

Keldas. (ON "kelda": spring or water). Circuit 1.8 miles/2.8km. Ascent 688ft/210m. Moderate but some steep sections. Start: Glenridding car park (turn right over bridge and right again along lane by stream). Fine views. Lanty's Tarn (Lancelot Tarn) is shallow, but a delightful place to sit by awhile.　　　NY 387169

Helvellyn via Striding Edge and Sticks Pass. Circuit 10 miles /16km. Ascent 2750ft/838m. Strenuous. Exhilarating ridge walk, dangerous in bad weather. Start: Glenridding.　　　NY 386169

WELL. St Patrick's Well. Like horse trough with ornate canopy and slate roof. St Patrick baptized the locals here AD 540. Ever after, place named St Patrick's Dale abbreviated later to Patterdale-Pattraicc's Valley.　　　NY 387166

38 18

ARCHITECTURE. A "Statesman's" farm. Glencoyne, 1629. Farmhouse and barn-cum-cow byre joined together in typical longhouse fashion. The front door opens onto a cross passage leading to the back door. Tall cylindrical chimneys. Crow-stepped gables which protect the roof in high winds. Several spice cupboards. Plaster panel bearing carved initials "T. H. D. H. 1629." of the Howard family. Now owned by National Trust. NY 384187

BIRDS. Winter-spring-summer: cormorant, red-throated diver, goldeneye, goosander, merganser, teal, little grebe, common and lesser black-backed gulls, nuthatch, Bewick's swan and lesser spotted woodpecker. Ullswater. NY 3818

FARM. Glencoyne. National Trust. Limited viewing by appointment. Phone 07684 82207. NY 384187

FISH. Ullswater (Ulfr's Water). About half of lake owned by Dalemain Estate and the rest between the National Park Authority, The National Trust and several private landowners. 7½ miles/12km long, ¾ mile/1.2km wide. 476ft/145m above sea level. Maximum depth 205ft/62.4m. Average depth 83ft/15.2m. Eel, perch, roach, brown trout, salmon and whitefish. Rarely caught is the schelly, also known as the skelly, gwyniad or freshwater herring. It is the smallest member of the salmon family and is also present in Haweswater and perhaps Red Tarn. Charr also haunt the deeps but few recently caught which may suggest its gradual demise. Fishing is free provided North West Water Ltd licence held. Boat hire—Glenridding or Pooley Bridge. NY 3818

MAMMALS. Pine marten. Red squirrel. Glencoyne Wood. NY 3818

PLANTS. Oak wood habitat. Glencoyne. N/T. NY 3818

TREES. Ancient oaks. Glencoyne Wood. N/T. NY 3818

WALKS. Seldom Seen. Circuit 3 miles/4.8km. Seldom Seen is a row of cottages built by the Greenside Mining Company in Glencoynedale and rarely visited, but they did provide shelter during Scottish raids. Glencoyne Farm—round chimneys and corbie gables, (N/Trust) is passed. Start: Glencoyne bridge. NY 387188

39 10

MINE. Caiston Glen Trial. Galena and blende. NY 394100

39 11

ARCHAEOLOGY. Oval enclosure of 1¼ acres/0.50ha of turf-covered bank inside of which are hut enclosures. Unexcavated but presumed Iron Age/Roman. NY 398116

39 12

ARCHITECTURE. Hartsop Hall now a farm. Two C16 windows. Originally built as a shelter for monks travelling between Furness Abbey and Lanercost Priory and then manor house of the Lancasters, Sir John Lowther, 1st Lord Lonsdale late C17 and long-time home of the Allen family, latterly tenants of the National Trust. Right of way through it. Dry-built barn of surface stone. NY 398121

MINE. Hartsop Hall Mine. C17 infrequently to 1942. Lead. 30oz/ 850g of silver per ton of lead metal. Minute amount of gold. Fluorspar, pale straw coloured, the only specimen of this mineral found in Borrowdale Volcanics.   NY 395120

39 14

MINE. Deepdale Iron Mine. Haematite. 200ft/61m above Deepdale Hall two levels and openworks.   NY 394143

39 15

EVENT. Sheep dog trials. Last Saturday of August. Patterdale.   NY 3915

MINE. Hagg Mine. Lead. Abandoned 1808 and no longer any visible signs.
     NY 390158

REFRESHMENT. White Lion. Patterdale. Phone 07684 82214. Edward Elgar, one of England's premier composers, stayed here with his wife Alice in 1916. Dr. C. W. Buck, his friend, recounted that Elgar penned a musical appreciation of the local splendour but the score has seemingly been lost or perhaps destroyed by Elgar himself.   NY 397159

Patterdale Hotel. Phone 07684 82231.   NY 396159

YOUTH HOSTEL. Goldrill House. Patterdale. 1970. On site of Lake District's first hostel 1931 which had previously belonged to T. A. Leonard (Refer NY 247204). Part roofed with grass sods, as in Scandinavia. Phone 07684 82394.
     NY 399157

39 16

ARCHITECTURE. Bank barn, fine example. Side Farm. Ullswater. NY 399163

CHURCH. St Patrick. Patterdale. 1853. Small. NE tower with saddleback roof and clock under eaves. Font with C14 base, C13 stem and C18 bowl. Communion set made from Glenridding silver. Bible of 1611 rebound in two volumes. Gonfalon—White Ensign from the Battle of Jutland. Embroidered tapestries, by local Ann Macbeth 1875–1948. One depicts The Good Shepherd with Hartsop, Deepdale, Caudale Moor and Kirkstone in the background. At the bottom of the panel are the music notes of "Jerusalem" which caused Queen Mary to burst into song when she saw the tapestry at a London Exhibition. Another's verse reads "Christ keep the mountain lands all the winter through, And bless the farms, and bless the school, and bless the fireside too." Porch notice reads "Helvellyn praises God, but please do not bring it into church on your boots."   NY 393161

FISH. Goldrill Beck (OE "golde": marsh marigold beside the stream) & Grisedale Beck. Brown trout. Free.   NY 3916

LITERARY. The Wordsworths often stayed at the home of their friends Captain & Mrs Luff of Side Farm, Patterdale.   NY 398163

TRANSPORT. Ullswater Navigation & Transit Co Ltd. Glenridding. Phone 07684 82229 or 0539 721626. A water-borne service commenced 1855. *Lady of the Lake* launched 1877 and *Raven* launched 1889. *Raven* cost £2,865, built in sections and transported to Penrith by rail and therefrom by horse-drawn wagons to Pooley Bridge, where it was assembled. Originally steam driven but converted to oil in 1930s. It's twin diesels each generate 142 h.p. to give maximum speed of 16 knots. One hour journey for the length of the lake from Glenridding pier to Pooley Bridge via Howtown.   NY 390169

WALKS. Place Fell and Ullswater shore from Patterdale. Circuit 8 miles/13km. Ascent 2250ft/690m. Strenuous, but a superlative walk.   NY 394161

Grisedale (Grise: a pig or boar). Circuit 4 miles/6.4km. Moderate. Glaciated valley with characteristic scratch marked rocks. Can be wet sections. Start: Grisedale.
                                                                                  NY 390161

39 17
MINE. Blowick Trial Mine. Hidden levels beside stream. Copper.   NY 399176

39 18
GEOLOGY. Rock bar. Silver Point. Ullswater.   NY 3918

Belle Isle, Windermere (Author)

Area 14 – Haweswater

40 11

GEOLOGY. Moraines. Caudale Bridge. Kirkstone Pass.   NY 4011

REFRESHMENT. Brothers Water Inn. Erected by the Revd Pearson. Phone 07684 82350.   NY 403118

WATERFALLS. Candale Beck near Brothers Water. Path from Caudale Bridge on A 592. 2 miles/3.21km. Circuit. Moderate.   NY 404116

40 12

BIRDS. Brothers Water. Winter: Ferruginous duck—rare.   NY 4012

FISH. Brothers Water. Once known as Broad or Broader Water but name changed on the drowning in 1785 of two brothers when they fell through the ice while skating. Wordsworth wrote of this in *The Prelude* 1805/6, line 231 Book VIII "Retrospect". Site of Special Scientific Interest. No boating allowed. ½ mile/0.8km long & ¼ mile/0.4km wide. 520ft/158m above sea-level. Maximum depth 70ft/21m. Eel, perch, brown trout & whitefish. No permit required. In 1947 given to the Treasury by the Earl of Lonsdale, in lieu of Death Duties, who made it an unconditional gift to the National Trust.   NY 4012

40 13

ARCHITECTURE. Low House Farm. C17. Hartsop (valley of the Deer). Good example of farm and byre built onto the living quarters.   NY 408131

Spinning galleries at Thorn House and Mireside Hartsop, an old lead mining village.   NY 409131

Fell Yeat, once The Bunch O'Birks Inn, on the old pack-horse trail to Kirkstone Pass. Hartsop.   NY 407130

Rare late C16 corn-drying kiln on a steep slope, Hartsop. Entrance to lower floor-heating area from south whilst drying chamber entrance above from higher ground to north. Spaced slate slabs on end formed the drying chamber floor and allowed the circulation of warm air to the damp grain spread on rough cloth.   NY 4013

LITERARY. Cowbridge. Brothers Water. Hartsop. Here Wordsworth wrote "The Cock is crowing, The stream is flowing, The small birds twitter." March 1802.   NY 402133

PLANTS. Deciduous habitat. Low Wood. Hartsop.   NY 4013

TREES. Relict of ancient forest. Low Wood. Hartsop. National Trust.   NY 4013

WALKS. Brothers Water. Circuit 2½ miles/4km. Easy. Woodside behind Hartsop

Waterfall. Haweswater. (Rosemary Liddle)

Hall scheduled as an Area of Special Scientific Interest. Start: the lay-by alongside the AA Box.   NY 403134

Brothers Water. Hartsop, Patterdale. Circuit 7½ miles/12km. Moderate. Start: NY 405132

40 14

ARCHITECTURE. Rare early C19 two-storey building with pigsty at ground level and "privy" above. Unusual two-storey L-shaped barn. Also has a barn across the slope and one down the slope. Beckstones. Patterdale.   NY 404149

MINE. Dubhow Copper Mine. 2 levels west of Angle Tarn. 1761–1860s infrequently.   NY 409144

WATERFALLS. Angletarn Beck. Hartsop. Park at Cow Bridge (NY 403134) then sign-posted track to Hartsop. After first building on left follow metalled road north and continue on a track when road bears east. A path then climbs the fell to the falls. 4½ miles/7.24km. Circuit. Moderate.   NY 408140

40 15

CHURCH. Ruin at Boardale Hause. Built by St Patrick C5 to establish worship of St Martin of Tours. Meeting point of pack-horse trains between Bore Dale and Patterdale.   NY 408157

40 16

LITERARY. Wordsworth Cottage near Rooking, Patterdale. In 1806 Wordsworth asked the Quaker, Thomas Wilkinson (1751–1836), to arrange the purchase of the 1670 farmhouse for him. Asking price was £1000 but Wordsworth would only pay £800. Wilkinson approached the Earl of Lonsdale for the additional £200 which so embarrassed Wordsworth that he never lived in the farmhouse but let it to a local farmer. In 1834 he sold it to the local inn keeper. Until her death in 1948 it was the home of Miss A. M. Macbeth maker of the embroidered tapestries in St Patrick's church. (Refer NY 393161).   NY 400160

PLANTS. Upland fell habitat. Place Fell.   NY 4016

VIEWPOINT. Ullswater from summit of Place Fell.   NY 405169

40 17

GEOLOGY. Borrowdale volcanic series. Place Fell.   NY 4017

41 10

MEMORIAL. Cairn inscribed "Hic Jacet, Mark Atkinson of Kirkstone Pass Inn. Died 14 June 1930. Aged 69 years." Caudale Moor.   NY 414101

41 12

MINE. Myers Head Mine. Hartsop. c1870s. Lead. 16oz/453g of silver per ton of lead metal. Not economic and the only Lakeland mine to be wholly overwhelmed by rate of flow of mine water. Shaft at confluence of Pasture Beck and Hayeswater Gill. (NY 416126) and 3 levels and shaft.   NY 410125

41 14

FISH. Angle Tarn. Maximum depth 29ft/9m. Eel, perch, pike & brown trout. Permit required—enquire locally. There is a very clear echo repeating four/five times from a point on the tarn's east shore. NY 4114

41 19

WATERFALLS. Scalehow Force. Ullswater. Take path behind Patterdale village hall, cross Goldrill Beck, through Side Farm and then NNW. 6½ miles/10.46km. Circuit. Easy. NY 414191

42 12

FISH. Hayeswater (OE "haeg": lake by enclosure). Depth 51½ft/16m. Perch and brown trout. Permit required—enquire locally. NY 4212

WATERFALLS. Hayeswater Gill. Hartsop. Path from gate at car park. 4 miles/6.43km. Circuit. Moderate. NY 426129

42 14

BIRDS. Heck Crag. Bannerdale. Eagles nested around here 1788. Female shot but male returned with another female. The male was shot 1789 and the female disappeared, so The Revd W. Richardson observed. After many years absence the golden eagle has returned and breeds in Riggindale closely monitored by wardens of the Royal Society for the Protection of Birds. NY 420149

42 15

ARCHAEOLOGY. Early type of large stone circle. Bannerdale. NY 423154

43 14

MAMMALS. Ancient red deer herd—200/300 wild stock, never having been enclosed. Summer grazing Yewgrove Gill, The Nab. Rutting Sept/Oct when the stags roaring may be heard. Later the herd disperses to Kentmere, Long Sleddale, Shap and Place Fells. Permit required. Rampsgill. Martindale Common. NY 4314

43 15

GEOLOGY. Alluvial fan. Martindale. NY 4315

43 16

ARCHITECTURE. Dale Head Farm. Martindale. 1666. Massively buttressed supposedly supporting a gallery, long demolished. NY 433165

Fleshing house, where deer are skinned. Martindale. NY 435169

GEOLOGY. Valley with glacial features. Martindale. NY 4316

HISTORICAL. The Bungalow. Martindale. The German Kaiser stayed here whilst on a deer shoot. The hunting of deer pursued since C13—de Lancaster family. NY 439162

43 17

LEGEND. In 1834 unaccountable noises both day and night heard in and within vicinity of (the now ruined) Henhow cottage. The tenant, a shepherd, had just left the cottage before day break when, over the nearby wall, he saw a woman carrying a child. He spoke with her and she told him that she had lived at that remote cottage years ago. She had been seduced by an older man, above her station. Her seducer had arranged to meet her locally to give her a potion. But it was too potent and killed the mother as well as the unborn child. She said that she was doomed to wander thus for a hundred years of which 40 had already passed. Later enquiries established a local clergyman to have been the seducer. Martindale.   NY 434177

43 18

ARCHITECTURE. The building known as Cotehow was once The Star Inn. Cruck built. Martindale.   NY 435188

CHURCH. St Martin. Martindale. 1633 on C13 site. Nave and chancel in one, oblong windows, plain bellcote. Jacobean lectern. Altar, pews and pulpit made by local craftsmen. C14 holy water stoup, reputed to be a Roman altar brought down from the High Street range, bears marks of arrow sharpening. From 1882 used only as a Mortuary Chapel but more recently used on St Martin's Day (4th July) and certain summer Sundays. Churchyard yews 600 years old, from which Martindale archers made long-bows to use at Agincourt and Flodden.   NY 434184

St Peter. Martindale. 1880/2. Red sandstone and slate. At 1000ft/305m above sea-level one of the highest and loneliest churches in England. Fine collection of stained-glass windows.   NY 434189

TREES. Yews, ancient, behind old church in alder woods. Martindale.   NY 4318

WALKS. Hallin Fell. 2.1 miles/3.5km. Ascent 721ft/220m. Easy. Start: old St Martin's Church. Martindale.   NY 434184

Martindale, Bannerdale & Angle Tarn. Circuit 6.8 miles/11km. Ascent 1443ft/ 440m. Strenuous. Start: St Martin's Church. Martindale.   NY 434184

43 19

ARCHITECTURE. "Corbie" (crow) stepped gables. Hause Farm. Martindale.
NY 434191

GEOLOGY. Basalt. Hallin Fell.   NY 433198

Calcite. Hallin Fell.   NY 433198

Rock bar. Hallin Fell.   NY 433198

MEMORIAL. Cairn on Hallin Fell in memory of Lord Brougham.   NY 435195

VIEWPOINT. Steep ascent from Martindale Church. Full view of geological formations of Ullswater. Hallin Fell.   NY 433198

44 10

FISH. Blea Water. Maximum depth >200ft/61m. (Only Wast Water and Windermere are deeper). Brown trout. Free.   NY 4410

GEOLOGY. Post Ice Age scenery. Blea Water above Haweswater.   NY 4410

44 11

HISTORICAL. Racecourse Hill, High Street. (ME "Brettestrete: the Briton's road). 2717ft/828m. Until 1835, venue for Hartsop, Kentmere, Mardale and Troutbeck shepherds' annual meeting to exchange strayed animals. Social occasion with horse racing and wrestling.   NY 441110

MAMMALS. Red deer, fell ponies. Riggindale.   NY 4411

PLANTS. Mountain habitat. High Street.   NY 4411

44 13

PLANTS. Upland fell habitat. Riggindale.   NY 4413

44 16

PLANTS. Upland fell habitat. Martindale.   NY 4416

44 19

WALKS. Howtown via Ullswater's eastern shore to Glenridding. One of Lakeland's best walks. Park Glenridding and take steamer to Howtown where walk commences. Easy. 6 miles/9.6km.   NY 443198

45 10

GEOLOGY. Borrowdale volcanic series. Haweswater.   NY 4510

PLANTS. Alpine meadow rue. Crags above Blea Water.   NY 4410

45 11

HISTORICAL. Mardale before valley flooded and resulting infrastructure, was remote and Outlaws lived in seclusion. From 1209 until 1885 when Hugh Parker Holme, the last descendant died, they had their own dynasty of Kings. Hugh Holme, the first King of Mardale, conspired against King John (in the Canterbury conspiracy) but on discovery of the plot had to take refuge in a cave in Riggindale—hence Hugh's Cave, Riggindale.   NY 456115

46 10

WALKS. Haweswater & Kidsty Pike. Circuit 8 miles/13km. Ascent 1700ft/518m. Strenuous. Extensive views. Start: south end of Haweswater but parking can be difficult.   NY 469107

WATERFALLS. Blea Water Beck and Small Water Beck. Haweswater. Path sign-posted Kentmere, from car park. Note glacial moraines. 3 miles/4.82 km. Circuit. Moderate.   NY 461104

Dudderick Force. Haweswater. Path alongside Mardale Beck from car park.
NY 464106

46 12
ARCHAEOLOGY. Castle Crag. Haweswater. Cairns and standing stones. Pre-Roman fortified site atop the crag. NY 469128

46 14
GEOLOGY. Hanging valley. Measand Valley. NY 4614

47 10
ARCHAEOLOGY. Cairnfields. Mosedale. NY 479102

47 11
HISTORICAL. Mardale, a small village, existed until 1929 when a dam was erected to retain the waters of the numerous fell becks. Water level raised by 95ft/29m creating a reservoir 4 miles/6.5km long. The C17 Church of Holy Trinity was destroyed and corpses re-interred at Shap. The 1713 school dismantled and rebuilt as a private residence at nearby Watergate Head. In very dry summers parts of Mardale village can be seen, north of The Rigg. The old field walls are still in remarkable condition and the bridge spanning the original stream through the village still stands. In 1984, when much of the drowned village was visible, the stream could be seen flowing through the arch of the bridge. NY 476118

47 12
VIEWPOINT. Panoramic view of Haweswater reservoir from Whiteacre Crag.
NY 479124

47 13
ARCHITECTURE. Haweswater Reservoir tower incorporates several windows from the drowned Mardale church. NY 479130

47 15
WATERFALLS. Fordingale Force. Measand Beck. Haweswater. From Naddle Bridge join a track (which is part of the Wainwright Coast to Coast Path) alongside Haweswater and when footbridge reached climb fell by indistinct path. 6 miles/9.65km. Circuit. Moderate. NY 471158

48 10
ARCHAEOLOGY. Cairnfields. Mosedale. NY 483102

48 11
WATERFALLS. Hopgill Beck and Rowantreethwaite Beck. Haweswater. Path opposite Wood Howe Island, sign-posted—Old Corpse Road. Public footpath to Swindale. Moderate. NY 483117

48 13
BIRDS. Golden eagle, in flight, perhaps best seen from vicinity of Haweswater

Hotel. In Riggindale, where the eagles have their eerie, the RSPB maintains an observation point on 24 hour watch from March to August. Public may view from 0800–1800hrs. Phone 09313 337 or 09313 376. NY 484139

Also might be seen—buzzard, goshawk, merlin, peregrine, tree pipit and green woodpecker. Largest RSPB Reserve in England at over 27000 acres/ 10926ha. Naddle Forest. NY 4813

FISH. Haweswater Reservoir (ON "hafr": a he-goat). Owned by North West Water Ltd. No boating. 4 miles/6.4km long & ½ mile/ 0.8km wide. 790ft/240m above sea-level. Maximum depth 198ft/60m. Average depth 135ft/41m. Charr, eel, schelly (specimen 2lb 1½ oz). brown trout & vendace. Day permits from Haweswater Hotel or Post Office, Bampton. NY 482138

MINE. Guerness Gill Mine. Copper. 1836–1852. Rock debris blocks entrance. NY 480134

TREES. Junipers growing on Borrowdale Volcanic Series screes. Haweswater. NY 4813

48 14

BIRDS. Blackcap, black grouse, buzzard, cormorant, red-throated diver. Ducks: mallard, merganser. Golden eagle, great crested and Slavonian grebes, common and lesser black-backed gulls, jay, kestrel, peregrine, raven, ring ouzel, rook, siskin, long-tailed tit, tree pipit, wheatear, great spotted & green woodpeckers. Haweswater. NY 4814

48 15

WATERFALLS. Measand Beck Forces. Haweswater. Path from Naddle Bridge. 1½ miles/2.41km. Circuit. Moderate. NY 485155

49 12

PLANTS. Acid moorland habitat. Swindale Common. NY 4912

49 14

LEGEND. Farmer Williams and his wife of Mardale (now under Haweswater reservoir) were expecting their first born when, at the very moment of birth, a huge boulder fell from nearby Wallow Crag into the lake below. The parents regarded it as an ill omen and that their baby son, Charles, would meet his death by drowning. As the years passed he grew up to be healthy and intelligent with an inclination to poetry. One evening, walking home in the gathering gloom he heard screaming and running across the fell he found a bull attacking a girl. He managed to distract the bull and they made good their escape. He walked Maria home and, over a period, they fell in love and became engaged but before they could marry she died of an illness. Unhappy Charles sought solace in his poetry and wandered the fells at all hours. One cold wet night he did not return to the farmstead. Next day he was found drowned at the very spot by Wallow Crag from whence the huge boulder had fallen years before, though his death appears to have been no unfortunate accident, as his last poem suggests:

And what is death, that I should dread
To mingle with the silent dead?
'Tis but a pang—and pangs are o'er;
A throb—and throbbing is no more;
One struggle—and that one my last:
A gasp—a groan—and all is past!

Wallow Crag. Haweswater.   NY 496149

49 16

MINE. Haweswater Mine. 3 levels. Copper.   NY 495160

49 18

WALL/FENCE. On way to Towtop stone circle look for curved construction. Such ancient "fences" were termed "painable", that is, every tenant had to repair his fences or be in "pain", and fined 6s.8d.(33p).   NY 4918

Area 15 – Bampton

50 12

GEOLOGY. Glacial featured valley. Swindale.   NY 5012

MAMMALS. Red deer & fell ponies. Swindale.   NY 5012

TREES. Native Oakwood. Swindale.   NY 5012

50 14

PLANTS. Acid moorland habitat. Naddle Forest.   NY 5014

50 15

ARCHITECTURE. Haweswater reservoir hollow—arch dam wall, the first of its kind in UK 1,550ft/472m long and 96ft/29m high. Reservoir fed by underground pipe-line from Ullswater. Supplies 60 million gallons of water daily to Manchester. William Wordsworth in his *Guide to the Lakes* wrote "Haweswater is a lesser Ullswater with this advantage, that it remains undefiled by the intrusion of bad taste."   NY 503156

LEGEND. A small cairn on Hugh Laithes Pike, Haweswater, reputed to be the last resting place of "Wicked" Jimmy Lowther—the first Earl of Lonsdale who died 1802 aged 66. Sir James, because of his position, entered into an unsuccessful arranged marriage but fell in love with the daughter of one of his tenant farmers. He maintained her in a style to which she was unaccustomed, at a residence in Hampshire but she, being a country girl, pined for her home county and eventually died. Sir James never recovered from her death. He turned to alcohol and although succeeding to the Lonsdale estate in 1784, became greedy and bitter. He was killed in a riding accident, unloved and unmourned. The original burial was not without difficulty on account of his restless Spirit which thereafter struck terror in the community. So the villagers disinterred the body and buried it under huge boulders on the Pike. The hauntings ceased though a weird figure is often seen by walkers at dusk.   NY 502152

PLANTS. Deciduous mixed habitat. Rare mosses—*Ptilium* and *Hylocomium umbratum*. Naddle Low. (North West Water Ltd. Permit required).   NY 5015

TREES. Coppice, sessile oak, primitive ash and birch. Naddle Low Forest. (North West Water Ltd. Permit required).   NY 5015

50 17

WATERFALLS. Howes Beck. Bampton. At Bampton telephone box take fell road towards Stanegarth Farm (NY 497177) and return via Hullockholme Farm. 4 miles/6.43km. Circuit. Easy.   NY 502177

51 14

PLANTS. Upland fell habitat. Harper Hills.   NY 5114

51 16

ARCHITECTURE. Thornthwaite Hall built for the Curwen family in C16, now a farmhouse. "L" configuration one arm of which is former pele tower. Mullioned windows.   NY 513163

WATERFALLS. Thornthwaite Force. Haweswater. At Naddle Bridge take ladder stile over S wall and cross drystone bridge and then a wooden bridge. Permissive path to left. 1 mile/1.6km. Circuit. Easy.   NY 512160

51 18

ARCHITECTURE. Bampton Hall. C16. Gableroofed square dovecot.
                             NY 515183

EVENT. Mardale Hunt and Shepherds' Meet—at St Patrick's Well Inn, Bampton—on the Saturday nearest 20th November annually. Used to be held at the Dun Bull Inn in the village of Mardale (now under Haweswater).   NY 515182

REFRESHMENT. St Patrick's Well Inn. Bampton. Phone 09313 244.
                             NY 515182

52 10

MAMMALS. Wet Sleddale. Herdwick sheep.   NY 5210

52 11

TOPOGRAPHIC. O/S Triangulation point inset at ground level near summit cairn on Seat Robert.   NY 526114

52 14

ARCHAEOLOGY. Possible site of a "Thing" mound, yet to be excavated. Talbert Head.   NY 529144

52 17

REFRESHMENT. The Crown & Mitre. Bampton Grange. Phone 09313 225.
                             NY 520179

52 18

CHURCH. St Patrick. Bampton Grange. (OE "beam-tun": the enclosed land with the tree). 1726–8. Part timber arcaded. Chancel restored 1885. One of only 10 churches in UK dedicated to this Saint. W tower. Font C12 though 1662 carved on it. Reredos—carved oak with inlaid panels of holly. Portrait of Reverend John Boustead (1776–1832) Master of Bampton Grammar School, said to have educated more students for the church than any other man in England; also portraits of Edmund Gibson, (1669–1748), who became Bishop of Lincoln and then London; Bishop Hugh Curwen (c1490–1568) Chaplain to Henry VIII, then Roman Catholic Archbishop of Dublin under Queen Mary and then turned Protestant upon enthronement of Elizabeth I. Painting of Mardale Church before valley flooded to form extended Haweswater Reservoir in 1935. The vicarage, opposite the church, houses the famous "Tinklar" library, many of its books written in Latin. NY 522180

GEOLOGY. Limestone. Knipe Scar. NY 5218

52 19

ARCHAEOLOGY. Stone circle in limestone pavement. Knipe Moor.
NY 528193

53 10

MINE. Sherry Gill Mine. Barytes. NY 538104

53 11

PLANTS. Upland fell habitat. Wet Sleddale. NY 5311

Rather rare spignel (*Meum athamanticum*). Wet Sleddale. NY 5311

53 17

MEMORIAL. Mary's Pillar. Erected 1854 by Thomas Castley of The Thorn, Rosgill in memory of his daughter who died aged 24. NY 538176

54 11

BIRDS. Wet Sleddale Reservoir. Winter; long-tailed duck. NY 5411

Cockley Beck Bridge, Wrynose Bottom. (Rosemary Liddle)

54 15

CHURCH. Shap Abbey, ("hep" or "heppe": heap [of stones]). Remains of the Abbey (dedicated to Mary Magdalene) founded by Premonstratensian canons in 1180 when they moved from Preston-in-Kendal. They were known as White Canons from the colour of their habits and were involved in the local community, even running a leper hospital at Appleby. It was the only Abbey founded in Westmorland and the last to be founded country-wide. In 1540 it was the last to be dissolved. Within the ruin of the chapel is the grave of an Abbot, indicated by a chiselled crozier in the stone. Circles incised into the floor suggest procession markers—used on Sundays and especial days. Much of the stone was plundered to build Lowther Castle. Boundaries of the fields hereabouts delineated as they were in medieval times. Ruins maintained by English Heritage.   NY 548153

55 14

CHURCH. Keld Chapel. C16. Simple rural place of worship. National Trust.
NY 554145

55 15

GEOLOGY. Shap. Gogglesby Stone. This stone of 12 tons & others, "the Thunder Stone" and "the Giant's footprint", formed part of an avenue of paired and similar stones of nearly a mile in length culminating in a stone circle, known as Karl Lofts. These stones, placed by Neolithic and Early Bronze Age people, dispersed by railway embankment.   NY 559151

56 19

ARCHITECTURE. High Hall, Little Strickland. 1600. The Crackenthorpe arms on panels adjoining massive fire-place.   NY 564195

Low Hall, Little Strickland formerly known as Little Strickland Hall. Renowned for splendid Tudor woodwork and beautiful plaster ceilings. Jacobean mantelpiece. Mullioned and transomed windows.   NY 564197

CHURCH. St Mary. Little Strickland. 1814. Y traceried lancets. C17 pews. Stone tablet known as the Thrimby Inscription 1695.   NY 562197

Area 16 – Wast Water

09 00

CHURCH. St Paul. Irton (enclosed land by the River Irt). 1856/7. Fine view north east. Tower with 8 bells, nave and chancel. Two north windows pre-Raphaelite. Brass memorial tablets to Sir Thomas and Sir Richard Brocklebank. Marble tablet to Skeffington Lutwidge, commander of HMS *Carcase* on a polar expedition in 1773. Serving under him was Horatio Nelson, then aged 14. C9 10ft/3m cross shaft in churchyard. The copy is prominent but the original is on the far side of the churchyard among tomb stones.   NY 092005

HISTORIC. Kirkland. Ancient trackways converge at early C9 Cross.

NY 092005

09 08

ARCHAEOLOGY. Sampson's Bratfull. Stockdale Moor. Long cairn—96ft/29m. long and 45ft/13m wide. East end 6ft/2m. high. Unexcavated. Cairnfields in vicinity.   NY 098080

10 00

ARCHITECTURE. Irton Hall. 1874. Sandstone. Elizabethan style—clock tower Victorian style. C14 Pele tower. Twenty five generations are said to have lived here. Now a private residence.   NY 105005

10 01

EVENT. The Biggest Liar in the World Competition. Held since 1974 in memory of Will Ritson (1808–1890) popular landlord of the Wasdale Head Inn who related such tall stories patronage increased substantially. 3rd Thursday in November. The Bridge Inn, Santon Bridge.   NY 109016

HISTORICAL. The River Irt, near Santon Bridge, once famous for pearls from the river mussel (*Margaritifera margaritifera*)—black and oval. The Romans made mention of this—and in 1692 the newly chartered Company of Pearl Fishers paid the villagers to search for them and marketed them in London for £800. They are rarely found today.   NY 1001

REFRESHMENT. The Bridge Inn, Santon Bridge. One of the venues for the annual competition to find the Biggest Liar in the World. Also at one time venue for another old Cumbrian entertainment The Gurning Thro a Braffin Contest, which is generally held at Egremont now. This contest consists of pulling funny faces with one's head enclosed by a horse collar. Phone 09467 26221.   NY 109016

10 05

ARCHAEOLOGY. Cairnfields. Hollow Moor.   NY 101054/103054/105055

11 02

TREES. Oakwood. Greengate, Wasdale.   NY 1102

12 02

MINE. Mecklin Park Mine. Haematite. Not commercial—closed mid 1880s.
NY 129020

12 03

REFRESHMENT. Strands Hotel. Nether Wasdale. Phone 09467 26237.
NY 125039

WALKS. Wast Water foot. Circuit 4¾ miles/7.6km. Moderate. Good weather essential for this superlative walk. Start: Strands village, Nether Wasdale.
NY 129039

12 04

CHURCH. Nether Wasdale ("nether": lower). St Michael and All Angels. 1552. Chapel of Ease to St Bees Priory. Low, nave and chancel in one. Some Georgian windows. Pulpit and Lectern C17 from York Minster. Oak panelling of flowers, fruit and cherubs. Relief of Royal Arms of George III. Painted texts on walls.
NY 124041

HISTORICAL. Maypole (beside the church) commemorates Queen Victoria's Jubilee 1897.   NY 125041

REFRESHMENT. The Screes Hotel. Nether Wasdale. Phone 09467 26262.
NY 125040

WALKS. Wast Water 5 miles/8km. Easy. Some wet ground. Steep screes 1700ft/518.2m. Start: road junction to east of Nether Wasdale then left to Easthwaite (clear view of Yewbarrow) alongside west shore rising to Greendale and back to start.   NY 124040

Nether Wasdale. Riverside and lake. 3½ miles/5.6km.   NY 123040

12 05

ARCHITECTURE. 1704 cruck built farmhouse. Windsor Farm. Wasdale.
NY 121057

INDUSTRIAL ARCHAEOLOGY. c1900 Threshing machine built into a bank barn. Harrowhead Farm. Wasdale.   NY 126055

13 00

REFRESHMENT. The Bower House Inn. C17. Eskdale Green. Phone 09467 23244.   NY 131003

13 05

BIRDS. Peregrine falcon. Buckbarrow crags.   NY 1305

HISTORICAL. Buckbarrow Farmhouse. Base for the Catholic Achille Ratti Climbing Club. Named after Achille Ratti, alpine climber, who later became Pope Pius XI.   NY 136053

14 00

ARCHITECTURE. Low Holme, Miterdale. House around small cobbled yard. Barns, hogg-house (for young sheep) and sheep dip. NY 143007

14 03

ARCHITECTURE. Lund bridge; pack-horse. NY 142039

British Nuclear Fuels Ltd pump house. Up to 11 million gallons of water (¼ inch of Wast Water's depth) extracted daily for use at Sellafield. NY 146039

14 04

ARCHITECTURE. Wasdale Hall. Built 1829/43 on a previous farm site (Daker End) for a Mr. Stansfield Rawson. Imposing views of Wast Water. Stone and timber construction, mullioned and transomed windows. Purchased by National Trust in 1959 and now let to Youth Hostels Association. NY 144045

NATURE RESERVE/TRAIL. Nether Wasdale-Lund Bridge-Woodhow-Ashness-High Birkhow. Circuit 2½ miles/4km. Start: SW of Wast Water. Roe deer. National Trust. Trail leaflets available from Cumbria Wildlife Trust. Rydal Road, Ambleside. Phone 05394 32476. NY 146047

VIEWPOINT. Towards Wasdale Head from Wasdale Hall. The outline of Yew-barrow, Great Gable and Lingmell form the emblem of the Lake District National Park, designated as such June 1951, covering 866 sq. miles. NY 143045

YOUTH HOSTEL. Wasdale Hall. Wast Water. Seascale. Phone 09467 26222. NY 145045

14 05

WALKS. Greendale Tarn. Wast Water. Circuit 5½ miles/8.8km. Strenuous. Start at Greendale. NY 144056

15 00

MINE. Ban Garth Mine. Eskdale. Haematite. 1845–1880. Uneconomic. NY 153008

15 04

GEOLOGY. Borrowdale volcanic series. Wast Water. NY 1504

15 05

VIEWPOINT. Wasdale. At this point perhaps the best view of the screes. NY 151053

16 00

ARCHITECTURE. Dalegarth Hall. Farm house, 5 huge round chimneys. C14—then known as Austhwaite, ancestral home of the Stanley family. The ceiling of one room adorned with stags and hounds. NY 169001

Stone ruin—peat house. Used for storing peat prior to sledging it down the valley for use as domestic fuel. Eskdale. NY 165008

FISH. Blea Tarn. Boot. Depth 16½ft/5m. Perch & brown trout. Free. NY 165009

MINE. Blea Tarn Mine. Haematite. Uneconomic—closed mid 1880s. NY 167007

16 02

WATERFALLS. River Mite tributary, below Burnmoor Tarn. Miterdale. The route starts at Eskdale Green from a lane near the school, north east. The walk of 6 miles/9.65km is a nature lover's paradise.   NY 161029

16 04

PLANTS. Upland fell habitat. Illgill Head.   NY 1604

16 05

PLANTS. Rare shrubby cinquefoil (*Potentilla fruticosa*). Illgill Head.   NY 1605

16 06

WALKS. Mosedale Horseshoe takes in Pillar. Circuit 12½ miles/20km. Ascent 4750ft/1450m. A classic Lakeland walk. Start: Overbeck bridge. Wast Water.

NY 168069

16 07

WATERFALLS. Nether Beck. Wast Water. After heavy rain quite spectacular especially where beck passes through steep sided deep ravine. 2½ miles/4.02 km. Circuit. Moderate.   NY 160070

16 08

WATERFALLS. Overbeck. Wast Water. Follow Path from Overbeck Bridge (NY 168068), return via lower slopes of Yewbarrow. 2½ miles/4.02km. Circuit. Moderate.   NY 167086

17 00

CHURCH. St Catherine. Boot (ME "bend in the valley"). C17. Small. Nave and chancel in one, bellcote. 150 years old pitch pipe. Treble bell C15. Large octagonal C14 font delicately carved with varied tracery (for 60 years used on a farm). In C15 chapel upgraded to Parish Church after petition to the Pope re travel difficulties to St Bees for baptisms and burials. Interesting churchyard memorials particularly one to Tommy Dobson, a bobbin turner, died 2 April 1910, aged 83, most famous huntsman of his day and held by many to have been a greater huntsman than John Peel. Founded Eskdale and Ennerdale Foxhounds in 1857. Relief carving of Tommy, a fox, a hound, a whip, a hunting horn and a brush (fox's tail). His funeral expenses, including conveyance from Langdale to Eskdale via Wrynose and Hardknott passes and coffin amounted to £6 8s. 6d. (£6.42). Memorial also to Willy Porter. Nearby, site of St Catherine's Day Fair—originally 5 December but now 25 November.   NY 176003

TRANSPORT. Dalegarth Station west to Ravenglass—the Ravenglass and Eskdale railway— 'La'al Ratty, after its builder, Ratcliffe. Track gauge 15in/38cm compared with British Rail gauge of 4ft.8¾in/1432cm. 7 miles/11.2km long. Line opened 24th May 1875 at the then gauge of 3ft/91cm for freight and passengers. Closed 1913 because the mines which it served closed due to over-production and low prices, but re-opened 1915 in stages. Mr W. J. Bassett-Lowke, the famous model engineer, converted the line to 15inch gauge. Previously line as far as Boot but miniature locomotives could not cope with gradient. 40 minute journey to Ravenglass. 5 steam locomotives (oldest 1894) & 7 diesel locomotives. Museum. Daily 0900–1850hrs: reduced Winter service. Phone 0229 226.   NY 174007

WALKS. Dalegarth-Stanley Force-Doctors Bridge-St Catherine's. 3.7 miles/6km. Ascent 360ft/110m. Woodland, waterfalls, plants and birds. Profusion of cryptogams, algae, ferns & mosses. Start: car park.   NY 172003

Blea Tarn. Eskdale. Circuit 5½ miles/9km. Ascent 800ft/244m. Moderate. Wilderness walk. Start car park, Dalegarth.   NY 173007

17 01

INDUSTRIAL ARCHAEOLOGY. Boot. Restored and working C16 bank flour mill. A mill was operating near this site C13.   NY 176012

MINE. Nab Gill Mine. Level 660ft/201m deep. High quality Haematite. 1845 but finally proved uneconomic and closed 1918. Near Boot.   NY 175012

MUSEUM. Boot. Restored and working bank mill. Open daily, not Saturdays, Easter to end September 1100–1700hrs.   NY 176012

REFRESHMENT. Burnmoor Inn. Boot. Some building of 1578. Phone 09467 23224.   NY 176011

17 02

ARCHAEOLOGY. White Moss. Eskdale. Cairns and cairned circles.
NY 173024

Brat's Hill. Eskdale. Stone circle and cairn circles.   NY 174025

17 03

ARCHAEOLOGY. Boat How, Eskdale. Hut circles/Terraces.   NY 177034

18 00

ARCHITECTURE. Bank barn—fine example. Low Birker. Eskdale.
NY 189005

Doctor Bridge. Pack-horse bridge widened 1734 so that the local doctor (Dr. Edward Tyson) could cross with his pony and trap. Eskdale.   NY 189007

18 01

FISH. Eel Tarn near Boot. Depth 6½ft/2m. Small brown trout. Free. NY 189019

INDUSTRIAL ARCHAEOLOGY. Water wheel. Gill Bank Farm. Eskdale.
NY 181019

18 02

WATERFALLS. Whillan Beck. Eskdale. Path starts at the Mill leading to Burnmoor Tarn. 5 miles/ 8. Km. Circuit. Moderate. NY 185025

18 04

FISH. Burnmoor Tarn. Depth 42½ft/13m. Perch, pike & brown trout. Free.
NY 1804

18 06

MAMMALS. Wasdale. Herdwick sheep. NY 1806

PLANTS. Oakwood habitat. Greengate. NY 1806

18 07

FISH. Wast Water (OE "Wassewater"). Owned by the National Trust. 3 miles/4.8km long, ½ mile/.80km wide. 200ft/60m above sea-level. Maximum depth 258ft/78.6m; average depth 135ft/41m. Charr, eel, perch, pike, salmon, brown & sea trout. Best locations are the shallows especially River Irt egress where modest runs of salmon and sea trout occur. Permit from The Warden, National Trust Campsite, Wasdale Road. NY 181075

WALKS. Wasdale Head. 3 miles/4.8km. Easy. Best walked after dry spell. Start from village, south to camp sign and then on to Lingmell Gill and return. Fine views of Scafell and Pikes Crags—a climbers playground. NY 182076

Sca Fell from Wasdale. Circuit 8½ miles/14km. Ascent 3950ft/1200m. Strenuous. Dangerous sections—Lord's Rake. Experience essential. Start: Brackenclose, the first hut of the Fell & Rock Climbing Club, opened 3rd October 1937 although the club was founded at Wasdale Head in 1886. NY 182075

18 08

ARCHITECTURE. Pack-horse bridge—known as Down in the Dale Bridge— with single arch and low parapets. Local stone. c1700. NY 187089

CHURCH. St Olaf (Martyr King of Norway) Wasdale Head (ON "vat(n)s dalr": the dale of the lake [now drained]). Seats 39. Chancel and nave in one. Bellcote. Plain mullioned windows, one etched—Napes Needle and "I will lift up mine eyes to the hills from whence cometh my strength." (Psalm 121). Served by the Vicar of Gosforth. Originally constructed of ships' timbers and walls held together with shells and burnt seaweed. 35ft.9inch x 14ft.2inch (10.94m x 4.32m). Walls 6ft.6inch/1.9m high. Churchyard memorials to climbers—Common grave of Henry L. Jupp (29); Algernon E. W. Garrett (27) and Stanley Ridsdale (26) plus grave of R. W. Broadrick who all died on Sca Fell (Scaw Fell) on 2lst September 1903. (Near foot of Lord's Rake a cross carved into the rock commemorates this tragedy). Great Gable claimed C. D. Frankland on 31st July 1937 and G. R. Speaker, a President of the Fell and Rock Climbing Club, on 20th September 1942. NY 188087

EVENT. Wasdale Head Shepherds' Meet. 2nd Saturday of October. Premier show of Sheep, Sheep Dogs and competitions for Shepherd's crooks & boots. Hound Trails, Wrestling & Fell Races. Wasdale Head.　　　　NY 1808

REFRESHMENT. Wasdale Head Inn. Phone 09467 26229. Originally Huntsman Inn 1856, later known as Wastwater Hotel. Centre of British rock climbing in its formative years. Since 1974 the accolade for The Biggest Liar in the World competed for annually in memory of Will Ritson (1808–1890) past landlord. (Shares venue with The Bridge Inn, Santon Bridge). His wife, Dinah, was one of the Fletchers of Nether Wasdale—whose kin had been landowners thereabouts for C7. It was Will's friendship with Professor John Wilson, a giant-sized wrestler, which gradually drew travellers to the area. (Refer SD 411989).　　　NY 186087

WALKS. Wast Water Head. Circuit 2½ miles/4km. Strenuous. Superb views of the highest fells in the UK.　　　　NY 185082

18 09

WATERFALLS. ¾mile/1.20km above Wasdale Head Inn. Cross pack-horse bridge and follow path right. Known as Ritson Force—after Will Ritson "the biggest liar in the world" (Refer NY 186087). Visitors are still told that the water is turned off during the quiet months to conserve electricity.　　　NY 185095

19 01

REFRESHMENT. Woolpack Inn. Eskdale. Oil painting of C18 ploughing scene. Phone 09467 23230.　　　　NY 190010

YOUTH HOSTEL. Holmrook, Boot. Phone 09467 23219.　　　NY 195010

19 02

FISH. Stony Tarn near Boot. Depth 16ft/5m. Small brown trout. Free.　　　　NY 198024

19 03

PLANTS. Upland fell. Eskdale.　　　　NY 1903

19 08

WALLS. River and ice worn rocks. Good example. Wasdale.　　　NY 1908

AREA 17 – Langdales

20 00

MINE. Spot How Gill Copper Mine. NY 205004

20 01

MINE. Taw House Copper Trials. Level started 1875 at NY 207013 and a further level at NY 205013

20 06

HISTORICAL. Sca Fell. 3,162ft/964m given to the National Trust by A. C. Benson, Master of Magdalene and G. G. Wordsworth who had bought it in 1925.
NY 207065

MEMORIAL. Carved cross 24ft/7.3m. from foot of Lord's Rake on Sca Fell marks site where 4 climbers died in a fall on 21st September 1903. First Lakeland fatality of roped climbers. They are buried at St Olaf's, Wasdale Head. (Refer NY 188087). NY 205068

21 01

ARCHAEOLOGY. Hardknott. Best preserved Roman fort in Cumbria, built circa AD 130. 3 acres/1.2ha. Regardless of terrain the fort followed the usual configuration of a square with rounded corners, each with an internal tower and central gateways to each side. Commandant's house, pair of granaries, bath block. Some of the remaining walls 5–6ft/1.5–1.8m high. Called Mediobogdum in Roman times, meaning "the middle of the bend". Fort built for Emperor Caesar Trajan Hadrian Augustus by the fourth cohort of Dalmatians. Possibly 500 men garrisoned the fort. Defensive ditches to the north. No evidence to suggest occupation beyond AD 197. Open daily all year. NY 218014

ARCHITECTURE. Brotherilkeld Farm (originally known as Butterilket, "budr Ulfkell": bothy of Ulfkell). Classic Yeoman farmhouse C17—interior well pre-served. On site of Norse settlement and once owned by Furness Abbey. Now owned by the National Trust but still farmed by the Harrison family. Not open to the public. NY 213014

EVENT. Eskdale Show. At Brotherilkeld Farm on last Saturday of September. Sheep, Hound Trail, Dogs, Fell Race, Handicrafts, Produce and Trade Stands.
NY 213014

GEOLOGY. Borrowdale volcanic series. Eskdale. NY 2101

MEMORIAL. Bridge over River Esk. Plaque in memory of Dick Marsh, Anglican Minister killed in climbing accident. NY 212013

21 02

WATERFALLS. Esk Falls and waterfalls on How Beck. From Brotherilkeld walk the sign-posted route to Esk Falls, and at pack horse bridge follow track on E side of Lingcove Beck. Further paths can be seen if the indistinct path is followed NE and on to How Beck. 8 Miles/12.8 km. Circuit. Moderate.   NY 214024

21 05

GEOLOGY. Erratics. Sampson's Stones, Upper River Esk.   NY 217054

21 06

TOPOGRAPHIC. Broadcrag Tarn. Scafell Pike. The highest tarn in England at 2746ft/836m above sea-level. Depth 1½ft/0.5m.   NY 213069

21 07

LITERARY. Scafell Pike at 3206ft/977m England's highest mountain—first recorded climb on 5th August 1802 by Samuel Taylor Coleridge, unaccompanied. At the summit he wrote a passionate love letter "From this sweet lounding Place I see directly thro' Borrowdale, the Castle Crag, the whole of Derwent Water, and but for the haziness of the Air I could see my own House"—not to his wife, but to Sarah Hutchinson (Wordsworth's sister-in-law) with whom he was in love. He then came down via Broad Stand.   NY 2107

MEMORIAL. Summit of Scafell Pike—3206ft/977m. "In perpetual memory of the men of the Lake District who fell for God and King, for freedom, peace and right, in the Great War 1914–18. This summit of Scafell was given to the nation, subject to any commoners' rights, and placed in the custody of the National Trust by Charles Henry, Baron Leconfield. 1919."   NY 215072

PLANTS. Mountain habitat. Scafell Pike.   NY 2107

21 08

HISTORICAL. Piers Gill, ravine east of Lingmell. Very difficult standard of climbing. In 1921 an injured walker, a Londoner named Cornelius Crump lay where he had fallen, for 20 days before rescue.   NY 212082

22 01

PLANTS. Mountain habitat. Hardknott Pass.   NY 2201

VIEWPOINT. Spectacular views of Scafell and Scafell Pike from Border End 1713ft/522m. Hardknott Pass.   NY 227019

22 03

WATERFALLS. A series of falls at Throstlegarth near confluence of Lingcove Beck and River Esk.   NY 227037

23 04

TOPOGRAPHIC. Embankment surmounted many years ago by a fence built by monks of Furness Abbey. At Lingcove Beck below Scafell on descent to Esk.   NY 2304

WATERFALLS. Series of falls on Lingcove Beck at the head of Mosedale. Good path to Stonesty Gill but indistinct to Swinsty Gill. Grand views. 4½ miles/7.2km. Circuit. Moderate. NY 235044

23 09

MINE. Grains Gill Level. Ruined building beside Gill and Level closed.
NY 235099

24 01

MINE. Cockley Beck Mines. Copper. C17. Levels at NY 245005 and NY 244001 and C19 shaft at NY 247013. Nearby—ruined building. NY 249013

VIEWPOINT. Cockley Beck bridge, into Duddon Valley. NY 247017

24 07

FISH. Angle Tarn, Langdale Fell. Maximum depth 50ft/15m. Brown trout.
NY 2407

24 09

MINE. Driedly Gill Level. 30ft/9.14m level. NY 247098

25 05

WATERFALLS. Whorneyside Force. Falls 100ft/30m. between precipitous rocks in Hell Gill. Oxendale. From Old D/G Hotel Great Langdale 4 miles/6.4km. Circuit. Strenuous. NY 259055

25 07

HISTORICAL. Beside Rossett Gill, Great Langdale the unmarked grave of a pack woman who perished in a storm nearly 200 years ago. This woman walked from valley to valley via the passes selling haberdashery etc., to the isolated country folk. The steepness of this pass to Esk Hause reflected in verse "If I were a lover, and loved a lass,/Who lived on top of Rossett Pass,/While I abode at Dungeon Ghyll,/I'd swear by all that's good and ill/To love and cherish her for ever and ever,/But to visit her—never!" NY 2507

26 03

HISTORICAL. c1860 Lanty Slee installed one of his many illicit whisky stills here. Red Tarn. NY 268037

MINE. Red Tarn Mine. Shallow pits and test bores for iron north of Red Tarn. c1870s. NY 268038

26 04

WATERFALLS. Browney Gill. Great Langdale. Park near Old Dungeon Ghyll Hotel and then by track to Stool End Farm (N/T) bearing left into Oxendale. 5 miles/8.04km. Circuit. Strenuous. NY 265043

27 00

MEMORIAL. Substantial cross commemorating the death of six airmen in the crash of their Halifax MK 5. No. LL505 on 22 October 1944. Great Carrs. There have been 20 or so such crashes in Lakeland with 50 lives lost.   NY 271009

27 02

HISTORICAL. The Three Shires Stone. Summit of Wrynose Pass. Signifies the meeting point of the counties of Cumberland, Lancashire and Westmorland prior to 1974 boundary changes which resulted in Cumbria. West side of stone states Lancashire and W. F. 1816 on east side. Stone originally known as Brandreth or Three Foot Brandreth. Illegal cock-fighting took place here.   NY 277027

27 05

ARCHITECTURE. Barn dry built with stones from Mickleden and Oxendale Becks. Stool End Farm, Great Langdale.   NY 276057

EVENT. Langdale Day. Sheep, Horses, Dogs, Hound Trail, Fell Race, Wrestling, Handicrafts, Produce, Vintage Machinery, Trade Stands etc., Stool End Farm, Great Langdale. 3rd Sunday August.   NY 277057

MEMORIAL. Seat on The Band bears plaque "Rest and remember the work of S. H. Hamer Secretary of The National Trust 1911–1934."   NY 273058

27 06

GEOLOGY. Moraine. Langdales.   NY 271065

27 07

ARCHAEOLOGY. Pike o' Stickle. Langdale Fell. Site of Mesolithic axe "factory". 2730–2550 BC. Discovered in 1947. Felsite a volcanic Tuff (extremely hard fine-grained rock formed from volcanic dust) easily shaped with granite hammers to form rough axe-head. Finish, using sandstone, applied at Ehenside Tarn site near Beckermet (NY 006069). Distribution over much of UK and near continent. A learned estimate suggests that the scree on Pike o' Stickle represents the waste products of 45,000/ 75,000 completed stone axes. About 200 axe-flaking sites have now been identified in the Langdale Pikes area and a further 350 lie between Bowfell, Scafell Pike and Glaramara. Lakeland may fairly be regarded as Britain's first industrial region.   NY 272072

INSECTS. Mountain ringlet butterfly on grassland habitat between Pike o' Stickle and Harrison Stickle. Rarely seen in cloudy conditions. Scarce. Great Langdale.   NY 2707

PLANTS. Mountain habitat. Langdale Pikes.   NY 2707

28 02

WATERFALLS. Greenburn. At Three Shires Inn, Little Langdale, follow lane sign-posted Tilberthwaite and then a path sign-posted Slaters Bridge beyond which the track contours Knotthead to reach the beck. Left track leads to Greenburn reservoir. 5 miles/8.04km. Circuit. Moderate.   NY 286023

28 05

ARCHITECTURE. To left of middle window is a small rectangular opening, a spy hole, operative at night when interior shutters closed. C16 cruck-built barn. Wall End Farm. Great Langdale.   NY 283055

MEMORIAL. Seat inscribed "William Herbert Morris 1880–1938". On summit of pass between Great and Little Langdale.   NY 289051

28 06

REFRESHMENT. Old Dungeon Ghyll Hotel. Great Langdale. C19, originally a "Statesman's" farmhouse. The public bar is the original cowshed. Given to the National Trust by the eminent historian G. M. Trevelyan. Phone 09667 272.
NY 286061

WATERFALLS. Great Langdale. 52ft/16m. Behind New Dungeon Ghyll Hotel.
NY 289066

29 00

WATERFALLS. Tilberthwaite. 54ft/16m. In wooded gorge.   NY 299008

29 01

MINE. Tilberthwaite Mine. Copper. C16–1942. Main entrance near waterfall on Tilberthwaite Gill. (Refer NY 305007). One working at   NY 299010

29 02

MINE. Greenburn Mine. Copper. c1845–1917. Two other workings hereabouts.
NY 290022

29 03

ARCHAEOLOGY. Little Langdale. Possible site of "Thing" mound at rear of Fell Foot Farm. Little Langdale.   NY 297033

Remains of Roman road which linked the forts at Galava (Ambleside), Mediobogdum (Hardknott Castle) and Glannoventa (Ravenglass) visible above ground below Hollins Crag on the Wrynose road. With diligence a significant proportion of the old road can be traced along the Wrynose and Hardknott passes, though farming down the Esk valley has obliterated most of its precise route to Ravenglass.
NY 291032

ARCHITECTURE. Arms of Fletcher Fleming (son of Sir Daniel) who lived here 1707–1716, under gable of Fell Foot Farm. Round chimneys. Fine panelling. Little Langdale.   NY 296033

HISTORICAL. Possible Viking "Thing" Mound, where Vikings gathered to administer justice on the orders of King Ethelred. Terraced hill NW of Fell Foot Farm, Little Langdale.   NY 297033

Lanty Slee, 1802–1878, died at Greenbank, his own small holding. (Refer NY 319032). Slate quarryman and infamous smuggler, said to have had a distillery and store place for illicit spirits at Fell Foot Farm, once an Inn. Little Langdale.
NY 299032

29 04

FISH. Blea Tarn. Little Langdale. Maximum depth 25ft/7.6m. Perch, pike & brown trout. Day permits from Blea Tarn Farmhouse.   NY 2904

PLANTS. Mosses—stag's horn clubmoss (*Lycopodium clavatum*), fir clubmoss (*Lycopodium selago*) and alpine clubmoss (*Lycopodium alpinum*). Clubmosses are an ancient group of ferns with only a few species. Small, creeping plants, branched stems & leaves. Spores June/Sept. Blea Tarn, alongside path to Brown Howe.
NY 297045

VIEWPOINT. Langdale Pikes from Blea Tarn.   NY 295043

WALKS. Blea Tarn-Brown Howe-Side Pike. Circuit 3.1 miles/5km. Ascent 1000ft/305m. Strenuous. Magnificent views of Langdale Pikes, Bow Fell, Crinkle Crags and Wetherlam. Start: National Trust car park, Blea Tarn.   NY 296044

29 06

ARCHITECTURE. Dog-leg staircase built into rectangular projection at rear of Millbeck Farm. Great Langdale.   NY 295066

REFRESHMENT. New Dungeon Ghyll Hotel. Great Langdale. Phone 09667 213.   NY 295064

WALKS. Langdales and Blea Tarn. Circuit 8 miles/12.9km. Strenuous. Wet areas. Wordsworth captured the views in "The Excursion." Start: NY 294063

Pike o' Blisco. Circuit 7½ miles/10.5km. Ascent 2099ft/640m. Grand views of the Langdales and its fells. Start: New Dungeon Ghyll Hotel.   NY 295064

Crinkle Crags (possibly ON "Kringla": a circle). Circuit 8 miles/13km. Ascent 2800ft/850m. Strenuous. Direction finding in mist difficult—small rock peaks separated by steep sided cols. Start: New Dungeon Ghyll Hotel. Great Langdale.
NY 295064

Langdale Pikes traverse. Circuit 8 miles/13km. Ascent 2450ft/750m. Strenuous. Start: New Dungeon Ghyll Hotel. Great Langdale.   NY 295064

WATERFALLS. Stickle Gill, Great Langdale. 128ft/39m cascades alongside path to Stickle Tarn. Path from car park close to New Hotel. 1 mile/1.6km. Circuit. Strenuous.   NY 294065

29 08

FISH. Codale Tarn. Depth 6½ft/2m. Brown trout. Free.   NY 297088

Area 18 – Ambleside

30 00

GEOLOGY. Chalcopyrites. Occurs Coniston mine. NY 3000

MINE. Tilberthwaite Mine. (Refer NY 299010). Deep adit entrance at Horse Crag Quarry. NY 305007

WALKS. Tilberthwaite to Little Langdale. Circuit 4 miles/6.4km. Ascent 1000ft/304m. Strenuous. Rough and wet areas. "Lanty Slee" had several illicit stills in this area. Start: Tilberthwaite quarry. NY 306009

30 01

ARCHITECTURE. Farm; green volcanic slate used. Tilberthwaite. NY 3001

Spinning gallery; Low Tilberthwaite. NY 305011

WALL. Bee Bole. High Tilberthwaite. NY 308013

30 02

ARCHITECTURE. Cruck built barn with threshing floor and separate cowbyre. Low Hall Garth. Little Langdale. NY 309029

BIRDS. Nest site of black-headed gulls. Little Langdale Tarn. NY 3002

HISTORICAL. Lanty Slee's (illicit whisky distiller & smuggler) caves on Betsy Crag, south of Little Langdale Tarn, late C19. In recent times Harry Griffin, author of Lake District books, discovered apparatus remains. NY 3002

30 03

FISH. Little Langdale Tarn. Maximum depth 68ft/21m. Vendace. Permit required—enquire locally. NY 3003

30 04

PLANTS. Upland fell habitat. Lingmoor. NY 3004

30 05

ARCHAEOLOGICAL. Remains of early farm settlement. Oak Howe. Great Langdale. NY 307057

HISTORICAL. Possible C17 plague pit roughly circular within triangular enclosure. It is said that a woman and her son lived near this spot. He went to London to seek his fortune but succumbed to the plague. His belongings were sent home but mother was then infected and died. The local people were so terrified that body left to mould where it lay instead of burial in consecrated ground. Oak Howe, Great Langdale. NY 307057

QUARRY. Greenstone. Spoutcrag. Great Langdale. NY 307052

30 06

ARCHITECTURE. Old farmhouse at Raw Head, Great Langdale now a climbing hut for the Fell and Rock Climbing Club. NY 304067

Peat houses where the fuel was stored after digging and drying. Rawhead. Great Langdale. NY 304068

30 08

FISH. Easedale Tarn. Maximum depth 60ft/18m. Eel, perch & brown trout. Free. NY 3008

30 09

WATERFALLS. Far Easedale. Grasmere. Follow Easedale Road from Grasmere village and then track sign-posted Far Easedale. 6 miles/9.65km. Circuit. Strenuous. NY 302099

31 00

TREES. A grove of rowans—mountain ash. Unusual. Holme Fell. NY 311009

31 01

ARCHITECTURE. Bank barn either side of farmhouse. Threshing floor. Holme Ground Farm now owned by the National Trust. NY 311012

CRAFTS. Slate ornaments and "furniture". Holme Ground Farm. NY 311012

31 02

QUARRY. Moss Rigg. Stone used in Chapel of Unity, Coventry Cathedral. Selected by Sir Basil Spence. NY 312024

31 03

ARCHITECTURE. Slaters Bridge in Little Langdale, marked the old boundary between Westmorland and Lancashire. Arguably the most interesting and attractive bridge in the Lake District. Built by nearby quarry slaters in C17. NY 312030

High Birk Howe. C16 Statesman's farmhouse but originally as a "two up and two down". Extremely rare timber and plaster chimney hood. Very low beamed ceiling. Barn roof has uncommon "Wrostler" interlocking slates at ridge. Little Langdale. NY 314033

HISTORICAL. Terraced cottages in Little Langdale known locally as Jam Row because the miners who lived there are said to have existed solely on bread and home-made jam on account of being so poor. NY 315034

Greenbank Farm, Little Langdale, once the home of "Lanty Slee" the notorious smuggler. His potent distillations, using potato peelings, from a still in the cellar the smoke from which vented via the farm chimney. Also an illicit still in nearby Atkinson Coppice. He transported the whisky to the Duddon via Wrynose, returning with salmon. NY 319032

REFRESHMENT. Three Shires Inn. Little Langdale. Phone 09667 215.

NY 316034

31 04

ARCHITECTURE. Baysbrown farmhouse—front wall faced with green slate.

NY 314049

31 05

ARCHITECTURE. Bridge over Great Langdale Beck, Thrang. Built 1818— John & Jane Atkinson.

NY 317053

VIEWPOINT. Perhaps the best view of the Langdale Pikes, from Great Langdale Beck.

NY 312058

31 06

BIRDS. Black-headed gulls colony. Summer. Lang How Tarn. Silver How. Grasmere.

NY 317068

31 08

GEOLOGY. Hanging valley. Sour Milk Gill Easedale.

NY 317088

PLANTS. Acid moorland habitat. Far Easedale.

NY 3108

WATERFALLS. Sourmilk Gill. Cascades of 58ft/18m and 36ft/11m over rocks. Far Easedale.

NY 318088

32 00

FISH. Yew Tree Tarn. Depth 10ft/3m. Brown & rainbow trout. Permit from Nicholsons Sporting shop, Coniston.

NY 3200

GEOLOGY. Coniston limestone. South side of Tarns Hows.

NY 3200

32 01

GEOLOGY. Roches moutonnées. High Oxen Fell.

NY 324019

LEGEND. Low Oxen Fell. Ghost of Betty Briggs, a Tilberthwaite farmer's daughter, who with Jack Snipe her suitor, attended a dance at Clappersgate. Walked home by another admirer, who is thought to have met an unexpected end from Jack Snipe who quite soon died of guilt and remorse.

NY 324019

32 02

WALKS. Stang End & Low Oxen Fell. Circuit 3 miles/4.8km. Easy hard surfaced tracks. Unfit for cars. Start: sign-post.

NY 328022

Hollin Bank-Hodge Close-Holme Fell and Yew Tree Tarn. Circuit 4 miles/6.5km. Ascent 820ft/250m. Moderate. Start 1.2 miles/2 km. South of Skelwith Bridge.

NY 329023

Black Crag. Circuit 4 miles/2.4km. Ascent 550ft/168m. Moderate. Good views— clear visibility essential. Unusual triangulation point on Black Crag bears the National Trust emblem. Start from west end of Tongue Intake plantation.

NY 328022

32 03

HISTORICAL. Iving How. In 1818 Wordsworth organised a syndicate to purchase land plots here which would give freeholders the right to vote—hopefully for his patron Lord Lonsdale. NY 321032

LITERARY. The Wordsworth children stayed with Betty Youdell and her quarryman husband John (mentioned in *The Excursion* Book V line 750...) whilst recovering from whooping cough for their Allan Bank home proved too cold and draughty. Sarah Youdell, daughter, was a maid at Allan Bank. The cottage is now a ruin. High Hackett. Near Grasmere. NY 324035

WATERFALLS. Colwith Force on River Brathay, between Langdale Tarn and Elterwater. Little Langdale. Fall 70ft/21m in deep tree covered ravine. Boletus fungi grow hereabouts. NY 328031

32 04

BIRDS. Winter: Slavonian grebe and whooper swans. Elterwater. NY 3204

FISH. Elterwater. (ON "Elptvatn": Swan Lake). Privately owned. Eel, perch, pike and brown trout. Permit from The Elterwater Hotel. NY 3204

INDUSTRIAL ARCHAEOLOGY. Low Wood Gunpowder Company of Kendal, owned by David Huddleston, manufactured 4–6000lbs/1814–2721kgs of gunpowder per week from 1824 to 1934, on the site of the now Langdale Timeshare properties. Originally water supplied by Langdale Beck but Stickle Tarn dammed and water piped 4 miles/6.4km. to works in 1824. In January 1863 six workers died after an explosion at the works and a further five died in 1868 and others in 1887 and 1903. NY 327049

REFRESHMENT. Britannia Inn. Elterwater. Amalgamated quarrymen's cottages of C17. Doorway sign depicts 100 gun warship c1682. Phone 09667 210. NY 325048

TOURIST INFORMATION CENTRE. Village shop, Chestnut Tree Corner. Elterwater. NY 328048

WALKS. Elterwater. Skelwith Bridge & Little Langdale. Circuit 5.6 miles/9km. Ascent 623ft/190m. Easy. Start: National Trust car park, Elterwater village. NY 329048

Little Langdale. Circuit 6 miles/9.5km. Ascent 450ft/140m. Moderate. Start: N/Trust car park, Elterwater village. NY 329048

Lingmoor Fell & Great Langdale. Circuit 6½ miles/10.4km. Ascent 1350ft/411m. Strenuous. Start: Elterwater village. NY 329048

YOUTH HOSTEL. Originally C17 farmhouse. Elterwater. Ambleside. Phone 09667 245. NY 327046

32 05

CHURCH. Holy Trinity. Chapel Stile. Great Langdale. First mentioned in 1571. 1857 in the style of C13 built of green slate from nearby quarry on Silver How. South tower, nave chancel and north aisle. East window is copied from Troutbeck (Jesus Chapel). Window by Edward Burne-Jones, William Morris & Ford Madox Brown. Churchyard grave of G. M. Trevelyan "Historian of England".   NY 321054

EVENT. Langdale Gala. Sheep, Dogs, Fell Races, Slate Dressing, Trade Stands. 1st Saturday of June. Chapel Stile.   NY 322053

WATERFALLS. Below Thrang Crag above Chapel Stile, Great Langdale. Path from Harry Place Farm (west of Chapel Stile). 2 miles/3.22km. Circuit. Moderate.
          NY 321057

Meg's Gill. Chapel Stile. Path from Holy Trinity church climbs beck, following a wall until it bears right. Follow indistinct path left to first fall and upwards, returning via Spedding Crag and Raven Crag. 2 miles/3.21km. Circuit. Moderate.
          NY 324059

32 07

WATERFALLS. Wray Gill. Grasmere. From village along road to Red Bank. After bridge take 2nd gate right sign-posted Langdale. 2 miles/3.21km. Circuit. Moderate.   NY 327074

Blindtarn Gill. Silver How. Grasmere. From Easedale Road follow a road until it curves right for Far Easedale. Cross Easedale Beck and follow signs to Blindtarn Moss. 3 miles/4.82km. Circuit. Moderate.   NY 322079

32 08

HISTORICAL. Blindtarn Gill Farm. Home of George and Sarah Green who, leaving a house contents sale at Langdalehead to walk the 6 miles/9.6km home across mountainous country, died on 19th March 1808 in White Gill (NY 2907) in a snow storm leaving 6 children. The eldest child, Agnes, 11 years of age, cared for her brothers and sisters for two days plus feeding, milking and other farm jobs, before setting out for help when the storm abated. Grasmere families took in the orphans due, in the main, to Dorothy Wordsworth's efforts—she also raised considerable funds to which Queen Charlotte contributed. Buried in Grasmere churchyard. Wordsworth wrote an elegiac stanza: "Who weeps for strangers? Many wept for George and Sarah Green ..."   NY 323082

MEMORIAL. Behind two barns in Far Easedale is a "natural armchair" in a group of rocks. A plaque reads "This scene was dear To the Heart of T. M. Scott. Hunc locum Multum amavit" (He loved this place very much). T. M. Scott, M. A. born 12 December 1891, died Easter 1950. Bachelor. For over 40 years he ran camps for Manchester Grammar School pupils.   NY 323089

32 09

LITERARY. John Ruskin visited Helm Crag, 1305ft/398m Grasmere, when aged 11. At the time he wrote "dark shadow shaded the fields at its feet, Made the cornfields wave browner and darkened the deep ..."   NY 327093

VIEWPOINT. Breathtaking views over Grasmere from Helm Crag. From below, the jumbled configuration of summit rocks create a silhouetted illusion of

"The Lion and the Lamb" (best seen from road south of Dunmail Raise) or "The old Lady at the organ" (best seen from Easedale Tarn or Tongue Gill). Its northern pinnacle is the highest point. NY 327093

33 00

GEOLOGY. Coniston Limestone. East side of Tarn Hows. NY 336005

INSECTS. Glow worm. Tarn Hows. NY 3300

MAMMALS. Badgers. Tarn Hows. NY 3300

33 03

ARCHITECTURE. Park Farm near Skelwith Bridge. Wall incorporating a stone upon which is carved the Alphabet. NY 335032

33 04

PLANTS. Tarn habitat. Elterwater. NY 3304

TREES. Bird Cherry—flowers late May/early June and then leaves are stripped by lackey caterpillars, which form large cocoons resembling cobwebs/tents. The larvae pupate and the tree grows further leaves for the remainder of the season. Elterwater. NY 332045

33 05

YOUTH HOSTEL. High Close Loughrigg. Ambleside. Phone 09667 212. NY 338052

33 06

ARCHITECTURE. Dale End, Grasmere. Farm house, part 1661 (roof and one fireplace) rest of later date. NY 336062

BIRDS. Winter: Goldeneye, Slavonian grebe and pochard. Grasmere. NY 3306

FISH. Grasmere. Owned by the National Trust. 1 mile/1.6km long & ½ mile/0.8km wide. 208ft/63m above sea-level. Maximum depth 75ft/22m. Bitterling (*Rhodeus amarus*) [introduced into Grasmere, depends on freshwater mussels for its reproduction], eel, perch, pike (a specimen at 28lbs/12.7kg) & brown trout. Permit from Grasmere Information Centre. NY 3306

GEOLOGY. Island on Grasmere—a drumlin. NY 338066

HISTORICAL. Grasmere Island. Cock fighting took place in the barn. The island's sale in C19 was a catalyst in forming the National Trust in 1885. NY 338066

Old Corpse Road from Huntingstile to Langdales. Grasmere. NY 334064

33 07

ARCHITECTURE. Small building next to St Oswald's lych-gate, once church school, built 1660. Wordsworth taught here for several hours daily in 1811. John Wordsworth had lessons here. In 1854 let to Sarah Nelson who made gingerbread to eke out a meagre income. Today the building, now owned by Gerald and

Margaret Wilson, is still used for the manufacture and sale of "Sarah Nelson's Celebrated Grasmere Gingerbread" and also rum butter, fudge, truffles and jams. The business has been conducted by only 3 families over 130 years. Open weekdays 0930–1730hrs and some Sundays 1230–1730hrs. Goods may be ordered by post. Phone 05394 35428.   NY 337074

Bank barn; Grasmere.   NY 331078

CHURCH. St Oswald. Grasmere (OE "graesmere": the grassy shore of the lake). St Oswald, King of Northumbria died 642 in the Battle of Masserfield at Hexham fighting the heathen Mercians. His head is buried in Durham Cathedral adjacent to St Cuthbert. C13 Tower and Nave. The Church served 3 parishes, each with its own entrance, a small gate for Langdale, lych-gate for Grasmere, and a lighted arch for Rydal & Ambleside. Interesting interior—murals of 1687 and, especially, the roof timbers. It is said that the latter inspired Wordsworth to write *The Excursion*: "Not raised in nice proportions was the pile,/But large and massy; for duration built,/With pillars crowded, and the roof upheld/By naked rafters intricately crossed,/Like leafless underboughs in some thick wood,/All withered by the depth of shade above..." Poor Box 1648 inscribed "S Oswaldes Poor Box". C12 sculpture. Memorial by John Keeble, Oxford theologian:

> To the memory of
> William Wordsworth
> A true philosopher and Poet
> who by the special gift and calling of
> Almighty God
> Whether he discoursed on man or nature
> Failed not to lift up the heart
> To Holy Things
> Tired not of maintaining the cause
> Of the poor and simple;
> And so in perilous times was raised up
> To be a chief minister
> not only of noblest posey
> But of high and sacred truth
> This memorial
> Is placed here by his friends and neighbours
> In testimony of
> Respect Affection Gratitude.

Churchyard—graves of William Wordsworth, 7 April 1770–23 April 1850, [William Shakespeare also died on St George's Day, 23 April 1616], his wife, Mary, died 17 February 1859, and his sister, Dorothy, died 25 January 1855, his son also called William 1810–1883 together with his wife, Fanny died 1888, plus his son Thomas aged 6½ (1806–1812) and his daughter Catherine aged 3 (born 1818), who died whilst the Grasmere Rectory was the family home. Grave of Dora Quillinan *née* Wordsworth. The Celandine was among William Wordsworth's favourite flowers and he penned a poem entitled "The Lesson" to its honour; representations of it are carved on his tombstone. Also graves of Hartley Coleridge died at Nab Cottage 1849 (son of Samuel Taylor Coleridge); Sir John Richardson, Arctic Explorer and Surgeon who fought with Nelson at Copenhagen and in America 1812 (1787–1865); Arthur Hugh Clough, (poet, born Liverpool 1819 and died Florence 1861; his works included *The Bothie of Tober-na-Vuolich*: A Long Vacation Pastoral), and his sister Anne Jemima, first Principal of Newnham

College, Cambridge; and George and Sarah Green, victims of a snow blizzard in 1808 in White Gill, Langdale (Refer NY 323082); and Sarah Nelson (of the gingerbread shop). NY 336074

CRAFTS. Weaving. Chris Reekie & Sons Ltd have been in Grasmere since 1949. The Old Coach House, Stock Lane, Grasmere. Open Mon/Sat 1000–1800hrs. Sun 1000–1230hrs. and 1415–1730hrs. Phone 05394 35221. NY 3307

Blacksmith; White Bridge Forge. Grasmere. Mon/Fri 0800–1800hrs. Sat 0800–1200hrs. Phone 05394 35414. NY 3307

Paintings of mountain scenery. Heaton Cooper Galleries. Grasmere. Oct/June weekdays 0900–1700hrs and Sun 1200–1700hrs. July/Sept weekdays 0900–1800hrs. and Sun 1200–1800hrs. Closed 23 Dec/2 Jan. Phone 05394 35280.

NY 3307

CUSTOMS. St Oswald. Grasmere. Rush-bearing. Prior to 1841 the floor of the church was unboarded and yearly on the Saturday nearest St Oswald's Day (August 5th), the local people brought fresh cut rushes to lay on the bare earth floor to provide warmth and dryness. The ceremony is not unique to Grasmere or Cumbria for such ceremonies are held in a dozen or more churches throughout the land. (Refer NY 374044). However, in Cumbria, only Ambleside, Warcop, Musgrave and Urswick continue the custom, though some not without a break. At Grasmere, as in other churches, rush-bearing was a boon day on which parishioners worked for the good of the community. Ale was provided and Grasmere's churchwardens' accounts for every year between 1682 and 1830 contain an entry for expenditure on rush-bearing ale, "1/–(5p) paid for ale bestowed on those who brought rushes to repair the church." Special hymns sung, one verse of which: "Our fathers to the house of God,/As yet a building rude,/Bore offerings from the flowery sod,/And fragrant rushes strew'd,/ May we their children ne'er forget/The pious lessons given,/But honour still, together met,/The Lord of earth and Heaven." NY 336074

HISTORICAL. In C15 and C16 Grasmere was a thriving centre for the fulling industry which cleaned and thickened the locally woven cloth. NY 3307

LITERARY. Allan Bank, Grasmere. Built 1805 by Crump, a Liverpool merchant. Home of the Wordsworths June 1808/May 1811. Coleridge often visited and De Quincey stayed for months but the Wordsworths were not happy in this cold house—"a temple of abomination" so wrote the Bard, until the landlord returned whereupon they then moved to Grasmere Rectory. Bequeathed to National Trust by Canon Rawnsley, who spent the last 3 years of his life here—died 28 May 1920. Now rented privately. NY 333077

The Old Rectory. Grasmere. Home of the Wordsworths 1811/1813 and where two of their children died. NY 336074

NATIONAL TRUST SHOP. Church Stile, Grasmere. C16 formerly an inn with cockpit. In 1799 S. T. Coleridge and William Wordsworth stayed here when on a walking holiday. NY 336074

REFRESHMENT. Red Lion Hotel. Grasmere. Originally coaching inn C18.
Phone 05394 35456. NY 336074

Wordsworth Hotel. Grasmere. NY 337075

TOURIST INFORMATION CENTRE. Church Stile, Grasmere. National
Trust. Phone 05394 35621. NY 336074

TRANSPORT. Rowing boat hire at Allonby's. Grasmere. Phone 05394 35409.
NY 334071

WALKS. Grasmere and Rydal Water. Circuit 5 miles/8km. Easy. Very pleasant stroll
known as the Wordsworth Walk. Start Grasmere Church. NY 336074

Easedale Tarn. Circuit 5 miles/8km. Ascent 620ft/188m. Moderate. Can be wet.
The Wordsworths used often to walk this route, especially to see "Churn-milk"
force (Sour Milk Gill). Start: Grasmere village. NY 335074

Helm Crag. Circuit 4 miles/6.4km. Ascent 1100ft/335m. Strenuous. Wet areas.
Outstanding views in clear visibility. Start: Grasmere village. NY 336073

Silver How. Circuit 3.4 miles/5.5km. Ascent 1246ft/380m. Strenuous. Clear visibility
essential to obtain panoramic views. Start: Grasmere village. NY 337074

YOUTH HOSTEL. Butharlyp How, Grasmere. Phone 05394 35316.
NY 336077

33 08

ARCHITECTURE. Goody Bridge House. Grasmere. 1690. Drip moulds to
lintels to keep window free from eaves water. NY 333081

LEGEND. Sir Walter Scott, when staying at neighbouring Dove Cottage with
the Wordsworths, clandestinely visited The Swan Inn to supplement the meagre
fare of his hosts who were abstemious. His deception ended embarrassingly when
the two men called at the inn to hire a pony and the landlord expressed surprise
as seeing Scott so much earlier than his usual time. NY 339083

LITERARY. Lancrigg Terrace, Grasmere. Wordsworth composed much of *The
Prelude* here. NY 332085

REFRESHMENT. Traveller's Rest. An old coaching inn at start of Dunmail
Raise. Grasmere. Phone 05394 35604/35378. NY 336089

Swan Inn. Grasmere. C17. Wordsworth wrote of the Inn: "… Who does not
know the famous Swan?…" (The Waggoner line 88). Phone 05394 35551.
NY 339083

WALKS. Allcock Tarn. Circuit 3 miles/4.8km. Ascent 900ft/274m. Strenuous.
Excellent views south & west. Start: Grasmere village. NY 339083

YOUTH HOSTEL. Thorney How. Ambleside. Phone 05394 35591.
NY 331084

34 00

INDUSTRIAL ARCHAEOLOGY. Lime Kiln. Sunny Brow. NY 343004

34 01

WATERFALLS. Pull Beck. Path from Sunny Brow (NY 343004). 3 miles/ 4.82km. Circuit. Easy.   NY 346016

34 02

MINE. Coniston United Mine. Shaft. c1850s. No mineralization. (Refer NY 358021).   NY 347021

34 03

BIRDS. Crossbills sometimes nest in the larchwoods around Skelwith Bridge.
NY 3403

CRAFTS. Green slate ware. Kirkstone Galleries Ltd. Skelwith Bridge. Ambleside. Phone 05394 33296. Workshop Mon/Fri 0800–1700hrs. Cafe, Shop and show-room open daily all year 1000–1800hrs, but mid-Nov to mid-March 1000–1700hrs. Parking available.   NY 348034

FISH. River Brathay—Skelwith Bridge and lower reaches. Brown trout. Permit from Grasmere Information Centre.   NY 3403

INDUSTRY. Kirkstone Quarries Ltd. Skelwith Bridge. Green-blue close grained slate dressed for many and varied purposes—exported world wide.   NY 343034

REFRESHMENT. Skelwith Bridge Hotel. Skelwith Bridge. Phone 05394 32115.   NY 344034

WATERFALLS. Skelwith Force, Skelwith Bridge. Despite the River Brathay's large catchment area of Wrynose, Langdale and Little Langdale Fells, the waterfall is only 20ft/6m high, though the volume of falling water is the greatest in the Lake District. The path to the force leads through mill yard behind Kirkstone Galleries Ltd.   NY 340034

34 04

FISH. Loughrigg Tarn. National Trust. Maximum depth 30ft/9m. Perch, pike (up to 15lbs/6.8kg), roach & brown trout. Day permits available at Tarn Foot Farm, where car parking is available.   NY 3404

34 05

VIEWPOINT. The best view of Grasmere, from SE side of Loughrigg Terrace— the ridge above the lake.   NY 3405

34 06

FISH. River Rothay. Perch, pike & brown trout. Permit from Grasmere Information Centre.   NY 3406

HISTORICAL. Coffin-stone, next to corner of a stone wall, opposite How Top Farm. Used as a temporary resting place for coffins along the old coffin track to Rydal Church.   NY 344068

Site of C13 fulling mill (to dress and finish local Herdwick wool for markets at Kendal) in Banneriggs Wood. Grasmere.   NY 344063

MAMMALS. Red squirrel. Banneriggs. Grasmere. NY 3406

NATURE RESERVE/TRAIL. White Moss Common. Rydal. Circuit 1½ miles/2.5km and also 2½ miles/4km. National Trust Guide obtainable at N/T Information Centre, Ambleside and also at Grasmere. Start: White Moss Common car park. NY 349066

REFRESHMENT. Prince of Wales Hotel. Grasmere. NY 341068

TREES. Grove of beech, John's Grove, named by Wordsworth in memory of his brother who drowned. Public access. Opposite the Grove is the site of the Wishing Gate. Wordsworth explained the origin of the name "from a belief that wishes formed or indulged there have a favourable issue." NY 344067

WHEELCHAIR WALK. White Moss Common to River Rothay, from car park. NY 348065

34 07

EVENT. Cumberland & Westmorland Wrestling, Races, Fell Running, Hound trailing, Cycling. Thursday nearest 20th of August. Showfield right of Stock Lane. Grasmere. NY 341074

FISH. Brown trout. Alcock Tarn, originally called Buttercrags until a Mr. Alcock stocked it with trout. Free. NY 349078

LITERARY. Dove Cottage, Town End, Grasmere. Built 1600s as The Dove &

Dove Cottage. Grasmere. (Rosemary Liddle)

Olive Bough Inn, but called Town End by the Wordsworths who rented it at £5 per annum plus 7/6 annual window tax, 1799/ 1808, and birthplace of three of their children. The cottage with a growing family, proved too small especially as Wordsworth was forced to work in that one room, common to all the family, to all visitors, and where the children frequently played beside him. Thereafter the home of Thomas De Quincey for next 28 years though for 12 of those years he used it purely to store his books. Open mid Feb/mid Jan. Daily 0930–1730hrs. Fee. Phone 05394 35544.   NY 342071

MEMORIAL. To William Wordsworth. Grasmere.   NY 341071

MUSEUM. Wordsworth Museum. Town End, Grasmere. Next to Dove Cottage in converted bank barn. Best collection in the world of Wordsworth's original material. Paintings exhibited. Local history. Preserved at the museum is "the Rock of Names"—William and Dorothy Wordsworth, Mary Hutchinson, Samuel Taylor Coleridge, John Wordsworth and Sarah Hutchinson had carved their initials on a rock slab which is now beneath Thirlmere's waters. Canon Rawnsley rescued fragments of this rock carving and built them into a cairn, originally near the Straining Well above Legburthwaite. Upstairs, re-creation of farmhouse interior of the period. Open daily mid Feb/mid Jan 0930–1730 hrs. Fee. Phone 05394 35544.   NY 342071

34 08

CHURCH. Our Lady of the Wayside, Catholic Church. 1964. Grasmere.
                                                                    NY 340082

LEGEND. Michael, a shepherd, married Isabel when late in life. His wife, twenty years younger than he, was just as industrious in caring for their small-holding. Their son Luke, took over from Michael, by then nearly 70 years of age. Their happy life was marred when Michael was called upon under a long-standing surety given for his brother's son, who had failed in business. To meet the legal commitment required the sale of half of the farm, the remainder then becoming unviable. Luke decided that he should work in the city in order to provide the necessary sums required. Before Luke left home father and son toiled long and hard bringing down rocks from the fell to build a sheep-fold beside the beck. For a time Luke sent money from London to help pay for the surety, while the now infirmed Michael struggled to keep the farm going until his son's eventual return. But gradually the funds no longer came for Luke had fallen into corrupt ways and became so ashamed that he went abroad and was never heard of again. For several years Michael tramped daily to the pile of rocks, too old to build for the future, and died in his 80th year. The farm was sold and the cottage on Green Head Ghyll was demolished. But the pile of rocks remains beside the beck. Michael's Fold. Grasmere. Wordsworth's "Michael" a Pastoral Poem.   NY 3408

MEMORIAL. Seat in memory of Tim Oldfield by whose efforts in 1950s local rights of way were entered on maps.   NY 345084

MINE. Greenhead Trial. No mineralization.   NY 346085

WATERFALLS. Greenhead Gill. Great Rigg. Grasmere. Route from Swan Inn on A 591, via a lane. At 2nd turn right follow a path sign-posted Greenhead Gill and Allcock Tarn. 1½ miles/2.41km. Circuit. Moderate.   NY 347085

34 09

MINE. Fairfield Mine. Haematite. c1700–1876. Provides Grasmere with water.   NY 340098

35 01

FISH. Drunken Duck Inn Tarn. Brown trout-fly.   NY 351013

MINE. Coniston United Mine. c1850s. No mineralization. Level.   NY 354019

QUARRY. Brathay Quarries produced the distinctive blue-black flagstone which face St Mary's Church, Ambleside and many other of the town's buildings.   NY 357016

REFRESHMENT. Drunken Duck Inn, formerly known as Barngates Inn. C16. Near Hawkshead. Phone 05394 36347.   NY 351013

35 02

MINE. Coniston United Mine. c1850s. No mineralization. Level.   NY 358021

35 05

MINE. Cavern near Ambleside. Result of slate quarrying. It is said that the whole population of Ambleside could fit into it with ease. Charlotte Mason Teacher Training College holds an annual carol service here—the acoustics are superb.   NY 355057

35 06

BIRDS. Winter: Pochard. Rydal Water.   NY 3506

FISH. Rydal Water once known as Rothaymere. Half owned by National Trust, the other half by Rydal Estates. Only scouts staying at Rydal Hall allowed to canoe on it. ¾ mile/1.2km long & ¼ mile/0.4km wide. 181ft/55m above sea-level. Maximum depth 55ft/16m. Bitterling (*Rhodeus amarus*) introduced into Rydal Water, depends on freshwater mussels for its reproduction. Charr, eel, perch, pike, roach, salmon and brown trout. Game Fishing licence required from North West Water Ltd. New Town House, Buttermarket Street, Warrington. Cheshire. Phone 0925 234000. Permit from Grasmere Information Centre.   NY 3506

LITERARY. Nab Cottage, Rydal Water. Built 1702. Now a guest house. Thomas De Quincey lodged here. De Quincey was born in Manchester in 1785 and educated at Bath, Manchester and Worcester College, Oxford. Died 1859 and buried in Edinburgh. His works include *Vision of Sudden Death, Confessions of an English Opium Eater* 1821/2, *On Murder as one of the Fine Arts* 1827. He married the landlord's daughter, Margaret Simpson, when he was 31, in Grasmere church in February 1817 after she had borne him a son the previous November and then moved into Dove Cottage. Although it was an enduring love-match (she died 20 years later) the union incurred the strong disapproval of the Wordsworths who thought marriage between one of the gentry and a "low-born" woman quite unsuitable. In 1818 De Quincey made Editor of Westmorland Gazette after its foundation but he was sacked 14 months later. In 1829 he became the owner of Nab Farm, where his family was then staying but the farm was sold in 1833 because De Quincey could not maintain interest payments on the mortgage. Hartley Coleridge, writer and poet, eldest son of Samuel Taylor Coleridge, poet, became tenant 1840 until his death here in 1849 at the age of 52. As a youth very frail and in the Southey household he lacked the discipline so necessary to develop his undoubted poetic genius. However, he went to Oxford though he himself said "with few habits but those of negligence and self-indulgence, with principles honest and charitable but little applied to particulars, with much vanity and diffidence, with wavering hopes and uncertain spirits, I was sent among men." He did well in examinations but failed to win University acclaim which made him more melancholy than ever. After some casual library work in London he "retired" to the Lakes, doing little for the rest of his life.   NY 355064

PLANTS. Tarn habitat. Rydal Water.   NY 3506

WATERFALLS. White Moss Common.   NY 350067

35 07

WALL/FENCE. Boundary fence between Rydal and Scandale. Built 1277, above Nab Scar, *en route* for Heron Pike by Cistercian monks of Furness Abbey. Remains of wattle and fence post.   NY 3507

35 08

MINE. Grasmere Lead Mine. 1564–1573. Several levels, shafts and openworks. Unsuccessful.   NY 350087

35 09

LITERARY. Greenhead Gill. Setting for Wordsworth's "Michael".   NY 3509

36 00

FISH. Blelham Tarn (ME "Blaylolme"). Depth 13ft/4m. Eel, perch, pike & brown trout. National Trust owned. Day permits from Low Wray campsite.
NY 3600

INDUSTRIAL ARCHAEOLOGY. Bloomery site. Blelham Tarn. NY 365006

INSECTS. Rare caddis (*Limnephilus xanthodes*). Rare raft spider (*Dolomedes fimbriatus*)—female up to 22mm and male 10/13mm. Adult spiders feed on damselflies and even tadpoles. Furness Abbey monks used to catch leeches for medicinal purposes. Blelham Tarn.   NY 3600

PLANTS. Tarn habitat. Blelham Tarn. (Cistercian monks of Furness Abbey used the tarn as a fishery). No public access for area is scheduled as a National Nature Reserve. Unique example of sphagnum bog developing from wet willow woodland. Buoys indicate experiments by The Freshwater Biology Association.   NY 3600

36 01

ARCHITECTURE. Huyton Hill School. Pull Woods, near Wray. Timber framed gabled mansion reminiscent of such houses in Cheshire.   NY 368019

36 03

ARCHITECTURE. Brathay Hall. C18. 5 bays. Semi-circular columned porch. Built for the Harden family and home of John Harden C19 watercolour artist, followed by the Redmaynes. Here, Miss Dorothy Blomfield composed the hymn "O Perfect Love". Now the Brathay Education Centre.   NY 367031

Brathay Bridge c1681, since widened. Clappersgate.   NY 367034

CHURCH. Holy Trinity. Brathay (ON "breith-a": broad stream—likely to flood.) 1836. Built by wealthy Giles Redmayne, of Brathay Hall, whose Italian business interests are reflected in the architecture. The church is not properly orientated due to the difficulties of the site. Flagged floor from Brathay Quarry (Refer NY 357016). SW tower. Utilitarian. Romanesque.   NY 362034

GARDEN. White Crags. Clappersgate. Created by Charles Henry Hough and his family c1900. Limited opening to public. Best late May and June. Azaleas, heathers, rhododendrons and many other trees and shrubs.   NY 366035

LEGEND. Old Brathay one time home of two highwaymen brothers named Gilbert alias Weston. Eventually discovered and hanged.   NY 367034

36 04

ARCHITECTURE. Loughrigg Brow. Ambleside. 1863. Gothic. Mullioned and transomed windows. Inscription above entrance reads: "God's Providence is my Inheritance."   NY 369044

LITERARY. Dr. Thomas Arnold of Rugby (1795–1842) built Fox How at the foot of Loughrigg Fell in 1833 as a holiday home and for his retirement, but he died 11 June 1842 when only 46. His fame rests on his achievement at Rugby, on the public school reforms associated with his name and on the far-reaching influence upon the English boarding-school system, to which he gave new life and popularity. He remained at Rugby for 14 years during which time he changed the character of the school and made it a model for others to imitate. His publications included *History of Rome* 1838–43 and *Oxford Lectures on Modern History* 1842. His eldest son, Matthew, an Inspector of Schools, lived for some time at Fox How after the death of his mother in 1872.   NY 365049

36 05

ARCHITECTURE. Cote How. C15. Spinning gallery.   NY 363059

HISTORICAL. Edward Quillinan and his wife Dora, (*née* Wordsworth) lived here when married in 1841. Dora died of tuberculosis in 1847. Loughrigg Holme.   NY 363053

LITERARY. Fox Ghyll near Rydal. De Quincey resided here from 1821–1825. It was also the residence of Rt. Hon. William Edward Forster (1819–1886). In

1850 he married Jane, eldest daughter of Dr Arnold of Rugby. Became Liberal M. P. for Bradford in 1861 and in 1865–66 was Under-Secretary for the Colonies. In 1870 entered the Cabinet and piloted the 1870 Education Act through Parliament. Was contender for Prime Minister after Gladstone retired in 1875 but withdrew. Resigned from Government in 1882.   NY 363051

36 06

ARCHITECTURE. Rydal Hall. Mainly Georgian though some C15. Once the seat of the Le Fleming family, one of the Lake District's biggest land owners, at one time. Large Bank Barns, one c1650, the other 1670. Underhousing and threshing floor. Rydal Park, private park of Rydal Hall can be freely walked through. The gardens are open all year Wednesday and Saturday 0900hrs to dusk. It is the venue of the Rydal Sheep Dog Trials on 2nd Thursday after 1st Monday of August. Now owned by the Diocese of Carlisle and used for conferences, holidays etc. Phone 05394 32050.   NY 366064

CHURCH. St Mary. Rydal (OE "ryge": the valley where rye was grown. ME "Rothay-Dale"). 1824. Built by Lady Ann Frederica Elizabeth Le Fleming at a cost of £1500. Octagon spire. Nave, chancel. Stained glass south window by Holiday. 1891. Plate c1670/90. Memorials to Thomas and Matthew Arnold. Wordsworth was Chapel Warden in 1833. The Wordsworths used the left-hand pew in front of the pulpit.   NY 364062

EVENT. Ambleside Sports. Thursday, early August. Cumberland & Westmorland Wrestling, Fell Races, Hound Trails etc., Rydal Park.   NY 3606

HISTORICAL. Dora's Field, Rydal. Known locally as the Rashfield on account of the rushes which once covered it. Wordsworth purchased this land in 1825 on which to build a home should he not continue renting (which he did all his life). He gave the field to his daughter Dora, in which she kept her pony. This is not the site of his poem "I wondered lonely as a cloud… A host of golden daffodils." The inspiration for the poem came from seeing the daffodils at Gowbarrow Park, Ullswater. Now National Trust. The entrance is through Rydal Churchyard.

NY 364062

During the 2nd World War Rydal Hall was retreat of the temporarily exiled Queen Wilhelmina of the Netherlands.   NY 366064

LITERARY. Rydal Mount, Rydal. In 1574 Rydal Mount is recorded in the Parish as a yeoman farmer's cottage owned by the Knotts and then the Keenes. It was greatly enlarged in the C18. It was rented by the then owner, Lady Diana Le Fleming of Rydal Hall who acquired it in 1812, to William Wordsworth in 1813. On May Day, William and Mary, three surviving children, his sister Dorothy and sister-in-law Sarah Hutchinson, moved into Rydal Mount which became their family home for 46 years. William Wordsworth died here in 1850,; his sister Dorothy died here 1855 and Mary, his widow, died here 1859. From here in 1841 Dora married Edward Quillinan, a Lieutenant in 3rd Dragoon Guards (a widower with two small children) of whom Wordsworth disapproved. Wordsworth landscaped the 4½ acres/ 1.82h of garden, much approved of by

Queen Adelaide (Dowager of William IV) who visited the Wordsworths in 1840. Adjoining is Dora's Field (National Trust) given by Wordsworth to his daughter. A mass of daffodils in spring. The house contains many of the poet's personal possessions, family portraits—including the only colour portrait of the poet's sister, Dorothy, and first editions of his works, (he was made Poet Laureate when aged 73 although he wrote no poetry during his term of office), genealogical tables, a case containing the sword of his brother, John, Captain of the *The Earl of Abergavenny*, sunk off Portland Bill in 1805 with tragic loss of lives. Now the home of Wordsworth's great, great grand-daughter, Mrs Mary Wordsworth Henderson—The Mount purchased from the Fleming family in 1969. Open March–October 1000–1730hrs. daily. November–mid January Thursday–Tuesday 1000–1730hrs. Phone 05394 33002. NY 364064

REFRESHMENT. Glen Rothay Hotel—Badger Bar. Rydal. Phone 05394 32524. NY 363062

36 07

WATERFALLS. High Falls and Buckstones Jump Waterfall. Rydal. Follow bridle path close to Rydal Beck for 2 miles/3.2km. High Falls (NY 366068) are reached through gate beside the path which follow upwards to Buckstones Jump on the fell beyond. NY 366077

36 09

WATERFALLS. Rydal Beck and High Fall. Track past Rydal Mount then east through gap in wall before gate into valley. 5 miles/8.04km. Circuit. Easy.
NY 362097

37 00

CHURCH. St Margaret. Wray. 1845. SE tower. Nave & chancel. NY 372007

37 01

ARCHITECTURE. Wray Castle. Built 1840–7 for £60,000. by Dr Dawson of Liverpool using his wife's inheritance from a gin fortune. Later he was bankrupted and the architect died an alcoholic. Towers/turrets/battlements. The castle sold for £25,000. Now owned by The National Trust and let to College of Marine Electronics; known as RMS *Wray Castle*. Interior viewable in July & August, by appointment only. Phone 05394 32320. NY 375010

LITERARY. Wray Castle. Rupert Potter rented castle 1892. His daughter, Beatrix Potter, already drawing animals, encouraged by the Vicar of Wray, Canon Rawnsley. NY 375010

TREES. Handsome specimens in the 64 acres/26ha of Wray Castle grounds, including a mulberry planted by Wordsworth—very near an unusual fern-leafed beech. NY 372010

WALL. Bee Boles. Low Wray Farm. NY 372011

37 02

GARDEN. Stagshaw. Ambleside. National Trust. Overlooks Lake Windermere. Many & varied azaleas, camellias, magnolias & rhododendrons. Created by Cuthbert Acland, Regional agent for National Trust for nearly 30 years who lived at Stagshaw cottages from 1959–1979. Open daily April–end June. 1000–1830hrs. July—to end October by appointment only. Phone 05394 32109. Very limited parking. NY 379027

37 03

ARCHAEOLOGY. Borrans Field (ON "heap of stones"), Ambleside. Galava Fort (remains of) AD 79, protected the road from Brougham over Hard Knott to Ravenglass. Original fort of turf and timber built by Agricola and replaced by a sandstone fort 270ft x 395ft (82m x 120m) housing 4 barracks, headquarters, commandant's quarters and a granary, with slated roofs and glazed windows in AD 100 by Emperor Trajan. It was attacked at least once. In 1963 a gravestone was found on the site (now in the Museum of Natural History and Archaeology at Kendal) inscribed "To the good gods of the Underworld/Flavius Fuscinus Retired/From the Centurionship/Lived 55 years: To the good gods of the underworld/Flavius Romanus, Record-clerk/lived for 35 years/killed in the fort by the enemy." Model of fort in Armitt Museum. (Refer NY 376043). Gold, silver and base metal coins unearthed plus bronze eagle, bronze bell and leather shoes. NY 373034

ARCHITECTURE. The Log House, Lake Road, Ambleside, now a shop selling casual and formal wear, together with a restaurant, is a Norwegian building transported from there in 1905 for Alfred Heaton Cooper's Coniston home. Re-erected here 1914. NY 377037

GARDEN. Hayes Garden Centre—established here for nearly 100 years. Ambleside. Phone 05394 33434. NY 376036

HISTORICAL. Croft Lodge 1830. Its boat house and harbour was site of Clappersgate port, from the wharves of which nearby quarried slate was transported. NY 371036

PLANTS. Deciduous mixed habitat. Skelghyll Wood. (Cumbria Trust for Nature Conservation. Permit required). NY 3703

TOURIST INFORMATION CENTRE. National Park Centre. Waterhead. Ambleside. Phone 05394 32729. NY 377032

TREES. Tulip trees beside lake. Waterhead. Ambleside. NY 3703

WALKS. Jenkin's Crag & Skelghyll. Circuit 3 miles/4.8km. Easy. Splendid views of The Old Man of Coniston through to Langdales and Lake Windermere. Start: path between Ghyll Head Hotel (left) and Romney Hotel (right), opposite Waterhead Hotel. NY 377032

Troutbeck & Wansfell Pike from Ambleside. Circuit 6 miles/ 9.7km. Ascent 1500ft/457m. Strenuous last half. Clear weather essential for panoramic views.

Skiddaw from Surprise View, Borrowdale. (Rosemary Liddle)

Start: path between Ghyll Head Hotel (left) and Romney Hotel (right), opposite Waterhead Hotel, Ambleside. NY 377032

YOUTH HOSTEL. Waterhead Ambleside. Phone 05394 32304. NY 377031

37 04

ARCHITECTURE. Bridge House, Ambleside. Tiny c1650 building on two floors (the main room being only 13ft/3.96m by 6ft/1.8m) spans Stock Ghyll in the centre of town. Built as a summer house and/or apple store-house for the now demolished Ambleside Hall (the home of the Braithwaite family), on Smithy Brow—east. Has been home for a family called Rigg with six children and also a tea-room, weaving shop, cobbler's, pigeon loft, leather store, antique shop and now, National Trust Information Centre. NY 376047

C15 and C17 cottages; earliest vernacular buildings in this area of the original settlement. How Head. Ambleside. NY 378047

CHURCH. St Mary. Ambleside (Hamal's dairy pastures by the river sand banks). 1850/4 designed by Sir G. Gilbert Scott to replace St Anne's. Broached spire of 180ft/54m. Interesting artefacts of C16 & C17. Monuments. Stained glass by Holiday. Mural (tempera applied directly on to plaster) of Rush-bearing Procession by Gordon Ransome, a student during 2nd World War when Royal College of Art evacuated to Ambleside. Bible of 1611 and a Bible presented by Wordsworth's widow. NY 374044

St Anne. Chapel Hill, Ambleside. 1812. West tower. Victorian tracery in lancets. On the site of an Elizabethan chapel. De-consecrated and now residential accommodation. NY 378047

CUSTOMS. Rush-bearing at St Mary. Ambleside. Originally held at St Anne's church on the Saturday nearest St Anne's Day, July 26. Since the de-consecration of St Anne's the parish church of St Mary celebrates the custom usually on the first or second Saturday in July for July 1 is the official celebration of when Mary visited her cousin, Elizabeth (Luke 1: 39–41). A Procession of the local people carrying garlands and rushes parade through the town. The Procession halts at the Market Square when, with emblems raised, the Rush-bearing hymn, written by Wordsworth's friend Revd Owen Lloyd in 1835, is sung. The custom of rush-bearing, said to have originated from a Roman fertility drama, has slowly died out now that rushes have ceased to be needed for warmth and dryness on bare earth floors. (Refer NY 336074). NY 374044

HISTORICAL. The Charlotte Mason College of Education, presently a teacher training college. Founded by Charlotte Mason in 1892 for training governesses. She was founder of P. N. E. U. (Parents' National Education Union.) Her motto was "Education is an atmosphere, a discipline, a life." She based her teaching on natural law and insistence that parents should assist in the education of their children. From Scale How moved to present site, at Green Bank 1891, which a year earlier had been the home of Mrs Dorothy Benson Harrison, daughter of Robinson Wordsworth, relative of William Wordsworth. Charlotte Mason was

Principal until her death in 1923. Thereafter, continued as a private educational establishment until purchased by Westmorland County Council in 1961.

NY 375049

The Old Stamp House, corner of Church Street & Lake Road, Ambleside was Wordsworth's office in his capacity as Distributor of Stamps for Westmorland.

NY 376044

Ambleside Market Place granted its first charter in 1650.   NY 377045

LITERARY. Harriet Martineau, agnostic with radical views but concern for the exploited poor, political economist and novelist, built The Knoll—lived here 30 years. Born in Norwich 1802 and buried in Birmingham 1876. One of 8 children whose father died when she was 24 leaving the family poor so she perforce to write despite ill-health for most of her life, leaving her deaf and with no sense of smell or taste. Best remembered for her *The Complete Guide to the English Lakes* 1855, *Illustrations of Political Economy* 1832/4, *Deerbrook* 1839 and *Autobiographical Memoir* 1877. Her death mask is displayed in the Armitt Collection (above Ambleside library) and also displayed is a sofa, covered in her exquisitely stitched needlepoint. Friend of Wordsworth, Charlotte Bronte (who stayed for a week between publication of *Shirley*, 1849, and *Vilette*, 1853), George Elliot (pseudonym of Mary Anne Evans) & Matthew Arnold.   NY 373048

MUSEUM. The two Misses Armitt, who lived at Rydal Cottage, researched the history of the Lake District and founded The Armitt Collection, a notable assemblage of books, papers, maps & guide books relating to the Lakes, by the Arnolds, both Collingwoods, Harriet Martineau, Beatrix Potter, John Ruskin, Wordsworth and others. Archaeological treasures from Borrans Field. The Armitt Trust, founded 1912 (William Heelis a founder member and his wife Beatrix Potter, who as a member, subsequently donated a unique collection of her Natural History paintings) incorporated the Ambleside Book Society, founded 1828 (of which Wordsworth was a member) and the Ambleside Ruskin Library, founded 1882. Open Monday/Wednesday/Friday, above the Public Library. Ambleside.

NY 376043

TOURIST INFORMATION CENTRE. National Park Information Centre. Old Court House. Church St Ambleside. Open daily. Easter–September. Phone 05394 32582.   NY 376044

National Trust Information Centre. Bridge House. Ambleside. Open daily. Easter–October.   NY 376047

WALKS. Stockghyll and Sweden Bridges. Circuit 5 miles/8km. Moderate. Waterfalls and rustic bridges. Start: Royal Yachtsman Hotel, Ambleside.

NY 377045

Todd Crag & Clappersgate. Circuit 3 miles/4.8km. Easy. Good visibility essential to enjoy panoramic views. Start: St Mary's Church into Rothay Park. Ambleside.

NY 374044

Rydal and summit of Loughrigg Fell. Circuit 6 miles/9.6km. Ascent 1000ft/305m.

Swaledale sheep. (Rosemary Liddle)

Herdwick sheep. (Rosemary Liddle)

Moderate. Very easy to get lost on this fell in mist. Viewpoint superb; almost all the high fells can be seen. Start: Ambleside Police Station.   NY 376046

Fairfield horseshoe. Circuit 11 miles/18km. Ascent 3300ft/1000m. Best clockwise with initial steep ascent of Nab Scar behind Rydal Mount. Strenuous. Great care necessary on Fairfield in mist as its summit is a large flat plateau. Start: Ambleside.
           NY 376046

An Environmental walk—Rothay Valley (ON "raudh a": red river) & Loughrigg. Circuit 2½ miles/4km. National Trust Guide obtainable at the Start: The Bridge House Information Centre, Ambleside.   NY 376047

37 05

LITERARY. Eller How, Ambleside, was a school run by Miss Anne Jemima Clough (sister of the poet Arthur Hugh Clough) who became Principal of Newnham College. One of her pupils was the future Mrs Humphrey Ward, authoress.   NY 379051

37 06

WATERFALLS. Scandale Beck. Ambleside. From the town take lane to Nook End Farm and follow beck upwards to High Sweden Bridge. 4 miles/6.43km. Circuit. Easy.   NY 379065

37 07

WALL. Incorporating terrain, traverse of rock. Stones horizontal regardless of slope; above Rydal.   NY 374077

38 01

EVENT. Windermere Record Attempts. All manner of amphibious crafts and water skiers vie for world records. 2nd week Oct. Low Wood Bay.   NY 385019

38 02

HISTORICAL. Low Wood Hotel originally called the Low Wood Inn. In 1847, local landowners, including William Wordsworth, Thomas Arnold and Professor Wilson (Christopher North), met here in collective opposition to the mooted extension of the railway from Windermere to Keswick through Low Wood. Wordsworth wrote a sonnet to the *Morning Post*: "Is then no nook of English ground secure From rash assault?..."   NY 385021

LITERARY. Dove Nest, Windermere. Now a holiday complex. On slopes of Wansfell. Between 1829–31 the home of the poet Felicia Dorothea Hemans *née* Browne 1793–1835 (buried in Dublin). Her principal works *The Seige of Valencia* 1823, *The Forest Sanctuary* 1825, *Records of Women* 1828 and *Songs of the Affections* 1830. She also wrote "The Boy stood on the Burning Deck."   NY 384025

TREES. Specimens of sequoia & Hondo spruce. Skelghyll Wood. Ambleside.
           NY 3802

VIEWPOINT. Jenkins Crag. Ambleside. On track which leads to Silurian

Skelghyll beds. Fine views of head of Windermere and distant Langdales, Crinkle Crags etc; National Trust. NY 384028

38 04

WATERFALLS. Stockghyll Force. Ambleside. 60ft/18m fall. At rear of White Lion Hotel. Victorian tourists delighted by spectacle, paid 3d to see it. Three local fulling mills were powered by the beck's water as were bobbin, corn, linen, paper and saw mills. NY 385046

39 00

HISTORICAL. During 2nd World War Short Sunderland flying boats were built on what is now White Cross Bay Caravan Park, Troutbeck Bridge. The homes accommodating war time workers demolished and The Lakes School built nearby. NY 396003

In the early 1800s John Longmore an engraver of Troutbeck, unfortunately mentally deranged, spent 6 years carving inscriptions into rocks. One reads "National Debt £800,000,000. O Save My Country Heaven, George and William Pitt." Another rock lists sixteen names including Burns, Scott, Garrick and Professor Wilson. Beneath is "The Liberty of the Press". Two of the rocks are dated 1835 and 1836 respectively. Crag Woods. White Cross Bay. Windermere. NY 391005

MEMORIAL. A white cross erected in the lake at White Cross Bay commemorates the drowning in 1853 of two young men. NY 3900

39 01

ARCHITECTURE. Wood Farm. Troutbeck. Round chimneys. Spice cupboards, one inscribed W. B. M.(William and Mary Birkett) 1685. Some walls 8ft/2.4m thick. Panelling below which are wall writings. NY 394015

LITERARY. Briery Close, formerly the home of Sir James and Lady Kaye-Shuttleworth, where Charlotte Bronte was staying in August 1850 when Mrs Elizabeth Cleghorn Gaskell (*née* Stevenson) first met her. That meeting is recorded in Mrs Gaskell's *Letters* edited in 1966 by J. A. V. Chapple and A. Pollard. She was born in Cheyne Walk, Chelsea in 1810 and died at Holybourne in 1865 and buried in Knutsford. Her works included, *The Life of Charlotte Bronte* 1857, *Mary Barton* 1848, *Ruth* 1853, *Cranford* 1853, *North and South* 1855 and *Sylvia's Lovers* 1863. NY 391019

TOURIST INFORMATION CENTRE. Lake District National Park Visitor Centre. Brockhole (OE "brocc-hol": Badger sett). Lake District wildlife, Geology & History etc., Lectures, exhibitions, displays, reference library, shop with leaflets, maps & books. Cafe rebuilt to original Edwardian style and renamed "Gaddums". Picnic area. Grounds landscaped by Thomas Mawson, a local landscape architect, who also designed those of Langdale Chase Hotel and Rydal Hall, open daily late March–early November. Parties by appointment only. Fee. Phone 05394 46601. House built 1899 by William Henry Gaddum a Manchester businessman. Later sold to Merseyside Hospital Council for use as a Nursing Home. In 1969 purchased by Lake District Planning Board for £65,000. Diversification of chimney stacks.

NY 390010

WHEELCHAIR WALKS. Provided at Brockhole. NY 390010

39 03

WATERFALLS. Hol Beck. Wansfell. Follow Robin Lane from Troutbeck Post Office and then Hundreds Road at the end of which lie the cascades. 3½ miles/5.63km. Circuit. Easy. NY 399034

39 09

WATERFALLS. Caiston Beck, below Middle Dodd, Red Screes. From near Kirkstone Pass car park (NY 402088) a Permissive path leads to Brothers Water. When track from N is met turn S on to it and follow up Caiston Glen. The secluded falls lie SE. 5 miles/8.04km. Circuit. Moderate. NY 393097

Area 19 – Kentmere

40 00

FISH. Holehird Tarn. Depth 10ft/3m. Carp, chub, perch, roach & tench. Along driveway to Holehird Cheshire Home. Day permits only obtainable from garden staff. NY 408008

Trout Beck. Perch & brown trout. Permit from Information Centres at Ambleside or Windermere. NY 4000

HISTORICAL. The records of the Ambleside Turnpike Trust for 1885 indicate that 21,480 carriages crossed over the bridge at Trout Beck. NY 403003

REFRESHMENT. Sun Hotel. Troutbeck Bridge. Phone 05394 43274.

NY 404002

40 01

WALKS. Town End-Skelghyll-Brockhole. Circuit 4 miles/6.4km. Easy Start: Wain Lane from road junction return via Mirk Lane. NY 405019

YOUTH HOSTEL. High Cross Castle, Bridge Lane, Troutbeck. Windermere. Phone 05394 43543. NY 405013

40 02

ARCHITECTURE. Bank barn with spinning gallery, two level access and mullioned windows. Above a door initials "G. E. B 1666." Belonged to the Browne family who stored therein their wool fleeces until sold. Town End. Troutbeck. NY 407022

Town End. Troutbeck. 1623. Built by George Browne for his newly-wed Susannah on site of previous house. Massive round chimneys. Wood mullioned windows. A fine example of a Yeoman farmer's house. Magnificent assemblage of intricately carved built-in furniture, much of it dated. The Browne family lived here for 318 years. Bee Bole, sheltered slate—slab ledge in the side of the house used to hold 3 small plaited straw skeps. Before sugar was imported from the Indies, honey was a staple sweetener and beeswax and mead would also be produced. From 1943 the house in care of the National Trust. Open April/end October Tuesday–Friday, Sunday, Bank Holiday Monday & Good Friday 1400–1800hrs or dusk if earlier. Last admission 1730 hrs; no electric light. Phone 05394 32628. NY 406023

Spinning gallery. Low Fold Farm. Troutbeck. NY 408027

Bank barn 1868. Unusual square ventilators to eaves, perhaps acting as Dovecot. Brow Head, Troutbeck. NY 407027

Bank barn with crow-stepped gables. High Fold. Troutbeck. NY 408028

40 03

WELL. St Margaret's Well, Troutbeck. The village consists of dwellings grouped around communal wells. Nearby are St James, St John and several springs.

NY 409033

40 06

WALKS. Woundale. 2 miles/3.2km to Pike How. Strenuous upper reaches. Entrance to this lonely valley is via a 5 barred gate 1½ miles/2.4km south of the Kirkstone Inn.

NY 409066

40 08

GEOLOGY. The Kirk Stone, so called from at least 1184 because of its supposed resemblance to a church, gave the pass its name; more church-like from north side. Wordsworth wrote of this in his "Ode to the Pass of Kirkstone": "This block—and yon, whose church-like frame, Gives to this savage Pass its name" (lines 47/48). Acoustic properties of the rocks hereabouts promote echoes.

NY 401086

REFRESHMENT. Kirkstone Pass Inn formerly known as The Travellers Rest. At 1481ft/451m one of the highest inns in UK. Built 1840 by Revd Sewell (1781–1869) of Troutbeck. Subsequent vicars of Patterdale held the Licence—it then being common practice for the clergy to own pubs. A burial place was found on digging the foundations. Phone 05394 33624.

NY 402080

40 09

MINE. Kirkstone Pass Mine. Behind waterfall west of road. Trials for copper.

NY 403093

41 00

ARCHITECTURE. Causeway Farm. Troutbeck. C17. First owners, the Philipson family. Much of original oak furnishings remain.

NY 416000

Near Orrest. (ON "Orrusta": battle). Windermere. 1707. Massive round chimney.

NY 419002

GARDEN. Lakeland Horticultural Society in the grounds of The Lake District Cheshire Home, built in 1869 for M. M. Dunlop. In 1889 Beatrix Potter holidayed here with her parents. Unusual trees/shrubs (eucalyptus, mulberry, tree of Heaven, tulip tree), Alpines and Heathers. Open daily all year. Free. Holehird. Troutbeck.

NY 410007

41 01

ARCHITECTURE. Longmire House. Troutbeck. Again a private residence, previously a farmhouse owned by the Longmire family since 1571. Spinning gallery. C16 window panes, one marked 1565, others with Tudor Rose, Tudor Royal Arms, a shield, initials G. B. and E. B. Panelling.

NY 413019

41 02

CHURCH. Jesus Church (formerly Chapel). Troutbeck (trout stream). On site of previous church 1562. West tower 1736, castellated in like manner to the tower of Grasmere Church. Nave & chancel in one. Unusual for a Lake District church—a gallery, with Hanovarian Coat of Arms. Lancet windows. Stained glass showing The Crucifixion and Our Lord as a clean-shaven young man by the illustrious artists Edward Burne-Jones, Ford Maddox Brown and William Morris. (It is said that Brown and Morris were fishing nearby as Burne-Jones was designing the beautiful east window. They ceased their labour and assisted Burne-Jones in his.) Royal Arms of George II (1737) above door. C16 & C17 carved woodwork in chancel from Calgarth Hall. Two collecting shovels 1692. Churchyard memorial to Reverend Sewell who built the Kirkstone Inn. NY 412028

41 03

ARCHITECTURE. Clock cottage—so called because of a clock attached to house end wall. Troutbeck. NY 414038

Spinning gallery. High Green. Troutbeck. NY 412035

Bank barn with unusual hipped roof into which is let a chimney stack. High Green. Troutbeck. NY 410033

REFRESHMENT. Mortal Man. Troutbeck. 1689. Originally The White House. The Inn sign portrays two local farmers; one undernourished and the other ruddy cheeked and rotund and reads, "Oh Mortal man that lives by bread, What is it makes thy face so red, Oh silly ass that looks so pale, 'Tis from drinking Sally Birketts ale." [Birkett at that time being the landlady]. The original sign was painted by the Yorkshireman Julius Caesar Ibbetson (1759–1817) Royal Academician, who lived in Troutbeck 1801–03. Phone 05394 33193. NY 411035

Queens Head. Troutbeck. 1617 coaching inn with spinning gallery now enclosed. Since 1780 a "Mayor of the Hunt" has been enthroned here most years at the Hunt Supper held in February. Originally the Mayor presided over village disputations. Mayor's chair in restaurant. An Elizabethan carved four-poster bed from Appleby Castle forms the "old bar". Phone 05394 32174. NY 414037

41 06

WATERFALLS. Woundale Beck and Trout Beck. Park at Town Head, follow Ing Lane to Hagg Bridge and Troutbeck Park Farm. Then across fell to waterfall on Troutbeck passing the Woundale fall at the edge of Hird Wood. 10 miles/16.09km. Circuit. Moderate. NY 418066

41 08

WATERFALLS. Woundale Beck below Hart Crag. Path from NY 409067. 4 miles/6.43km. Circuit. Moderate. NY 410084

41 09

HISTORICAL. John Bell's Banner. Kirkstone Pass. 2474ft/754m. So called because hereabouts John Bell was stationed to turn the quarry during the hunt. (Banner meaning boundary). NY 410098

42 00

WALKS. Applethwaite Common. Circuit 4 miles/6.4km. Easy. Start on road between Ings and Troutbeck. NY 424006

42 05

ARCHITECTURE. Hagg Bridge. Troutbeck. Dry-stone hump-backed bridge with interesting passage way in west side. NY 421054

Troutbeck Park. Troutbeck. Rare early C19 two-storey building once used as pigsty at ground level with "privy" above. Barn wall has 5 rows of stone "throughs" which bind the walls together. NY 420057

WATERFALLS. Hagg Beck. Troutbeck. Track; Ings Lane, at Hagg Bridge bear right. 4½ miles/7.24km. Circuit. Easy. NY 425056

42 06

MAMMALS. Red deer. Fell ponies. Troutbeck. NY 4206

43 00

ARCHAEOLOGY. High Borrans. Iron Age settlement site about 160yards/ 146m square. Traces of walls, hut circles and a stone with cup markings. NY 437009

ARCHITECTURE. High House. Ings. C16. Massive round chimneys. Walls 9ft/2.7m thick. Stained glass dated 1562. Originally family home of Richard Braithwaite second son of Sir Thomas of Burneside. NY 438005

43 01

ARCHAEOLOGY. Troutbeck. Settlement site. NY 437010

43 05

ARCHAEOLOGY. Remains of Roman road, known as The Scot's Rake. Ill Bell range. NY 4305

43 08

BIRDS. Peregrine falcon nest site. Froswick. Kentmere. NY 4308

44 06

BIRDS. Golden eagle has nested on Rainsborrow Crag. Kentmere. NY 4406

HISTORICAL. Hill-side enclosures known as Grassings, most likely stocked with Galloway cattle in C18 and C19. Kentmere. NY 4406

44 07

HISTORICAL. Kentmere Reservoir. 1848. Helped to regulate the speed of the River Kent, which is the fastest flowing river in UK, falling 1000ft/304m in 25 miles/40km. Its power utilised to run 15 fulling mills and quarries along its course and at Staveley in particular, mills producing bobbins, cotton, gunpowder, woollens & snuff. NY 4407

44 08

WATERFALLS. River Kent waterfall Lingmell Gill. Park at Kentmere church follow track to reservoir and beyond to Kentmere Common. 8 miles/12.8km. Circuit. Easy, then moderate from reservoir.   NY 441089

44 09

WATERFALLS. On River Kent below Hall Cove, Kentmere. From Kentmere church follow track to reservoir and beyond, to the falls. 9 miles/14.48km. Circuit. Easy, then moderate from reservoir.   NY 440095

45 00

MEMORIAL. Williamson's Monument. High Knott. Hugill. Cairn with inscribed tablet "In Memory of Thomas Williamson of Height, in Hugill. Gent who died February 13th 1797. Aged 66 years." Erected 1803.   NY 454001

MINE. Pool Scar Trial. No mineralization.   NY 459008

45 01

CRAFTS. Pottery by Gordon Fox. Sawmill Cottage. Kentmere.   NY 454016

INDUSTRIAL ARCHAEOLOGY. The Diatomaceous clay resulting from the deposited skeletons of microscopic plants (Diatoms) was used in the manufacture of egg-shell finish paint, face powder, floor coverings, insulation bricks, metal polish, paper, plastic, rubber & sound proofing material. Waterford Bridge Kentmere.   NY 456019

MINE. Staveley Mine. Lead. Abandoned 1895. Several exploratory levels hereabouts.   NY 457017

45 02

EVENT. Kentmere Sheep Dog Trials. Millrigg. Last Sunday of August.
                                   NY 458022

GEOLOGY. Kentmere Tarn, now drained, contained Britain's one of two known deposits of Diatomite. (Refer also Skeggles Water, NY 4703). In 1955 and 1959 whilst excavating the Diatomite, the Cape Asbestos Co Ltd. found two perfectly preserved dug-out 4 man canoes of oak; carbon dated as of C14. The better one now in National Maritime Museum and the other, in fragments, now in Kendal Museum.   NY 4502

45 03

GEOLOGY. Glacial lake drained in 1870. Kentmere.   NY 4503

45 04

ARCHITECTURE. Kentmere Hall, now a farmhouse C15. C14 Pele tower (in ruins) vaulted cellar, staircase to 4 storeys. Ancestral home of the Gilpins.
                                   NY 451042

CHURCH. St Cuthbert. Kentmere (the lake of the River Kent). 1866, but roof beams C16 and Norman windows. West tower. Nave and chancel in one. Church named after the C7 hermit who, previously a shepherd in the Lammermuir Hills, died as Bishop of Lindisfarne. Memorial (by Keswick School of Industrial Arts in 1901) to Bernard Gilpin, noted church reformer of C16 "faced the persecution of the Church and the anger of the Queen for truth and duty" having declined the offer of the position of Bishop of Carlisle in order to devote himself to his living at Houghton-le-Spring, Durham. NY 457041

HISTORICAL. Kentmere Hall. Tradition has it that King John awarded the Hall to Richard Gilpin for killing a certain ferocious wild boar. The family produced many heroes, William, killed at Battle of Bosworth Field 1485 and Bernard, born here 1517, noted churchman influential in the progress of the Reformation and known as The Apostle of the North. Sent to the Tower where certain death awaited but, on the journey, his horse fell and Gilpin broke his leg. Before being fit enough to resume his journey Queen Mary I had died and on authority of Elizabeth I he resumed his position of Archdeacon of Durham. He died 1583 at Houghton-le-Spring, Co Durham after being trampled on by a bull in Durham market place. NY 451042

LEGEND. Hugh Hird, a giant of a man, son of a nun expelled from Furness Abbey when she was pregnant lived at Hird House, Troutbeck (NY 419058), in Tudor times. Above the kitchen chimney at Kentmere Hall he alone positioned the 30ft/9m long & 13inch/0.33m by 12inch/0.3m thick beam, 6ft/1.82m above ground level. On account of his prodigious strength King Edward IV summoned him to Court, where he defeated the King's wrestlers in contest. In 1682 while up-rooting a large old tree he died aged 42. NY 451042

WALKS. Kentmere village to Kentmere Reservoir completed 1848 to provide water power to drive machinery along 15 miles/24km of the River Kent. Circuit 6 miles/9.6km. Easy. Parking restricted at Church. Good views of High St. fells. Start walk on quarry tracks and meadow paths. NY 457041

Kentmere, Hartrigg, Kentmere Reservoir & Overend. Circuit 6.5 miles/105km. Ascent 672ft/205m. Moderate. Start: St Cuthbert's Church. Kentmere.
NY 457041

Kentmere Horseshoe. Circuit 12 miles/19km. Ascent 3650ft/1100m. Strenuous. Magnificent views. Start: Kentmere Church. NY 457041

45 06
ARCHAEOLOGY. British Settlement site. Tongue House. Kentmere.
NY 452069

45 07
MAMMALS. Badgers' sett for generations. Tongue Scar. Kentmere. NY 453071

45 09
GEOLOGY. Coniston Limestone. Kentmere. NY 4509

Post Ice Age scenery. Small Water. NY 4509

46 00

ARCHAEOLOGY. Burial mound. Elf Howe, Kentmere. Folk lore believed elves to dwell in burial grounds.   NY 467002

46 02

ARCHAEOLOGY. Mill Riggs. Kentmere. Fortified Celtic site. Hut circles within 4 entranced rampart; ¾ acre site.   NY 461025

46 03

HISTORICAL. Temp Hotel does not now cater for the traveller but was once the Kentmere Inn. It made legal history as first inn to lose its licence [House of Lords lawsuit Sharp v Wakefield] due to out of hours drinking and lawlessness with which the local police were quite unable to deal. Kentmere.   NY 460039

46 04

WATERFALLS. Force Jump. Kentmere. Path from High Lane Kentmere to Longsleddale and after a few yards path sign-posted Mardale. West at next farmhouse to join Low Lane. Further on, east through gate in wall. 2 miles/3.21km. Circuit. Easy.   NY 461044

46 05

FARMING. Overend Farm. Fields continuously down to grass for past 150 years—Kendal Corn Rent Act 1834.   NY 464057

46 09

GEOLOGY. Andesite. Harter Fell.   NY 462095

47 03

GEOLOGY. Skeggles Water. Contains one of two known deposits of Diatomaceous clay. Planning Permission not granted for extraction. (Refer also Kentmere Tarn NY 4502).   NY 4703

47 07

WATERFALLS. River Sprint. Longsleddale. From Sadgill 3 miles/ 4.8km. From Green Quarter Kentmere, over Hollow Moor. 8 miles/ 12.8km.   NY 477078

47 08

INDUSTRIAL ARCHAEOLOGY. Scant remains of cottages, engine shed and light railway. Wrengill Quarry. Longsleddale.   NY 475085

WATERFALLS. At junction of River Sprint and Wren Gill. Longsleddale. Quarry road from Sadgill. 5 miles/8.04km. Circuit. Moderate.   NY 477084

Forces Falls. Swindale. A series of 9 falls. Park near Swindale Foot (NY 521138) and follow Swindale Lane (an old corpse-road from Mardale to Shap) to Swindale Head. 1 mile/1.60km further on the falls are reached, passing Hobgrumble Gill (NY 501113) a vertical fault of several hundred feet. 5 miles/8.04km. Circuit. Moderate.   NY 477084

48 05

GEOLOGY. Silurian series. Longsleddale.   NY 483057

Calcite. Longsleddale.   NY 480057

49 00

WATERFALLS. A series of 3 in Dockernook Gill. Longsleddale. Track from Docker Nook Farm. 2 miles/3.2km. Circuit. Easy.   NY 498009

49 03

ARCHITECTURE. Wad's Howe. Longsleddale. Rare two storey pig-sty/"privy" although latter function now separate.   NY 496032

49 05

GEOLOGY. Coniston limestone. Stockdale. Longsleddale.   NY 491053

Wrynose Pass. (Rosemary Liddle)

AREA 20 – Shap Fells

50 01

GEOLOGY. Valley with glacial features. Longsleddale.   NY 5001

50 02

ARCHITECTURE. Yewbarrow Hall. Longsleddale. C14 tunnel vaulted massive Pele tower adjoined to C17 house. Walls 8ft/2.4m thick.

     NY 504026

Kilnstones Farm, Longsleddale. C16. On site of earlier dwelling inhabited by monks 1263. Originally exterior stone steps led to a loft in which pack-men took a break from their long journeys over the fells. Small building once used as a pigsty on the ground floor with a "privy" on the first floor and a hen-house on the second floor.   NY 502020

CHURCH. St Mary. Longsleddale (OE "slaed": a valley). 1863. Nave, chancel and bellcote. Lancet windows. Chalice 1571 when a record of the church mentioned. C18 oak locker.   NY 501028

LITERARY. Longsleddale is said to be the "Long Whindale" in *Robert Elsmere* 1888 by Mrs Humphrey Ward.   NY 5002

TREES. Native oak woods. Site of Special Scientific Interest. Also broad leaved woodlands. Longsleddale.   NY 5002

51 00

ARCHITECTURE. C17 pack-horse bridge. Nether House. Longsleddale.

     NY 516001

52 02

BIRDS. Bannisdale. Winter: Hen harrier. Occasional.   NY 5202

GEOLOGY. Silurian series. Bannisdale.   NY 5202

52 07

TOPOGRAPHIC. O/S Triangulation point inset at ground level. Great Yarlside.

     NY 524077

53 01

ARCHAEOLOGY. Remains of Hut Circles encompassed by low parapet. Lamb Pasture. Bannisdale.   NY 532019

ARCHITECTURE. Lowbridge House, Bannisdale. 1837. Barge board gables. Family home of the Fothergills.   NY 538011

Grizedale Forest 'architecture'. (Rosemary Liddle)

53 09

GEOLOGY. Erratic; massive granite boulder known as Gray Bull. Wasdale Pike.

NY 539092

54 01

ARCHITECTURE. Forest Hall. Fawcett Forest. On the site of an ancient hall, mostly demolished, remainder of which is used for farming purposes. (Fawcett is mutation of Faudside, an old manorial name; Forest refers to unenclosed moorland devoid of trees).

NY 548012

54 04

ARCHITECTURE. Borrowdale Head. Fawcett Forest. C17. Interesting interior plasterwork.

NY 544042

Salving House, Borrowdale Head, restored. It provided shelter during the autumnal "doctoring" of sheep in bygone days. Each sheep's wool was methodically parted in strips exposing the skin to which was applied a mixture of tar and butter (17lbs/7.7kg of Stockholm tar to 1 gallon/4.5 litres of butter). "Salving" sheep flocks against the dreaded scourge of "Scab" superseded by use of sheep dips, developed in early C20. Compulsory dipping since 1906 has virtually eradicated the disease. "Saving the ship for a ha'porth of tar" is a misquotation; its origin is "salving the sheep ...".

NY 544042

Watergate at NY 274129 (Author)

Area 21 – Ulpha

08 96

ARCHAEOLOGY. Roman fort—Glannaventa, Ravenglass. C4 coins found on site.
SD 088962

TRANSPORT. Ravenglass & Eskdale narrow gauge railway. 40 minute journey to Dalegarth Station from Ravenglass. Daily all year though restricted service in winter.
SD 086966

10 93

REFRESHMENT. Brown Cow Inn. c1800. Waberthwaite. Phone 0229 717243.
SD 106932

10 95

CHURCH. St John Evangelist. Waberthwaite (ON "veithi-buth": hunting/fishing lodge in the clearing). Nave & chancel in one. Bellcote. Windows C16 and C17. Box pew 1807, pulpit 1630. Interesting font. Fragments of C10 cross shaft in vestry and churchyard. Cup and Paten 1576. Altar frontal cover bears the inscription "Vae mihi si non verum praedico" (Woe betide me if I do not speak the truth). Served as chapel for Muncaster Castle and service times dictated by the tides.
SD 100951

10 96

ARCHAEOLOGY. To the west of Muncaster Castle is Walls Castle (SD 088961) the tallest standing Roman building in the north of England. Its sandstone walls 12ft/3.6m high. Once the bath house of Glannaventa, a Roman Fort which lasted for over 300 years, linked with Waterhead, Ambleside by the Tenth Highway (the Wrynose/Hardknott Pass road). Said to have been the home of the Penningtons before they built their castle.
SD 103963

ARCHITECTURE. Muncaster. Modern house enclosing castle built 1258 by Gamel de Mulcastre. C14 pele tower.
SD 104965

BIRDS. British Owl Breeding & Release Scheme. In grounds of Muncaster Castle.
SD 103963

CASTLE. Muncaster. C13 but rebuilt for the 4th Lord Muncaster (of the Pennington family, whose home it still is) in 1862/6 by Anthony Salvin, the fashionable architect of the time. A gold coin of Theodosius I (379–395) discovered in foundations. Library with ribbed ceiling. Drawing room coved ceiling. Billiard room panelling from *Fighting Temeraire* the wooden battle ship painted by the artist J. M. W. Turner. Some stone chimney pieces are Elizabethan. Furniture, tapestries & paintings, one of which is of Thomas Skelton, the Castle's Jester in C17. His antics coined the words "tomfool/tomfoolery". 7 inch/17cm in diameter, glass bowl enamelled in white & gilt, known as a "luck" bowl, of which there are several in Lakeland. King Henry VI gave this bowl to Sir John Pennington who sheltered the King for 9 days after the Lancastrian defeat at Hexham in 1463. This particular "Luck" ensures a male heir, which has held good to this day from the C15. Arboretum. Pele Tower; ground floor has working model trains, other toys and children's reading material. Also a unique collection of Russian soldiers in various States/regional costumes. Bird Garden. Spectacular grounds. Castle open April– Sept. Tuesday–Sunday + Bank Holiday Mondays 1300–1600hrs. Gardens and Owl Centre 1100–1700hrs. Phone 0229 717203/717614.   SD 103963

CHURCH. St Michael. Muncaster (OE "Mula": a personal name—Mula's stronghold). C12. Low; with bellcote. Chancel lower. Mullioned windows in nave. Stained glass by Holiday 1882 & 1887. The west windows are one of the few "Doom" windows in the country, showing both the "saved" and the "lost" at the Last Judgement. Memorials to the Penningtons. C15 east window has Pennington Arms, a mountain cat, carved outside of it. Interesting artefacts C17 & C18. Tablet inscribed "Holie Kinge Harrye gave Sir John a brauce wrkyd glass cuppe… Whylles the familie shold keep hit unbrecken they shold gretely thryve". Churchyard—C10 Cross shaft and wheel head, in the grounds of Muncaster Castle.   SD 104966

EVENT. Muncaster Country Fair & Sheepdog Trials. Muncaster Castle main gate. Sheep, Fell Race, Archery, Clay Pigeon Shooting, Vintage Machinery, Trade Stands etc., August Bank Holiday Monday.   SD 104966

INDUSTRIAL ARCHAEOLOGY. Muncaster. 1455 Corn mill restored 1970s and now working; stone ground flour on sale to the public. Probably a mill on this site before the 1400s. Mill Race over ¾ mile/1.2km. Long, fed by the River Mite. Overshot wheel 13ft/3.9m diameter. 3 pairs of mill stones. Large kiln for drying grain prior to milling. Open April, May, September & October daily except Saturdays 1100–1700hrs. June to August 1000–1800hrs. Fee. Phone 0229 717232.   SD 106964

LEGEND. The ghost of a young carpenter is said to haunt the Tapestry Room of Muncaster Castle. Sir Ferdinand Pennington paid his jester, Thomas Skelton, allegedly a vicious and evil man, to kill the young man who sought to court his daughter. As proof that he had carried out his master's instruction he presented him with the head of the deceased.   SD 103963

NATURE RESERVE/TRAIL. Muncaster Castle. Circuit 2 miles/3km. Passes one of the largest Heronries in the UK—on the Esk estuary. Trail open Easter to October every afternoon except Friday. Guide available at the start.   SD 103963

TREES. Over 100 species in Muncaster Castle Park.   SD 1096

10 97

MINE. Brackenwalls Gill Iron Mine. 2 levels open at SD 102977 and a level and surface workings at   SD 105977

11 90

MINE. Middle Kinmont Mine. Haematite.   SD 118905

11 91

CHURCH. St John Baptist. Corney (OE "Cran": a Heron—hence Heron Island). Bellcote, nave and chancel. Churchyard—gravestones to Richard Pullin died aged 97 and John Noble who died in 1772 at the age of 114. Sundial 1882—gift of Edward Troughton, Corney's famous scientist of 1800s.   SD 112913

11 97

MONUMENT. Chapels Wood. Muncaster. Octagonal tower on promontory overlooking the Esk valley. Three storeys, cross arrowslits, lancet windows & pyramidal roof. To King Henry VI. Shepherds found the King at this spot after his defeat and escape at the Battle of Hexham in Northumberland. Tower built by the Penningtons of Muncaster Castle, to whom the King gave a small glass bowl for his "deliverance"—still on display to this day.   SD 111974

12 97

ARCHITECTURE. Cropple How Farm near Muncaster has the only known surviving plastered woven wattle chimney-hood. The plaster made of clay, dung and straw.   SD 129977

12 98

MONUMENT. Ross's Camp. Muncaster Fell. Erected 1883 at spot where shooting parties stopped for refreshment.   SD 121986

13 90

ARCHAEOLOGY. Corney Fell. Long cairn. Cairnfield.   SD 130903

MINE. Buckbarrow Beck Mine. Copper. 1 level.   SD 136908

13 91

VIEWPOINT. To north west and Isle of Man from Corney Fell 1216ft/370m.   SD 136914

WATERFALLS. Buckbarrow Beck. Corney Fell. Delightful small waterfall between Whit Crags and Prior Park. Path ¼ mile/0.4km N of Buckbarrow Bridge, walk E for 1 mile/1.60km.   SD 137911

13 95

ARCHAEOLOGY. Barnscar. Birker Moor. Settlement site—the so called City of Barnscar or Bardscar. Enclosures. Large hut circles. In C19 early Bronze Age collared urns found under some of the cairns.   SD 133959

13 99

ARCHITECTURE. Cottage—sandstone lintel has decorated markings of the original owner, a blacksmith.   SD 134998

WALKS. Muncaster Fell-Muncaster Mill. Circuit 4.6 miles/7.5km. Ascent

557ft/170m. Moderate. Best to leave car at Muncaster Mill Station on the Ravenglass and Eskdale miniature railway; entrain to Irton Road Station and walk back to start point over Muncaster Fell. Walk starts- SD 137999

14 93

WATERFALLS. Rowantree Force. Waberthwaite Fell. Can be approached by a 3½ mile/5.6km track from Fell Lane near Grange (SD 121938) or by a 4½ mile/7.2km track from SD 179927 at Bigert Mire. SD 145938

14 98

HISTORICAL. On fell above Brant Rake—a hole, approximately 4ft/1.2m diameter and 2ft/0.6m deep. Stone lined and with provision for a lid. Used for keeping fighting cocks in for several days before a contest. SD 1498

MINE. Brant Rake Mine. Haematite. Closed mid 1880s. SD 149985

14 99

REFRESHMENT. George IV Inn. Eskdale Green. C16. Originally named Tatty Garth due no doubt to a nearby potato field, but re-named King of Prussia. Changed to its present name on hostilities with Germany in 1914. Remains of Roman bath house. SD 149998

15 96

ARCHAEOLOGY. Devoke Water, Birker Fell. Cairnfield. SD 151969

FISH. Devoke Water. Largest tarn in the Lake District serves as reservoir for Millom whose Angling Association controls the fishing rights. Legend has it that in C13 Furness Abbey monks stocked the tarn with red trout imported from Italy. SD 1596

PLANTS. Acid moorland habitat. Devoke Water. SD 1596

15 99

MAMMALS. Eskdale. Herdwick sheep, no wool on broad white face, no fringe and long fleece, coarse in summer and fine in winter. Of all the sheep breeds the Herdwick is best able to withstand the worst ravages of a Lake District winter. Ewes have lived for weeks under snow-drifts, surviving by sucking their own wool rich in fat, emerging possibly with a healthy lamb. The wool is hardwearing and is used in tweed manufacture, in the past known as Hodden Grey; and its meat is considered a delicacy. "Herdwyck" derived from tradition of leasing land to a tenant with a "herd" of sheep. Sheep take a long time to know best grazing and shelter on the fells so flock not moved on change of land owner. The flock said to be "heafed", belongs to the farm. Of all sheep breeds the Herdwick has the strongest "homing" instinct and is unlikely to survive if removed from its particular fell. Herdwicks (not unlike the Scandinavian primitive Goth sheep) were introduced by Norse settlers C10. Cumbrian sheep counting numbers, one to ten; Yan, Tyan, Tethera, Methera, Pimp, Sethera, Lethera, Hovera, Dovera, Dick. These are distinctly similar to words used in Old Welsh, Celtic and Breton. SD 1599

16 96

ARCHITECTURE. Abandoned Quaker settlement. Woodend near Devoke Water. SD 167963

16 98

WATERFALLS. Red Gill. Eskdale Green. Park near High Ground Farm (SD 168981) and follow road towards Eskdale Green. After crossing Black Beck take indistinct path north west leading to Red Gill. 2½ miles/4.02km. Circuit. Moderate. SD 165987

17 90

MINE. Bowscale Beck Mine. Copper. Now in a very dangerous condition. SD 172909

17 91

MINE. Logan Beck Mine. Copper. Extensive levels and deep flooded shafts. SD 173916

17 94

MINE. Hesk Fell Mine. Copper. Extensive; 3 levels. SD 175942

17 97

WALKS. Devoke Water. 3 miles/4.8km. Exposed, rough & wet terrain. Superb views. Good visibility essential. Best late summer and early autumn. Start: SD 171976

17 99

MAMMALS. Red squirrel. Eskdale. SD 1799

WATERFALLS. Stanley Ghyll. 37ft/11m fall. 1½ Miles/2.4km from Trough House car park beyond Dalegarth Hall. SD 174995

18 90

WALKS. Beckfoot-Mill Brown-Beckstones. Circuit 4.3 miles/7km. Ascent 475ft/ 145m. Easy. Start: road junction between Beckstones and Beckfoot. SD 187900

18 91

GEOLOGY. Rocks showing glacial scratches. Just past Frith Hall. SD 186916

HISTORICAL. Frith Hall—ruin of C15 Hunting Lodge, later an inn and now a farm (looks like hill-top ruined castle). In C18 marriages in style of Gretna Green performed here. Legend has it that a man was murdered at the inn and his ghost still haunts the ruins. Hudleston family of Ulpha Old Hall. SD 186916

18 92

ARCHITECTURE. C15 farm house with ruined tower—possibly a Pele Tower. Old Hall Farm. Ulpha. SD 182925

LEGEND. Fleeing from a wolf, the lady of the Manor fell to her death in the gorge, the spot thereafter known as Lady's Dub. Hence the fell's name of Ulpha (ON "ulf-haugr": Wolf hill). Near to Old Hall Farm. Duddon.   SD 182925

MINE. Ulpha Copper Mine. Stonegarth Wood. c1860.   SD 186924

18 93

PLANTS. Upland fell habitat. Ulpha Fell. (National Trust).   SD 1893

18 99

MINE. Gill Force and Gate Crag Mines. Haematite. Uneconomic— closed mid 1880s.   SD 180999

WATERFALLS. Birker Force. Eskdale. Park at Trough House car park (NY 172002) and follow track sign-posted Birker Fell. Pass through two gates and then path east sign-posted Boot and Upper Eskdale. 4 Miles/6.43km. Circuit. Easy to strenuous.   SD 187999

19 93

CHURCH. St John. Ulpha (ON "ulf-haugr": Wolf hill). Possibly much older than C16. Low, nave & chancel in one, bellcote. East Windows C17. C17 and C18 wall paintings. Royal Arms of Queen Anne. Unique fruit wood altar and, unusually, a crucifix. Pitch pipe. The church is lauded in Wordsworth's Sonnet XXXI "The Kirk of Ulpha to the Pilgrim's eye is welcome as a star". Lych-gate near to which is a stoup inscribed "J. G. 1766"—most probably of John Gunson, a local farmer. Grave stone to memory of a Whitehaven man "who perished on Birker Moor during the pelting of the pitiless storm on the lst January 1826".
    SD 198932

REFRESHMENT. The Travellers Rest. Ulpha.   SD 197933

TOURIST INFORMATION CENTRE. Post Office. Ulpha. Phone 0229 716255.   SD 197934

19 94

WATERFALLS. Crosby Gill, near Ulpha. Enchanting though small. Best approach is through Low Wood. 2 miles/3.2km. Circuit. Easy.   SD 195949

Area 22 – Torver

20 92
INDUSTRIAL ARCHAEOLOGY. Bloomery—iron smelting forge of C15. Cinder Hill. Duddon. SD 202921

21 90
ARCHITECTURE. Barn with lst floor granary and built-in wooden corn bins. Rare. Hawes Farm. Broughton Mills. SD 214906

21 95
WALKS. Dunnerdale to Seathwaite. Circuit 2¾ miles/4.4km. Easy. Start: SD 213953

22 90
ARCHITECTURE. Fine examples of tile-hung farmhouses—Broughton Mills. Hesketh Hall SD 223908 and Hobkin Ground. SD 228908

REFRESHMENT. Blacksmith Arms. Broughton Mills. C18. Mounting block. Phone 0229 716824. SD 222906

22 92
MINE. Dunnerdale Mine. Yielded 6,555 tons of iron ore between 1872 and 1874. SD 228924

22 95
REFRESHMENT. Newfield Inn. Seathwaite. Dorothy & William Wordsworth stayed here in 1804 where for 4s.6d.(22½p) in total, they secured beds, supper, breakfast, ale and stabling. The bar's slate floor, from Walna Scar quarry, shows clearly the different eruptions of volcanic dust. Phone 0229 716208. SD 227959

22 96
ARCHAEOLOGY. Tiny Druid circle atop Wallowbarrow Crag. SD 222968

BIRDS. Wallowbarrow Crag. Golden eagles showed interest in this site during 1960s. SD 224967

CHURCH. Holy Trinity. Seathwaite (ON "saer": a lake in a clearing). 1874. Bellcote. Aisleless. Royal Arms of George I. Revd Walker worked hard to bring up 12 children but cared for his congregation just as much. Church contains a chair he himself made. Outside the porch is a stone used by the the parson for clipping sheep inscribed "This stone was used/at Gateskell Farm/About the middle of the /18th Century as a Stool/For clipping sheep by/The Revd Robert Walker/Vicar of the/Parish of Seathwaite/Revered by the Title of/WONDER-FUL WALKER." SD 229961

MEMORIAL. Churchyard Grave of "Wonderful Walker" (formerly school-master at Loweswater) Revd Robert Walker, Rector for 66 years. Born Seathwaite 1709 and died 1802 aged 92. Kindly despot of the parish and despite stipend of only £50/annum left over £2000 at his death—much from his work on local farms, sheep clipping, harvesting etc., and his home-brewed beer which he sold to his congregation on Sunday afternoons. SD 229961

22 97

WATERFALLS. Grassguards Gill and Wet Gill. Dunnerdale Forest. From Forestry Commission car park take Permissive path on north bank of River Duddon. 4 miles/6.4km. Circuit. Easy. SD 228978

22 98

ARCHITECTURE. Grassguards. Farm with cobbled yard, on Viking site reputedly. Owned by the Sankey family of late. SD 224981

23 91

WALKS. Upper Lickle near Broughton Mills. Circuit 4 miles/6.5km. Moderate. Quiet & remote. Start: Appletree Worth Beck. SD 239919

23 93

GEOLOGY. Dam or barrage of hexagonal rhyolite across stream. Stephenson Ground. SD 235932

INDUSTRIAL ARCHAEOLOGY. Cylindrical stone lined pit for potash. Bracken burned in late September, resultant ash used for fleece washing or for "fulling" in Broughton Mills. Stephenson Ground. In C16 tenants of certain landowners (in the Lickle valley William de Lancaster) were granted permission to enclose "their" land/ground hence—Carter, Hobkin, Jackson Stanton and Stephenson Ground etc. SD 235931

23 94

VIEWPOINT. Caw (1735ft/528m) Dunnerdale. Wide views. SD 230944

23 96

WATERFALLS. Tarn Beck, just below Seathwaite Bridge, Duddon Valley. Park at Seathwaite church and walk ¼ mile/0.40km upstream. SD 231963

23 99

BIRDS. Barnacle goose, buzzard, merlin, nightjar. Owls: barn, long-eared, short-eared and tawny. Raven, shelduck, sparrow hawk, stonechat, tree pipit, turtle dove. Warblers: garden, grasshopper and wood. Woodpeckers: great and lesser spotted. Spring/summer. Duddon Valley. SD 2399

GEOLOGY. Birks Bridge. Pools, known as "dubs" carved into rocky river bed by abrasive action of swirling water and rocks. Note "flow-through" holes in the parapet of the bridge. SD 234993

WALKS. Birks Bridge-Seathwaite-Dunnerdale. Circuit 6 miles/ 9.6km. Moderate. River Duddon—majestic. Wordsworth's sonnet "The River Duddon"— "Whence that low voice? A whisper from the heart ..." Woodland, fell, riverside and farmland. Start: Birks Bridge. SD 236995

Seathwaite Tarn. Circuit 4 miles/6.4km. Moderate. Some wet areas. Sundew (insectivorous plant) near tarn. Good views down River Duddon plus impressive rock formations. Start: north of Birks Bridge. SD 237995

Dunnerdale Forest–Wallowbarrow–Seathwaite–Tarn Beck. Circuit 6 miles/10km. Ascent 836ft/255m. Moderate. Picturesque. Start: Froth Pot car park. SD 235995

Harter Fell (ON "herter" or "hjartar": the fell of the stag). Circuit 7½ miles/12km. Ascent 2450ft/ 750m. Strenuous. Panoramic views. Start: Birks Bridge.
SD 236995

WATERFALLS. River Duddon. Cascades and deep pools. Birks Bridge Rapids.
SD 234994

24 92

GEOLOGY. Metamorphosed rock exposed at landslip. Appletree Worth.
SD 242922

Coniston Limestone. Appletree Worth. SD 2492

24 98

WATERFALLS. Tarn Beck below Seathwaite Tarn. Dunnerdale. Path starts SD 234984 between Troutal Tongue and High Tongue bearing left to reach Tongue House Farm where a track leads to the falls. Return via Brow Side. 3 miles/4.82km. Circuit. Moderate. SD 240985

25 90

INDUSTRIAL ARCHAEOLOGY. Bloomery site above Climb Stile. Woodland. SD 259901

25 93

GEOLOGY. Coniston limestone. Broughton Moor. SD 2593

25 98

FISH. Seathwaite Tarn. Depth 79ft/24m. Charr and brown trout. Furness Fishing Association controlled. SD 2598

26 93

GEOLOGY. Drumlins and Roches moutonnées. Green Rigg. Torver.
SD 269931

26 94

ARCHAEOLOGY. Bleaberry Haws. Stone circle, 17ft/5m diameter, of seven stones. SD 268945

Bleaberry Haws. Long dyke. SD 2694

26 95

PLANTS. Acid moorland habitat. Torver High Common.   SD 2695

26 96

FISH. Blind Tarn. Depth 23ft/7m. Coniston. Charr & brown trout. Free.
SD 262967

26 97

FISH. Goatswater. Coniston. Depth 47ft/18m. Brown trout. Charr—a member of the salmon family, elusive. Usually caught using plumb line down to 80ft/24m. Free.   SD 266976

GEOLOGY. Dow Crag 2552ft/778m. First climbed 1886 by W. P. Haskett Smith & J. W. Robinson. Fine echoes obtained from opposite shore of Goats Water.   SD 263978

26 99

MINE. Seathwaite Tarn Mine. Copper. 3 levels. Uneconomic and closed c1850.
SD 261993

27 90

BIRDS. Nightjar nest site. Beacon.   SD 2790

FISH. Beacon Tarn. Maximum depth 30ft/9m. Charr, perch, pike & brown trout. Free.   SD 275903

PLANTS. Sundew and butterwort (insectivorous plants) around boggy area of Beacon Tarn.   SD 275903

VIEWPOINT. Beacon Crag. Coniston Water. 836ft/254m.   SD 277907

27 92

GEOLOGY. Fossils—Graptolites (having internal skeletal frame) found in disused quarry near Hazel Hall. Coniston.   SD 270927

27 93

CRAFTS. Fell workshop; pottery, sculpture and wood. Brocklebank.   SD 279938

27 94

ARCHAEOLOGY. Ring cairns on summit of Hare Crags. 100ft/30m diameter with 6ft/1.8m wide bank. Entrance on south east. Torver.   SD 279949

27 96

ARCHAEOLOGY. Enclosures and cairn sites. Torver Beck. Coniston.
SD 276963

PLANTS. Acid moorland habitat. Little Arrow Moor.   SD 2796

WATERFALLS. Banishead Quarry. Torver. Park near bridge over Torver Beck and follow metalled road/bridle-path towards disused quarries. 3¼ miles/5.23km. Circuit. Easy.   SD 278960

27 97

QUARRY. Bursting Stone Quarry. Coniston. Active. Borrowdale Slate. Owned by Burlington Slate Company, named after Lord Burlington who became Duke of Devonshire. In 1771 he acquired several quarries in the area.   SD 279973

27 99

ARCHITECTURE. Well preserved Goose Bield. Its corbelled dry-stone bell-shaped walls served as a fox trap when baited with a dead goose. At approximately 1700ft/518m. on Great How Crags, Levers Water, Coniston.   SD 275998

FISH. Levers Water. Maximum depth 100ft/30m. Brown Trout. Free. SD 2799

HISTORICAL. Levers Water. Coniston. Provided head of water to the mine water wheels, now a reservoir.   SD 2799

Simon's Nick—yawning chasm on Coniston Fell. Simon Puchberger, a German miner about 1600, perished in this stope/nick following a blasting accident.
    SD 279990

28 90

WALKS. The Beacon & Beacon Tarn. Circuit 3¾ miles/6km. Ascent 700ft/213m. Moderate. Wet areas. The Tarn is 26ft/8m deep & contains brown trout. Blawith Fell beacon 835ft/254m provides excellent viewpoint of whole length of Coniston Water. Start: Blawith Common.   SD 289909

28 92

TREES. Juniper bushes, our only native cypress. Its wood, known as "savin" is fragrantly scented, the charcoal of which was used in manufacture of gunpowder C19 and the bitter green berries are still used in the flavouring of gin. Ripe berries are black and extremely sweet. Torver Low Common.   SD 282924

WATERFALLS. Torver Beck, near Coniston Water. Park just below garage on A 5084. Follow left bank of beck upwards. 3½ miles/ 5.63km. Circuit. Easy.
    SD 287926

28 93

WALKS. Torver Low Common. Circuit 2½ miles/4km. Easy. Possible wet areas. Start: lay-by opposite Torver Mill garage then south to path junction, take righthand track up to & around disused reservoir and return.   SD 285932

28 94

CHURCH. St Luke. Torver (ON "torfi's ergh": the peat pastures of...). 1884. Very low with squat buttressed central tower. Weathervane—large green fish. Has Consecration Papers signed by Archbishop Cranmer in 1538 prior to which time the dead had to be carried to Ulverston.   SD 285943

REFRESHMENT. Church House Inn. Torver. Phone 05394 41282. SD 284942

Wheel Gate Hotel. Torver. Phone 05394 41418.   SD 284942

28 96

ARCHAEOLOGY. Ring cairns/Cremation burials. 1000 BC. Henge site; stone bank on 3 sides with 4th side being Torver brook. The burial site was excavated by W. G. Collingwood in 1909, when 2 urns containing bone ash & teeth of a child plus small fragment of woven cloth discovered. Banishead Moor.   SD 285967

28 98

WATERFALLS. Levers Water. Coniston Fells. 54ft/16m. Best views from bridge below falls. (Refer SD 282991).   SD 283987

YOUTH HOSTEL. Coniston Copper Mines. Previously "Red Dell" mines office and manager's home. Phone 05394 41261.   SD 289986

28 99

MINE. Copper mines valley, Coniston. Old engine shaft, ruins of winch house & water wheel. Nearby is tunnel entrance—very dangerous to proceed further than restraints. Peacock ore (blue/green copper ore) hereabouts.   SD 289991

WATERFALLS. Levers Waterfall. Coniston Fells. Start from road opposite Coniston Post Office leading to Coppermines Valley track. 3½ Miles/5.63km. Circuit. Moderate. (Refer SD 283987).   SD 282991

29 90

BIRDS. Coniston Water. Winter: Great northern diver. Scaup.   SD 2990

29 91

LEGEND. Peel Island reputed to have been the hide-out of Adam de Beaumont's band of Yorkshire outlaws who terrorised the locality 1346/1363.   SD 295919

LITERARY. Peel Island. Coniston Water. Formerly known as Montague Island after the Lords of the Manor. Ancient inhabitation remains have been found. National Trust owned and landing by boat permitted. Setting for Wildcat Island of Arthur Ransome's *Swallows and Amazons* 1931, which he wrote when staying at the Newby Bridge Inn.   SD 295919

W. G. Collingwood M.A., F.S.A. One time Professor of Fine Art at Reading University was also President of the Cumberland and Westmorland Antiquarian Society. Wrote several books, *The Lake Counties, Lake District History,* etc., He was an authority on Norse. His character "Thornstein of the mere" lived on Peel Island.   SD 295919

29 92

INSECTS. Large caddis (*Anthripsodes nigroervosus*). Oxen House Bay. Coniston Water.   SD 292921

29 97

PLANTS. Rare royal fern (*Osmunda regalis*), parsley fern, black-stalked spleen-wort. Church Beck. Coniston.   SD 296979

29 98

GEOLOGY. Roches moutonnées beside Church Beck. Coniston.   SD 294982

Coniston limestone—fossils. Church Beck. Coniston.   SD 294980

MINE. Coniston Copper Mines. They extend to Levers Water (SD 280993). Some cobalt ore and nickel. From Roman times. In 1850s output was 3,000 tons of copper pyrite per annum but steady decline thereafter due to foreign competition. Closed 1915. Many lodes the principal of which is known as Bonser Vein at 1530ft/466m below the surface.   SD 290985

WATERFALLS. Church Beck, Coniston. Best seen just before Miners Bridge.
SD 294981

Tarn Hows. (Rosemary Liddle)

AREA 23 – Hawkshead

30 94

BIRDS. Cormorant roost. Fir Island. Coniston Water.   SD 306942

LITERARY. Arthur Ransome lived at The Heald on Coniston Water 1940–45.
SD 307942

30 95

INDUSTRIAL ARCHAEOLOGY. Bloomery site. Hoathwaite Beck, where it flows into Coniston Water.   SD 303953

30 96

ARCHITECTURE. Coniston Hall. C16 farmhouse with 4 massive square & round chimneys: quite unusual for such a remote house to have four hearths. The Le Flemings lived on this site from 1250. Their wealth accumulated from the Coniston copper mines which they owned plus vast tracts of the surrounding area. The family moved to Rydal Hall in C18—the Wordsworths were their tenants at Rydal Mount. Wordsworth wrote of the Hall in *The Prelude*, book II.   SD 305963

EVENT. Coniston Country Fair. Country pursuits & Trade Stands. 1st Sunday in August. Coniston Hall.   SD 305963

HISTORICAL. Bowmanstead, so called after its garrison of bowmen (archers) for the defence of Coniston Hall. Coniston Water.   SD 301968

30 97

CHURCH. St Andrew. Coniston (ON "Kunungstun": the King's manor). 1819. On site of original building 1586. Embattled west tower. Chancel and embattled bays 1891. West window stained glass by Kempe. Plate 1632.   SD 302976

Sacred Heart of Jesus. Roman Catholic. 1872. Coniston.   SD 301974

CRAFTS. Little Arrow Pottery, Coniston. Daily except Wednesdays during summer.   SD 3097

MEMORIAL. Coniston. "In Memory of Donald Campbell C. B. E. who died on January 4th 1967 while attempting to raise his own world water speed record on Coniston Water". His record of 260.35 mph/418.98km accomplished in 1959.   SD 303976

John Ruskin (1819–1900) buried in NE corner of St Andrew's churchyard beneath an Anglo Saxon style cross, the head of which is Tilberthwaite slate and the shaft of Elterwater slate. Designed by his secretary W. G. Collingwood to represent a pictorial biography. Bears among its decoration by a Mr Miles a Swastika (sign of the Scandinavian God of Thunder) and a menorah (7 branched candelabrum used in Jewish worship—but here representing *The Seven Lamps of Architecture* which he wrote in 1849). SD 302976

MUSEUM. Ruskin Museum. The Institute. Yewdale Road. Coniston. Local history—in particular, Ruskin, Lake District minerals. Greek lace pattern, brought back by Ruskin, now rarely crafted in the Coniston area though popular at turn of century. Original drawings by the late Alfred Wainwright, Lakeland's best known author of guide books. Open March/Oct. Daily 0930–1730hrs. Fee. Phone 05394 41387. SD 3097

REFRESHMENT. Black Bull Inn. Coniston. C16. The artist, J. M. W. Turner stayed here 1797 and De Quincey often visited. Landlord in late C18, John Robinson, married one of "Wonderful Walker's" daughters. Phone 05394 41335. SD 301975

Crown Hotel. Coniston. Phone 05394 41243. SD 302976

Sun Hotel. Coniston. C18. Donald Campbell used the hotel as a base during his several attempts at the World Water Speed Record. Phone 05394 41248. SD 301975

TOURIST INFORMATION CENTRE. 16 Yewdale Road, Coniston. Open April–October 1000–1700 hours. Phone 05394 41533. SD 304975

WALKS. One of the starting points for ascending "The Old Man of Coniston"— very possibly from the Welsh "Allt Maen", steep or high rock; also in Elizabethan times a miner was known as an "Old Man". 2631ft/802m. Disused slate quarries and copper mines along the way. SD 300976

Walna Scar and west shore of Coniston Water. Circuit 7 miles/11 km. Moderate. Wet areas. Takes in Bronze Age road between Coniston and Seathwaite. Slag from ancient bloomeries might be found on shore-line. Start: Coniston village. SD 300976

Wetherlam and Old Man of Coniston. Circuit 7½ miles/12km. Ascent 3825ft/ 1170m. Strenuous. Start: Coniston village. SD 300976

Coniston Copper Mines Valley & Levers Water. Circuit 4 miles/6.4km. Strenuous. Pre C16 mines but closed C19 & C20. Some shafts 1000ft/304m deep. Start: Black Bull Inn. Coniston. SD 300976

30 98
MAMMALS. Badgers. Yewdale Fells. Coniston. SD 301982

YOUTH HOSTEL. Holly How. Far End. Coniston. Phone 05394 41323. SD 303981

30 99
PLANTS. Upland valley habitat. Yewdale. SD 3099

WATERFALLS. The White Lady. White Gill. Coniston. The falls, between Mart Crag and Yewdale Crag can be seen from Coniston village though in dry periods they disappear. There is an old lime-kiln near the foot of the waterfall. SD 3099

31 95

HISTORIC HOUSE. Brantwood. Coniston Water. Originally a cottage 1797 (now the entrance hall & study). Chief home of John Ruskin, from 1872 until his death on 20 January 1900. Purchased unseen from J. W. Linton, a wood-engraver and poet and Mrs Linton the novelist, for £1500. Much building work in this period. When he came to inspect his purchase he found "a mere shed of rotten timber and loose stone". Splendid views of Coniston Water from his turret bedroom. The remaining art collection includes work by William Henry Hunt, Burne-Jones & Samuel Prout, as well as some of Ruskin's drawings and paintings. Documents, furniture and Wainwright exhibition. Bookshop. Refreshments. The coach house contains his boat *Jumping Jenny*. Open mid-March to mid-November daily 1100–1730hrs. Mid-November to mid-March, Wednesday to Sunday 1100–1600hrs. Fee. Phone 05394 41396. SD 313958

LITERARY. John Ruskin, writer on social subjects and art, born Hunter Street, Holborn, London 1819. Educated Christ Church College, Oxford where he won the Newdigate prize for poetry. Married Euphemia Chalmers Gray in Perth 1848 but she divorced him for non consummation of the marriage. She then married John Millais the painter in 1854. Between 1855–8 Ruskin was involved in the building of University Museum, Oxford. In 1869 he became Slade Professor of Art at Oxford. Died 1900—buried St Andrew's Churchyard, Coniston. Memorials in Westminster Abbey, London, Keswick (Area 7. 26 22) and Oxford. Best works: *The King of the Golden River* 1841, *Modern Painters* 1843, *The Stones of Venice* 1851–3, *The Winnington Letters* (edited by V. A. Burd in 1969), *Fors Clavigera* 1871–84 and *Praeterita* 1885–9. His influence felt by such people as Marcel Proust, Octavia Hill (a joint founder of the National Trust), Leo Tolstoy and later, Mahatma Gandhi. SD 312958

NATURE RESERVE/TRAIL. Brantwood. Coniston Water. John Ruskin's home 1872–1900. Ruskin's stone seat. Ice house. Beck Leven trail in oak woods. Circuit 3½ miles/5.5km. Easy. Open Easter–October daily except Saturdays. From November to February by appointment only. Guide available at house. Woodland garden for the disabled. SD 312958

PLANTS. Quillwort—unusual habitat, normally at altitude. Coniston Water. SD 311958

WATERFALLS. Brantwood. Follow yellow markers on Nature Trail (small fee). 4 miles/6.43km. Circuit. Easy. SD 312954

31 97

FISH. Coniston Water. Owned by Rawdon-Smith Trust.(Old name—Thurstainwater/Thurston Water). 5¼ miles/8.4km long, ½ mile/0.80km wide. 143ft/43m above sea-level. Maximum depth 184ft/56m. Average depth 79ft/24m. Charr, eel, perch, pike & brown trout. No permit required. Boats may be hired at Coniston village. 10 mph/16km per hour speed limit—though attempts at official and international speed records approved. SD 3197

HISTORICAL. Tent Lodge. In 1805 a tent was erected here (then known as Townson Ground) to accommodate the very pretty Elizabeth Smith, born 1776, died of consumption 1806, aged 29. She was accomplished in French, German, Greek, Hebrew, Italian, Latin, Spanish and also knowledgeable in Arabic & Persian. Her translation of the Book of Job won meritorious acclaim. The June 1846 edition of *The Englishwomen's Magazine* stated that "she was a living library". Alfred Tennyson, poet, stayed at Tent Lodge while on honeymoon in 1850.

SD 318974

The Labyrinth, once a well tended maze long overgrown. Coniston.   SD 313979

TRANSPORT. *Gondola*. Twin cylinder 60 horsepower engine—near silent steam power and very smooth. Unable to sail in windy conditions. Built 1859 at a cost of £1,100 to a design of Sir John Ramsden by Jones & Quiggan of Liverpool for Furness Railway Co., the Chairman of which was the Duke of Devonshire of Coniston Hall—hence the ducal coronet surmounted by a bifurcated serpent atop the curved prow. 85ft/30m long and with a beam of 14ft/4m, accommodating 86 passengers. In service until 1937 when the hull served as a house-boat. In 1963 she sank but has been lovingly restored by the National Trust to her former glory of Victorian splendour, at Vickers shipyard at Barrow in Furness. Re-launched in 1980—the ceremony performed by Mrs Howell, great granddaughter of Captain Hamill, Master of the *Gondola* from 1863–1913. Phone 05394 412888. Water Head Pier. Coniston Water. If a demand—sailings from mid March to the end of October.   SD 311972

31 98

ARCHITECTURE. Spinning gallery. Cruck built. Boon Crag Farm. Coniston.

SD 316984

TREES. Arboretum—specimen Himalayan silver fir, western hemlock & mountain hemlock. Monk Coniston Hall. Private.   SD 3198

VIEWPOINT. Of Coniston Water from grounds of Monk Coniston Hall now a Holiday Fellowship Centre. Previously home of James Garth Marshall, M. P. for Leeds, scholar in the geology of the area.   SD 318983

31 99

ARCHITECTURE. Yew Tree Farm. Near Coniston. Excellent example of a typical Cumbrian spinning gallery. The rear of the farmhouse is cruck built with new wing added 1743. National Trust. No access.   SD 319998

INDUSTRIAL ARCHAEOLOGY. Pot lime kiln near High Yewdale Farm. Coniston.   SD 315997

WALKS. Holme Fell. Coniston. Circuit 3 miles/4.8km. Ascent 900ft/295m. Moderate. Good view Yewtree Farm, long view of Coniston Water and panoramic views of surrounding high fells. Start: Shepherd's Bridge.   SD 314999

WALL. Double row of bee boles. High Yewdale Farm. Coniston.   SD 315997

32 90

TREES. Some lime trees 1000 years old along Bell Beck, Linsty (ON: path of the limes) Hall Wood.   SD 329902

32 91

INDUSTRIAL ARCHAEOLOGY. Bloomery site. Satterthwaite Moor.

SD 328916

32 96

BIRDS. Mallard and teal nesting site. High Man Tarn. Grizedale Forest.

SD 329964

32 99

FISH. The Tarns—Tarn Hows. Perch, roach and rudd. Permit required—enquire locally.   SD 3299

VIEWPOINT. Tarn Hows, created in the main by Man.   SD 329996

WALKS. Glen Mary, Tarn Hows & Tom Heights. Circuit 3 miles/ 4.8km. Ascent 700ft/213m. Moderate. Best in good weather—mid week to avoid crowds. Start: lay-by north of gill.   SD 322999

Tarns Hows. A N/T Survey found that only 1 in 10 visitors walk around the tarn. Circuit 2¾ miles/4.5km. Ascent 600ft/180m. Easy. Start: National Trust car park.

SD 326995

WATERFALLS. Tarn Hows. 3 spectacular falls. Park N of Glen Mary Bridge and take path through Lane Head Coppice. 2½ miles/ 4.0km. Circuit. Moderate.

SD 326999

33 90

INDUSTRIAL ARCHAEOLOGY. This area, known as Force Forge from its early iron forges—some C17. Two bobbin mills, subsequently developed, the north mill was on original site; the south mill now a private residence.   SD 339909

33 91

WATERFALLS. Rusland Force near Satterthwaite.   SD 339911

33 92

ARCHITECTURE. Satterthwaite. Bank barns, near church, converted to other uses.   SD 338923

CHURCH. All Saints. Satterthwaite (the summer farm in a clearing). 1840 on site of earlier church. Short castellated tower. Diagonally angled south west porch—unique. Overall built of dressed slate. Lych-gate.   SD 338924

REFRESHMENT. The Eagles Head. Satterthwaite. Phone 0229 860237.

SD 338922

33 94

ARCHITECTURE. In 1970 the barns and stables of the demolished Grizedale Hall converted to The Theatre in the Forest at which top actors and musicians are billed. Seating for 229 people. Bookings—phone 0229 860291.   SD 335944

BIRDS. Black grouse. Grizedale Forest.   SD 3394

CAMPSITE. In ornamental grounds of Grizedale Hall demolished 1957. During the Second World War the Hall was used as prisoner of war camp for German Officers. Franz Von Werra, *Luftwaffe* pilot, was the only escapee from here but soon recaptured. Then sent to Canada from where he escaped to USA and returned to Germany, via Mexico, Peru, Bolivia, Brazil and Spain reaching Berlin 18 April 1941. On 25 October 1941 his plane dived into the sea. He is presumed to have drowned. Film made of his exploits, *The One that Got Away*.   SD 336942

FISH. Grizedale Beck. Brown trout. Permit by post from The Forestry Commission. Grizedale. Ambleside.   SD 3394

GEOLOGY. Silurian series. Silurian Way trail. Grizedale Forest.   SD 3394

MAMMALS. Deer—red and roe and polecat. Observation hides—permit required. Also Deer Museum open daily March–November. Grizedale Forest. Phone 0229 860373.   SD 3394

MUSEUM. Forestry Commission; local industries & trails. Grizedale.   SD 3394

NATURE RESERVE/TRAIL. Silurian Way. Circuit 9 miles/15.5km. Steep and rough sections. Guide obtainable from start at Grizedale Visitor Centre.
SD 335944

Millwood Forest trail. Circuit 1 mile/1.6km. Guide obtainable from start at Grizedale Visitor Centre.   SD 335944

PLANTS. Pinewood habitat. Grizedale. (Forestry Commission. Permit required).
SD 3394

WHEELCHAIR WALK. Provided at Grizedale Visitor & Wildlife Centre. Grizedale. Hawkshead. Phone 0229 860373.   SD 335944

33 98

CHURCH. Baptist Chapel 1678—restored. Graveyard. Hawkshead Hill.
SD 338987

WATERFALLS. Above Hawkshead Hill. 20ft/6m fall. Park at Hawkshead Hill and walk east through gate on right taking the right-hand path to a farm then right again to a gate giving access to the beck. 1½ miles/2.41km. Circuit. Easy.
SD 336985

33 99

MEMORIAL. "National Trust. The Tarns are given in memory of Sir James Scott of Yews and of Anne Lady Scott 1930." Originally several small tarns called Monk Coniston Tarns. c1919 dam built and marshland drowned, to provide a head of water to power Coniston's saw mill. One of the finest views of Lakeland from this point. Tarn Hows.   SD 330996

VIEWPOINT. Superb view of the south lakes and tarns in good weather. Hawkshead Hill.   SD 336992

34 94

FISH. Grizedale Tarn. Depth 6½ft/2m. Minnow, 3-spined stickleback. SD 346943

34 98

ARCHITECTURE. Hawkshead Hall. Manor House of Furness Abbey monks c1410—traceried window in gate-house. From C16–C18 the home of the Nicholson and Copely families.   SD 349988

HISTORICAL. C15 Courthouse, Hawkshead. Once held by Furness Abbey. Local life and history; coppicing, charcoal burning, local iron industry & charr fishing. National Trust. April to end October. 1000–1700hrs. Free admission. Key from National Trust Shop. Main Square, Hawkshead.   SD 349989

34 99

ARCHITECTURE. C16 cruck-built barn. Field Head Farm. Hawkshead.
SD 348999

35 95

HISTORICAL. Esthwaite Hall. Birthplace of Edwin Sandys 1519–88. For his support of principles of Reformation imprisoned in Tower of London by Queen Mary. Later appointed to provide new translation of the Bible. Became Bishop of London and then Archbishop of York 1576. Founded Hawkshead Grammar School.   SD 358958

35 96

ARCHITECTURE. Esthwaite Lodge. 3 bays & Doric porch.   SD 354968

LITERARY. Francis Brett Young (1884–1954), physician, novelist and poet, spent his summers at Esthwaite Lodge between 1928–1933. Wrote *The House under the Water* 1932. He also wrote *Deep Sea* 1914, *The Dark Tower* 1914 and *White Ladies* 1935.   SD 354968

YOUTH HOSTEL. Esthwaite Lodge. Hawkshead, Ambleside. Phone 09666 36293.   SD 354968

35 97

BIRDS. Winter: greylag geese, tufted duck. Esthwaite Water.   SD 3597

FISH. Esthwaite (ME "Estwater": the eastern clearing). Owned by the Sandys family. 1½ miles/2.4km long and ¼ mile/0.4km wide. 217ft/66m above sea-level. Maximum depth 80ft/24m. Controlled by Hawkshead Trout Farm. Foldgate. Hawkshead. Phone 09666 541. Bitterling* (*Rhodeus amarus*), charr, eel, perch, pike, roach, rudd, salmon, brown & rainbow trout. Rowing boats may be hired.

---

* Bitterling introduced into these waters—depends on freshwater mussels for its reproduction.

Permit—from Post Office Hawkshead. Game Fish Licence from North West Ltd. New Town House, Buttermarket St. Warrington, Cheshire. Phone 0925 234000.

SD 3597

LEGEND. North shore of Esthwaite Water—oval shaped tarn named Priest's Pot so called because just enough water to satisfy a Priest's thirst. Very possibly the Hawkshead Hall monks' fish pond. SD 357978

PLANTS. Very rare North American aquatic (*Hyrilla lithuanica*). Likely introduction by botanist. Esthwaite Water. SD 358975

WALL. Flagstones, behind Hawkshead church. SD 351979

35 98

ARCHITECTURE. Hawkshead Hall. Gatehouse C15. Stepped gables. Built by Furness Abbey monks, from which they conducted an extensive woollen business. Justice administered from here. Gallows sited on nearby hill. A niche over the entrance contained a statue of St Mary, Patron of Furness Abbey. SD 350988

Minstrels Gallery. C15. Originally the Crown & Mitre. Hawkshead. SD 352983

Town Hall 1790. Market Square, Hawkshead. Used to be five open-arched shops called The Shambles, from which butchers exhibited their wares on market day. Many C17 houses and some still have external stone staircases. SD 352982

Barn c1850. Cattle underhousing, grain/hay above. Contiguous to Town End Cottage. Colthouse. SD 359981

Beckside Cottage. Colthouse. 42 paned C18 window—only one pane opens for ventilation. SD 358983

CHURCH. St Michael and All Angels. Hawkshead ("Haukr-Saetr", the homestead of Haukr). C15. Murals—James Addison (of Kendal church fame) credited with painting north aisle ("sentences of Scripture decently flourished") 1680. William Mackreth added the one over the pulpit c100 years later. Effigies of the parents of Archbishop Sandys of York in chapel at east end of north aisle. The Archbishop who founded Hawkshead Grammar School in 1585, rebuilt the north aisle in 1578. By north door hangs a "Burial in Wool Certificate". (An Act of Parliament decreed woollen shrouds for the dead in an effort to stimulate the wool industry. "Corps was nott put in wrapt or wound up or buryed in any shirt shift sheet or shroud made or mingled with flax hempe silke haire gold or silver or other than what is made of sheeps wooll only"). More than 200 such certificates were issued. Peal of 8 bells—2 added in 1958 to the 6 of 1765 cast by James Harrison of Barrow, Lincolnshire. 1693 sun dial complete save for gnomon, in NE corner of churchyard. Church situated on higher ground commanding wide views of fells and Esthwaite Water. Originally whitewashed but roughcast removed 1875 to reveal Silurian stone with sandstone to windows and doors. Alongside east wall are stone seats upon which Wordsworth used to sit. SD 351980

Methodist Chapel. Hawkshead. Quaint. Originally a Unionist chapel (for all Denominations) dedicated 20 November 1862. SD 352983

Friends Meeting House. Colthouse. 1688 and still used as such today. Georgian windows to front. A separate meeting room for women was above lobby. Interesting C18 furniture. Burial ground of 1658, one of the earliest in the country.
SD 359982

EVENT. Hawkshead Agricultural Show. Sheep, Horses, Ponies, Show Jumping, Hound Trailing, Carriage Driving, Handicrafts, Produce, Trade Stands etc., 3rd Tuesday of August.
SD 3598

GEOLOGY. Slate fence; Colthouse.
SD 357984

INDUSTRIAL ARCHAEOLOGY. Remains of part of a circular building for a "Horse engine/Gin". No machinery remains. Town End. Colthouse.
SD 359981

LITERARY. Grammar School, Hawkshead. Founded 1585 by the then Archbishop of York, Edwin Sandys as The Free Grammar School. Granted its Charter in 1588 by Queen Elizabeth I to educate 100 scholars. Wordsworth educated here with his brothers, 1779/1787. William left here to go up to St John's College, Cambridge. A desk bearing his initials is on view. Reconstructed rooms as they were in C18. Housekeeping ledger (showing board at 12 guineas per annum) of Ann Tyson, with whom Wordsworth lodged before she moved to Colthouse in 1784. He made reference to the Tyson's property in Colthouse in *The Prelude*— "Nor that unruly child of mountain birth,/The froward brook, who, as soon as he was boxed/Within our garden, found himself at once ..." [Book IV 50–53]. Wordsworth's first recorded poem honoured the Grammar School's Bicentenary.

Windermere from Orrest Head. (Author)

Open March–October Monday–Saturday 1000–1700hrs (closed 1230–1330hrs). Sunday 1300–1700hrs. Fee.   SD 352982

Anne Tyson's cottage, now named Wordsworth Lodge. Hawkshead. Wordsworth and his brothers also boarded here while at the Grammar School.   SD 354980

Anne Tyson's cottage—Greenend. Colthouse. Here Wordsworth and his brothers lodged following the death of Hugh Tyson, a joiner, in 1784, the widow having moved from Hawkshead.   SD 357983

MUSEUM. Beatrix Potter Gallery. Main Street. Hawkshead. Housed in her husband's solicitors offices—a selection of her original drawings and illustrations for her childrens books. Open April–end of October Monday to Friday 1030–1630hrs. Entrance by timed ticket. National Trust. Phone 05394 36355.   SD 352983

NATIONAL TRUST SHOP. Main Square, Hawkshead. Phone 05394 36471.
                                                                SD 353982

REFRESHMENT. Red Lion (known as Pig & Whistle in C15). Hawkshead. Below front eaves two small busts of local men, man with whistle and man with pig. Phone 05394 36372.   SD 352982

Queens Head. Hawkshead. C16. Curious artefact in the form of a giant clog. Phone 05394 36271.   SD 352983

TOURIST INFORMATION CENTRE. National Park Centre. Main car park, Hawkshead. Leaflets, maps, guides, nature trails etc., Open daily Easter–September. Phone 05394 36525.   SD 353981

WALKS. Hawkshead-Blelham Tarn-Wray Castle & Latterbarrow. Circuit 6 miles/ 9km. Ascent 885ft/270m. Moderate. Panoramic view from Latterbarrow. Some steep sections and possible wet areas. Start: Hawkshead car park.   SD 354981

35 99

ARCHITECTURE. Belmount. Late C18. 5 bays, doorway with Tuscan column.
                                                                SD 352993

HISTORICAL. Outgate, Hawkshead. Supposedly named thus, being point where commons began and enclosures ended.   SD 356998

LEGEND. Outgate, Hawkshead. Supposedly home of a witch who transformed herself into a hare. Despite regular chasing by the local pack of hounds—was never caught.   SD 356998

REFRESHMENT. The Outgate Inn. Hawkshead. Phone 05394 36413.
                                                                SD 356998

36 95

PLANTS. Lake habitat. Esthwaite Water.   SD 3695

REFRESHMENT. Tower Bank Arms. Near Sawrey. National Trust owned. Beatrix Potter illustrated the pub in *The Tale of Jemima Puddle-Duck*. Phone 05394 36334.   SD 368957

36 96

GEOLOGY. Drumlin. East of Esthwaite Water. SD 3696

37 90

ARCHITECTURE. Low Graythwaite Hall. C16 Seat of the Rawlinsons. Interesting topiary. SD 372909

LEGEND. Silver Holme Island, Lake Windermere, reputed to be repository of a silver horde. SD 377907

37 91

ARCHITECTURE. Graythwaite Hall. Elizabethan but much remodelled other than at rear. Gothic windows, arches and interesting gables. House not open to the public. SD 371913

GARDEN. Graythwaite Hall. Present home of the Sandys family. 7 acres/2.8ha of formal garden landscape by Thomas Mawson a Victorian who published his treatise *The Life and Work of an English Landscape Architect*. Azaleas & rhododendrons. Open daily April–June 1000–1800hrs. Phone 05395 31248. SD 371913

37 93

INDUSTRIAL ARCHAEOLOGY. Site of iron-furnace 1711 but later site of a bobbin mill and, latterly, a joiners. The Forge, Cunsey Beck. Windermere. SD 378937

37 95

ARCHITECTURE. Fold Farm. Far Sawrey. House dated 1700, good example of the period. Round chimneys, thick rendered walls. Slate built barns. SD 379954

CHURCH. St Peter. Far Sawrey (the far sour muddy lands). 1866/72. North east tower, aisleless, transepts & lancet windows. Interesting stained glass, especially one of the Good Samaritan; St Celia window, south wall, portraying Beethoven music score. Stands in open fields. SD 378951

HISTORIC HOUSE. Hill Top, Near Sawrey. C17. Beatrix Potter's farmhouse, which she purchased as an investment when aged 39 and just prior to her engagement to Norman Warne, the publisher, against parental wishes. He died within a few months. Now owned by National Trust. Her furniture, china and paintings on view. Most of her best loved books were written here. Open April to end of October on Mondays, Tuesdays, Wednesdays and Saturdays 1000–1730hrs. Sundays 1400–1730hrs. The House is closed on Thursdays & Fridays but the shop is open daily 1000–1300 & 1400–1730hrs. Phone 05394 36269.

SD 370955

LITERARY. Beatrix Potter, born 1866 in London and died 22 December 1943. From 1896 lived with parents at Near Sawrey in rented house (Eeswyke). She bought Hill Top in 1905—but never lived there, retaining the tenant, John Cannon, as farm manager. Thereafter she used the house as a retreat. Until 1913, when she married William Heelis, solicitor, whom she had engaged for property transactions, she wrote and illustrated 13 or so books *The Tale of Peter Rabbit* 1900, *The Tale of the Tailor of Gloucester* 1901, *The Tale of Squirrel Nutkin* 1903, *The Tale of Tom Kitten* 1907, *The Tale of Samuel Whiskers* 1908, *The Tale of Jemima Puddle-Duck* 1908. Also the *Journal of Beatrix Potter* 1881–1897 edited by L. Linder in 1966. Thereafter, she devoted herself to farming matters especially the breeding of Herdwick sheep and the buying up of farm property, eventually to be passed to the National Trust. Through her generosity and far-sightedness over 4000 acres/6437 hectares of the Lake District have been preserved for the nation.

SD 370955

REFRESHMENT. Sawrey Hotel. Far Sawrey. C17 originally a farmhouse, the stables of which is now the Claife Crier bar, after the locals ghost of Claife Heights (Refer SD 373988). Phone 05394 433425. SD 379955

TOURIST INFORMATION CENTRE. Post Office, Far Sawrey. SD 378955

37 96

FISH. Moss Eccles Tarn. Depth 15ft/4.5m. Brown trout. Fly only. Bag limit. Permit from Tourist Information Centre Hawkshead. SD 3796

LITERARY. Castle Cottage, Near Sawrey. Beatrix Potter's home from her marriage in 1913 to William Heelis until she died 1943. William, a solicitor, known to older folk as Apple Billy, his family originating from Appleby. SD 374962

37 97

MAMMALS. Red and roe deer. A red stag, shot, recorded 30 stones /190kg, exceeding by 14 stone/88kg the record of the Scottish Monarch of the Glen. Claife Heights. SD 3797

NATURE RESERVE/TRAIL. Claife Heights, Lake Windermere. Woodland Walk. Deer—red and roe. SD 3797

VIEWPOINT. Wise Een Tarn. Near Sawrey. Panoramic view of distant Langdales. SD 3797

37 98

LEGEND. Crier of Claife named after a "spirit". One stormy night the ferryman heard calls from the opposite bank so he rowed across the lake. Next morning he returned without a passenger, speechless with horror and several days later died without uttering a word. On stormy nights thereafter the "crying" could still be heard. Eventually a monk from Lady Holme Island exorcized the "spirit" in a disused quarry. The Crier is commemorated by a bar so named, in the Sawrey Hotel. The Crier of Claife may have been the unhappy spirit of Thomas Lancaster who, in 1671, administered arsenic to his wife, six children and a servant at their home in Threlkeld. As was the custom he was brought back to his birth-place, High Wray (SD 3799) and hanged from the door-frame and then placed on the gibbet at Sawrey Causeway, close to the ferry. SD 373988

37 99

ARCHITECTURE. High Wray. Village Hall—until 1931 a school. The teacher's cramped living quarters above the single classroom.   SD 373999

38 92

BIRDS. Mute swans. Grassholme Island. Windermere.   SD 382925

38 93

INDUSTRIAL ARCHAEOLOGY. c1711 weir and head race. Cunsey Beck Bridge. Windermere (Refer SD 378937).   SD 381935

38 95

WALKS. Claife Heights. Waymarked track starting between Windermere Ferry and Hawkshead. Magnificent views.   SD 385955

Claife Heights (ON "kleif": steep slope). Windermere. Circuit 10 miles/16km. Ascent 1550ft/470m. Start: SD 388954

38 96

NATURE RESERVE/TRAIL. Ash Landing Reserve. Marsh, meadow (acid and calcareous) and scrub. Managed by Cumbria Wildlife Trust.   SD 386962

PLANTS. Small balsam (*Impatiens parviflora*). Rare in the Lake District. Windermere.   SD 3896

38 98

HISTORICAL. Sir Henry de Hane Segrave died at Belle Grange on Friday 13th June 1930 following a crash earlier that day in his speedboat Miss England II just after breaking American held world water speed record, with a speed of 98.76mph/ 158.93kmh. His engineer was killed outright.   SD 387989

38 99

HISTORICAL. Old paving visible of previous horse and carriage road from Hawkshead to Windermere ferry. Near Belle Grange.   SD 385990

39 91

MAMMALS. Roe deer. Badgers. Great Tower Plantation given to the Boy Scouts Association by Mr. W. B. Wakefield. Windermere.   SD 3991

NATURE RESERVE/TRAIL. Scout camp. Great Tower. Windermere. Roe deer. Collection of skulls and skins.   SD 3991

VIEWPOINT. Panoramic views from Ludderburn Moss 733ft/223m. Pleasant picnic area.   SD 397910

39 94

ARCHITECTURE. Storrs Hall, now a hotel, Bowness on Windermere. 1808/ 11—some c1790, when it was home of Sir John Legard. Designed by J. M. Gandy of Lancaster Castle fame. Five bay Doric porch. Octagonal garden house 1804 built to commemorate Admirals Duncan, St Vincent, Howe and Nelson.

SD 393942

HISTORICAL. Storrs Hall, originally home of Sir John Legard. A later owner Colonel John Bolton was clandestine smuggler of rum and slaves, using a passage from the shore to the cellars of the Hall. He amassed a fortune from the Liverpool slave trade by exporting locally made gunpowder to Africa in exchange for negroes. In C18 he brought the newly introduced light-weight plough from Scotland which reduced labour to one man and two Clydesdale horses.

SD 393942

LITERARY. Storrs Point. Regatta held here in 1825 organised by Colonel Bolton to celebrate Sir Walter Scott's 54th birthday, with a procession of more than 50 gaily decorated barges following Wilson's flagship (Refer SD 411989). Attended by the future Prime Minister George Canning, Southey, John Wilson and Wordsworth.

SD 391942

39 95

ARCHITECTURE. Ferry House, originally a hotel 1879 on site of earlier inn until 1869 venue for annual wrestling promoted by Professor Wilson (Refer SD 411989) but now headquarters of The Freshwater Biological Association.

SD 391956

Waterloo Gardens c1810, adjacent to ferry landing Lake Windermere. Pyramidal roof, overhanging timber floor. Carved window lintel.

SD 391957

HISTORICAL. Ramp Holme (where garlic or "ramp" grows). In C13 known as Rogerholm but in C18 known as Berkshire Island after its then owner, The Earl of Suffolk and Berkshire.

SD 394952

INSECTS. In 1960 new British water-beetle (*Stenelmis caniculatus*) discovered near Ferry House, Windermere.

SD 391956

Large caddis (*Athripsodes nigroervosus*). Windermere.

SD 391956

TRANSPORT. Windermere ferry service for more than 500 years. Originally a small boat propelled by oars and much later, in 1860 a larger steam powered vessel and then, in 1970 diesel. 47 persons and 11 horses drowned 19th October 1635 as they crossed Windermere after attending a fair and a wedding. Possibly the sad event resulted in the Legend of the Crier of Claife. (Refer SD 373988). Daily service on *The Drake* except Christmas Day & Boxing Day. 0650–2150hrs. Sundays and winter service 0950–2050hrs. 10 minute—700yd/640m crossing.

SD 395958

39 96

ARCHITECTURE. Belle Isle (corruption of "Isabella" Curwen) previously known as Brentwood (OE "brennan": to burn hence firewood) but later, The Holme and later still, Long Holme. On site of Roman villa. 1774—unique cylindrical 20 bed-roomed house. Dome with lantern. Unfluted Ionic columns. Building started by John Plaw for Thomas English a wealthy Nottingham merchant who, ridiculed by the locals, lost heart in the project and sold it. Completed in 1781 by John Christian Curwen—cousin of Fletcher Christian of *Bounty* fame. Under seige during Civil War by Parliamentary troops—relieved by owner, Huddleston Philipson who himself was laying seige to Carlisle at the time. In 38 acres. Owned by the Curwens since 1781. J. C. Curwen maintained a fleet of vessels crewed by his scarlet uniformed private navy. Many paintings, some by Reynolds and Romney. Now a Conference Centre but parties of 20 plus may visit the island by appointment with Mrs Curwen. Wordsworth disapproved of the architecture but relented somewhat when his son, John, married Isabella Curwen. SD 393965

BIRDS. Windermere—all year. Cormorant, red-throated diver. Ducks: goldeneye, mallard, merganser, pochard, shelduck, teal and tufted. Nuthatch and whooper swan. SD 3996

HISTORICAL. Robert Philipson (Robert the Devil), a Cavalier, lived in earlier house on Belle Island. In the Civil War, pursuing Roundheads, he stormed Kendal Church where still hangs his hilted sword and helmet. SD 393965

NATURE RESERVE/TRAIL. Belle Isle shore. Circuit 2 miles/3km. Certain days May–September. Guide available at house. Red-breasted merganser breeds. SD 393965

WALKS. West side of Windermere lake from Bowness, by ferry and thence Lakeside.

Topiary at Burneside. (Author)

Return by steamer. 7 miles/11km. Easy but if water level high, detours by road unavoidable. Several good vantage points to view up the lake.   SD 398965

39 97

CHURCH. St Mary. In 1256 a hospital, later an Augustian Chantry dedicated to The Virgin Mary, was founded here by Walter de Lyndesay, and abolished by Edward VI. The island then purchased by the Philipsons of Calgarth Hall. Ruin—none above ground. Lady Holme Island, Windermere. National Trust.
SD 398975

HISTORICAL. Hen Holme Island named after its colony of moorhens.
SD 397974

Lady Holme Island named after "the lady chapel of Tholme".   SD 398975

39 98

FISH. Windermere ("Vinandr's" lake and later Wynandmere). Owned by South Lakeland District Council. The lake's normal capacity is 313.674 million litres and the area covered is 3639 acres/1473ha. Water takes c9 months to travel from its intake to Newby Bridge and River Leven. 10½ miles/16.8km long & 1¼ miles/2km wide. 130ft/39m above sea-level. Maximum depth 219ft/67m off Wray Castle. Average depth 78ft/24m. Bullhead, charr, eel, minnow, perch (specimen caught—4lbs/1.8kg), pike, roach, rudd, salmon, 3-spined stickleback, stone loach, tench, brown and sea trout. No permit required except for game fish, obtainable from North West Water Ltd. New Town House. Buttermarket Street, Warrington, Cheshire. Phone 0925 234000. During 2nd World War small perch (c 1oz) caught in their thousands in one netting (perhaps 5 million all told) then canned and sold as "Perchines". Surviving perch now grown to specimen proportions.   SD 3998

HISTORICAL. During winter of 1894/5 Windermere was frozen end to end for 16 weeks to a depth of 18 inches/45cms. 100,000 people ventured on to the ice as well as a coach and four. During 1928 and 1964 the lake again froze over. In 1911 a Mr. Foster from Oldham was the first person to swim the length of Windermere.   SD 3998

39 99

ARCHITECTURE. Calgarth Hall. The Park known as "calfgarth" in 1365. Near Troutbeck Bridge. C16. Much rebuilt after Civil War. 2 mullioned and transomed windows S side. Some walls 7ft/2.1m thick. Round chimneys. Interior; Jacobean plaster ceiling 1st floor. Some of the Hall's woodwork is in Jesus Church, Troutbeck. (Refer NY 412028). Hall now residential apartments.   SD 399997

LEGEND. Calgarth Hall. The Squire and local Magistrate, Myles Philipson, (whose family had resided at Long Holme, now Belle Isle) owned the Hall and its considerable estate but he coveted the land belonging to Kraster and Doreen Cooke, which adjoined its boundaries. The scheming Squire, having had his several offers to purchase rejected, invited the Cookes to dinner but the next morning had them arrested for theft of an item of his dinner service. The other dinner guests and Philipson gave false testimony which resulted in the Cookes' execution on the gallows. Just before she died Doreen Cooke uttered a curse "Guard thyself, Miles Philipson; thou thinkest thou has managed grandly, but that tiny lump of land is the dearest a Philipson has ever bought or stole, for you will never prosper, neither your breed—your schemes will wither, the side you take will lose, Philipsons will own no land, and while Calgarth shall stand we will haunt it night and day, Never will ye be rid of us." It manifested in two skulls frequently appearing, gyrating, floating and gambolling before the Squire, his family and his guests, always followed by calamitous events. Despite being caught and crushed, burned or fragmented, the skulls always returned to a recess at the head of the stairs at the Hall. Notwithstanding his land aquisition the Squire's wealth dissipated and his health deteriorated. Upon his death the skulls then only appeared at Christmas and on the anniversary of the Cookes' execution. The legend formed the basis of Miss Strickland's *How Will it End?* and the poem "Folkes Speech of Cumberland" by Dr Alexander Craig Gibson (1869) "...To Calgarth Hall in the midnight cold Two headless skeletons crossed the fold..." The Hall eventually bought by Dr Watson, (born 1737 and died here 1816) Bishop of Llandaff, who exorcized the demented spirits.   SD 399997

Moot Hall, Keswick. (Rosemary Liddle)

AREA 24 – Windermere

40 90

LITERARY. Arthur Ransome (1884–1967) writer of stories for children wrote *Swallows & Amazons* while living at Low Ludderburn 1925–35. (Small white-washed cottage behind yew trees on a bend). In 1924 he had married Evgenia Petrovna Shelepina, Trotsky's secretary, after his long awaited divorce from Ivy Constance Walker. Public welcome to view.   SD 404908

40 94

ARCHITECTURE. Blackwell School near Bowness on Windermere. 1900. Much gabled. Imitative Tudor. Fine drawing room with Oriel overlooking the lake.   SD 400945

Spinning gallery. Bellman Houses. Winster.   SD 405942

40 96

CHURCH. St Martin. Bowness on Windermere (Bowness—Bulness meaning the bull's promontory—where the parish bull was kept). C15. Clerestory C16. Consecrated 1483 after a fire: the font bears marks of the fire. Believed to have original floor 5ft/1.5m below the nave. Colourful interior. Stained glass—east window C15—in tracery central fragments of C14. Virgin and Child glass dated 1260 from Cartmel Priory. East window shows armorial bearings of local families including John Washington of Warton, died 1407. The mullets and bars (stars & stripes) now on American flag for he was great, great, great, great, great, great, great, great, great, great grandfather of George Washington—born 22 February 1732, died 14 December 1799. Inaugurated as First President of the United States of America 1789. South aisle—memorial dated 1816 to Bishop Watson of Llandaff, by Flaxman. Interesting artefacts. Unique in church memorials a wooden statue of St Martin carved by local craftsmen over 300 years ago—St Martin was a Roman soldier who gave his cloak to a beggar. The Latin text of 1629 between arches, placed there by Christopher Philipson, Junior, Gentleman, commemorates the Gunpowder Plot "This is a day more famed as each year brings it round. Rejoice, ye who are good. The mischief conspired in Stygian gloom has been made an empty tale at the hand of Providence. England, which was to be conspicuous for the greatness of its ruin, may now sing hymns, since she has remained free by the grace of Heaven". C16 quotations from Coverdale's Bible (1535) also on the walls. Rare copy of a Bible known variously as the Breeches, the Braine Pan, or the Cratch Bible. Refers to unorthodox rendering of certain words: "breeches" for aprons (Genesis 3:7), "braine pan" for skull (Judges 4:53) and "cratch" for manger (Luke 2:7 & 10). Churchyard—common grave of 47 people drowned 19 October 1635 when Windermere ferry capsized. SD 402968

Mickleden Vale, Langdales. (Rosemary Liddle)

EVENT. Windermere Marathon. Start & finish Bowness promenade, last Sunday in October, annually. SD 402968

HISTORICAL. Belsfield Hotel, Bowness. Built 1845 & purchased by Henry William Schneider in 1860 from Baroness de Sternberg. Sneider, Chairman of Barrow Steelworks & Shipyard (now Vickers) daily left his home for his office preceded by his butler, Pittaway, carrying breakfast on a silver salver, and embarked on his steam launch *Esperance*. At Lake Side he boarded his personal railway coach (he owned the railway) for his journey to Barrow. Evening time would see the procedure reversed. *Esperance* (built at Rutherglen) may be seen at the Windermere Steam Boat Museum. She is the oldest yacht on Lloyd's Register of Shipping. Arthur Ransome wrote of the *Esperance* as Captain Flint's house-boat in *Swallows & Amazons*. SD 402968

MEMORIAL. To Mountford John Byrde Baddeley, author of the *Thorough Guide to the Lakes*. The headstone was conveyed from the summit of Scafell Pike. Bowness Cemetery. SD 401963

REFRESHMENT. New Hall Inn, Robinson Place, Bowness on Windermere. Built 1612 adjacent to The Smithy to which beer was passed through a purpose made hole in the wall—hence its now popular name of Hole In't Wall. In 1852 Tom Longmire, Champion Wrestler of England who won 174 Belts, was landlord. Charles Dickens reputed to have supped here. Phone 05394 43488. SD 404969

TOURIST INFORMATION CENTRE. National Park Centre. Leaflets, displays etc., Glebe Road, Bowness Bay, Bowness on Windermere. Open daily Easter–September. Phone 05394 42895. SD 401967

TRANSPORT. Bowness Bay Boating Co., ply the lake daily, except 25th December. Scheduled services to Waterhead, Ambleside. Selected trips also. Phone 05394 43360. SD 402967

VIEWPOINT. Biskey Howe, Bowness on Windermere. Accessible from Lake Road by several footpaths. Seating provided. Sunset viewing, of Windermere, highly recommended. SD 408969

WALKS. Brant Fell & School Knot. Circuit 5 miles/8km. Easy. Start: St Martin's Square. Bowness. Panoramic views. SD 403969

40 97

CRAFTS. Pottery, leatherwork, metalwork, brass rubbing, jewellery & clock restoring. Craftsmen of Cumbria. Fallbarrow Road, Bowness. Phone 05394 42959. Open daily Easter–Sept 0930–1800hrs. SD 403972

EVENT. Model boat rally at Windermere Steamboat Museum 3rd weekend of May. Also a Motorboat Rally 1st weekend of August. SD 402976

MUSEUM. Rayrigg Road. Bowness on Windermere. Historic Lake Transport— steamboat museum opened 1977 by the Prince of Wales. Perhaps most important exhibit *Dolly*, 1850, being the oldest mechanically propelled boat in the world, raised in 1962 after some 60 years submerged under Ullswater. *Kittiwake* & *Osprey* passenger trips. Beatrix Potter's rowing boat. Ferry boat *Ann*, a wherry, once used to ferry goods/people across Windermere. *Esperance* built 1845 (Refer SD 402968) in 1941 sank in 20ft/6m of water near Blake Holme, a small island S end of Windermere but salvaged by T. C. Pattinson shortly after. Open Easter–end October daily 1000–1700hrs. Fee. Phone 05394 45847.   SD 402976

WALKS. Bowness on Windermere, Matson Ground & Lickbarrow. Circuit 5½ miles/8.8km. Easy. Start: The Hole in't Wall inn.   SD 403973

WATERFALLS. Rayrigg Cascades. Although only a 13ft/3.96m fall, quite charming.   SD 406975

40 98

ARCHITECTURE. Rayrigg Hall. Windermere. c1700. Bow windows. Inside Elizabethan panelling.   SD 403981

Spiral staircase housed in semi-circular structure at rear of Low Millerground Farm. Windermere.   SD 402988

HISTORICAL. Sycamore tree bears metal plaque recording that "Queen Adelaide and suite landed here July 2th 1840 and ascended Rayrigg Bank attended by the Revd Fletcher...". She, the Dowager Queen of William IV who died aged 71 in 1837, renamed the hill—Queen Adelaide's Hill. Windermere.   SD 401982

Indistinct remains of corn mill, mid C14. C17 bell turret. Ferryman summoned by bell pull from Belle Grange opposite.   SD 402988

VIEWPOINT. Queen Adelaide Hill. Windermere. 259ft/79m. Sunset viewing highly recommended.   SD 403986

41 90

NATURE RESERVE/TRAIL. Barkbooth, Windermere. 30 acres/12.5ha of undulating fell with outcrops of Silurian rock. Tarn. Roe deer and glow worms. Permit required from Cumbria Wildlife Trust. Church Street, Ambleside.

SD 415906

41 92

ARCHITECTURE. Bryan House Farm. Winster. 2 fine bank barns.   SD 416928

HISTORICAL. Jonas Barker and his son and grandson (the latter until late C18) made much valued grandfather clocks. Bryan Houses. Winster.   SD 417928

Remains of bank and ditch indicating ancient forest. Winster.   SD 410928

41 93

CHURCH. Holy Trinity. Winster (ON "vinstri": the left-hand river). 1875. Low—bellcote, nave & chancel in one. Stained glass c1875. Interesting texts on 5 wooden tablets, dated 1796. Pitch-pipe in glass case. Churchyard war memorial.

SD 417930

REFRESHMENT. Brown Horse Inn. Winster. Phone 05394 43443.

SD 418936

Hill Top. Near Sawrey. (Rosemary Liddle)

WALKS. Winster. Circuit 5 miles/8km. Moderate. Very peaceful area of the Lake District. Start near church. SD 416930

41 96

GARDENS. Matson Ground House near Bowness. Flowering shrubs, rock & water gardens. Open daily (not Sundays) April–September. SD 416966

VIEWPOINT. Windermere from Brant Fell. SD 410961

41 97

ARCHITECTURE. Helm Farm. Bowness on Windermere. 1691 spinning gallery. SD 413970

CHURCH. St John Evangelist. Lake Rd. Windermere. 1886 in style of C13. Large. No tower. Cruciform and aisleless. Screen—carved by the Vicar and parishioners 1896 on. Stained glass by Holiday in west and north west windows— 1905/8. SD 412978

MEMORIAL. Baddeley's Clock. Windermere. Squat slate clock tower is memorial to Mountford John Byrde Baddeley B. A., well-known author of the *Thorough Guide to the Lakes* who died 1906. He is buried in Bowness Cemetery. SD 410978

WALKS. Adelaide Hill, Windermere. (Named after Queen Adelaide). 3½ miles/ 5.6km. Easy. Fine views of Wetherlam, Crinkle Crags, Bowfell, Langdale Pikes, Fairfield range, Red Screes, Thornthwaite & Ill Bell. Start north of Police Station then west on sign-posted footpath. SD 412978

41 98

CHURCH. St Mary. Ambleside Road, Windermere. 1850/82—resulted in no cohesive architecture but well worth viewing. SD 410987

CRAFTS. Lakeland Brass Rubbing Centre, facilities available. Free. Open daily March–October. Windermere. SD 4198

LITERARY. Between 1807 and 1812 Elleray was the home of John Wilson. Demolished in 1869 and present building on the site is a girls' school. Wilson was born in Paisley 1785, died 1854. Poet, essayist, critic and Professor of Moral Philosophy at Edinburgh University. Wrote under the pen name Christopher North in *Blackwood's Magazine* "Noctes Ambrosianae" papers. "The Isle of Palms and other poems" 1812. Great friend of Will Ritson (Refer NY 186087). Admirer of Wordsworth and friend of Coleridge, Southey, De Quincey and Sir Walter Scott. SD 411989

TOURIST INFORMATION CENTRE. Victoria Street, Windermere. Open Easter–October daily 0900–2100hrs. November–Easter daily 0900–1800hrs. Phone 05394 46499. SD 413987

41 99

MEMORIAL. To Arthur Heywood. Land given for public use—Orrest Head. Windermere. SD 414993

VIEWPOINT. Orrest Head. Windermere. 784ft/238m. The best location to see Lake Windermere from end to end. Enter the second of two gates immediately below Windermere Hotel and follow zig-zag path to the summit.   SD 414993

42 94

MINE. Knipe Tarn Mine. Barytes and galena. Of the level and shaft there is now no trace.   SD 423942

42 96

FISH. Cleabarrow Tarn. Depth 8ft/2.5m. Common & mirror carp & tench. Windermere, Ambleside & District A. A. Permit from Smyth's Records, Ash St. Bowness. Phone 05394 43750.   SD 424962

42 97

PLANTS. Rare butterfly orchid. School Knott, Windermere.   SD 4297

42 99

ARCHITECTURE. The Common Farm. Windermere. C17. Former home of the Williamsons, zealous C18 Quakers. Unusual double spice cupboard.

SD 422996

43 94

INDUSTRIAL ARCHAEOLOGY. Gilpin (bobbin) Mill. Ruinous condition. Waterwheel. Near Crook.   SD 433942

43 99

CHURCH. Mislet near Windermere. C17 Quaker Meeting House until C18. William Williamson, of Common Farm made provision in his will for a school to be maintained (Refer SD 422996).   SD 432996

44 90

INDUSTRIAL ARCHAEOLOGY. Disused corn mill of 1829 on River Gilpin fully preserved but now a field study centre. Crosthwaite.   SD 441908

44 91

ARCHITECTURE. Spout Farm. Crosthwaite. C18. Some mullioned windows. Round chimneys. Stone "ball" finial. 1709 spice cupboard.   SD 444917

CHURCH. St Mary. Crosthwaite (Cross in a clearing). 1878. Rock-faced tower. Apse. C16 artefacts. A wall shows plan of pew seating in time of Henry VIII.

SD 446911

REFRESHMENT. The Punch Bowl Inn. Crosthwaite. Phone 04488 234.

SD 446912

44 96

MINE. Borwick Fold Mine. Lead. Engine-house ruins.   SD 442969

44 98

CHURCH. St Anne. Ings (ON "en": outlying pasture land). 1743. West tower. Nave & chancel in one. Unusual fine Italian marble floor. Painting over Communion Table of Last Supper. Cup & Cover Paten 1634. The outer door has lock dated 1682 plus a wrought iron key—all that remains of earlier church founded by Thomas Birkett in 1511. Dorothy & William Wordsworth quite taken with the church when visiting on 6th October 1802 and Wordsworth included the church's greatest benefactor, Robert Bateman, in his poem "Michael" (line 258). Wordsworth's epitaph for Robert Bateman engraved on a brass plate in the church.

SD 446986

EVENT. Lake District Sheep Dog Trials. 1st Thursday of August. Ings, Stavely.

SD 4498

HISTORICAL. Robert Bateman, born at Ings of poor parents, with the help of villagers and through his constant endeavour became sole proprietor of a large city merchanting house with overseas interests. Whilst amassing great wealth abroad he yearned to return to Westmorland and had had built Reston Hall to this end. Before leaving Leghorn, Italy, he paid for marble to be sent to Ings church. He then boarded one of his own ships bound for England. In the Strait of Gibraltar, the villainous captain threw Bateman overboard and returned to Italy with all Bateman's possessions, and disappeared.

SD 446986

44 99

HISTORICAL. Grassgarth records Norse system of land holding. A unit of land—a "grass" (about 8 acres/3ha) considered sufficient to support one horse, three cows, seventeen sheep and twenty geese during the winter. During the summer the animals were released onto adjoining fells to allow grass to grow and be harvested as hay.

SD 442996

45 90

BIRDS. Winter: Siskins. Crosthwaite Woods.

SD 4590

45 93

ARCHITECTURE. Low Fold Farm. Crook. C17. Mounting block. Implement collection of bygone days and a Roman mill.

SD 450936

45 94

HISTORICAL. Crook Hall. (Previous to re-building known as Twatterden Hall). Once owned by the Philipson family who also owned Belle Isle. During the Civil War, the Royalist Robert Philipson, nick-named Robin the Devil, was besieged on Belle Island by Parliamentary forces commanded by a Colonel Briggs. Colonel Huddleston Philipson (Robert's brother), broke the seige after eight days. In an act of revenge the two brothers endeavoured to kidnap Colonel Briggs who was at prayer in Holy Trinity Church, Kendal. The affronted congregation chased them out. Whilst the brothers escaped, Robert's helmet and sword were seized and are displayed, to this day, in the church.

SD 452945

45 95

CHURCH. St Catherine. Crook. 1887. West tower of Late Perpendicular style but plain. The C1620 bell tower at SD 450947 is all that remains of the old church.

SD 451951

45 98

ARCHITECTURE. Reston Hall. Ings. Built 1743 for Robert Bateman, benefactor of Ings church who died in mysterious circumstances in the same year. Seven bay front. Fine interior.

SD 455988

WALKS. Staveley-tarns-River Kent. Circuit 6 miles/9km. Moderate. Potter Tarn & Gurnal Dubs Tarn dammed, their waters used for Staveley's paper mill. Start from the quarry lay-by.

SD 456986

46 91

ARCHITECTURE. Broadoak. Underbarrow. 1565. Porch date-stone. Fine oak staircase. Original leaded pane to stair window.

SD 468918

46 92

CHURCH. All Saints. Underbarrow. 1869. Looks odd.

SD 463926

HISTORICAL. Underbarrow, birthplace of Edward Burrough, a Quaker. When 19 he met and was influenced by George Fox (Founder of the Society of Friends). At the age of 28 he died in Newgate Prison.

SD 460920

INDUSTRIAL ARCHAEOLOGY. Greenridge Mill, Underbarrow. Saw mill equipment complete. 13ft/4m overshot wheel.

SD 463923

REFRESHMENT. The Punch Bowl. Underbarrow. Phone 04488 234.

SD 468922

46 94

CRAFTS. Woodturning, needlecraft, knitting, picture framing. Gifts and local crafts. Open 7 days a week 0930–1800hrs (winter 1700hrs). Phone 04488 268. Low Crag. Underbarrow Road. Crook.

SD 461941

46 95

REFRESHMENT. The Sun Inn. Crook. Phone 0539 821351.

SD 464951

Originally an old Coaching Inn now The Wild Boar Inn. Crook. Phone 05394 45225.

SD 465951

WALKS. Start from The Wild Boar Inn, along River Gilpin. 2 miles/3.2km. Full of historical interest. Crook.

SD 465951

46 96

ARCHITECTURE. Ashes Farm. Fine 1737 house, added to at different times. On site of a chapel. Decorated chimney piece. Walls 3ft/0.9m thick. Coat of Arms dated 1737 above gateway. Owned in 1750s by Robert Philipson.

SD 469969

Hollin Hall. Staveley. Barrel vaulted Pele Tower of c1450. Extensions by Robert

Philipson. Stepped gables, round chimneys. Some of the interior panelling removed by Le Flemings to Rydal Hall.   SD 466961

46 98

CHURCH. St James. Staveley (the lea where staves were obtained). 1864. Nave, chancel, bell-turret. Slender tower on west buttress. Some C15 glass in north lancet. The three east lancets, designed by Sir Edward Burne-Jones and made by Morris & Co, are strikingly beautiful, the figures being set against a very dark blue. Medieval font. C17 chest.   SD 469986

CRAFTS. Stonework. John Williams. Low Holme, Staveley near Kendal. Visitors by appointment. Phone 0539 821505.   SD 4698

Individual oak and mahogany furniture. Peter Hall Woodcraft. Danes Rd. Staveley near Kendal. Phone 0539 821633. Open Mon/Fri 0900–1700 hrs. Show room only, Saturdays 1000–1600hrs.   SD 4698

46 99

ARCHITECTURE. Scroggs Farmhouse. C17. Staveley.   SD 469993

47 91

REFRESHMENT. Tullythwaite House; farmhouse teas. Phone 04488 397.
                                                              SD 472915

47 98

CHURCH. St Margaret. Staveley. 1388. Body of the church demolished 1865 and only the tower now remains; preserved. Let into a wall a plaque commemorates a meeting of local farmers in 1620 protesting against a decision by James I to divest them of their titles to certain tracts of land.   SD 472982

FISH. River Kent. Staveley. Brown trout. Permit from Newsagents. Staveley.
                                                              SD 472983

REFRESHMENT. The Eagle & Child. Staveley. Phone 0539 821320. SD 473980

48 91

GEOLOGY. Limestone escarpment. Underbarrow.   SD 4891

MAMMALS. Badgers. Scout Scar. Kendal.   SD 4891

PLANTS. Limestone habitat. Underbarrow.   SD 4891

Orchids: bird's nest, early purple, early marsh, fly, frog, fragrant, greater and lesser butterfly, twayblade. Polypody, green spleenwort and moon-wort ferns. Scout Scar. Kendal.   SD 4891

TREES. Whitebeam (*Sorbus aria*). Tough wood, used by millers for wheel cogs and for present day tool handles.   SD 486919

48 92

QUARRY. Millstone Quarry at roadside near Scout Scar. The evenly bedded limestone used by local gunpowder firms for their mill stones.   SD 484924

WALKS. Scout Scar & Helsington, near Kendal. Circuit 5½ miles/ 9km. Moderate. Limestone escarpment. At the top are many disc-shaped stones which give a musical note when struck. Botanical interest. Fine views through 360 degrees. Start: Scout Scar car park.   SD 489923

48 93

ARCHITECTURE. Cunswick Hall, now a farmhouse. Rebuilt but some C15 exists. Gateway with Tudor Royal Arms.   SD 486934

HISTORICAL. Cunswick (originally Conneyswicke) Hall. Seat of the Leyburnes from C14–1715. Katherine Parr resided at the hall for a time.   SD 486934

LEGEND. Roger, son of Sir Charles de Leyburne owner of Cunswick Hall, betrothed to Helen, daughter of Sir Allan Bellingham of Burneside Hall, murdered his father as they returned from Burneside Hall, on a dark and stormy night, in order to claim his inheritance and marry. Sir Allan disbelieved Roger's explanation that his father had fallen into the flood waters and washed downstream. Shortly afterwards Reginald Duckett of Grayrigg Hall, (of whom Roger was jealous for his evident regard by Helen, and who was fortunate to escape unhurt after Roger's hired assassins had died in their attempt to kill him), walking with Sir Allan by the river, found the body of Sir Charles with an evident dagger wound. They accused Roger of murder, to which he confessed, later dying by his own hand. Sir Allan then remembered that Sir Charles had told him that all the Leyburnes would rest peacefully save for one, whose body would whiten the rocks on Cunswick Scar and thereafter haunt the Hall.   SD 486934

PLANTS. Deciduous mixed. Cunswick.   SD 4893

48 94

ARCHITECTURE. Low Brundrigg. Crook. C17 farmhouse original family home of the Dixons. Spice cupboard. Royal Stuart Arms above fire-place plus initials "G. D; A. D. 1667". Carved cist initialled "A. I. D. 1714". Oak panelling. Court room with oak benches around the walls.   SD 484949

48 98

MINE. Frost Hole Trials. Lead, small amount of argentiferous galena found, 8oz/226g of silver per ton of lead ore.   SD 489986

NATURE RESERVE/TRAIL. Dorothy Farrer's Spring, Staveley. Permit required from Cumbria Wildlife Trust. Church Street, Ambleside.   SD 480983

WATERFALLS. North of Spring Hag near Stavely.   SD 488986

49 92

VIEWPOINT. Scout Scar near Kendal. One of the finest views of the mountains from the south. The "umbrella" erected 1912 as memorial to King George V.
                                                                      SD 495920

49 93

PLANTS. Rare lesser butterfly orchid (*Platanthera bifolia*). Cunswick.   SD 4993

TREES. Oak wood. Cunswick. SD 4993

49 94

HISTORICAL. C19 turnpike toll house, Kendal to Windermere at Plumgarth. It is recorded that in 1844/5, 12,000 passenger vehicles paid tolls for using the road. SD 492948

49 95

ARCHITECTURE. Tolson Hall. Burneside. Built 1638 by Thomas Tolson, a tobacco merchant. C19 barge board to gables. Interior—1638/9 plasterwork. C17 glass. Imposing entrance. SD 496954

MONUMENT. Burneside. Obelisk to celebrate William Pitt and the British Victory at Waterloo. Erected by James Bateman of Tolson Hall. 1814. SD 494954

49 97

ARCHITECTURE. Godmond Hall. Burneside. C17 Pele tower. SD 499978

High Hundhowe. Burneside. C17. SD 495978

Mire Foot. Burneside. C17. SD 498976

Winster Valley. (Rosemary Liddle)

AREA 25 – Kendal

50 90

ARCHITECTURE. Helsington Laithes Manor. Kendal. C15 with additions during C16/17/18. Fine plaster tracery in drawing room. Chapel—pre-Reformation three light window. SD 507908

50 95

ARCHITECTURE. Burneside Hall. 1275. C14 embattled pele tower. Fortified walled courtyard. Remains of moat. C16 gatehouse. SD 509959

Hollins Farm. Burneside. 1687. Cruck-truss in west wing. Bedroom fire-place overmantels plaster work. (Thought to have been The Holly Bush Inn at one time). SD 503953

CHURCH. St Oswald. Burneside (pronounced "Burnieside"-ON Brunolf's hill). 1880. Nave & chancel in one—aisles. 12 clerestory windows. Tower. Richly carved doorway and reredos with carved flowers, the latter by village craftsmen. Plate. Unusual and interesting artefacts. SD 504957

INDUSTRY. Croppers Paper Mill. Burneside. In production since 1833, bought in 1845 by James Cropper of Viking forbears, whose name is in Iceland's *Landnama Bok*. SD 506959

REFRESHMENT. The Jolly Anglers. Burneside. Phone 0539 732552.
SD 505957

50 98

VIEWPOINT. From Potter Fell, north of Burneside. SD 503986

51 90

ARCHAEOLOGY. Alavna (corruption of Alauna) Roman Fort, Natland. An important post from the reign of Agricola to late C4. 500ft/152m long by 400ft/122m wide: early timber fort replaced by stone circa AD 135. Although only green mounds remain important treasures have been found—an altar and an inscribed gravestone to a soldier of the 20th Legion. The inscription's ending states that anyone burying another body in his grave shall incur a fine. Both in the British Museum. SD 515907

INDUSTRIAL ARCHAEOLOGY. Helsington Mill. On the site of medieval corn mill, once used for marble polishing but, over a century ago, used in snuff preparation by Gawith, Hoggarth & Co.,Ltd. A long established Kendal business.
SD 514904

51 91

YOUTH HOSTEL. Highgate. Kendal. Phone 0539 724066. SD 513912

51 92

CHURCH. Holy Trinity. Kendal ("Cherchebi": Kirkby [Churchtown] later known as Kirkby Kendal—The Dale of the River Kent). On C8 site. In 1189, Scots massacred all the town's citizens sheltering within the church during one of their Border raids. C13 with extensive rebuilding. Largest Parish Church in England. 80ft/24m high tower; peal of 10 bells. 5 aisles, one of which is called the Flemish Aisle because it accommodated Flemish weavers who settled in Kendal in the Middle Ages. Anglian Cross shaft. Above the High Altar is featured the Corona of 1970. North aisle roof has painted angels, unusual in a northern church. The Parr Chapel contains a black marble tomb thought to be of Sir William Parr, grandfather of Katherine Parr, Henry VIII's sixth wife. Gonfalon collection—Westmorland Regiment's Colours since its inception in 1755. Memorial plaque to George Romney the eminent painter, who died in Kendal 15 November 1802 and interred at Dalton in Furness, his birthplace. Father Thomas West was buried just outside the Strickland chapel (according to W. G. Collingwood)—see Literary below. SD 516921

St George. Castle St. Kendal. 1839. The west front's two polygonal towers originally supported low spires but removed 1927. Canted ribbed ceiling to nave. SD 519929

Quaker Meeting House. 1816. Stramongate, Kendal. Since 1660 Quakers have been influential in Kendal and much of the town's industry was founded by them during C18 and C19. SD 517928

EVENT. Kendal Gathering; three week festival of concerts, bands, choral music, chamber music and shows. Late August, concluding with a Torchlight Procession 2nd week of September. Kendal Sheep Dog Trials; last Sunday of August. Kendal Festival of Jazz and Blues; 2nd and 3rd week November. Northern International Festival of Mime and Visual Theatre; end of April. Kendal Folk Festival on August Bank Holiday. SD 5192

FISH. River Kent. Kendal. Brown trout. Free. Much of the river from source to sea is controlled by Angling Associations but they may be prepared to grant permission. Details at local Information Centre. SD 5192

HISTORICAL. Site of motte and bailey, a wooden stockade built 1092 by Ketel De Tailbois, 3rd Baron of Kendal. Castle Howe. Kendal. SD 512924

INDUSTRY. Kendal's motto is "Pannus mihi panis" (wool is my bread). Kendal Green worn by bowmen. Cloth first dyed yellow with dyer's broom (*Genista tinctoria*) and then blue with woad. Red dye produced from processed mountain lichen—later, damson stones—hence the abundance of such trees in the Lyth Valley. SD 5192

LITERARY. Father Thomas West (real name Thomas Daniel) became a Jesuit Priest in 1751. His *Guide to the Lakes* published in 1778. Died at Sizergh aged 62 on 10 July 1779 and buried at Holy Trinity, Kendal. SD 516921

MONUMENT. Kendal. On site of C11 Norman motte and bailey castle, commemorates 1688 Revolution. Castle Howe, Kendal. SD 513924

MUSEUM. Abbot Hall. Kendal. Built 1759 for Colonel George Wilson of Dallam Towers, by John Carr of York at a cost of £8000. As a gallery since 1962 and run by Mary Birket, curator, from 1968–86. Lake District life and history. Archaeology. Art Gallery. Open May to October Monday–Saturday 1030–1700hrs & Sunday 1400–1700hrs; November to April Monday–Friday 1030–1700hrs & Saturday & Sunday 1400–1700hrs. Fee.   SD 516921

NATIONAL TRUST SHOP. 18 Finkle Street. Kendal. Phone 0539 731605.
                    SD 516927

REFRESHMENT. Ring O' Bells. Kendal. 1741. Beside the church gate, it is the only public house built on consecrated ground. Phone 0539 720326.
                    SD 516921

WALKS. Woodland trail; Serpentine Woods from Serpentine Road. Kendal.
                    SD 5192

Underbarrow & Cunswick Scars. Circuit 7 miles/11km. Ascent 625ft/190m. Moderate. Limestone pavement. Panoramic views. Start: Kendal.   SD 515926

51 93

ARCHITECTURE. Castle Dairy. 26 Wildman Street, Kendal. Served the castle while Katherine Parr in residence. Built 1564 it is the oldest inhabitable stone built house in the area; owned by Anthony Garnett. Carved oak beams and hand-carved four-poster bed. Some C16 glass. Open Easter–September Wednesdays only 1400–1600hrs. Fee. Phone 0539 722170.   SD 519931

CHURCH. St Thomas. Stricklandgate. Kendal. 1837. Embraced west tower. Lancet windows. Short chancel, aisleless.   SD 514931

CRAFTS. Weaving. Susan Foster. 9 Windermere Road, Kendal. Open Wednesday, Friday, Saturday 1000–1700hrs. In August Monday to Saturday. Phone 0539 726494.   SD 5193

HISTORICAL. Katherine Parr's silver bound prayer book, measuring just over 2in x 1½in (6cm x 4cm) kept in Mayor's parlour in Kendal Town Hall. May be viewed by appointment.   SD 514932

MUSEUM. Station Road, Kendal. Fossils. Natural History. Cumbria collection. Dioramas. Geology. Originated 1796 from private collection of Mr. Todhunter. Open Spring Bank Holiday–October Monday–Saturday. 1030–1700hrs. Sunday 1400–1700hrs. Rest of year Monday–Friday 1030–1700hrs, Saturday & Sunday 1400–1700hrs. Fee. Phone 0539 721374.   SD 518932

TOURIST INFORMATION CENTRE. Town Hall. Highgate. Kendal. Phone 0539 725758.   SD 514932

51 96

INDUSTRIAL ARCHAEOLOGY. Oakbank Bobbin Mill, disused.
                    SD 518964

52 92

CASTLE. Kendal. Remains of curtain wall. 3 towers, one round & two oblong. All C13. Built by William Rufus. One owner was Thomas Parr, father of Katherine Parr who was born at the castle in 1510. Her brother died without heirs in 1571 and the castle abandoned shortly afterwards. Not until 1896 was it acquired for the town to mark Queen Victoria's Diamond Jubilee.   SD 522924

HISTORICAL. Katherine Parr, widow of Edward Nevill, Lord Latimer, wed Henry VIII when she was 31—as his sixth wife and he, her third husband. (Katherine of Aragon, widow of his elder brother Arthur—divorced; Anne, daughter of Sir Thomas Boleyn—beheaded; Jane, daughter of Sir John Seymour—died in childbirth of a son, afterwards Edward VI; Anne, sister of William, Duke of Cleves—divorced; Catherine Howard, niece of Duke of Norfolk—beheaded). Katherine Parr was a cultivated and strong minded woman with strong Protestant leanings and may have been responsible for her stepson, Prince Edward, being educated by radically Protestant tutors, and encouraged learning in her stepdaughters; she herself had a book published, *The Prayers Stirring the Mind unto Heavenly Meditations* 1545, a most unusual distinction for any UK monarch. Twice widowed, she outlived the King, married again and died within days of the birth of her daughter, Mary. She is buried in the chapel adjoining Sudeley Castle (Gloucestershire), the now much restored residence of her fourth husband, Thomas Seymour. He was brother of the late Queen Jane and therefore uncle to the future King Edward VI.   SD 522924

52 93

EVENT. Westmorland County Show. Livestock, Sheep, Horses, Ponies, Show Jumping, Dogs, Hound Trail, Fell Race, Agricultural Exhibitions, Vintage Machinery, Cumberland and Westmorland Wrestling, Carriage Driving, Handicrafts, Trade Stands etc; 2nd Thursday September. The Showground, Kendal.   SD 521936

52 95

ARCHITECTURE. Gilthwaiterigg Hall. C15. 2 ancient windows in west wing.   SD 521952

CHURCH. Dodding Green. Skelsmergh. Originally private residence of William Dodding C14. It was extensively renovated by Robert Stephenson in C17 who left it in Trust for a Catholic priests' home. Until 1791 Mass celebrated in secret room and then present chapel built on lessening of religious persecution. Gravestone beside drive of early priest in charge.   SD 529954

52 96

ARCHITECTURE. Coppice How Farm. Skelsmergh. Early cruck construction.   SD 525969

52 99

HISTORICAL. Garnett Bridge. Long Sleddale. Once a thriving mill village; woollen mills, corn mill and bobbin mill.   SD 524992

53 90

REFRESHMENT. The Station Inn. Oxenholme (the land where oxen were kept). Phone 0539 724094.   SD 536900

53 95

ARCHITECTURE. Skelsmergh Hall. C15. Home of the Leyburne family for over 400 years and now a farm. Pele tower, tunnel vaulted. Jacobean house adjoining has mullioned and transomed windows. Rare Bible box. Stuart period panelling. 1711 cradle.   SD 531958

CHURCH. St John Baptist. Skelsmergh (ON "Skjaldmar's" [a personal name] shieling). 1871. Bellcote, nave & chancel.   SD 533954

53 96

FISH. Skelsmergh Tarn. Depth 16½ft/5m. Roach & rudd. Free.   SD 533966

53 98

ARCHITECTURE. Selside Hall. Kendal. C14. Original seat of the Thornburghs. Double vaulted basement. Walls 4ft/1.2m thick. Priest hole. Transomed windows.   SD 534989

INDUSTRY. Watchgate Water Treatment Plant, Selside. Draws water from Haweswater, Thirlmere, Ullswater and Windermere to supply vast area from Barrow to Manchester. Largest such plant in Europe.   SD 530982

LEGEND. Selside Hall. Troublesome ghost of C16 and C17 which frequently extinguished all candles and lamps, thought to have been the spirit of a sheepstealer hanged from a yew tree in the grounds of the Hall some years previously.
                                    SD 534989

53 99

CHURCH. St Thomas. Selside. (ON "selju-saetr": the Willow sheiling). 1838. Tower. Lancet windows. Interesting artefacts.   SD 535992

54 91

MEMORIAL. On Monument Hill, Hill Top (now Holme Park school), New Hutton. 1766. Memorial to Midge, a mare reputed to have won all races in which she was entered.   SD 547913

54 95

FISH. Patton Mill near Kendal. Trout rearing farm.   SD 5495

55 90

ARCHITECTURE. Strawberry Bank. New Hutton. Interior—C17 fine stucco panels.   SD 558909

55 91

MUSEUM. Hall House Historic Collection. New Hutton. Kendal. Farm machinery, steam driven vehicles/implements, musical instruments etc., Open March–September, Sunday–Thursday. 1100–1700hrs. Fee. Phone 0539 721767. SD 552916

55 92

BIRDS. Fisher Tarn. Winter: Smew. SD 5592

55 98

FISH. Whinfell Tarn. Depth 10ft/3m. Chub, eel, perch, pike, roach, rudd & tench. Permit from adjacent farm. SD 557981

56 91

CHURCH. St Stephen. New Hutton (the [new] farm on the spur of land). 1828 on site of 1730 chapel. Embattled W tower with Arms of prominent families. Lancet windows. Atop churchyard gate pillars two stone greyhounds from the now demolished Sleddall Hall. SD 563912

Little Langdale. (Rosemary Liddle)

Area 26 – Bootle

10 87

FISH. River Annas. Bootle. Brown trout. Members only of Millom & District Angling Association.   SD 1087

10 88

ARCHITECTURE. Village Cross 1897. Bootle. About the smallest market town in England it is noted in The Domesday Book, its market charter is dated 1346.

SD 106885

CHURCH. St Michael and All Angels. Bootle (OE "buthl"; the dwelling). 1837 some Norman. Cruciform. Pinnacled tower. Font inscribed RB and carved lettering "In Nomine Patris Filii et Spiritus Sancti". Small brass and effigy in full armour to Sir Hugh Askew (Henry VIII's cellarer) died 1562. Knighted at Battle of Musselborough in 1547 by King Edward VI. "Here lyeth Sr Hughe Askewe late of the seller to Kynge Edward the VI which Sr Hughe was maid knyght at Muskelbrough felde in ye yere of oure Lord 1547 and dyed ye second day of Marche In the yere of oure Lord God 1562". Pedestalled sundial.   SD 106885

REFRESHMENT. Kings Head. Bootle. Phone 06578 239.   SD 108882

High Lodore Farmhouse, Borrowdale. (Author)

10 89

HISTORICAL. Remains of Seaton Nunnery, early C13 Benedictine foundation dedicated to St Leonard.   SD 101897

11 83

CHURCH. St Mary. Whitbeck (ON "vithir": withy beck). Restored in 1883. Dual bellcote. Nave & chancel in one. 6ft/1.8m high effigy of Lady of Annaside C14.   SD 119839

11 84

WATERFALLS. Black Combe. Path from St Mary's Church, Whitbeck. 3 miles/4.82km. Circuit. Moderate.   SD 119847

13 82

CHURCH. St Mary. Whicham (OE "ham": Hwita's home). Restored 1858. Norman doorway. Nave & chancel in one. Double bellcote, each bell over 500 years old. Plate 1628. C17 east window. 1917 Victoria Cross.   SD 135826

MINE. Whicham Trial. Copper pyrites.   SD 130829

WALKS. Black Combe—most north westerly fell, giving panoramic views over Lakeland and into Scotland and Isle of Man. Circuit 7½ miles/12km. Ascent 1945ft/592m. Moderate. Start: Whicham Church.   SD 135826

13 85

VIEWPOINT. From summit of Black Combe (1970ft/600m) the most extensive view in Britain according to Colonel Mudge F. R. S. (1762–1820) distinguished mathematician and surveyor. In clear weather may be seen; 14 counties, Isle of Man and Mourne mountains in Northern Ireland. "View from the Top of Black Combe" (Wordsworth 1813) describes the view in detail.   SD 135855

15 85

MINE. White Combe Beck Mine. Copper. Several levels and surface works.
                                                                        SD 152857

16 88

MINE. Raven Crag Trial. Copper pyrites.   SD 168883

17 84

REFRESHMENT. The Punch Bowl Inn. The Green. Phone 0229 772605.
                                                                        SD 178846

17 88

ARCHAEOLOGY. Impressive large stone circle (consisting of 55 stones, the largest 7ft/2.1m high) in natural amphitheatre, locally known as Sunkenkirk but Ordnance Survey records as Swinside. Neolithic. Possibly ceremonial or for astronomical purposes.   SD 172882

MINE. Black Beck Mine. Copper.   SD 173888

18 83

MINE. High Brow Sulphur Mine. Iron pyrites. c1851. SD 182835

19 88

INDUSTRIAL ARCHAEOLOGY. Duddon Bridge. Remains of charcoal-fired iron furnace (40ft/12m high) of 1736 together with massive iron-ore store and workers' cottages. SD 197884

LITERARY. Duddon Bridge. Wordsworth—Sonnets 1806 to 1820. SD 199882

19 89

ARCHITECTURE. Duddon Hall. C19. Ornate with Doric details. Interesting garden. SD 194896

WALKS. Duddon Hall. Circuit 5¼ miles/8.4km. Easy, but one short steep ascent. Start: SD 192896

Loughrigg from Ambleside. (Author)

Area 27 – Broughton/Furness

20 85

WALKS. Duddon sands. Circuit 4¾ miles/7.6km. Easy, mainly on level country lanes. Start: lay-by near Foxfield railway station.   SD 208854

20 87

CHURCH. St Mary Magdalene. Broughton in Furness. (Broughton—OE "broctun": the enclosure by the brook). C15. Red sandstone. Some windows C16. SW tower 1900. Fine Norman door. Interesting font. Unusually, has ring of 10 bells. Clock bears lettering "Watch, for ye know not the hour".   SD 209875

REFRESHMENT. High Cross Inn. Broughton in Furness. C16. Settle inset with C18 prints. Phone 0229 716272.   SD 209876

21 86

WALKS. Heathwaite Settlement. Circuit 5 miles/8km. Easy. Panoramic views. Start: SD 217869

21 87

ARCHITECTURE. Broughton Tower, Broughton in Furness. Sir Thomas

Holy Trinity Church. Grange. (Author)

Broughton and generations before, resident here. He was slain at Battle of Stoke field near Newark on Trent 6 June 1487 which marked the end of the Wars of the Roses. Large mansion erected by the Gilpin Sawreys around the C14 Pele tower. The Sawrey family were Puritans and almost alone among their kinsfolk supported Cromwell during Civil War. Now a special school.　　SD 213879

MONUMENT. In memory of John Gilpin, who gave land for the market. Erected by his widow in 1810. Broughton in Furness.　　SD 212875

REFRESHMENT. Manor Arms. Broughton in Furness. Phone 0229 716286.
SD 212875

Old Kings Head. Station Road, Broughton in Furness. C16 Manorial Courts held here as well as meetings of Church Wardens and "The Twenty-four". Phone 0229 716293.　　SD 211874

Black Cock Inn. C16. Prince Street, Broughton in Furness. Phone 0229 716529.
SD 212875

WALKS. Broughton in Furness, Latter Rigg & Woodland. Circuit 5½ miles/9km. Moderate. Quiet Natural History walk. Start from Market Square, Broughton in Furness.　　SD 212875

Broughton to Broughton Mills alongside River Lickle. Circuit 5 miles/8km. Moderate. Some wet areas. Many stiles and gates. Start: Broughton in Furness Market Square, then road to Coniston & Torver, then through wicket gate on right.　　SD 212875

22 86

ARCHITECTURE. Causeway End Bridge. Parapet carvings by Thomas Dawson a postman who, whilst waiting for the mails, carved: "Happy land. A sensible man won't offend me and no other can. Be kind to the poor. Shelling green peas. England for ever. England expects every man this day will do his duty. I can paddle my own canoe. Do not stop long at the fair. They laugh best who laugh last. Put your shoulder to the wheel. Nil Desperandum".　　SD 224866

23 84

REFRESHMENT. Greyhound Inn. Grizebeck. C18. Phone 0229 89224.
SD 239849

24 89

CHURCH. Woodland. 1891. Nave, bellcote and apse.　　SD 248891

25 87

ARCHAEOLOGY. Cairnfields. Heathwaite.　　SD 255875

25 88

ARCHAEOLOGY. Cairn. Kirkby Moor.　　SD 257880

26 89

ARCHAEOLOGY. Cairnfields. Woodland Fell.　　SD 267890

2 round cairns of 20ft/6m & 40ft/12m diameters. Some excavation C19 proved sepulchral. White Borran. SD 266890

27 84

ARCHAEOLOGY. Ring cairn 100ft/30m diameter with 9ft/2.7m wide bank. Entrance on south west. Keldray. SD 279842

28 85

LITERARY. Arthur Ransome lived at Lowick Hall 1947–50. He worked on and greatly improved this Norman Manorial Hall when he became Lord of the Manor. SD 286859

28 88

CHURCH. St John Baptist. Blawith (pronounced "Blaith"). 1863. Nave, bellcote & chancel. Lancet windows. Church recently closed. SD 289883

Remains of a chapel built c1560. Blawith. SD 288882

29 85

REFRESHMENT. Farmers Arms. C14. Spinning gallery. Huge round chimneys. Many old oil paintings. Lowick Green. Phone 0229 861277. SD 298853

29 86

CHURCH. St Luke. Lowick (ON "lauf-vik": the shady creek). 1885 but records indicate a chapel prior to 1577. Sandstone dressed. W tower. Lancet windows. S wall has 1828 sun dial. SD 290861

EVENT. Lowick and District Agricultural Show. Livestock, Sheep,, Horses, Fell Ponies, Show Jumping, Hound Trail, Fell Race, Wrestling, Carriage Driving, Vintage machinery, Produce, Handicrafts, Trade Stands etc., lst Saturday of September. Lowick. SD 2986

FISH. River Crake at Lowick Farm. Lowick Bridge. Perch, pike, salmon, brown & sea trout. Permit from Lowick Farm. SD 292864

REFRESHMENT. Red Lion Inn. Just off A 5084 at Lowick Bridge. Phone 022985 366. SD 293865

29 88

INDUSTRIAL ARCHAEOLOGY. Ancient furnace forge complex still traceable. From here cannon balls were manufactured—used by the Duke of Cumberland in the 1745 Rebellion. Nibthwaite. SD 295883

29 89

INDUSTRIAL ARCHAEOLOGY. High Nibthwaite. Coniston Water. C18—quayside facilities for transporting copper from Coniston to Ulverston. Charcoal furnace for iron. SD 292897

Area 28 – Newby Bridge

30 84

CHURCH. Wesleyan chapel. 1863. Spark Bridge.   SD 301848

REFRESHMENT. The Royal Oak. Spark Bridge. Phone 0229 861286.

SD 306849

31 82

INDUSTRIAL ARCHAEOLOGY. Greenodd at mouth of River Crake, formerly an important port. Shipped out was copper ore and slate from Coniston's industries and cotton was shipped in for the cotton mill at Backbarrow. Some of the old staithes remain.   SD 316827

31 83

LITERARY. Arthur Ransome lived at Hill Top, Haverthwaite, from 1963–65.

SD 315834

31 84

CHURCH. Baptist Chapel. Tottlebank (OE "totian": to peep, hence look-out hill). Spark Bridge. Founded 1664 by Colonel Roger Sawrey of Broughton Towers. Its isolation due to The Five Miles Act 1665, which prohibited worship by non-conformists within such distance of a corporate town. Rebuilt C18. Benches lateral to lectern. Recently restored.   SD 315845

31 86

CHURCH. Holy Trinity. Colton (ON "col-tun": the village on the River Cole). Founded by Archbishop Sandys in 1578. Enlarged in C18. W tower. Nave & chancel in one. Communion rail C17. Plate 1571. Dickson memorial windows by Holiday. One bell medieval possibly from Conishead Priory, Ulverston. Royal Arms of George III. Wall clock 1829. Copy of Bishops Bible 1577—a "treacle" Bible, so called because of a misprint in Jeremiah 8:2—"Is there no tryacle [instead of balm] at Gilhead". Sun dial 1764 with 1886 base, in churchyard. Beside footpath to the church is St Cuthbert's Well used for baptisms. Mounting block.   SD 318861

32 82

INSECTS. Purple hairstreak butterfly. Roudsea Wood.   SD 3282

PLANTS. Rare fly orchid (*Ophrys insectifera*), rock rose, the rare yellow sedge (*Carex flava*), royal fern, adder's tongue, herb paris, bog rosemary, ploughman's spikenard and lilies-of-the-valley. Roudsea Wood.   SD 3282

32 84

WALKS. Rusland Pool & River Leven. Circuit 6½ miles/10.5km. Easy. Estuary, woodland, riverside & farmland. Start: Pool Foot.   SD 328843

32 85

REFRESHMENT. White Hart Inn. Bouth. Old "hooker" ring (used for tying up horse drawn coaches) still affixed to wall. Remarkable collection of stuffed mammals. Phone 0229 861229.   SD 328855

32 87

ARCHITECTURE. Barn originally with water wheel which powered a threshing machine in upper storey. Low Longmire Farm. Bouth.   SD 327871

33 85

INDUSTRIAL ARCHAEOLOGY. Gunpowder works of Messrs F. C. Dickson, developed c1850 but closed 1929 after yet another devastating explosion. Between 1867 and 1911, 27 workers died in eight explosions. Black Beck. Bouth.
                                                                         SD 333858

33 87

NATURE RESERVE/TRAIL. Hay Bridge. There is also a Deer Museum here, as well as exhibits of birds, butterflies and moths. Declared a Nature Reserve in 1971 by Helen Fooks as a memorial to her husband Major Herbert Fooks, formerly game warden of Grizedale Forest. The Reserve includes parts of Rusland Moss as well as open fell, farmland, woodland, pond, stream and tidal river. Open daily by appointment only, as the grounds and museum essentially serve to teach those schools, organizations and individuals interested in natural history. Apply Warden Deer Museum, Low Hay Bridge. Bouth-by-Ulverston. Phone 0229 860412.
                                                                          SD 3387

33 88

NATURE RESERVE/TRAIL. Rusland Moss. An area of raised bog and woodland controlled by Nature Conservancy Council. Permit required.
                                                                         SD 334886

PLANTS. Lowland moss habitat. Rusland Moss. (Nature Conservancy. Permit required).   SD 3388

TREES. Pines, native. Rusland Moss. (Nature Conservancy. Permit required.
                                                                          SD 3388

33 89

CHURCH. Rookhow. Rusland. A monthly Quaker Meeting House 1725. Accommodation, stables, gig house. Well preserved.   SD 332896

St Paul. Rusland ("Hrolds's or Hrolf's land"). 1745. Virtually rebuilt save for tower. Aisleless. Nave, tower and chancel. Stained glass by Hardman. Originally a chapel of ease for Colton. Churchyard grave of Arthur Ransome (1884–1967) and his wife Evgenia. Also burial place of the Romney family, the painter lived at one time at nearby Whitstock Hall.   SD 338897

INDUSTRIAL ARCHAEOLOGY. Stoney Hazel. Built 1718 the ruins of this Finery forge is the only complete specimen of its type in Britain. 550yds/490m north of High Bridge on Force Beck. Permit to view from Lake District Special Planning Board, Brockhole. SD 336897

34 83

CRAFTS. Low Wood near Haverthwaite. In 1849 gunpowder works, there are now glass engravers, joiners, engineers, antique dealers & sculptors. Open Tuesday to Sunday. SD 346836

INDUSTRIAL ARCHAEOLOGY. Low Wood Gunpowder Works. Haverthwaite, alongside River Leven. 1799–c1931. Site overgrown. Devastating explosion 1863 killed six and heard in Keswick, 30miles/48km distant. SD 346836

34 84

CHURCH. St Anne. Haverthwaite (ON "hafri": oats, hence clearing where oats are grown). 1824. West tower, nave & chancel. Traceried windows. Memorial tablet to George Dickson, accidentally shot in Montevideo when a bullet fired at another man passed through his body and hit Dickson. Churchyard slab to William Fell of the 52nd Light Infantry in Wellington's campaigns. SD 348842

REFRESHMENT. Angler's Arms. Haverthwaite. Phone 05395 31216. Popular for obvious reasons as a riverside pub, near the fast flowing River Leven and its confluence with Rusland Pool. SD 345841

TRANSPORT. Lakeside & Haverthwaite railway. Steam trains. 3½ miles/5.6km. In River Leven valley. Station be-decked in Victoriana. Phone 05395 31594. Open daily Easter–October. Museum. Haverthwaite. SD 349842

34 87

TREES. Beech, famous plantations. Rusland Valley. SD 3487

34 88

EVENT. Rusland Valley Horticultural Show. Fell Race, Hound Trail, Handicrafts, Produce, Trade Stands etc., 3rd Saturday of August. Rusland. SD 3488

GARDEN. Rusland Hall. Landscaped by Capability Brown. Specimen trees. White peacocks. Open daily (except Sundays) April–September. Phone 0229 860276. SD 340888

HISTORIC HOUSE. Rusland Hall near Satterthwaite. Built by the Rawlinson family. Georgian. Five bays, 2½ storeys and Tuscan columned doorway. Hall reputed to have been used by counterfeiters of golden guineas from the Greenburn copper, in C17. Exhibition of photographs and vintage photographic equipment, music and self playing musical instruments. Upright and grand pianos, pianolas and a pneumatic orchestrelle organ of the period preceding the gramophone. Open daily (except Sun days) April–September. Phone 0229 860276. SD 340888

INDUSTRIAL ARCHAEOLOGY. Bow fronted mill, the Old Tannery. Oak bark ground by mill-stone walked round by a pony. 300yds/250m south east of Rusland Hall. In ownership of National Park Authority. SD 341887

35 83

ARCHITECTURE. Bigland Hall. Mostly 1809. Roman Doric portico.

SD 355831

BIRDS. Nest site of red-breasted merganser. Bigland Tarn.   SD 356831

FISH. Bigland Tarn. Brown & rainbow trout. Bag limit. Day permits from Bigland Hall Estates Office. Phone 05395 31361.   SD 356831

35 84

ARCHITECTURE. The White Waters Hotel, Backbarrow. The Lakeland Village Time Share complex formerly a corn mill in C16 then the Ainsworth cotton mill where child workers ill treated, working 6 days a week from 0500–2000hrs & later. In 1890 Lancashire Ultramarine Co established a Blue works. Reckitts took over the company in 1920 continuing production of industrial blue (indigo mixed with lime), including "Dolly Blue" for laundering, until closure 1981.   SD 357849

INDUSTRIAL ARCHAEOLOGY. Iron-making from a bloomery forge in 1685 to blast furnace and refining. The site is not open to the public. Backbarrow.

SD 357848

35 85

MAMMALS. Roe deer. Backbarrow Wood. Newby Bridge.   SD 3585

35 87

FISH. Boretree Tarn near Finsthwaite. Perch, pike & brown trout. Maximum depth 40ft/12m. Controlled by Lonsdale Angling Club who issue membership tickets.   SD 3587

PLANTS. Pinewood habitat. Yewbarrow.   SD 3587

TREES. Mixed woodland. Yewbarrow.   SD 3587

35 88

MAMMALS. Mountain hare. Rusland Fells.   SD 3588

36 83

FISH. Bigland Lake. Perch, pike, rudd, roach & tench. Day permits from Bigland Hall Estate Office.   SD 364834

36 86

ARCHITECTURE. Newby Bridge. Built 1652 to replace wooden structure. Slate, five arches—initial cost £90. The adjacent weir controls the level of Windermere.   SD 369863

Tower above Newby Bridge—a Folly. Erected by James King of Finsthwaite House in 1799 to commemorate the Battles of Camperdown, Cape St Vincent and The Nile. Inscribed "To honour the officers, seamen and marines of the Royal Navy, whose matchless conduct and irresistible valour decisively defeated the fleets

of France, Spain and Holland, and promoted and protected Liberty and Commerce".
SD 369869

FISH. River Leven. Stretch at Newby Bridge, opposite Swan Hotel. Brown trout. Permit from Swan Hotel.
SD 369863

REFRESHMENT. Swan Hotel. Newby Bridge. Original—1622, much extended. Columned doorway. Phone 05395 31681.
SD 369864

Newby Bridge Hotel. Phone 05395 31222.
SD 369862

36 87

CHURCH. St Peter. Finsthwaite (Finn's field). 1724. Buttressed central tower with squat spire. Timber framed porch. Fine coloured ceiling. Beautiful reredos by Salviati of Venice. Stained glass. Plate c1710. Monument. Churchyard—grave of Clementina Johannes Sobiesky Douglass, of Waterside. Died May 1771 aged 26. The Princess Clementina was possibly the illegitimate daughter of Prince Charles Edward Stuart [Bonnie Prince Charlie] and his mistress Clementina Walkenshaw, daughter of John Walkenshaw, an aide to the Prince.
SD 368878

INDUSTRY. Around this area the art of charcoal burning is still practised by one, Walter Lloyd. He may be seen at work on his kilns or merely resting in his horse-drawn caravan where he will probably be making tool handles or pegs. Finsthwaite.
SD 3687

36 88

FISH. High Dam. Finsthwaite. Depth 33ft/10m. Man-made to supply water to Stott Park bobbin mill. Perch, rudd & brown trout. Free.
SD 3688

36 89

BIRDS. Black grouse. Green Hows Tarn.
SD 3689

37 85

CHURCH. St Mary. Staveley-in-Cartmel (OE "staef-leah": where staves were obtained). 1793. Restored 1897. Earlier church 1618. Open timber roofed interior with some timber posts.
SD 379859

37 86

HISTORICAL. Birthplace of Edmund Law (1703–87) Bishop of Carlisle. Staveley-in-Cartmel.
SD 3786

37 87

TRANSPORT. Lakeside and Haverthwaite railway. Steam trains. 3½ miles/ 5.6km. River Leven Valley. Open daily Easter–Oct. Lakeside. Lake Windermere.
SD 378874

Windermere Iron Steamboat Co based at Lakeside. Phone 05395 31188. *Lady of the Lake* the first steam yacht (made of wood) on the lake 1845 but ran aground in 1861 and wrecked. *The Lord of the Isles* (also of wood) launched 1846 but irreparable damage caused when it caught fire in 1850. Both these boats were owned by the Windermere Steam Yacht Company. In 1858 this Company merged with the Company we know today, whose initial fleet consisted of the iron paddle steamers *Firefly* and *Dragonfly*. In June 1869 the Furness Railway Co. opened a line from Plumpton Junction (near Ulverston) to Lakeside when the screw steamer *Swan* was launched followed by *Teal*. *Tern*, built for £5000 by Forrestt and Sons of Wyvenhoe, Essex, with room for 600 passengers in first and third class accommodation, launched 1891 and *Swift* 1900. The original *Tern* is still in use though *Swift* now houses Sir Malcolm Campbell's car which in 1935 broke the land speed record at 301mph/484kmh. Also shown is a full-size replica of Donald Campbell's hydroplane used in his tragic last attempt at the world water speed record in 1967. [In 1959 his record breaking runs recorded a mean of 260.35mph/418.98kmh]. *Swan* and *Teal* replaced late 1930s by boats which bear the same name. ¾ million passengers carried annually, between April to October. The length of Windermere sailed in 1½ hours, calling at Bowness and Ambleside.

SD 379874

37 88

INDUSTRIAL ARCHAEOLOGY. Bobbin Mill built 1835 by John Harrison, a gentleman farmer. Decommissioned 1971 but re-opened as a museum 1983. Guided tours and demonstrations of bobbin making, once a most important industry in this area supplying bobbins to Lancashire's cotton-mills. A large mill might need to set up 10 million bobbins of which 10% per week required replacing. Open Easter–October Monday–Saturday 0930–1830hrs. Sundays 1400–1830hrs. During October closes at 1630hrs. Fee. Phone 05395 31087. Low Stott Park. Finsthwaite.

SD 373882

38 86

ARCHITECTURE. Boat Houses. Fell Foot. Windermere. Built 1860 to resemble "Gothic" castles with castellations, portcullis and water gates. Here Colonel Ridehalgh moored his steam yachts *Britannia* & *Fairy Queen*, both opulent vessels of their time.

SD 381869

TOURIST INFORMATION CENTRE. National Trust. Fell Foot Country Park. Windermere. Cafe. Picnic area. Open daily Easter–October. Phone 05395 31273. Park open all year.

SD 381869

38 87

BIRDS. Winter: Long-tailed duck. Windermere. SD 3887

38 89

BIRDS. Winter: Black-necked grebe. Blake Holme. Windermere. SD 3889

39 87

WALKS. Gummer's How, St Anthony's Chapel & Cartmel Fell. Circuit 4 miles/6.4km. Fine views of Winster valley. Start: SD 398876

39 88

VIEWPOINT. Gummer's How (ME "gimmers-how": pasture hill where gimmers/sheep were fed) 1054ft/321m. Superb view over south lakes and tarns in good weather. Car park opposite. SD 391885

39 89

BIRDS. Nest site of buzzards, sparrow hawks & long-eared owls. Blake Holme Plantation. Windermere. SD 3989

Area 29 — Levens

40 83

REFRESHMENT. The Crown Hotel. High Newton. Phone 05395 31793.

SD 401830

40 84

CHURCH. Cottage dated 1677 used to be a Quaker Meeting House, illegal at the time, 22 years before William & Mary's Act of Toleration. Small room with look-out window over porch. Closed c1920. The burial ground is opposite Height. Stones only record dates of death of local followers, the Hunters, Nashes, Teasdales and Windsors. Newton Fell. SD 402845

40 87

ARCHITECTURE. Boat house near Sow How farm bears a weather vane in shape of a pig. SD 401879

41 84

HISTORICAL. In 1748 John Wilkinson built a forge and furnace at Wilson House, near Lindale on the River Winster (SD 4280). He smelted haematite ore using peat dug from Winster Mosses transported by his invention, an iron boat. Locals scoffed when one sank in Helton Pool as it was then known. His inventions carried him much further afield, even to working with the Darbys of Coalbrookdale. His eventual last resting place was in an iron coffin in Lindale churchyard. He died 14 July 1808 aged 80. SD 4184

41 86

ARCHITECTURE. Thorphinsty Hall. Earliest reference to it dated 1275. Varied chimneys. Some windows mullioned. Doors dated 1705 and 1708. SD 415862

41 88

ARCHITECTURE. Hodge Hill. Elizabethan manor house, home of the Philipsons. Round chimneys. Spinning gallery. Carved C17 document cupboard and spice cupboard. Carved chamber door inscribed "B. P. A. 1692". Cartmel Fell.

SD 419882

CHURCH. St Anthony. Cartmel Fell (ON "katr": rocky soil). c1505. St Anthony was patron saint of charcoal burners. Unfinished west tower. Roof—low pitched and saddleback. Nave and chancel in one. Some original windows from Cartmel Priory, that of St Anthony shows the Saint holding picture of a pig. Rare seven Sacrament window. Good woodwork & three decker pulpit of 1698. Rare pre-Reformation Crucifix, mutilated, one of only 3 surviving in England—on display in Kendal Museum. Cup of 1808 together with Elizabethan Cup and Cover Paten. Farmers pew 1696 marked "WH"— William Hutton of Thorphinsty. Bench with children's "Fox and Geese" game carved upon it. Tombstone records the death of Betty Poole, aged three "Underneath this stone A mouldring Virgin lies, who was the Pleasure once of Human Eyes...". Churchyard has mounting block and hitching post. Arrow sharpening slits in porch. This pretty church, built by local farmers to save a walk of 7 miles/11km to Cartmel Priory is "Browhead Chapel" in *Helbeck of Bannisdale*, a novel by Mrs Humphrey Ward.

SD 417881

41 89

REFRESHMENT. The Hare & Hounds. Bowland Bridge. Excellent food. Phone 04488 333. SD 418896

Mason's Arms. Strawberry Bank, Cartmel Fell. A vast range of world famous beers. Excellent food. Phone 04488 486. SD 414894

42 83

HISTORICAL. Blea Crag Bridge—site of a murder and the hanging of the murderer on nearby Gallows Hill. "Richard Taylor was buryed whoe suffered the same day at Blakeragge bridge end for murthering wilfully Rich. Kilner of Witherslack. April 1576." SD 423837

42 86

PLANTS. Grass-of-Parnassus, marsh violet, lesser clubmoss. Winster valley.

SD 4286

42 87

ARCHITECTURE. South House. Pool Bank. C17. At rear mullioned & transomed windows, some walled up. Fine oak partitions of "Muntin & Plank" type. Wooden spinning gallery. Canopied porch, above which initials "I. H. K" John and Catherine Hartley, the first family to live here who were farmers of statesman class. SD 429877

INSECTS. Butterflies: brown argus, common & holly blue. Meadowbrown & wallbrown. Copper. Fritillaries: high brown, dark green, pearl bordered and small-pearl bordered. Grayling, heath—large & small. Dingy skipper. Moths: Rare barred tooth-striped moth, galium carpet moth, clouded magpie, Portland dagger, blossom underwing, white-marked moth & butterbur moth. The Winster valley.

SD 4287

42 88

ARCHITECTURE. Cowmire Hall. Crosthwaite. C17, built on to a C16 Pele tower its walls 4ft/1.2m thick with double-arched vault below. 6 bays. Latin inscriptions etched at bottom of one of the east window lights, translated "Pray for the souls of Miles Brigg (and of Johana his wife) benefactors of this Church". Another reads "Wilm brigg goeth to London vpon tusday XIth day of Aprill God protect hym". The first owners, the Brigg family, were benefactors of Cartmel Fell Church. SD 427887

43 83

GARDENS. Halecat. Witherslack. Home of Michael and Fortune Stanley—well known re Grasmere Games. Shrubs/trees. Splendid views of Morecambe Bay. Open all year Monday-Friday 0900-1630hrs. Sunday 1400-1600hrs in summer only. Free. Phone 044852 229.   SD 434835

43 84

ARCHAEOLOGY. Viking sword found in the area. Now in Kendal Museum. Witherslack.   SD 4384

ARCHITECTURE. Nether Hall. Witherslack. C16 but much rebuilt 1933. Walls 5ft/1.5m thick. Pack-ponies stopped overnight and their loads were lifted off (and on) by means of pulleys-in a shed in the grounds, which is now incorporated into the present kitchen.   SD 439844

CHURCH. St Paul. Witherslack (ON "vithar-slakki": wooded dell). 1671. Plain Gothic in delightful position. Tower—one handed clock. 1768 on south face. Richly carved and canopied pulpit, originally a three-decker. Royal Arms of Queen Anne 1710. Churchyard—1757 sun dial initialled J. B.(John Barwick) and also those of John & Peter Barwick. John, under whose Will the church was built, born 1618 and died 1669. He was an ardent Royalist, became Dean of St Paul's and is buried there. Peter was the physician to Charles II and was one of the few who ministered to the sick during the Plague of 1665. He died 1705 blind for the last 11 years of his life. Both John & Peter were born in Witherslack. Outside the church gate is Dean Barwick's school 1678 and the Master's House.   SD 432842

43 85

NATURE RESERVE/TRAIL. Whitbarrow. Buzzard, nightjar, raven, wood-cock, great spotted & green woodpeckers. Limestone plants: blue moorgrass & lesser meadow rue. Fox, red & roe deer. Start just before entrance to Witherslack Hall, following signed footpath to Lord's seat. Keep to public right of way as this is private land.   SD 437859

43 86

ARCHITECTURE. Witherslack Hall. Built 1874 as a hunting lodge by Lord Derby of Liverpool. The previous owner, Captain Stanley, linked to the Derbys. (Refer SD 434837). Now a private school for boys with learning and behavioural difficulties. Large. Red/grey stone. Tower. Many gables. Mullioned and tran-somed windows.   SD 436862

TREES. Large mixed woodland. Whitbarrow.   SD 4386

43 87

INSECTS. Butterflies: argus, fritillary, brimstone, hairstreak. Whitbarrow Scar.
                                                                          SD 4387

MINE. Whitbarrow Scar Trial level east of Pool Bank. c1753.   SD 436877

43 88

BIRDS. Curlews' nest site. Whitbarrow Scar.   SD 4388

44 84

INDUSTRIAL ARCHAEOLOGY. Bobbin/corn mill with 22ft/7m narrow type pitchback wheel. Potash pits. Witherslack.   SD 448842

44 87

MEMORIAL. The summit cairn on Lord's Seat, Whitbarrow, bears a stone tablet "This Reserve Commemorates Canon G. A. K. Hervey 1893-1967. Founder of the Lake District Naturalists' Trust".   SD 443871

PLANTS. Limestone habitat. Whitbarrow. (Cumbria Trust for Nature Conservation. Permit required).   SD 4487

45 85

PLANTS. Pinewood habitat. Whitbarrow. (Cumbria Trust for Nature Conservation. Permit required).   SD 4585

45 87

ARCHITECTURE. Flodder Hall, Lyth. Now a farm. C17. Picturesque. Large round chimneys. 1865 porch bears the inscription "Si sapiens fore vis: Sex serva quae tibi mando; Quid loqueris et ubi De quo cui quomodo quando". (If you wish to be a wise man, do these six things I command; watch what you say, where, of whom, how and when you say it). Very possibly originated by Samuel Knipe, died 1645. An oak beam in the hall bears "1606 Tobias Knipe". 4 sets of stairs.   SD 458877

45 88

ARCHITECTURE. Drawell Farm. Lyth. C17. Open timbered ceiling to kitchen. Spice cupboard.   SD 458882

48 85

ARCHITECTURE. Nether Levens, farmhouse, originally known as Low Levens Hall. C16 but parts much older, possibly C12. Mullioned and transomed windows—roundels of Preston and Wilson families arms. Massive round chimneys. Ruined C14 Pele tower. Reputed tunnel to Levens Hall. Dovecot.   SD 488851

CHURCH. St John Evangelist. Levens. 1828. Commissioned by Mary Howard of Levens Hall. 3 Bell turret, octagonal top and spire. Nave and chancel. Lancet windows. Original three bells, clapperless, preserved.   SD 485857

REFRESHMENT. The Hare & Hounds. Levens. Old world charm. Phone 05395 60408.   SD 485856

48 86

CHURCH. Methodist Church formerly Wesleyan chapel. 1892. Levens.   SD 487861

48 87

ARCHITECTURE. Peat hut. Lane End Farm. Sizergh.   SD 487872

48 88

BIRDS. Tree sparrow. Park End. Brigsteer.   SD 4888

CHURCH. St John. Helsington (OE "haesling-tun": the enclosed land of hazels). 1726. Nave & chancel in one, bellcote. E wall mural by Marion D'Aumaret 1920. Wordsworth quotation at gate: "Engelberg, the Hill of Angels" from Tour on the continent 1820.   SD 489889

48 89

BIRDS. Corncrake has bred in this area. Brigsteer.   SD 4889

GEOLOGY. Limestone pavement. Brigsteer.   SD 4889

PLANTS. Deciduous mixed habitat. Brigsteer.   SD 4889

REFRESHMENT. The Wheatsheaf. Brigsteer. Phone 04488 254.   SD 481897

49 83

ARCHITECTURE. Heversham Hall, now a farmhouse. Since 1614 owned by the Wilson family and tenanted by the Handley family since 1876. C14 and later ruined Pele tower. Trefoil-headed mullioned windows. Oak panelled banqueting room.   SD 494833

The original Heversham Grammar School of 1613 is a cottage standing alone on hillside behind the church, now used as a class room for the nearby "new" school.   SD 498835

CHURCH. St Peter. Heversham (said to derive from "Haefar" a C7 Anglian Chief; "Eureshaim" in Domesday records). 1869 with some interior work of C12/13. Important monastery in C8. Many C17 artefacts. Tablet to Lady Dorothy Bellingham (died 1626) underneath which is a carving of the lady. Part C9 cross-shaft in the porch. Churchyard sun dial 1690.   SD 496834

HISTORICAL. Heversham, birthplace of Richard Watson (1737-1816). Professor of Chemistry and, later, Bishop of Llandaff. Died at Calgarth Park and buried Windermere churchyard. Another old boy of Heversham Grammar school became Bishop of Ferns, Ireland. Another famous pupil of the school was Ephraim Chambers, born 1680 (at Melton, near Crooklands—1740). Noted for his 2 volume *Cyclopaedia* in 1728. He was also first editor of the *Literary Magazine* started 1735. He is buried in Westminster Abbey cloisters, the inscription on his tomb are his own words.   SD 4983

Cockpit in field above the Old school Heversham. Diameter 17ft/5m. Raised bank for spectators. Cock-fighting made illegal 1835. Cock-fighting since Henry II regarded as a moral building "sport" in the north of England, analogous to the "playing fields of Eton" in the south of the country. Cock-pits were often sited near to the school or church. Such fights generally supervised by a master to whom pupils paid a "cock-penny" to provide prize money. Cock fights were known as Mains.   SD 498835

REFRESHMENT. Blue Bell Hotel. C16 Princes Way, Heversham. Phone 05395 62108.   SD 495833

49 85

HISTORIC HOUSE. Levens Hall. The site occupied in 1188 by the Redmaynes of Levens, followed by the Bellinghams in 1489. Alan Bellingham lost ownership of it in a game of cards to Colonel James Grahme of Netherby in 1688, and by descent in 1885 to Mary Howard and Richard Bagot and is today the home of the Bagot family. Largest Elizabethan House in Cumbria. Norman Pele tower. Interesting chimney pieces, one depicts the 4 Seasons, the 4 Elements and the 5 Senses. Italian plaster ceiling with interlocked quatrefoils. Leather wall hangings. Cromwellian armour. Carolingian furniture. Items of Napoleon, Nelson and Wellington. Steam engine display in outbuildings. Herd of black fallow deer and Bagot goats (these Schwarzhal goats so named after Richard II presented some to the ancestors of the present family, whose manorial crest bears the male's scimitar horns.) Gardens designed by Monsieur Beaumont, gardener to King James II (he also designed Hampton Court Gardens). It was he who planted the 1½ mile/2.4km long avenue of oaks. Magnificent topiary. Gardens open daily. Access to park at all times. Earliest known Ha-Ha (OE "haya": hedge), a wall with its top at ground level and its base in a deep ditch. Its construction deprived deer and livestock access to the home garden while allowing unimpeded views across the landscape from the house. House open daily Sunday to Thursday 1100-1700hrs Easter-end September. Phone 05395 60321.   SD 496851

LEGEND. A gypsy who died of starvation on the steps of Levens Hall after being refused a meal, cursed the owners saying that no heir would be born until a pure white fawn was born in the deer park and until the River Kent ceased to flow. One and a half centuries later, in 1895 during the severe winter weather, the river froze and a white fawn was born—subsequently a son was born. The Grey Lady, as she is known, still haunts the grounds and surrounding areas—seen quite recently. Another ghost haunts Levens Hall, that of a black woolly dog which makes a nuisance of itself to visitors. However only one person at a time sees it and it then disappears into a room, without trace. This century there have been random sightings in the Hall of the Pink Lady, wearing mob cap and pink print patterned dress. No specific portent attached to sightings.   SD 496851

LITERARY. Mrs Humphrey Ward (1851-1920) *née* Mary Augusta Arnold, granddaughter of Dr Thomas Arnold of Rugby, stayed at Levens Hall during the winter of 1896/7, while writing *Helbeck of Bannisdale* 1898. She used the Hall and Sizergh Castle as models for *Bannisdale*. She also wrote *Robert Elsmere* 1888 and *Marcella* 1894.   SD 496851

TREES. Oaks, fine avenue of. Yews, ancient topiary. Levens Hall.   SD 4985

WALKS. Lancaster & Kendal canal. Circuit 6½ miles/10.5km. Easy. Parkland, riverside & canal tow-path. Start near Levens Hall. SD 496853

49 87

CASTLE. Sizergh Castle, near Sedgwick. C13/14. Seat of Strickland family since 1239. Mrs Horneyold-Strickland still in residence. Fine, furnished Pele tower, with unusual attached higher turret. Several C16 benches. Some fine Elizabethan carved overmantels, 5 carved before 1580. Good English and French furniture. 2 handed sword dated 1340. Stuart relics. Family portraits. Katherine Parr also lived here whilst twice widowed before she married Henry VIII. Grounds with large rock garden constructed of local limestone by Hayes Nurseries of Ambleside in 1926. National Trust. Open Sunday, Monday, Wednesday and Thursday 1400-1745 hrs. April to the end of October. Phone 05395 60070. SD 498878

49 88

INDUSTRIAL ARCHAEOLOGY. Lime kiln. Holeslack Farm. SD 493884

Wordsworth fountain. (Rosemary Liddle)

Area 30 – Stainton

50 84

ARCHITECTURE. Hincaster Hall. C16 extended C18. Round chimneys. Stone mullioned windows—7 lights to hall window. Some walls 7ft/2.1m thick. Roof may have been thatched, on account of its steep pitch.   SD 506848

50 85

MAMMALS. Fallow deer herd. Levens Park.   SD 5085

50 86

ARCHAEOLOGY. Cairn circle beside the River Kent in Levens Park. Burials—2 flint knives and Beaker pottery. The funerary site (sealed by a mound) built in an area of previous settlement of which flints of an earlier date have been found.   SD 505862

ARCHITECTURE. Gothic mansion 1871 by George Henry Brettargh Yeates—on some maps as Brettargh Holt. In 1937 it became the Levens Hotel; during the war an evacuation centre and then a Nursing Home. In 1971 became a Convent of the Sisters Noviciale (the Salesian Order). Linked now with diocese of Lancaster, of Hexham and of Newcastle and used as a conference centre and retreat. Near Levens Bridge.   SD 506866

50 87

INDUSTRIAL ARCHAEOLOGY. Ruins of gunpowder works Sedgwick. Appositely, ammunition stored here during the last war.   SD 509879

REFRESHMENT. Strickland Arms Hotel. Sizergh. Phone 05395 60239.   SD 500872

51 83

ARCHITECTURE. Deepthwaite bridge. C17.   SD 518834

51 85

ARCHITECTURE. Sellet Hall. Stainton. C17. 3 bay front. Mullioned and transomed windows. Fine "well" staircase.   SD 518855

51 86

ARCHITECTURE. Sedgwick House. 1868. Tower. Was the home of Jacob Wakefield (a Mayor of Kendal and whose family was instrumental in developing the local gunpowder industry), but is now a school.   SD 510869

51 87

INDUSTRIAL ARCHAEOLOGY. Ruins of gunpowder works opened 1764 by John Wakefield. Site superseded by that across the river. Sedgwick.   SD 512878

52 85

ARCHITECTURE. Stone foot-bridge C17. Stainton.   SD 524859

CHURCH. Independent chapel. 1698. Stainton (a place on stony ground). Pulpit bears date of building.   SD 526859

52 87

CHURCH. St Thomas. Crosscrake. 1875. On site of 1190 church foundations. Blue Westmorland slate. Unusually large sanctuary which incorporates stone from original building.   SD 524870

52 89

BIRDS. Enid Maples Bird Sanctuary. Grassgarth. 7 acres/2.8ha of 70 year old woodland with pond. Permit required from Cumbria Wildlife Trust. Church Street, Ambleside. (Access off A65 at junction to Natland).   SD 526897

CHURCH. St Mark. Natland (ON "nata": nettle, hence infested wood). 1909 though founded on C12 site. West tower and stair turret. Interior roof, segmented and plastered. Tie beams and curved queen posts. East window tribute to civilian and military who suffered in 2nd World War, designed by Gerald E. R. Smith. South window memorial to a father killed on the Somme and his son, taken prisoner at Arnhem, died of his wounds.   SD 521892

53 83

CHURCH. St Patrick. Crooklands (ON "krokr": land on bend in the river). 1852. Previous to chancel rebuild in 1892 was known as St Gregory's. Tower has gargoyles dating from Henry VIII when there was an old chapel on this site. Stair turret. Large cross, the light from which can be seen from the M6. Superb hill position. Plate 1832/6.   SD 537835

HISTORICAL. In 1652, George Fox preached in the old chapel (see above), to the "Seekers" of Westmorland who later formed the nucleus of the Quaker church.   SD 537835

INDUSTRIAL ARCHAEOLOGY. Milton Mill, Crooklands. Its gear in running order though not worked. Collection of farm tools. Drying kiln. Owned by Mr. Hayhurst whose family worked in the mill for generations. Permission to view from Mr. Hayhurst. Milton Mill Farm.   SD 530830

NATURE RESERVE/TRAIL. Along canal bank from Crooklands to Stainton.   SD 534835

53 88

ARCHAEOLOGY. Castlesteads. The Helm. Hill fort—several ramparts and enclosures. Perhaps pastoral farmsteads, of unknown date, though considered to have been a Brigantes encampment.   SD 531887

54 83

ARCHITECTURE. Preston Patrick Hall. C14. On site of C12 Abbey for

Premonstratensian Canons, later moved to Shap. Interesting windows and door-ways. Court room in which early Quakers were tried for non-payment of tithes. Until C16 owned by the Curwen family of Workington then passed by marriage to the Prestons.   SD 545837

54 87

ARCHITECTURE. Birkrigg Park. 1742. Bays. Flat window frames.   SD 542871

54 89

ARCHITECTURE. Bleaze Hall, now a farm. Old Hutton. Built 1600 by Roger Bateman, cloth manufacturer. Bequeathed to Henry Bateman of pack-horse train fame, London, York and Scotland. Now home of the Bentham family. Mullioned and transomed windows. Some parts remain of exquisite plaster ceilings and Jacobean fittings. Has ancient "Dobbie-Stone" (a prehistoric stone three faced hammer head with central hole), its "charm" preventing disturbance to the household by evil spirits.   SD 549891

INDUSTRIAL ARCHAEOLOGY. Lye-kiln in the lane leading to Bleaze Hall. In years past, bracken ash from the kiln together with fat or oils was boiled, the resulting interaction of oil and caustic potash produced a soft soap.   SD 549892

LEGEND. During the C13 the daughter of the family living in the medieval dwelling on the site of the present Bleaze Hall died of sorrow when her lover did not return from the Crusades. The funeral cortège has been seen on numerous occasions (none recent) passing around the Hall.   SD 549891

55 88

CHURCH. St John Baptist. Old Hutton (the [old] farm on the spur of land). 1873. Small apse. Bell-turret. Chalice 1459 (lodged elsewhere). C14 window from previous church on this site.   SD 559886

HISTORICAL. A house in Old Hutton bears a plaque stating that John Wesley lodged there October 1749 during his first visit to Westmorland as he journeyed from Leeds to Whitehaven.   SD 559886

Glossary

ARCHAEOLOGY

Approximate chronological divisions:

		Years ago		
Eolithic				[1]
Palaeolithic:	Lower	300,000	– 100,000	[2]
	Middle	100,000	– 35,000	
	Upper	35,000	– 11,000	
		Years BC		
Mesolithic:	Earlier	10,000	– 8,000	[3]
	Later	8,000	– 4,500	[4]
Neolithic:	Earlier	4,500	– 3,200	[5]
	Later	3,200	– 2,400	[6]
Bronze Age:	Early	2,400	– 1,400	[7]
	Middle	1,400	– 950	[8]
	Late	950	– 700	[9]
Iron Age:	Early	700	– 450	
	Middle	450	– 150	[10]
	Late	150	– AD 43	[11]

[1] Earliest period of human culture.

[2] Old stone age. Emergence of man as a tool making animal. Hand axe and flake tools. Gradual climatic changes alternating between ice cold and temperate.

[3] Middle stone age. Climate improved after last glaciation and most of ice melted. Sparse vegetation replaced by low bushes and trees and eventually forest.

[4] Separation of Britain from the Continent about 6000 BC.

[5] New Stone Age when the hunting economy changed to a farming one. Forests cut down to make space for crops.

[6] Beaker people.

[7] Food vessels of decorated course pottery. Flint and stone continued in use.

[8] Metal working developed.

[9] Hill forts and land boundaries. Less ritual burial.

[10] Early Iron Age Hallstatt traders introduced weapons and tools. The wheel much in evidence. Hill forts strengthened with better defences-discord between communities.

[11] Celts	1000 BC	–	AD 600
Romans	AD 1	–	AD 500
Anglo Saxons	AD 300	–	AD 1000
Vikings	AD 600	–	AD 1300

ARCHAEOLOGY

Bailey. Courtyard surrounded by defensive perimeter.

Burial mound. Neolithic or Bronze Age.

Cairn. Pyramid of rough stones as memorial or to waymark a path.

Cairnfields. Mostly Bronze Age, mounds of stone accumulated during the clearance of land for farming.

Cup Markings. Cup-shaped depressions (in rock) encircled with rings often with lines cutting across the rings and linking the depressions. Generally attributed to the Iron Age. Whilst their meaning is not clear to us they may have had the purpose of ensuring fertility and life.

Henge. A circular ritual monument of the Late Neolithic and Early Bronze Age. Ditch all around and a bank of earth or stone outside it. Earlier ones have single entrance and later and larger ones, two to four.

Hill fort. Fortified settlement site of Late Bronze Age and (mainly) Iron Age. Defended by earth ramparts or stone walls. External ditches.

Hut circles. Relics of prehistoric dwellings. Circular plan. Low walls of stone. Conical roof of thatch, reed or grass. Some huts used for storage others for dwellings with a central hearth. Some buildings surrounded by perimeter walls, others not. Around these huts may be fields—of square configuration for the simple plough (an Ard) of Bronze Age and Iron Age man necessitated ploughing at right angles to the initial shallow furrow.

Motte. Conical mound, usually large in diameter.

Ring cairn. Neolithic and Early Bronze Ages. Circular area within which burials sometimes made.

Stone circles. Late Neolithic or Bronze Age. Ring bank of piled stones, with one entrance. Some locations have groups or circles. Their purposes are thought to be in connection with observations of the sun, moon and stars—marking the seasons, certainly associated with religion and ritual whilst some acted as meeting and trading places.

Transhumance. Seasonal moving of livestock to another region, that is, from valleys in winter to high fells in summer.

Tumulus. Burial mound—usually earth covered.

Unenclosed huts. Neolithic or Bronze Age.

ARCHITECTURE

Arcade. Roof supported by a series of arches.

Bank barn. Two storied farm building built into natural slope of land so that carts could be wheeled into the upper floor from ground level, creating a feed/storage floor over the animals beneath.

Barge board. Sloping board, often carved, along a gable roof covering the rafters which overlap the walls.

Barrel vault. Continuous semicircular arched vault.

ARCHITECTURE

Bay. Space between windows or pillars.

Boss. Carved projection at the intersection of ceiling ribs.

Bressumer. Large beam supporting masonry over a large hearth.

Buttress. Brick or stone structure supporting a wall.

Castellated. Castle-like. Battlemented.

Chimney Hood. Huge canopy extending into living quarters 6ft/ 1.8m above the floor gradually narrowing to a flue in the roof space. Constructed of lath and plaster—the earliest of woven wattle coated with a mixture of clay, cow-dung and straw. Joints of meat hung therein to cure in the smoke. In wet weather sooty droplets fell upon those below "hallan-drop", hence the custom even now of countrymen wearing their caps while sitting by the fire.

Cist or Kist. Wooden box for sacred utensils.

Clapper bridge. Large slabs of stone, some making rough piers with larger slabs laid on top.

Corbel. A bracket or projecting beam, supporting a weight.

Corbie. "Crow" stepped gables. Type of roof end used especially with slate/stone walls.

Crenellate. Furnish with battlements.

Cruck built. Crucks (blades) are pairs of massive incurved timbers, from a single tree, forming arches from ground level (full cruck) to support the ridge beam. In the most primitive construction, walls were non-load bearing. Later, in C17 larger buildings had several crucks, standing on a timber cill or padstone to resist damp. To allow additional interior space and, therefore, upstairs room, the construction was erected on a low wall (raised cruck) and roof members supported by tie or collar beams. Crucks were pegged together at the apex while on the ground and then raised into the upright position.

Dormer Window. Window erected above plane of neighbouring roof.

Finial. Ornament at tip of ridge or a pinnacle.

Fire-house. Farmhouse living accommodation furnished simply—table and seating and built-in wall bread/spice cupboard.

Fire Window. Small window beside the chimney hood.

Gable. Triangular section or the end of a wall of a house.

Hallan. Straight passage connecting farmhouse front and back door.

Hearth Tax. Levied from 19 May 1662 until 1689, collected at 2/-(10p) per hearth in 2 instalments on Lady Day (25 March) and Michaelmas (29 Sept). Some exemptions—those in receipt of poor relief etc.

Heck. One side of mell formed by a partition.

Hospice. House of rest for travellers especially one kept by a religious order.

ARCHITECTURE

Ionic column. Shaft fluted in 24 semicircular flutes with fillets between them. In Classical Architecture an Order is an entire column consisting of base, shaft, capital and entablature. The 3 Greek kinds are Doric, Ionic and Corinthian. Composite and Tuscan are Roman developments of the Greek originals.

Jamb. Upright post of a frame in an opening.

Lime Mortar. Lime, not cement, as a constituent of the mix.

Lintel. Timber or stone placed horizontally over a doorway, window or other opening through a wall to support the wall above.

Mell. Short passage between hallan and fire-house.

Mullion. In Gothic architecture, vertical division between the lights of windows, screens etc.

Oriel. Projecting portion of a room and its window supported by corbels. From Latin "Orat-Oriolum" (little place for prayer).

Outshot. Additional small room under lean-to roof.

Palladian. C18 style based on the Italian architect Andrea Palladio (1518–80).

Pele or Peel or Pile (palisade). Stone tower or fortified dwelling capable of being defended against any sudden marauding expedition. Tower usually 3 storey; windowless ground floor for cattle, first floor living quarters and battlemented second floor (roof).

Windermere from Adelaide Hill. (Rosemary Liddle)

ARCHITECTURE

Priest hole. Secret hiding place let into fabric of a building to hide Roman Catholic priests.

Rannell-balk. Wooden beam across hearth from which pot-hangers suspended.

Slope Stone. Slate slab holed to take wooden rails or beams. Precursor of gates.

Spinning gallery. An open-sided gallery attached to a farm-stead or wool barn. Provided well-lit working area for spinning or for the drying of fleeces in the sheltered but airy conditions.

Transom. Horizontal mullion or cross bar in a window.

Tunnel Vault. A barrel vault—semi cylindrical.

Tuscan column. See Ionic.

Window Tax. Imposed 1696 on house occupiers to help meet the cost of reminting the damaged coin of the realm. It replaced Hearth Tax (q.v.). Each household paid a basic 2/- (10p) and those with between 10 and 20 windows paid a further 8/- (40p). A new Act in 1747 imposed an additional 6d (2½p) on houses of 10 to 14 windows and 9d extra on 15 to 19 windows; those house-holds with more than 19 paid 1/- (5p) per window. In 1825 those with less than 8 windows made exempt. (Scotland exempted altogether in 1707). The tax was abolished 1851.

CHURCH

Apse. Termination (of a church) usually in semicircular from surmounted by a demi-cupola.

Baluster. A small pillar, swelling in the centre or towards its base.

Baptistery. That part of a church in which baptism was performed by immersion. Can be a separate building.

Bellcote. A turret raised over the west end of small churches and chapels that have no towers in which to hang bells. This is distinct from the smaller turret at the east end of the nave for the Sanctus Bell.

Capital. The head of a column, pilaster. In Classical Architecture the Orders have each their respective Capitals, which differ considerably from each other.

Castellated. Battlemented.

Chalice. Sacred vessel used in celebration of the Eucharist.

Chancel. From "cancelli" —a lattice. A term long ago used to denote a choir—its name derived from the "cancelli" or stone screen, by which it was enclosed.

Classical. Formal, precise style based on Rome and Greece.

Clerestory. Wall under church roof pierced with row of windows.

Collar beam. Horizontal transverse timber connecting the mid-points of the sloping rafters of a pitched roof.

Corbel. A projecting bracket supporting a pier, cornice or column.

Cross. It was the custom before the Reformation to erect a large cross in the middle of the churchyard. Few survive.

CHURCH

Crossing tower. Tower above transepts.

Cupola. A dome covering a square, circular or polygonal base.

Decorated Style. C14 English Gothic style. Windows often contained ornamental tracery or divisions. Decorative mouldings.

Early English. C13 English Gothic style, with pointed arches and lancet windows.

Embraced tower. Buttresses clasp the corner.

Eucharist. Christian sacrament in which bread and wine are consecrated and consumed.

Flagon. Large vessel with handle, spout and lid, to hold consecrated water for Eucharist.

Font. Vessel containing consecrated water used in administration of baptism.

Gargoyle. Projecting spout to throw water from a roof off the wall. Usually situated in the cornice although sometimes on the fronts of buttresses—Early English or Decorated style. Often carved into figures or animals.

Gnomon. Arm of a sun-dial or similar object that casts a shadow to indicate the time.

Gonfalon. Banner, often with streamers, hung from a crossbar.

Gothic. C13/15 style, with pointed windows and arches.

Hagioscope. A hole bored through a wall or pier to allow a view of the altar.

Hammerbeam. Bracket supporting weight of a wooden arched roof.

Hatchment. Achievement of Arms in diamond/square-shaped frame. Distinguished a person's rank and position in life. Carried at the head of that person's funeral cortège.

Headstones. The practice of erecting memorial headstones became common from beginning of C17. Usually undecorated save for figure of an angel. By the end of the C17 classical shapes and motifs were incorporated. In Victorian times it was the fashion to celebrate death ostentatiously, with very elaborate headstones, allowing bereaved family to make a statement of affluence and to identify the grave plot emphatically.

Hogsback Coffin. In use before the Danes invaded and up to Norman conquest. Low with curved tops carved to represent tiles in imitation of the long low cottages of northern England. Exquisite scroll figure work often portrayed.

Lancet. Narrow window with pointed arch, obtuse at its point. So called for its resemblance to a surgeon's lancet—C13.

Lectern. Reading desk.

Lych-gate. Roofed gateway into Church yard, which shelters the coffin and bearers awaiting the priest who meets them on consecrated ground. Derivation—Lich, meaning corpse (Anglo-Saxon).

CHURCH

Misericord. Projecting bracket on the underside of stalls. Fitted with a hinge which, when turned up, formed a projection which could be used as a rest for the tired or infirm during long services. Often carved with mythological beasts and birds as well as religious figures.

Missal. Book of Prayers or book containing the years service of Mass.

Nave. Western body of a church between the aisles extending from the choir to the principal entrance. Derivation of nave—the centre of anything or "navis" so called from its vaulted roof resembling in shape an inverted ship.

Neo-classical. Late C18 style reviving the precision and symmetry of Greece and Rome.

Norman. Late C11/12 style, introduced to England from Normandy.

Paten. Shallow dish used for bread at Eucharist.

Perpendicular Style. C15 English. Larger windows, flatter arches with vertical and horizontal members to retain glass.

Pilaster. A square column or pillar, set in a wall but projecting from it: for decoration.

Pulpitum. The great screen which closed the west end of the quire.

Queen post. A pair of vertical (or nearly so) timbers placed symmetrically on a tie-beam and supporting side purlins (pairs of timbers some way up the slope of a roof).

Quire. The place where the monks' fundamental work (the Opus Dei) was carried out.

Recessed spire. Thin spire rising from the centre of a tower roof, well inside the parapet. (Needle spire).

Reredos. The wall or screen at the back of an altar.

Rood-screen. A wooden or stone screen, usually one bay west of the pulpitum (q.v.) with an altar against its western face.

Runic-Runes. Scandinavian—claimed to be invented by Woden. The Vikings & Anglo-Saxons used this written script for divination (insight into or discovery of the unknown or the future by supernatural means). The last Rune Master practised in Iceland in C17. The Runic alphabet consists of 16 letters, their curves changed into straight lines to facilitate engraving on hard surfaces. Could be said to be the forerunner of the modern trade mark.

Steeple. Spire atop a tower.

Stoup. Small niche with a basin at church entrance placed there for holy water.

Tomb chest. Stone coffin. Medieval funerary monument.

Transept. A transverse nave, passing in front of the choir and crossing the central nave of a church. Sometimes called the "cross", each of its parts to right and left of the nave referred to as "cross-aisles".

CHURCH

Triptych. A form of picture, generally depicting a religious theme, in three panels—a centre panel and two hanging doors, painted on both sides. Originally portable altars of medieval nobility.

Venetian window. A form of window also called a Palladian window.

GEOLOGY - including Mineralogy.

Agglomerate. Volcanic material composed of angular rock fragments embedded in a hard matrix of fine ash.

Alluvial fan. A roughly triangular deposit of material formed where a mountain stream enters a lake or sea. Scree fans develop in a similar manner.

Andesite. Fine-grained volcanic lava with a glassy matrix and high silica content. Frequently contains feldspar, rarely quartz.

Antimony. Brittle silvery-white element used especially in alloys.

Apatite. Transparent, translucent or opaque, occurring in veins with quartz, feldspar and iron ores. Crystals are hexagonal. Can also be white, violet or yellow. Glows in ultra violet light.

Arenite. Sandstone—comprising quartz, feldspar and rock fragments. Classified on the basis of average relative proportions of these 3 main components—in this case less than 15% matrix.

Arête. Sharp mountain ridge.

Arsenic. Brittle steel-grey semi-metallic element. A virulent poison.

Augite. Square or octohedral crystals usually dark green-black. Hard.

Barytes. Barium sulphate. Tabular crystals forming veins in rock. Usually colourless to white but can be grey, yellow or brown. Can be found in whorl or "cock's comb" configuration.

Basalt. Dark coloured lava, sometimes dark green or black. Very fine grained. In silica but usually containing feldspar.

Biotite mica. Randomly distributed small dark flakes. Gives granite rocks dark speckles. Quite soft.

Bismuth. A reddish-white easily fusible metallic element.

Borrowdale Volcanic Series. (BVS). Colouration—green. Solidified lavas and tuffs; their relative hardness and resistance to erosion resulting from igneous sources. Occurs in a broad band across the centre of the Lake District.

Breccia. A sedimentary conglomerate with sharp-edged and angular fragments.

Calcite. Transparent or opaque. Also known as Iceland spar when in clear crystalline form. Fine crystals. In this condition it refracts light, making print appear double. Masses of this mineral occur with limestone. Where it exists in veins of rock it may be coloured by impurities.

Cerussite. Most frequently occurs as radiating or cruciform crystals in lead veins.

Chalcopyrites. Copper pyrites. Brassy appearance. Brittle. Crystalline infrequently.

GEOLOGY - including Mineralogy.

Chiastolite. Slate is a good example of the effect of pressure on fine-grained sedimentary clay and shale. Heat produces crystals of new materials, one type of which is chiastolite. Easily recognised by the very fine grained dark inclusions arranged in a characteristic cross-shape.

China clay. In Lakeland a decomposed hypersthenite-feldspars in granite rocks partially or completely altered by extremely hot water to fine flaky mineral of which kaolin is one.

Coal. Hard opaque black or blackish mineral. Mainly carbonised plant matter, in seams or strata below the surface of the earth. Conversion in successive stages from peat through lignite (soft brown coal), hard brown coal to bituminous hard coal and anthracite. Used as a fuel.

Cobalt. Silvery-white metallic element similar in many respects to nickel.

Conglomerate. Erosion resulted in masses of different sizes of rounded pebbles and small boulders, set in a matrix of silica, iron and lime compounds. Looks like rough concrete mix.

Coniston Limestone. Calcite, dolomite and various silica. Forms a "shore-line" between B. V. Series and Silurian Series.

Diorite. Uncommon. Dark igneous rock containing fragments of a softer black lead-like substance—plumbago.

Dolerite. Medium grain, crystalline igneous rock. Surface outcrops often develop a reddy brown colouration.

Dolomite. Colourless mineral forming fine to coarse-grained aggregate. Occurs as a physical and chemical change of limestone.

Drumlin. Boulder debris—remains of glaciation.

Erratics. Stone or boulder transported by a glacier for a considerable distance from its place of origin and deposited in unusual surroundings.

Fault. Displacement of strata.

Feldspar. Found in almost all igneous rocks. Several types—determined by their chemical composition, but all are fundamentally aluminium silicates. Usually present in acid igneous material and can form long crystals. Where these are pink they are termed orthoclase feldspar. Plagioclase feldspar forms tabular crystals.

Felsite. Fine-grained. Hard. Found on Pike o' Stickle and other locations in Langdales and elsewhere, where it was shaped to form rough axe-head. (Refer NY 272072).

Fluorspar. Alternatively known as fluorite. Occurs as glassy, lustrous crystals or may be coloured by impurities, blue, green or violet. Fairly rare in the Lake District.

Gabbro. Coarse-grained and dark coloured igneous rock—often speckled appearance.

Galena. Lead sulphide. Lead ore. Sparkling silvery cube-shaped crystals if freshly broken.

GEOLOGY - including Mineralogy.

Garnet. Found in metamorphic rocks. Sometimes occurs in granites. Semi-precious gem stone from clear, flawless crystals and is extremely hard—is used as an abrasive.

Granophyre. An igneous rock. Medium grain size of granite family in which quartz and feldspar are intergrown.

Graphite. Crystalline allotropic form of carbon. Originated from carbon monoxide gas, reaction catalysed by iron oxide, pyrite, iron silicates and quartz.

Haematite. Oxide of iron, often occurring in kidney-shaped masses. Weathers to a red colour which spreads to nearby rocks. When broken, it shows a fine radiating structure. Much used in early iron industry.

Hanging valley. A tributary valley left high above the main valley floor after over-deepening of the main valley and the retreat of a glacier. Its stream reaches the valley by forming a waterfall. The same effect is produced by differential erosion by the main stream glacier and its tributary stream glacier.

Hornfels. Medium/fine-grained granulose rock produced by thermal metamorphism.

Kettle moraine. Depression in landscape formed by glacial ice melting, leaving sedimentary deposits.

Linarite. Sulphate of lead and copper, found in brilliant blue crystals. Linarite occurs altered to cerussite. Name derived from Linares, Spain, where is is alleged to be found.

Magnetite. Often small black octagonal crystals, shiny, found in gabbro.

Malachite. Fairly commonly encrusting rock surfaces in different shades of green granular material.

Mica. White or silvery flakes, sometimes with yellow or brown colouration. Transparent or translucent and hexagonal. Common as the shining particles in granite and also as the dark form called biotite, which is quite soft.

Microgranite. Light coloured finer grained than granite and of speckled appearance due to small black crystals of biotite mica.

Moraine. Accumulated material transported by ice and deposited at a later time. This debris may form a lateral moraine on the valley side or a series of moraines, each representing a temporary halt by the glacier. The last of these produces a lateral moraine which can be so large as to dam the end of the valley and hold back water to create a lake.

Penrith Sandstone. Quartz arenite in which the grains are coated with iron hydroxide.

Pyrite. Sometimes cube-shaped or as a thin layer at surface joints. Pale brassy yellow which weathers to very deep yellow metallic lustre.

GEOLOGY - including Mineralogy.

Quartz. Although colourless and transparent, often appears as grey rounded crystals hexagonal or pyramidal, sometimes coloured by impurities. Characteristic glassy appearance. Extremely resistant to weathering. Often in acid rock and in veins of sedimentary deposits.

Rhyolite. High silica content, acidic, usually light coloured, fine-grained rock of volcanic origin. Many variations exist determined by granite-like crystals incorporated. Hexagonal. Similar to Giant's Causeway in Ireland.

Roches moutonnées. Rocks in the path of a glacier smoothed and shaped by ice action. (French—"sheep rocks", because of their comparable shape). They may show scratch marks made by stones in the moving ice.

Rock bar. A layer of hard rock that may deflect the path of a glacier, which created the shape of a lake.

Scheelite. A form of tungsten.

Schist. Metamorphic rock in which mica is abundant. Arranged in parallel layers which tend to split off into thin flakes. They are named according to their most prominent mineral.

Silurian Series. Fine-grained grits and shales. In southern area of Lake District separated from Borrowdale Volcanic Series by a narrow band of Coniston Limestone.

Skiddaw slates. Oldest visible rocks—500/550 millions years old extremely fine grained and easily fragment. Colouration—blue/grey. Form major part of the north and north-western fells, some in south-east of region (near Ullswater) and south-west (Black Combe).

Slate. Extremely fine-grained. Cleavage planes. Can be black and shades of green, blue or brown.

Spotted slate. (Shales). Metamorphosed clay rocks recognised by spots about 0.02in/0.5mm to 0.1in/3mm across. In some instances the spots are small concentrations of iron ore.

Stone stripes. Caused by alternate freezing and thawing which tends to sort out small and large stones into lines. Arctic and sub-arctic frost phenomena.

Syenite. Medium to coarse-grain intrusive igneous rock. Can be white, grey, pink and red. Of granite family, in which quartz and feldspar are intergrown.

Tungsten. Steel-grey heavy metallic element with very high melting point, used for filaments of electric lamps and for alloying steel. Its only location outside of Cornwall is in Lakeland's Carrock Fell.

Truncated spur. A spur of land ending abruptly as if cut off at tip.

Tuffs. Compacted and hardened volcanic dusts.

Wolfram. An ore of tungsten, found as tabular or prismatic black crystals which have a slight lustre.

Zinc blende. Common name for sphalerite. Quite commonly found as rough and brittle crystalline masses. In mining days known as Black Jack.

SIMPLE GEOLOGICAL MAP OF THE LAKE DISTRICT

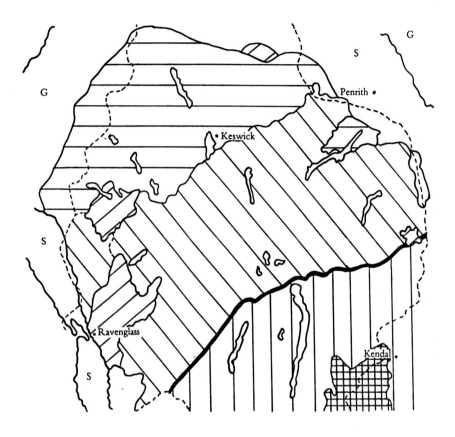

[═] Skiddaw Slates
[\ \ ] Borrowdale Volcanics
[/ /] Igneous Intrusions
[S] New Red Sandstone

[| | |] Silurian Series
[▬] Coniston Limestone
[▦] Carboniferous Limestone
[G] Millstone Grit/Coal Measures

INDUSTRIAL ARCHAEOLOGY.

Bloomery. An open air hearth where charcoal was used in smelting red haematite ores to obtain wrought iron. This direct reduction method used from prehistoric times until C15. All that now remains are occasional pieces of slag.

Horse Engine House/Gin case. Early form of horse-powered threshing machine provided an alternative to the use of wind and water mills. A horse tethered to a bar trotted a circular path, turning a crown wheel and pinion geared via a shaft and universal joints, to a wheel of the grinding-stones or other machinery. The gearing increased the speed to a final ratio of approximately 100:1. A special building was attached to the end of the barn, usually with rounded ends and sometimes its roof was supported only by pillars and open to the yard.

LANGUAGE — DERIVATION/DEFINITION.

Derivation of words and their meanings as applied to places in the Lake District and also to its agriculture. Names derived from Celtic (related to Gaelic and Welsh)—[C]; Old English-Anglo-Saxon—[OE]; Old Norse (Viking)—[ON]; Middle English (forerunner of dialect)—[ME]; Dialect—[D].

A. [ON] "River": *e.g.* River Liza.

Ay. [ON] "stream": *e.g.* Rothay, Brathay.

Acre. [OE] "accer", [ON] "Akr": As large a strip of land as could be ploughed by a yoke of oxen in a day. The acre was standardized by Edward 1 at 40 rods long x 4 rods wide or 4840 sq. yds. Regional variations persisted—6760 sq. yds in Westmorland and 7840 sq. yds in Ireland. (1 Rod = 16½ ft/5.02m).

Angul. [OE] "hook/angle": *e.g.* Angle Tarn.

Applethwaite. [OE] "aeppel", [ON] "epli": Clearing with an apple tree.

Ard Crags. [D] "dry/parched" crags.

Arnr. [ON] "Eagle": *e.g.* Erne Crag.

Askr. [ON] "Ash": *e.g.* Askham (Among Ash trees).

Band. Ridge or tongue of land dividing two lower tracts.

Bank. [ON] "banki".

Bannerdale. [ON] "bein-vith-dal": the dale with the holly tree.

Barf. [D] "barrow".

Barrow. [OE] "beorgh", [ON] "berg": small hill or mound.

Bee bole. Rectangular recess in wall into which was placed a small bee-hive of wickerwork or straw. C16/17. Before sugar was imported from the Indies, honey was a staple sweetener, also produced was bees-wax and mead.

Bekkr. [ON] "stream": *e.g.* Troutbeck (Trout stream).

Belde. [ME] "hut, animal shelter": *e.g.* Nan Bield pass.

Be(o)rgh. [OE] "Small hill": *e.g.* Yewbarrow (Hill for yews).

Bergh. [ON] "hill": *e.g.* Gowbarrow (Windy hill).

LANGUAGE — DERIVATION/DEFINITION.

Bessyboot. [D] "Bessy's sheepfold" (bucht).

Bield. [D] "den or shelter".

Biggin. [ON] "building".

Birki. [ON] "birch tree": *e.g.* Birkfell, Birkness.

Biskey How. [D] "Bishop's hill".

Blacksail. [ON] "blakk-seyla": dark mire or stream.

Blaen. [C] "peak": *e.g.* Blencathra (Peak with chair).

Blar. [ON] "dark blue": *e.g.* Blea tarn.

Blen. A headland.

Blencathra. [C] "saddleback".

Blencow. [D] "blenk": to glimmer.

Bord. [OE] "a board or shield": i.e. a plateau: *e.g.* Border End.

Borrans. [C] "boirean": a burial mound—hence a pile of stones; sometimes spelled barrans, borance, borwens or burghanes.

Bottom. Lowest or innermost part of a valley.

Bowfell. The bow-shaped fell.

Bowland Bridge. The bridge probably named after its builder.

Brandling. Local name for a salmon parr (immature).

Brandreth. Local name for a tripod. The English Place Names Society suggest that it may have applied to the hill upon which a beacon was sited.

Brant. [OE] "brant", [ON] "brattr": steep.

Brantwood. Land cleared by burning.

Brocc. [OE] "badger": *e.g.* Brockbarrow (Badger hill).

Brycg. [OE] bridge.

Bu. [ON] "bu": dwelling.

Bur. [OE] "the dale with the cottage": *e.g.* Boardale.

Burgaesan. [OE] "Burial place": *e.g.* Borrans.

Burh. [OE] fortified place.

Burthwaite. The clearing with the cow-shed.

Butere. [OE] "butter": *e.g.* Buttermere (q.v.).

Buth. [ON] "booth": herdsman's temporary shelter.

Bygg-garthr. [ON] "barley-field".

Byr. [ON] "village/hamlet": *e.g.* Lazonby, Glassonby.

Caer. [C] "fortified place": *e.g.* Carlisle. (The Caer of Luel).

Caester. [OE] "ancient fort": *e.g.* Papcastle (Hermit's castle).

Cairn. A pile of stones.

Calgarth. The calf enclosure.

Cam. A ridge.

LANGUAGE — DERIVATION/DEFINITION.

Carr. [ON] "kjarr": thicket in a swamp-land now reclaimed.

Carroc. [C] "rock". *e.g.* Carrock Fell.

Caudale. [ON] "kalfadalr": the calf dale.

Caucee. [ME] "clear high path": *e.g.* Causey Pike.

Caw. [D] "calf": *e.g.* Caw fell.

Cherry Holme. An island in Ullswater where once cherries grew in abundance.

Claife. [ON] "kleif": steep hill or path: *e.g.* Claife Heights.

Clough. [OE] "cloh": deep wooded ravine.

Cockshoot. A clearing cut in a wood which could be used for shooting game as it went through it. (*e.g.* Cockshot Wood, Borrowdale. Area 7 NY 266226).

Coledale. [ON] "kola-dalr": the charcoal-burning dale.

Combe. [OE] "cumb": deep rounded valley.

Copp. [OE] "point on ridge": *e.g.* Cop stone.

Cove. [OE] "cofa": combe/hollow.

Crake. [C] "creic": rocky.

Crinkle Crags. [ON] "kringla": convoluted ridge line.

Cumba. [C] "closed in valley": cwm.

Cumberland. Spelled "Cumbraland" in C10 and Cumerlandes in C16. The land of the Cwmry (the Welsh).

Dael. [OE] "valley": *e.g.* Mosedale (Valley of peat bogs).

Dalr. [ON] "large valley". [Belgic] "deylen": to distribute.

Dash. [ON] "dask": blow/buffet: *e.g.* Whitewater dash.

Deepdale. [ON] "djupdalr": the deep valley.

Devoke. From old Irish "Duffrock": the little dark one.

Doat. The apportioned-out pastures.

Dod. [ON] "toddi": a limb. [ME] "rounded hill top": *e.g.* Great Dodd.

Dore. "Door/gate": consequentially a mountain pass or gap in a ridge: *e.g.* Lodore, Mickledoor.

Doup. A cavity.

Dub. Small pool/pond/deep pool in a river.

Dudden. The dark stream.

Dun. [C] "hill fort": *e.g.* Dunmallet (Mallock's fort).

Ea. [OE] "river": *e.g.* River Eamont (River meeting).

Earn. [OE] " Eagle": *e.g.* Erne Crag.

Eik. [ON] "oak": *e.g.* Aiken Knott.

Elri. [ON] "Alder": *e.g.* Ellergill.

Esk. [C] water.

Eyre-a. [ON] "stream with gravely banks": *e.g.* Aira Beck.

LANGUAGE — DERIVATION/DEFINITION.

Feld. [OE] "open land": *e.g.* Bromfield (Brown land).

Fell. [ON] "fjall": originally mountain now rough high land.

Finsthwaite. [ON] Finn's clearing.

Fitz Park. Fits Park—the riverside meadows.

Fleetwith. [ON] "fljot-vithr": the wood by the river.

Flume. Usually of wood—a chute to direct water from its source to another point.

Fold. [OE] "fald/falod": small walled enclosure, for animals.

Force. [ON] "fors/foss": waterfall.

Frith. [ON] "fyrthe": a fir wood.

Garth. [OE] "geard": enclosed land/paddock.

Gate. Path or road.

Geiti. [ON] "goat": *e.g.* Gatesgarth.

Gill. [ON] "gil": a wooded valley, usually containing a stream. Wordsworth wrote of such a place as a "Ghyll".

Gillercombe. [ON] "gildre": a trap. Indicates that traps or snares may have been set in this combe.

Gimmer. Sheep aged between its first and second shearings.

Glaramara. [ON] "gliufr": a chasm. The shieling at the chasms.

Glyn. "wooded valley": *e.g.* Glencoyne (valley with reeds) cawn-reeds.

Goat. A gap.

Gowbarrow. [ON] "gol-berg": windy hill.

Grain. [ON] "grein": a side-valley.

Grassings. [ON] system of land-holding. Unit of land a "grass" (about 8 acres/3 ha) considered sufficient to support one horse, three cows, seventeen sheep and twenty geese during the winter. During the summer the animals were released on to the adjoining fells to allow grass to grow and to be harvested as hay. Hill-side enclosures.

Great Gable. [ON] "mikill gafl": the great gable, for from Wasdale the shape of the mountain resembled the gable of a building.

Greenburn. The green valley.

Gres-garthr. [ON] "The grassy enclosure": *e.g.* Grass Guards.

Greta. [ON] "grjot-a": the rocky river.

Grike. [D] "narrow cleft or ravine".

Griss. [ON] "swine": *e.g.* Grizedale.

Ground. [ON] "grund": enclosed land apportioned to tenant farmers in Middle Ages. Pronounced "grund". *e.g.* Stephenson's Ground.

Gymbr. [ON] "a yearling sheep": *e.g.* Gimmer Crag.

Hafri. [ON] "oats": *e.g.* Haverthwaite.

Haga. [OE] "hedge" hence an enclosure; also [ON] "hagi".

LANGUAGE — DERIVATION/DEFINITION.

Hagg. [ON] "hogg": part of a wood which has been cleared.

Hals. [ON] " narrow pass": *e.g.* Esk hause.

Hardknot(t). [ON] "hard-knutr": the rough or craggy hill.

Harter Fell. [ON] "hjartar fjall": the hart's fell.

Hassness. The headland with the narrow path.

Haugr. [ON] "hill/mound": *e.g.* Gummer's How (Gurnar's hill).

Hause. [ON] "hals": narrow ridge/entrance/path.

Hawes. The hills/mounds.

Head. [OE] "heafod": a stream's source/hill/headland.

Heaf. A northern term for sheep pasture.

Heaning. [ON] "hegna": to fence, hence enclosed pastures.

Hegdale. Near Rosgill. "Dale of the Bird-cherry". Local name of this tree is "Heckberry".

Hell Gill. [ON] "hellir": cave. The cavernous gill.

Helm Crag. [ON] "hjalmr": a helmet.

Hestr. [ON] "stallion": *e.g.* Hest Holme (former name of Derwent Island, possibly where horses corralled).

Heughscar. [OE] "Hoh": a projecting hill/rough fellside.

High Street. Named after the road which runs along the ridge formerly named The Britons' Road.

Hirst. [OE] "hyrst": wooded hill.

Hlith. [OE] "hlith": hillside.

Hogg hole. An escape route in a high wall, for sheep, in time of blizzard.

Hoghouse. [ME] "hog": yearling sheep. Shelters for sheep are placed in high intake fields.

Hole. [OE] "holh": hollow place.

Hollins. [OE] "holegn": holly-tree.

Holme. [ON] "holmr": an island or land liable to flooding.

How. [ON] "haugr": mound/knoll or larger—*e.g.* Silver How.

Hreys. [ON] "raise/pile of stones": *e.g.* Dunmail Raise.

Hryding. [OE] land clear of trees.

Hugill. [ON] "ha-geil": the high glen.

Hryggr. [ON] "ridge": *e.g.* Loughrigg (Ridge above lake).

Ill Bell. [ON] " illr": steep/rough.

In-bye land. [ON] "by"-land. Enclosed land nearest to the farmhouse. Alternative— "In-field".

Ing. [ON] "eng": outlying pasture land.

Ingtun. [OE] "township": *e.g.* Workington.

LANGUAGE — DERIVATION/DEFINITION.

Intake. [ON] "intak": enclosed land especially high moorland pastures.

Jenkin crag/hill. "Jenkin" a local pet name for John.

Kambr. [ON] "cock's comb": projecting spur: *e.g.* Cam Spout (waterfall).

Keld. Spring or marshy area.

Kelda. [ON] "well/spring": *e.g.* Threlkeld (The serf's well).

Kidh. [ON] "the young of the goat": *e.g.* Kidsty Pike.

Kirkja. [ON] "Church": *e.g.* Kirkoswald (Oswald's Church).

Kirkstile. [ON] "kirk": church.

Knock. A hill.

Knot(t). [OE] "cnotta": rocky outcrop on high land.

Krokr. [ON] "curve/bend": *e.g.* Crook (sited on a river bend).

Langdale. [OE] "the long valley".

Langr. [ON] "long": *e.g.* Langthwaite (long clearing).

Lathe. [ON] "hlatha": Barn or shelter for storing.

Latrigg. [ON] "latr": an animal's lair in a hill enclosure.

Launchy. Lancelot or Lawrence: *e.g.* Launchy Gill.

Leah. [OE] "meadow in clearing": *e.g.* Stavely (staves cut).

Leik-skeithr. [ON] "a place set aside for games": and now sheep-dog trials: *e.g.* Hesketh.

Leven. [C] "llyfn": smooth.

Levens. [ON] "lauf-nes": leafy promontory.

Lic. [OE] "corpse": *e.g.* Lickbarrow (a burial mound).

Liza. [ON] "lios-a": the sparkling stream.

Load. [OE] a "way"; *e.g.* Loadpot Hill.

Longstrath. [OE] "strod": the long marsh.

Low. [OE] "hlaw": now, high land with rounded summit.

Lundr. [ON] "small wood": *e.g.* Morland (Wood on Moor).

Lyp. Elevated look-out. Burial place.

Man. Cairned summit.

Manesty. [ON] "Mani": a personal name. Man's path.

Measand. [ON] "mjosund": a narrow channel of water.

Meir. [ON] "sand dunes": *e.g.* Cartmel (sand bank by rocky ridge).

Mellbreak. [C] "meall breac": the speckled hill.

Meloc. [C] "small hill": *e.g.* Watermillock—hill for sheep grazing. (Water=wether+meloc).

Mere. [OE] "boundary": *e.g.* Mere brook.

Mere. [OE] "Lake or pool": *e.g.* Thirlmere (Lake in hollow).

Mickleden. [OE] "micel-denu": the great valley.

LANGUAGE — DERIVATION/DEFINITION.

Mile. Originally a variable measure in England between 4854ft/1479m and 6600ft/2011m. The standard mile of 5280ft/1609m was laid down in 1593.

Moel. [C] "round grassy hill": *e.g.* Mell Fell.

Mont. [ME] "mound": *e.g.* Egremont.

Moss. [ON] "mosi": a bog.

Myrr. [ON] "swampy ground": *e.g.* Mirethwaite (Clearing in boggy ground).

Nabbi. [ON] "promontory": *e.g.* Skelly nab.

Naes. [ON] "headland": *e.g.* Ashness.

Niew. [OE] "new": *e.g.* Newbiggin (new building).

Nook. [ME] "noke": small farm.

Ongull. [ON] "hook/angle": *e.g.* Angle Tarn.

Orrusta. [ON] " a battle": *e.g.* Orrest Head.

Outgate. [D] "ootyat": the path or gate leading to the fell-pastures.

Pannage. The right to feed pigs in the manorial woods or the payment made for that right.

Pate. Badger.

Pearroc. [OE] enclosure.

Peel. Well fortified.

Pen. [C] "hill": *e.g.* Penrith—hill by a ford.

Penruddock. [C] "pen rhuddawc": the ruddy (soiled) hill.

Piers. [ME] "Peter".

Pike. [ME] "sharp summit": *e.g.* Langdale Pikes.

Pike o' Stickle. [ON] "stikill": sharp point.

Plaesc. [OE] "marshy puddle": *e.g.* Place Fell.

Ra. Boundary post.

Raise. Elevated position.

Rake. [ON] "rak": cattle or sheep track—usually steep.

Rannerdale. [ON] "hrafnar-dalr": the Raven's dale.

Ravenglass. [C] "rann gleis": land allotted to a man named Gleis.

Ridding. [ON] "rithja": to clear land of trees.

Rigg. [ON] "hryggr": extended high land with steep flanks.

Riggindale. The dale below the ridge.

Robinson. Named after Richard Robinson who purchased land hereabouts after dissolution of the monasteries. In 1557 his son sold off his father's estate and thereafter Robinsons Fell known as Robinson.

Rosthwaite. The clearing with the cairn.

Rothay. [ON] "rautha": trout stream.

Saetr. [ON] "summer pasture/farm": *e.g.* Seatoller (Olvar's shieling).

LANGUAGE — DERIVATION/DEFINITION.

Samson's Bratfull. A great stone-mound.

Savin. Juniper.

Sca. Cliff.

Scale. [ON] "skali": outlying temporary shelter.

Scandale. [ON] "skam-dalr": the short dale.

Scarth. Break in a ridge creating a pass.

Scearp. [OE] "sharp/rough/rugged": *e.g.* Sharp Edge.

Scree. Bank of loose rock on fellside.

Sel. [ON] "hill with a hut": *e.g.* Sellafield.

Sergeant Man. Very probably so named from the erection of the cairn by the Land-sergeant of Egremont.

Shap. [OE] "heap": pile of stones.

Sharrow. [OE] "scaru-hoh": the boundary hill.

Shieling. Grazing-ground for cattle. Small hut for shepherds.

Shoulthwaite. [ON] "hjol-tveit": the wheel clearing.

Sike/syke. [OE] "sic", [ON] "sik": sluggish stream, one that usually runs dry in summer.

Sinen. [D] "to dry up": *e.g.* Sinen Gill.

Sizergh. The dairy-farm of Sigrid.

Skali. [ON] "outlying hut": *e.g.* Winscale (hut in windy place).

Skelgill. The gill with the shieling.

Skelwith. [ON] "skiallr": gushing "noisy" water in the wood.

Skirsgill. [ON] "skyrsi": bad omen. The haunted gill.

Skogr. [ON] wood.

Skitha. [ON] "a landslide": *e.g.* Screes i.e. shale deposits on a fell side.

Skuti. [ON] "a rocky ridge": *e.g.* Scoat Fell.

Slack. [ON] "slakki": shallow valley.

Slape. Slippery.

Sockbridge. [OE] "soca-bred": boardwalk over the marsh.

Spoony. [OE] "spon": wooden roofing/shingle.

Spout. [ON] "spyta": to spit. Therefore, waterfall.

Sprinkling Tarn. [OE] "sprenta-burn" (corrupted): the gushing stream.

Stake Pass. The pass marked out by stakes.

Stanley Gill. Named after the Stanley family of Dalegarth, Eskdale C14.

Stede. [OE] "site of": *e.g.* Castlesteads.

Stickle. Sharp-pointed.

Stigr. [ON] "steep path": *e.g.* Sty Head.

Stile. [OE] "stigel": hill path but now the point at which a wall is climbed.

LANGUAGE — DERIVATION/DEFINITION.

Stock Gill. [ON] "stokkr": tree stump. May also have referred to a fulling mill.

Stool End. The farm at "the end of the ridge": (The Band, Bowfell).

Storrs. [ON] "storth": undergrowth.

Stott Park. [ME] "stot": bullock.

Strands. [OE] "strand": the lake shore.

Strickland. [OE] "stirk": sheltered pasture used for fattening young cattle.

Striding Edge. Only passable by being "astride" of.

Stybarrow Dodd. Hill with a steep path.

Sty Head. The top of the path.

Sunder. [OE] "remote/separated": e.g. Cinderdale.

Sweden Bridge. [ON] "svithingr": singed i.e. land cleared by burning.

Swinside. [ON] "svin": swine. The swine beck.

Tarn. Mountain lake.

Thak. [ON] "reed thatch": e.g. Thackthwaite.

Thing mound. Vikings gathered at such a point to promulgate laws and administer justice.

Thorpe. [ON] "farm or hamlet".

Thrangr. [ON] "narrow passage/path".

Thveit. [ON] "pasture at valley head": e.g. Stonethwaite (stone clearance).

Thwaite. [ON] "tveit": clearing in a wood or forest but in Lake District a field sloping down to a mire or mere.

Tilberthwaite. [OE] "Tilli's stronghold".

Tjorn. [ON] "small lake": e.g. Tewit tarn (Peewit's tarn).

Toddi. [ON] "bale of wool": refers to a fox's brush (tail). e.g. Tod Crag.

Ton. [OE] "tun": fence then enclosed land and extended later to manor, village or town.

Tongue. [OE] "tunge", [ON] "tunga": tongue shaped piece of land.

Trod. [D] "pathway": e.g. Moses' Trod.

Tun. [OE] "enclosed farm": e.g. Ulverston (Ulfr's farm).

Ullock. [ON] "ulfra-leikr": place where wolves play.

Ullscarf. The wolf's pass.

Vath. [ON] "ford": e.g. Skelwith (ford at noisy place).

Vik. [ON] "a creek or inlet": e.g. Piel (watch tower) Wyke.

Vithr. [ON] "wood": e.g. Witherslack (wooded hollow).

Waeter. [OE] water.

Wall End. [ON] "vollr": the end of the pasture before the start of the fell.

Wath. A ford.

LANGUAGE — DERIVATION/DEFINITION.

Westmorland. The people of the western moorlands - the land of the Westmoringas.

Wether. [ON] "vethr": a gelded ram.

Whitbarrow. [ON] "hvitr": light-coloured/white.

Wick. [OE] "dairy farm": e.g. Keswick (cheese farm).

Withig. [OE] "willow": e.g. Wythop (valley with willow trees).

Wra. [ON] "remote corner": e.g. Wray.

Yewbarrow. [OE] "eowu-beorg": hill where ewes were pastured.

Yr. [ON] "yew-tree".

MINES

Adit. Access tunnel into rock/earth. Also provides ventilation, a haulage route and a course for water discharge.

Cross-cut levels. Right angled tunnel to the main vein direction.

Drift. Horizontal tunnel.

Feather Working. A "feather" was a D shaped section 6 inch/15cm iron bar. Two "feathers" were inserted into a hole drilled into the rock using a hammer and an iron bar called a jumper. A wedge called a stope or plug was inserted between the flats of the "feathers" and hammered. The resulting vibration shattered the surrounding rock. Method used in the Elizabethan era.

Leat. Along the mountain sides, artificial watercourses to direct water to propel water-wheels which provided driving energy via geared cog wheels/pulleys etc.; for various mine machinery—e.g. water pumps, ore crushers etc.

Level. A tunnel driven to and along a vein. May not have immediate connection with the open air.

Lode. A principal vein containing ore minerals.

Openworks. A vein excavated in the open air.

Outcrop. Surface exposure of a vein.

Shaft. A pit excavated beside a vein or follows its downward direction.

Stope. Overhand-vein material removed from above level.

Underhand-vein material removed from the base of the level.

Vein. Fissure in country rock containing minerals.

REFRESHMENT—INN NAMES

The Law in the Middle Ages dictated that inns should show distinctive signs/symbols to assist the mainly illiterate population differentiate between the many inns of those times. Many inn names descend through heraldry from religious symbols which, in turn, descended from the Bestiary of the period; today, these attractive theories may sometimes rest upon insecure foundation.

Beehive. Long been a symbol of industry.

REFRESHMENT—INN NAMES

Black Bull. The Gin Act of 1736 caused taverners to drape their signs in black velvet or to add "Black" to the inn name. Also cognisance of the House of Clare.

Black Cat. Heraldic—the wild cat being the crest of the Penningtons—Barons Muncaster. Also religious house founded by St Francis in 1213.

Black Cock. Descriptive of male black grouse.

Black Lion. Heraldic—re Queen Philippa of Hainault, wife of Edward III. (She founded Queen's College, Oxford.)

Blacksmiths Arms. Important person in the community—making tools in peacetime and weapons in time of war.

Blue Bell. Common. Uncertain whether the flower is an heraldic bluebell or a bell painted blue.

Britannia. Roman name for Britain. The Royal Navy has used this name for some of its vessels since 1682. The female figure supporting a shield is of Frances Stewart, Duchess of Richmond, who was formerly mistress of Charles II.

Brown Cow. Common and not illustrative.

Brown Horse. Derivation obscure.

Bush. Used by the Romans to indicate a wine shop in the form of a bunch of evergreens, such as ivy.

Castle. Common inn name for centuries. Could be part heraldic or nearness to such a building but more likely because it was easily recognisable. At one time associated with Spain and indicated that a tavern sold Spanish wines.

Crown. Does not necessarily infer royal patronage but most probably does demonstrate loyalty to the reigning monarch.

Crown and Mitre. Symbolised the monarch and the Church.

Dog and Duck. Mainly refers to duck hunters and their retrievers. In some instances refers to Charles II time up to early C19 when duck, with their wings pinioned, were thrown into water and spaniels sent in to hunt for them. The only means of escape for the duck was to dive.

Dog and Gun. Meeting place of the shooting fraternity.

Drunken Duck. In Victorian times the landlady found 6 ducks apparently dead outside the cellar door. She had nearly finished plucking them when she noticed signs of life. She then remembered that she had seen the ducks drinking near to a leaking barrel and realised that they were actually drunk. To restore warmth to their denuded bodies she knitted each a woollen jacket to wear until their feathers grew again.

REFRESHMENT—INN NAMES

Eagle and Child. After the Arms of the Stanleys. In C14 Sir Thomas Lathom, family ancestor, had an illegitimate son through a liaison with the daughter of a Yeoman named Oskatell. Determined to introduce the offspring into his family he conceived a ruse to the effect that the baby was placed near an eagle's nest on his estate and whilst walking with his wife they would discover the child. He then persuaded his wife to adopt it. Despite the deception he left his wealth to his daughter Isobel who had married Sir John Stanley who benefited from the estates. Their crest thereafter reflected both triumph and injustice.

Eagles Head. C15 Christian and heraldic symbol. At one time associated with Germany and indicated that the tavern sold German wines.

Farmers Arms. A meeting point for predominantly local farming community.

Fish. Fishing "par excellence".

Gate. Proximity to a toll gate/church gate.

George and Dragon. Refers to England's Patron Saint, who lived in C3 or C4. Legendary fight with a dragon and rescue of a maiden caused thousands to be baptized.

George III. Since 1714 six kings have borne this name.

Globe. At one time associated with Portugal, and indicated that a tavern sold Portugese wines.

Gloucester Arms. Duke of Gloucester, later Richard III, stayed in Penrith 1471 while repairs effected to nearby castle.

Grange. In early times a "granary".

Greyhound. Heraldic reference to dukes of Newcastle—also refers to coursing.

Hare and Hounds. In common usage. Most probably a meeting place for coursing community. Also compliment to Lord of the Manor.

Highland Drove. Recalls the days when Highland cattlemen drove their herds south to English markets.

Horse and Farrier. Oftimes, in remoter parts, a publican would combine his trade with that of shoeing and doctoring horses.

Horse and Jockey. A favourite British sporting pastime.

Horse Shoe. Originally said to be protection against witches.

Kings Head. Popular. Usual head shown on inn sign is that of Henry VIII but at least eight other monarchs are shown.

Jolly Anglers. Perhaps signifies happy and slightly, but pleasantly, intoxicated fishermen.

Lamplugh Arms. Maybe refers to an enclosure or a church but exact derivation unknown.

Manor Arms. Its meaning now obscure.

REFRESHMENT—INN NAMES

Mason Arms. The Company of Masons was granted a Coat of Arms in 1473. The Cartmel Fell inn took its name from Kendal Masons who met here clandestinely in C18.

Mill. May indicate the inn's nearness to a stream or its past function.

Newby Bridge Inn. Probably named after the bridge's builder—Nuby or Newbury, popular in the Cartmel Fell area.

Newfield. Derivation obscure. Maybe because building on reclaimed land.

Norfolk Arms. Derivation obscure.

Oddfellow's Arms. Originally referred to Independent Order of Oddfellows (Manchester Union), a countrywide social and benevolent society.

Old Crown. Maybe one of the oldest inn signs but it does not invariably signify that the house was Crown property.

Outgate. Historically where commons began and enclosures ended.

Pack of Hounds. Maybe a meeting point of such.

Pheasant. Patronage of thirsty sportsmen (of these birds) courted by nearby hostelry.

Prince of Wales. Refers mainly to Queen Victoria's eldest son, Edward (1841-1910). In 1901 he became Edward VII.

Punch Bowl. c1630 the drink "Punch" became popular in England and its ingredients were usually mixed in and served from a bowl.

Queens Head. Originally of Elizabeth I. By Royal Proclamation in 1563 all such signs followed an approved example.

Red Lion. In C14 John o'Gaunt ordered that the heraldic red lion be displayed on public buildings when James I (also James VI of Scotland) ascended the throne.

Royal Oak. After restoration of Charles II to the throne he declared that his birthday, 29 May, be celebrated as Royal Oak Day, for it was in an oak tree (the Boscobel Oak, Shiffnal, Salop) that he hid, with his aide Colonel Carless, and escaped the Roundheads, following the Battle of Worcester in 1656.

Salutation. Originally referred to The Annunciation.

Ship. Derivation obvious but localised meanings.

Sun. Long used to express an inn's favourable location i.e. facing south.

Swan. Since C14. Alluded to the bird or part of a Coat of Arms, favoured by Henry VIII and Edward III.

Swinside. A place where swine/pigs were kept.

Three Shires. Approximate meeting point of the old counties of Westmorland, Cumberland and Lancashire.

Tower Bank Arms. Local derivation.

Travellers Rest. Travellers in bygone days using horses and coaches required nourishment for themselves and especially for their steeds.

REFRESHMENT—INN NAMES

Trout. Freshwater fish valued for sport and eating and such an inn usually located near to fishable water.

Two Lions. Heraldic—family association with strength and courage (of a lion).

Wheatsheaf. Common since C17. One of the devices on the Arms of the Brewers' Company.

White Hart. Heraldic—Richard II 1377/1399. Innkeepers showed their allegiance by displaying the device. Also there is an ancient legend related by the Roman author, Pliny, that Alexander the Great captured a White Stag and placed a gold collar around its neck.

White Lion. Heraldic—referring to Edward IV, the earls of March or the Duke of Norfolk.

Woolpack. Bale of wool weighing 240lbs/108kg.

Yew Tree. Archers bows were made from this tree and thus very important to our forebears. During reign of Henry V an Act was passed to preserve such trees.

Brathay Bridge. (Rosemary Liddle)

Index

ARCHAEOLOGY

ARCHITECTURE

Little Langdale. Low Hall Garth	[18]	30 02
-dry built. Great Langdale. Stool End	[17]	27 05
Hartsop Hall	[13]	39 12
-with granary. Broughton Mills	[22]	21 90
-with underhousing. Colthouse	[23]	35 98
-with water wheel (originally). Bouth	[28]	32 87
Barrow House. Derwent Water	[7]	26 20
Barton Hall. Pooley Bridge	[9]	47 25
Beacon. Penrith	[5]	52 31
Belle Isle. Windermere	[23]	39 96
Belmount. Hawkshead	[23]	35 99
Bigland Hall	[28]	35 83
Birkrigg Park	[30]	54 87
Blackwell School. Bowness	[24]	40 90
Bleaze Hall. Old Hutton	[30]	54 89
Blencow Hall	[4]	44 32
Boat House. Sow How Farm. Upper Alithwaite	[29]	40 87
Borrowdale Head	[20]	54 04
Brackenburgh Tower	[4]	47 38
Brathay Hall	[18]	36 03
Brettargh Holt	[30]	50 86
Bridge. Borrowdale. Ashness	[12]	27 19
Borrowdale. Grange	[12]	25 17
Causeway End-carved inscriptions	[27]	22 86
Clappersgate	[18]	36 03
Deepthwaite	[30]	51 83
Eamont Bridge	[10]	52 28
Eskdale. Doctors bridge	[16]	18 00
Great Langdale	[18]	31 05
Little Langdale. Slaters	[18]	31 03
Longsleddale. Pack-horse	[20]	51 00
Lund. Pack-horse	[16]	14 03
Newby	[28]	36 86
Pooley Bridge.Treble-arched	[9]	47 24
Scale Bridge. Double-arched	[11]	16 17
Seatoller	[12]	25 13
Sosgill. Naddle Fell	[8]	31 21
Stainton	[30]	52 85
Stockley	[12]	23 10
Troutbeck. Hagg	[19]	42 05

ARCHITECTURE

ARCHITECTURE

ARCHITECTURE

CHURCH

CHURCH

CHURCH

EVENT

GEOLOGY—including Mineralogy

GEOLOGY—including Mineralogy

HISTORICAL

HISTORICAL

INDUSTRIAL ARCHAEOLOGY

INDUSTRIAL ARCHAEOLOGY

INDUSTRY

INSECTS

LEGEND

LITERARY

MEMORIAL

MEMORIAL

War Memorial. Borrowdale Parish	[12]	25 14
Summit of Great Gable	[12]	21 10
Scafell Pike	[17]	21 07
White Cross Bay. Troutbeck Bridge	[18]	39 00
Williamson, Thomas	[19]	45 00
Wilson, Anthony & Jessie–Thornthwaite	[7]	22 25
Wordsworth, Children–William/Thomas/Catherine	[18]	33 07
Dorothy–Cockermouth	[1]	12 30
Grasmere. (Refer Church)	[18]	33 07
John–Father of W.W. (Refer Church)	[1]	12 30
Mary–Grasmere. (Refer Church)	[18]	33 07
Stone of Parting–Grisedale Tarn	[13]	35 12
William–Grasmere	[18]	34 07
William–Grasmere. (Refer Church)	[18]	33 07

MINE

Ambleside Cavern	[18]	35 05
Bassenthwaite. Beckstones Mine and level	[7]	21 26
Carl Side Trial	[7]	25 26
Dead Beck Trial	[2]	26 31
High Mill Trial	[2]	23 31
Robin Hood Mine	[2]	22 33
Windyhill Mine	[7]	21 26
Woodend Mine	[7]	21 27
Birkside Gill Copper Mine	[13]	33 12
Blencathra. Mine	[7]	29 26
Blease Gill Trial-level	[8]	31 26
Saddleback Old Mine	[8]	33 28
	[8]	34 27
Threlkeld Mine	[8]	32 26
Borrowdale. High Close Mine	[12]	24 17
Bowness. Borwick Fold Mine	[24]	44 96
Buttermere Fell. Dalehead Mine	[12]	22 15
Buttermere. Beckside Trial	[11]	19 15
Blackbeck Trial	[12]	20 13
Buttermere Mine	[11]	18 15
Low Wax Knott Trial	[11]	18 14
Caldbeck Fells. Braefell Mine	[2]	29 35
China Clay Mine	[3]	31 34
-1818 Level	[3]	31 34
Driggith Mine	[3]	32 35

MINE

PLANTS

QUARRY

REFRESHMENT

REFRESHMENT

REFRESHMENT

WATERFALLS

WELL

WHEELCHAIR WALKS

ANNE STRANGE christmas 2001.